35—

E
185.93
.M6
F73
1999

FREEDOM'S WOMEN

BLACKS IN THE DIASPORA

Darlene Clark Hine

John McCluskey, Jr.

David Barry Gaspar

GENERAL EDITORS

FREEDOM'S WOMEN

BLACK WOMEN AND FAMILIES IN CIVIL WAR ERA MISSISSIPPI

NORALEE FRANKEL

INDIANA UNIVERSITY PRESS

Bloomington and Indianapolis

This book is a publication of

Indiana University Press
601 North Morton Street
Bloomington, IN 47404–3797 USA

http://www.indiana.edu/~iupress

Telephone orders 800-842-6796
Fax orders 812-855-7931
Orders by e-mail iuporder@indiana.edu

The paper used in this publication meets the minimum requirements of American National Standard for Information Sciences—Permanence of Paper for Printed Library Materials, ANSI Z39.48-1984.
Manufactured in the United States of America

Library of Congress Cataloging-in-Publication Data

Frankel, Noralee, date
    Freedom's Women : Black women and familes in Civil War era Mississippi / by Noralee Frankel.
        p.   cm. — (Blacks in the diaspora)
    Includes bibliographical references and index.
    ISBN 0-253-33495-0 (cl : alk. paper). — ISBN 0-253-21278-2 (pa : alk. paper)
    1. Afro-American women—Mississippi—History—19th century. 2. Afro-American families—Mississippi—History—19th century. 3. Mississippi—History—Civil War, 1861–1865—Afro-Americans. 4. United States—History—Civil War, 1861–1865—Afro-Americans. 5. Freedmen—Mississippi—History—19th century. 6. Mississippi—History—Civil War, 1861–1865—Social aspects. 7. United States—History—Civil War, 1861–1865—Social aspects. 8. Reconstruction—Mississippi—Social aspects. I. Title. II. Series.
E1855.93.M6F73 1999
976.2'00496073—dc21   99-25526

1 2 3 4 5 04 03 02 01 00 99

Dedicated to

LETITIA WOODS BROWN,

to whom all things were possible.

CONTENTS

PREFACE

This book examines the experiences of African American women, particularly within families, during the Civil War and for the first five years of Reconstruction in Mississippi. Trying to squeeze three-dimensional human beings into a two dimensional page represents a frustrating challenge. Until writing in holograms becomes possible, authors continue to be forced to divide people's lives into categories that inevitably oversimplify. Thus in this book, I separate into a preface and seven chapters the topics of slavery, war experiences, work, relationships between men and women, families, and communities. At the same time, I am also aware of the complex interactions among these topics, particularly the connection between private lives and public policy.

As historian Thomas C. Holt has written, "We can write no genuine history of the black experience . . . without groping for the textures of their interior worlds. But having done that, we then must establish linkages between that interior world and the external developments and movements in the larger world: for only in that way can that history lay any claim to centrality in the national experience. . . . We must do history inside out and back again."[1] Emancipation and the resulting personal freedom experienced by individual slaves led to a broad social and political revolution. The lives of African American women who accepted and defied conventional definitions of private and public spheres reveal the connections and tensions between interior worlds and the larger world.

How emancipation affected freedpeople is a more complex question once gender becomes a category of historical analysis. Examining the links between interior lives and exterior events through the lives of women ultimately refines our understanding of the process of emancipation. During slavery, family, community, and culture all sustained slave men and women. Without minimizing their positive effects, however, slavery was a horrifying system under which people were literally bought and sold, and where labor was also capital. In this context, the notion of a personal or private life for those in slavery is misleading. The struggle of freedpeople to establish private lives involved gendered decisions about work, family, and community participation.

As freed women and men strove during Reconstruction to minimize the interference of former slave owners, practically everything considered private became a public issue: marriage, mobility, parenthood, housing, and control over African American women's sexuality. Experiences such as pregnancy, nursing, the preparation of meals, and washing clothes that were certainly viewed as private by freedwomen became areas of heated debate between employers and employees. As Ada Hurtado has pointed out, "the political consciousness of women of Color stems from an awareness that the public is personally political."[2] These issues became more politicized as freed women and men attempted to define freedom for themselves. Their belief in emancipation strengthened African American resolve to confront hostile white southerners in the public arena of voting booths and state legislatures.

As the book examines the change and continuity between slavery and freedom and the meaning of freedom, it looks at issues involving family and work. The questions surrounding family and labor are tied to what freedom meant to former slave men and women. Newly freed slaves understood the potential of freedom and they constructed their own definitions of the term apart from what white northerners or white southerners wanted for them.[3] For all the slaves, from the youngest to oldest, freedom meant residing with one's family without the threat of a member being sold. Former slaves also expressed the desire to "do like dey please wid no boss over dem, an' den dey wanted to go places an have no patroller ketch dem."[4] They interpreted freedom as living where one chose and owning land or earning wages when one was employed. They anticipated changes in working conditions and developed an intolerance for attempts at physical coercion by employers. Freedom became identified with different housing arrangements—during Reconstruction cabins were dispersed rather than lined up in rows in the quarters as they had been during slavery. Implicit in all the definitions of freedom was the desire to gain a life without servitude to white people that was crystallized in one African American domestic servant's statement to her mistress that "answering bells is played out."[5] Freedpeople tied emancipation to development without white interference in issues of common interest to members of the African American community.[6]

One of the most contested areas between African Americans and whites after the war was work. Historians have explored the ways in which free labor during Reconstruction transformed the status of former slaves but they have failed to pay close attention to gender issues during this crucial period of African American history. During slavery, the master ultimately determined work organization and schedules, although plantation owners sometimes delegated the responsibility to overseers. Slave women and men constantly tried with limited success to gain some control over their labor.

White employers and African Americans did not agree on how free labor should affect the newly emancipated African American men and women. After the war, former slave women and men assumed they would have more autonomy over their working lives. For freedwomen, the fight for more control over their labor took on an additional urgency because they wanted and needed more time for their families. Freedpeople negotiated between the limitations of restrictive labor conditions imposed by former masters and their desire for more independence through land ownership. They refused to accept the white southern belief that only labor for whites constituted legitimate work for African Americans. Thus, while defining themselves as a free people, African Americans began to struggle against the white perception of African Americans laborers whose entire lives revolved around labor for whites.

Just as freedpeople maintained their own definition of free labor, so also did they assign their own cultural values to marriage in ways that imbued it with both similar and different meanings than the meanings white middle-class planters assigned the institution.[7] Although tremendous change occurred with the introduction of legalized marriage, attitudes about marriage that were formed during slavery were more important in shaping postwar relationships than historians have recognized. In light of new evidence found in the pension records of African American widows of Civil War soldiers, a reexamination of how freedpeople reacted to legalized marriage seems in order. Although most historians who have recently written about the Civil War have concluded that freedpeople universally embraced legalized marriage, my evidence suggests more varied responses. There was more than one pattern of African American marital norms. Freedpeople based their new conceptualization of marriage on slave unions that had no legal standing but were acknowledged by the community and on the legal system of marriage newly open to freedpeople after the war. They did not solely rely on legal definitions of marriage based on marital law and marriage contracts. They developed notions of gender within the family and household as well as codes of sexual morality based on their own community standards. Freedpeople tolerated intimate relationships outside of legal marriages in certain specified circumstances, did not define illegitimacy as any child born outside of wedlock, and recognized the termination of a relationship even when the couple did not obtain a legal divorce. Using the language that they developed as slaves, they referred to informal marriages as "took-ups" and nonlegal divorce as "quitting."

The continued reliance of freedpeople on community standards to define marital relationships reinforced the racist beliefs already held by upper-class and middle-class whites that African Americans were universally immoral. Whites rarely appreciated the complex structures and nuanced relationships between freedmen and freedwomen. Whites saw most freedpeople just as they had seen slaves, as promiscuous and uncontrolled. Emancipation intensified and solidified such beliefs among whites. Such attitudes both justified violence and the disenfranchisement of African American men and informed local, state, and federal policy that affected African American men and women. Whites thus used the private realm of sexuality to justify decisions about who should exercise political power in the public sphere.

Along with attitudes toward marriage, historians have explored questions about the nature of African American families after the war. Emancipation ended the master's authority over the slave family. The new male head of the African American family gained limited authority and more economic responsibility. Historians have recently speculated that African American families were patriarchal after the war. Such theories refuted the idea that the African American family had been a matriarchy. Patriarchy, however, implies more legal and social power than the heads of African American families actually exercised. The free African American family was neither matriarchal nor patriarchal.

The families of freedpeople can be accurately described as male-headed. The use of the term "male-headed" raises questions about power relationships between men and women. It is difficult to determine where power resided in individual families but historians are mistaken when they assume that agreement between men and women meant that wives always deferred to their husbands. Too often gender differences become an issue for historians when disagreements between men and women emerge in the sources. Agreement can also signal divergent views based, in part, on gender. Freedmen and women, for instance, supported the Republican party but emphasized different reasons for doing so, even as they agreed on the same overall goals.

Male-female relationships need to be examined within a discussion of African American extended families. Marital disagreements between husbands and wives did not always weaken the African American family and sometimes such discord strengthened extended family connections. Communities contained and mediated these conflicts. African American communities were not based exclusively on the stability of individual nuclear families; the African American definition of family was more broadly conceived.

How freedom changed the circumstances of freedpeople was limited by the economic and racial realities. Ultimately economic conditions, political disenfranchisement, and racial hostility thwarted the freedom that African Americans had wanted. Freedwomen's lives in Mississippi were bounded by class considerations. They were very poor, barely making a living as agricultural workers and/or domestic laborers. Rural freedpeople constituted the vast majority of the African American population in Mississippi. Generalizations made about them do not apply to the African Americans who lived in cities; members of this group had often been free before the war.

Typical of these women was Lucy Brown. Each chapter of this book begins with the continuing story of Lucy Brown. While enslaved to one of the wealthiest slave owners in Mississippi, Lucy Brown married fellow slave Thomas Brown and bore several children. During the war, Lucy's husband Thomas enlisted in the Union army and Lucy lived in a federal camp established for former slaves. Reunited in Vicksburg, Lucy and Thomas legally married with a Union army chaplain officiating. After her husband died during the war, Lucy, with her only surviving child Clara, worked both as a field hand and a domestic servant after the war. Following her husband's death, Lucy became intimate with another African American soldier, Frank Dorsey, and later with a married man, Robert Owens. Sometime after these two relationships concluded, Lucy married Reuben Kelly, a freedman.[8]

As with each individual, Lucy Brown's life was unique even though she lived through the same historical events as her contemporaries did. Like thousands of other enslaved people in Mississippi, Lucy Brown spent part of the Civil War behind the Union lines. Her work experiences after slavery were similar to those of the majority of African American women in rural Mississippi. Her acceptance of intimate relationships both inside and outside marriage was not uncommon.

National events such as the war, the end of slave labor, and legalization of marriage for formerly enslaved people helped shape Lucy Brown's life. Though she made personal choices, her race, class, and gender largely defined the context in which options presented themselves. Much more than a victim of oppression, Brown was an active participant in her own life. Her survival speaks to the quiet heroism, with all its foibles, of the human spirit.

Episodes in Lucy Brown's life also act as a reminder that history happens in confusing ways and is not easily sorted into neat topics. Lucy Brown's story comes from her Civil War widow's pension file and her testimony shows the complicated process of determining historical truth from primary sources.[9] Lucy Brown's slave owner's daughter left memoirs that verify much of the factual information about Brown's war experiences that is contained in her pension file.[10] The memoirs include the story of the attempt of Brown's owners to move their slaves during the war to keep them from being freed by Northern soldiers and the discovery of that ploy by the Yankees. Brown also mentioned the same events in her pension testimony given in 1879 and again in 1897. Truth prevailed only in parts of the pension record, however. The pension examiner determined that Brown and her daughter lied when they denied Brown's second marriage. Brown confessed to misleading federal officials about her remarriage because she feared losing her pension. In the pension record, there was disagreement among freedpeople over the identity of the man who officiated at Lucy Brown's wedding. Memories fade, documents in a variety of sources are contradictory, and pieces of evidence emphasize one issue while ignoring others. These truths, half-truths, and lies make the work of historians intellectually challenging, frustrating, and fun.

Regardless of where one starts in writing history, except perhaps for the authors of the Bible, one always starts in the middle. There remain gaps in our knowledge of slave women's lives in Mississippi and how gender shaped the slave experience and sharecropping. Small-town and urban experiences of African American women also need more exploration. Many useful, creative, and brilliant books have been written on subjects covered in this book. Each historian approaches the topics and themes in different ways but relies heavily on the literature already extant. As one will see from my narrative and my footnotes my debt to my colleagues is enormous. The stories of African American women and men in this book are told more effectively because of their work.

ACKNOWLEDGMENTS

On the day I found a labor contract which indicated that several extended families had lived on a plantation in Warren County, Mississippi, I excitedly ran up to a historian, engrossed in his own research, whom I had met once or twice. Madly waving my treasure, I yelled "Look at this!" The poor man looked at it vaguely and mumbled, "That's nice."

My friends and colleagues have been putting up with this kind of obsession from many, many years. They have endured long monologues on my source material and ever-changing theories about race and gender. In the end, the following dedicated people read drafts of this manuscript and made thoughtful and insightful comments. Even when these gracious people contradicted each other, they forced me to rethink and better formulate my evidence and arguments. They are: Linda De Pauw, Laura Edwards, Malvina and Herbert Frankel, Sandria Freitag, Emily Fry, Gay Gullickson, Robert L. Harris, James O. Horton, Susan Lesser, Marie Tyler McGraw, Nell Irvin Painter, Joseph Reidy, Leslie Schwalm, Peter N. Stearns, Ronald Walters, Rosemary Wozniak, and Judith Zinsser. Kathy Babbitt has been an exacting and creative editor. The anonymous reader for Indiana University Press was also very helpful. May whoever it was "live long and prosper." William E. Kost provided much support, financial and otherwise, including a splendid sense of humor. Elizabeth Jennifer Frankel Kost helped me keep my priorities straight by once complaining that a book was "like having a baby in the house." I also want to thank our cats: the late Supply and Demand, and the much alive Nancy and Drew who kept me company while I wrote. Funding for the writing of this book was made possible, in part, by a summer fellowship from the National Endowment for the Humanities, an independent government agency, and a fellowship from the American Council of Learned Societies.

The historians Jacqueline Hall, Nancy Hewitt, and Elsa Barkley Brown have eloquently conveyed the reality of multiple and partial voices and truths. Ultimately, a book must speak with one voice, the author's. Authors must, as I do now, take sole responsibility for the "good, the bad, and the ugly" in their texts.

Many historians told me that I would not find much material on African American women due to the lack of sources. By the end of my research, I opened boxes and files praying that they would be devoid of any reference to freedwomen. Primary material for this book was abundant. Although it failed to answer all my questions and it provided me with lots of additional queries which I could not answer, the material was always rich. I want, especially, to thank the staffs at several archives: the National Archives and Records Administration (NARA); the Southern Historical Collection, University of North Carolina; Department of Archives and Manuscripts, Louisiana State University; Duke University Library; Amistad Research Center, Dillard University; Howard Tilton Memorial Library, Tulane University Library; and the Department of Mississippi Archives and History. They were very helpful, particularly all the poor souls who pulled all my records from their various nooks and crannies.

This book is dedicated to Letitia Woods Brown who rigorously trained me in the study of African American history and compassionately guided me in my real life. Although I know she would have argued with me over much of the conceptualization of this book, her faith in my ability as a historian allowed me to write this manuscript. I miss her very much.

FREEDOM'S WOMEN

SLAVERY

*"They were recognized as man
and wife by their master and by all
who knew them"* [1]

On a Fourth of July several years before the Civil War, Charles Clark's slaves celebrated their day's respite from cotton cultivation by attending the slave wedding of fellow slaves Lucy Young and Thomas Brown. According to the memoirs of Charles Clark's daughter, their slaves usually held a "big barbecue and dance" on the fourth, so the addition of a wedding made the holiday even more festive. More than twenty years later, Clark's former slaves recalled attending the couple's nuptials and even the holiday dinner, but they disagreed over who actually performed the ceremony. Henry Young thought that "John Marshall a colored preacher" led the service because "Marshall used to marry all the colored, he had them stand up and read a book to them." Lucy Young Brown and several other freedpeople clearly remembered Parson Frank Montgomery, a preacher and Charles Clark's brother-in-law, as the officiating clergyman. Nevertheless, everyone on the plantation in Bolivar County, Mississippi, considered Lucy and Thomas Brown to be husband and wife, even though slave marriages were not legally recognized. [2]

The work and family life of slave women was gendered but often not in conventional nineteenth-century ways. These women frequently labored in the fields at assigned tasks different from men. They were also responsible for traditional domestic functions for their families, such as cooking and cleaning, but they executed these in what little "spare" time masters gave them. The slave owners and overseers, particularly in states of the lower south such as Mississippi, considered women's field labor to be more important than the domestic work the women performed for their own families. Although nurturing slaves, especially children, increased masters' potential labor and capital because slaves could be sold, masters minimized the significance of women's family roles.

Even though underappreciated, the labor of female slaves included their reproductive function, which in the view of slaveholders, was equivalent to their field labor because both generated capital. A typical slave owner's list of plantation's assets included "hands, breeding women, children, mules, stocks, provisions, farming utensils of all sorts."[3] Slave owners considered slave children to be an investment because they grew into valuable field hands who potentially could also be sold if the master required capital.

Although such factors, which made it possible for masters to sell family members, made maintaining a private life difficult, slave men and women married in slave ceremonies. They referred to each other as husband and wife even though their marriages had no legal standing. Their marriages were recognized by slave communities. Slave women and men formed their own notions of what marriage and family meant even when their definitions differed from those of the masters.

Slavery Comes to Mississippi

"Mississippi was in all respects a curious state," historian W. E. B. DuBois explained. "It was the center of a commercialized cotton kingdom. . . . Mississippi plantations were designed to raise a profitable cotton crop, and not to entertain visitors. Here and there the more pretentious slave manor flourished, but [it] smacked more of the undisciplined frontiers."[4] In the antebellum period, slave owners headed southwest to states such as Mississippi just as northerners sought their fortunes in the Midwest. The spread of settlers and slavery in Mississippi was only made possible by the vigorous earlier removal of Native Americans from their land.[5]

In the nineteenth century masters often moved only their most productive slaves into the state from older, established plantations to the east. With the onset of greater cotton production in Mississippi, slave masters increased the importation of slaves into the state. Between 1850 and 1860, Mississippi imported slaves at a rate that was almost 13 percent higher than the rate at which slaves were exported from the state.[6] Plantations in Mississippi maximized the number of bales of cotton to be sold by using the cotton gin, which removed seeds more efficiently than they could be removed by hand, and by growing an improved hybrid cotton, Petit Gulf.

Petit Gulf cotton was easier to pick and more disease resistant than other varieties. [7]

In 1860, Mississippi contained 436,631 slaves, more than half of them females. There were only 775 free African Americans.[8] The majority of the slaves in Mississippi resided on plantations with over fifteen slaves. The majority of the African American population lived in the Delta in the northwest part of the state, areas of the river lowlands and the Natchez District that rest in the southwestern part of the state, and the Black Prairie or Tombigbee Prairie in the northeast.[9] The Black Prairie was part of the Alabama Black Belt. Like the Delta, the soil there was very fertile and slavery flourished. Plantations were first developed in the river lowlands and Natchez District; the Delta was settled last. Constant flooding made antebellum planters reluctant to establish plantations on the flat rich soil on the Delta. Levees were built and plantations that relied on slave labor spread.

Slaves who were brought to Mississippi in the decades before the Civil War were familiar with the pain of being separated from their families.[10] Slave owners and/or slave traders forced younger slaves to migrate from the Upper South to create new plantations in Mississippi. Male slaves between the ages of 15 and 39 were much more likely to be imported than any other age group.[11] According to historian Allan Kulikoff, when slave owner Leonard Covington moved from Maryland to Mississippi he "apparently wanted youths on his new plantation, for he left behind in Maryland, seven of his slaves . . . older than thirty." Kulikoff concluded that "a number of the older children probably left parents on the Maryland plantation."[12]

Because slave owners considered the elderly to be too frail and useless, extended families rarely came into new territories together. Other slaves entered the state via slave traders. Slaves universally hated slave traders and remembered their encounters with them for years. As one freedwoman bitterly recalled, she was "brought . . . by the negro traders just like they bring cows and horses here now."[13] One historian has concluded that by 1860 almost all the "adult Mississippi slaves had been either forced migrants to that state" or were only "first-generation Mississippi-born slaves. Only 32,814 slaves had lived in that state in 1820."[14] The number had increased more than thirteen times by 1860.

In spite of the slave traffic from the older slave states and its breakup of families, by the start of the war, some three-generation families lived on larger more established plantations. The majority of the slaves resided on or near plantations large enough for slave families to develop.[15] The

Mississippi African American population was quite young and so the potential for families to grow was high. Young adults who were brought into the state started new families after they completed their forced immigration to Mississippi.

Work under Slavery

Once slave owners established plantations in Mississippi, masters used gender as one organizing principle of both agricultural and domestic slave labor. Slave owners on larger plantations depended on a division of labor based on ability, sex, and age. Overall, female slaves provided more agricultural labor on plantations than did male slaves because the men also served as artisans and carried out other work.[16] Masters and overseers placed slaves in work gangs for cotton cultivation. As opposed to other places in the South where planters used other ways to organize slave labor, Mississippi planters relied on gangs. Plantations used the slave labor of men and women efficiently. By 1859, Mississippi produced more cotton than most other southern states.[17] Most modern historians of slavery agree on the system's profitability in the years before the war.[18]

On Mississippi cotton plantations with an extensive slave population, slave men plowed and slave women, older children, and elderly men hoed ("chopped") cotton.[19] Because plowing with animals required greater strength than hoeing, slave owners preferred that slave men rather then women plow. Although hoeing day after day strained the back, it required less upper arm and leg strength than plowing. Plowers also contended with willful plow horses and even more obstreperous and cantankerous mules. Even so, a few women plowed on plantations, particularly when women composed a large portion of the prime field hands. Although the majority of slave women toiled as hoers, some may have preferred plowing to hoeing because plow hands received certain privileges.[20] Plowers rode to the fields on plow animals while other laborers walked. Slave men and women especially welcomed riding those few acres from the fields after a long day. On some plantations, plowers also received longer rest breaks during the day.[21] While traveling in northern Louisiana within ten miles of the Mississippi border northerner Frederick Law Olmsted vividly described the grouping of laborers often used in Mississippi as slaves proceeded to the fields: "First came, led by an old driver carrying a whip, forty of the largest and strongest women I ever saw together; they were all in a simple uniform dress of a bluish check stuff, the skirts reaching a little below the knee; their legs and feet were bare." He noted, "[T]hey carried themselves loftily, each having a hoe over the shoulder, and walking with free, powerful, swing like 'chasseurs' on a march." The gender division was clear. "Behind them came the cavalry, thirty strong, mostly men, but a few of them women, two of whom rode astride on the plow mules. A lean and vigilant white overseer on a brisk pony brought up the rear."[22]

The cotton cycle dictated the slave masters' seasonal organization of the agricultural labor on larger plantations. During the early spring, slave women removed branches and twigs, helping to clear fields. In Mississippi slaves planted cotton during April. After two or three weeks hoe gangs thinned and weeded the plants. Then the fields were cultivated and hoed again, sometimes in alternating rows, which meant that slaves of both sexes worked in the fields at once, even if in separate gangs. When the plowers finished, they helped with the hoeing. This alternating cycle continued into July.[23] Hoers kept weeds and grass cleared from cotton plants and broke up the soil near the roots. If they were not hoed, young cotton plants choked from grass and suffocated in packed dirt, which inhibited the growth of their roots.[24] Slave women also hoed crops with a complementary growing season to cotton, including corn, sweet potatoes and peas.[25] During the month of August, when cotton needed less care, slaves harvested corn.

As plantation records show, slave owners on cotton plantations used male and female slaves for other different tasks. James Allen's plantation book cited, "women, cleaning up horse lot—men making fence," or two days later, "women at manure—men making fence;" later "men around pasture fence, women knocking stalks."[26] Similarly, on another plantation, on April 21, "John with women clearing up thicket;" May 13, "Henry with the women hoeing corn."[27] This work schedule varied according to factors such as weather.

Specialization of labor of the gang system decreased during the cotton harvest.[28] Historians have failed to reach agreement about whether men or women picked the most cotton. In the 1860s, one author, relying on impressionistic evidence, argued that "women are usually the best pickers."[29] Later historians refuted this finding, stating that male slaves picked more cotton per day but that women harvested more overall. Women provided most of the labor because women picked cotton while masters employed some male slaves in other work.[30] On one plantation, slave women picked cotton while the men were "making [animal] pens and fixing scaffolds."[31] More recently, another historian found that men and women averaged similar amounts per day.[32] Slaves gathered about one hundred and fifty pounds per day although some outstanding pickers harvested twice that amount.[33]

Agricultural labor influenced all aspects of a field hand's life. As with many preliterate peasant cultures, men and women sometimes recalled significant events in their lives in terms of their work. One woman, remembering the birth of her two girls, stated, "Lula was born about the last of cotton picking time a year and half before Leanna."[34] Similarly, a male freedman recalled a couple being married in "cotton-picking" time.[35] Reflecting on the age of her daughters, one freedwoman remarked that Sarah was born when "the hands were then scraping cotton," while Cora "was born in July a day or two before the 4th. The 4th. was a holiday with us and she was a day or two old that day and when I got up they were picking the first cotton and I turned to help."[36]

On larger plantations, female slaves worked as either domestic or agricultural hands. House slaves cooked, cleaned, washed, sewed, and cared for white children. Historian James Cobb related Mary's work day on the Doro plantation of Charles Clark (Lucy and Tom Brown's master). Before breakfast, Mary milked the cows, cooked both breakfast and food for "some of other servants, . . . made the beds, dusted, washed the dishes . . . and nursed her own" baby. After breakfast, she straightened up the kitchen, made dinner, "washed dishes, cleaned the dining room, washed a large batch of clothes and hung them out, and began preparing supper. After supper she milked for the second time that day, nursed her child, cleaned the kitchen and retired."[37] Domestic slaves interacted with field hands through work and family.[38] During cotton picking masters sent their house slaves to the fields when they needed additional workers to gather in the crop.[39] Additionally, domestic and field hands intermarried.

Despite the dual function of slave women as laborers and child bearers, slave owners, traders, and buyers appraised male slaves at a higher value than female slaves.[40] At an 1861 convention in Ripley, Mississippi, planters codified the economic distinction between female and male slaves. A slave was considered to be worth $100 at birth and $50 for each year after that "until the maximum value of $1000 is reached for males and $800 for females." After the age of 35 for male slaves, $40 was deducted per year until the age of 60. For female slaves, $32 was deducted per year after the age of 30 until the age of 55.[41] Given that both male and female slaves lost four percent of their monetary value a year, women were worth less at their maximum value and the decline in their worth started earlier.

This gendered difference may have stemmed from the women's drop in fertility after age 30. In contrast, it was not until slave men turned 35 that slave owners considered them to be less suited for physical labor.[42] Some masters developed other rating systems for their workers. They considered slave children to be one quarter of a hand, and as the children grew older they advanced until they became a whole hand. Slave owners designated as "half hands pregnant and nursing women."[43] Slave masters saw their female slaves in terms of their work and their potential value. Slave women viewed themselves as members of slave families.

In spite of their work schedule, slave women found time for their families. One planter's wife sympathetically recalled a slave wife's devotion to her husband: "[S]he cared for his comfort, washed and ironed and made his clothes."[44] After either field or house work, slave women performed many of the domestic chores of their family such as clothes-washing at night or on Sundays.[45] Occasionally, if the weather prohibited field work, particularly during the late fall or winter, women used the time to do their familial tasks. James Allen wrote on rainy days toward the end of November 1860, "hands in cabins," and again in February 1862, "early this morning it rained, snowed, & sleeted . . . women in cabins." Such citations were rare.[46] Generally, inclement weather did not break work schedules. Slave women fulfilled their domestic chores as conscientiously as time and the master permitted. Breakfast and dinner were cooked communally and eaten cold in the fields, although women often prepared supper in the evening for their individual families.[47]

Although freedwomen tried to fulfill their role as slave wives and mothers, Mississippi planters showed limited concern toward pregnant and nursing slave women. In the 1850s the fertility rate in Mississippi was lower than in upper southern states, suggesting that planters traded higher fertility rates for more work in the fields.[48] Masters dictated nursing schedules. Women sometimes nursed their babies in the fields after they finished hoeing or plowing a row.[49] On other plantations, slave women left their field work as often as four times a day to go to the slave nursery to feed their babies for approximately half an hour before returning to the work.[50] On the plantation on which Caroline Taylor lived as a slave, slave mothers nursed their babies four times a day for the first four months of the infant's life, and after four months, three times a day.[51]

At the dictates of slave owners, the majority of women did not care for their own children during the working day.[52] Elderly slave women with the help of older children looked after young children during the day. On one place, "from 1853 until March 1864," Amanda Edward served this function; she had "general management of taking care of the children born on the plantation." She also nursed the sick and "was usually present or immediately saw the children that were born" because she attended the mothers and their babies "at the time of their birth."[53]

Masters sent older children to the fields for simple tasks, placing the supervision of these preadolescents with adult field hands.[54] When trying to determine a child's age, African Americans sometimes associated a given age with a task performed by a child. Such recitations showed the labor functions of even small children during slavery. A freed woman recalled one child who "was a small child . . . large enough to bring a small bucket of water and do light-chores."[55] Similarly, Martha Johnson discussed the ages of her children, Fanny, three months old, "was a suckling little thing," Sam was three years old, "Foll was a pretty good sized boy—big enough to pick up chips, could tote little tin buckets of water if somebody drew it for him, Hudson could go after the cows. Jenny was the only one old enough to work in the fields."[56]

Parents viewed their children as more than potential workers. Families were one way for slave men and women to try to maintain a private world in which they exercised some control. Within the confines of slavery, men and women married and started families in part as a protest against the demeaning and dehumanizing aspects of slavery. Slave men and women believed in the future enough to establish their own family heritage. They often symbolized this beginning with a wedding.

Slave Marriages in Mississippi

Although without legal status because laws deprived slaves of the right of contract, slave marriages were common.[57] According to the pension files of widows of Civil War soldiers, slave marriages occurred frequently throughout the 1850s.[58] In most cases, slaves needed the consent of their master to wed. To reinforce his role as paternalist and to remind slave couples of his authority to legitimate slave matches, the slave owner sometimes chose to officiate at slave weddings. Once Harriet and Job Paul's master gave his permission, "he would read the ceremony out of a book."[59] Susan Alexander recalled her master asking her "if she was willing to take Allen as her husband and do for him all that a woman should and he Allen the same."[60] Occasionally, other whites, such as overseers, performed the service.[61]

Slave preachers also served as ministers. A "fellow slave" who was "a plantation preacher" conducted the marriage ceremony of Henry and Elizabeth Ellison, "with the consent of their owner."[62] Similarly, in Washington County, "a colored preacher was allowed to come to a plantation and marry couples after they got their owner's consent."[63] When slave preachers officiated over the slave nuptials, the ceremonies often occurred in the slave quarters and were less elaborate than when slave masters officiated. Rhetta Blair recalled "a colored preacher married us in Chappel Cross church. . . . We didn't have any supper."[64]

In contrast, some slave weddings, particularly those of favorite household slaves, were quite elaborate and included food and dancing accompanied by slave fiddling. One freedperson remembered being married in "my white folks house. . . . We had a right nice wedding and had plenty to eat."[65] In many instances masters exercised their authority by choosing the person who would conduct the ceremony. When Susan Drane married, her slave mistress, Mrs. Howcutt, arranged an elaborate marriage for her, with the "Rev. Mr. Samsome who was then pastor" of a church in Canton performing the ceremony. The slave-holding family with "a large number of invited guests" attended the nuptials held in their parlor and provided "a grand supper" afterward.[66] Masters on occasion released slaves from work when marriages were celebrated.[67] Marriages often took place at holidays. David and Marie Anderson "were married together with a number of other colored people on Christmas day," the most popular time for slave weddings.[68]

Other couples simply began living together with their master's permission but without a wedding ceremony. Slaves and southern whites commonly referred to these relationships as "took up." Technically, all marriages during slavery were "took up" because laws forbade legal marriages for slaves.[69] As one pension file recorded, a couple "were married to each other at Rankin County, Mississippi by taking up with each other as man and wife with the consent of their masters about the year 1853."[70] Planters and slaves considered slave marriages without a ceremony to be as valid as those that began with wedding ceremonies. One slave father explained that when his daughter married, "I gave my consent and both the owners agreeing, he came on a certain night and they went to bed together and after that time he visited and cohabited with her as his wife. . . . There was no formal ceremony, but they considered themselves husband and wife and were so regarded by others." He elaborated on the seriousness of the relationship by adding, "I was married in the same way and lived with my wife until her death and had seven children."[71]

Slave owners more often interfered with a slave's selection of a mate if the intended spouse lived on another plantation.[72] Cross-plantation marriages complicated the economic interests of the master, particularly the owner of the slave husband. Given that slave children inherited the status of the mother and lived with her, only the woman's owner financially benefited from the labor or sale of children. Even though most masters opposed them, cross-plantation marriages occurred with spouses who were usually within walking distance of a few miles. Julia Murry explained that "Nicholas Thomas had been courting me for about a year and my white folks tried to run him off the place, as they did not want their young women to marry off the plantation, but finally when they found they could not make him stop coming they consented that we should be married."[73] Talbert Royal explained he and his future wife "lived five miles apart and I asked her master for her and he consented to our marriage."[74] Typically the husband traveled at least twice a week, usually on the same nights each week, to see his wife. As one freedwoman explained, "At first he came to our place on what was called wife night Wednesday night and from Saturday night to Monday night."[75]

Although masters rarely exercised their power to interfere with the slaves' selection of a marriage partner, they always retained that right. During the war, a gang of white men assaulted Lewis Carroll when he traveled to see his wife on another plantation. The ruffians probably feared that an enslaved male traveling alone would seize the opportunity to flee to the Yankees. After the incident, Lewis Carroll's master insisted that Lewis give up his wife and take a wife on the same plantation, "so that he would not have to go off the place at night."[76] Forced to quit his wife and forbidden to visit her again, Lewis Carroll complied and sought out the father of a slave women whom he was willing to marry. The woman's father objected because of Carroll's existing cross-plantation marriage, but their owner insisted. Slave and master definitions of what constituted a binding marriage sometimes clashed.

Couples married to establish stability in their lives. They knew however that slavery threatened their marriages. Susan Smith lived with her slave husband from 1843 to 1846, but her "old master objected to me having a lover or husband" and moved her to his plantation in Alabama. When he died, her young master "brought me so I could have the man whom I wanted for a husband" and he reunited her with her spouse.[77] The Bureau of Refugees, Freedmen, and Abandoned Lands, commonly known as the Freedmen's Bureau, a federal agency established by Congress to aid former slaves, kept marriage registers of freedpeople. These logs provide an indication of slave marital longevity. Historian Herbert Gutman analyzed data from the Mississippi marriage records of 1864–1865 and determined that approximately 18 percent of the slave marriages ended involuntarily.

Gutman reported that, of freedpeople over 20 years of age who registered their marriage in this period, one in six "had been separated from a spouse by force;" and of men over 30, one in four, and for women, one in five.[78] Using other Mississippi Freedmen's Bureau records, historian John Blassingame determined that almost 39 percent of the slave marriages recorded in Mississippi were "broken by the master."[79] These figures probably represent the statistical range of the number of marriages broken by slave owners. Slave movement from the Upper South to the Lower South probably explains many of these forced separations.

Attitudes toward Slave Marriage

In spite of the nonlegal status and fragility of slave marriages, the surrounding community, including slaves from neighboring plantations, acknowledged the validity of slave marriages.[80] As one former slave holder commented, "[T]hey were recognized as man and wife by their respective masters and their families and by their acquaintances generally." Other former slaves said of their friends' marriages, "their marriage was never questioned by their friends or acquaintances."[81]

Slave men and women sometimes used different criteria and norms than slave owners when determining a slave's marital status. Masters defined slave marriages by whether they sanctioned the marriage. The slave community recognized the master's power to marry slaves to each other, but it also considered the quality of a relationship between the slave man and woman. The complicated and atypical intimacies of Charles Hutchins are an example of how slaves and masters defined which slaves were "husband" and "wife" and which were not. In the early 1850s, Charles and his wife Bridget married with the consent of their master. While living with Bridget, Charles began an intimate relationship with another slave woman, Maria. Their owner, E. J. Quince, "tried to prevent [it] but could not." To break up the relationship, Quince gave Maria to his daughter as a wedding present, effectively removing her from the plantation. Soon after, Charles became attracted to another woman, Susan, and once again the master intervened, explaining, "I also tried to prevent and hold him to his lawful wife but finding I could not do so and the war coming on I suffered Charles and his lawful wife to separate." Charles lived with Susan and occasionally visited Maria until he fled to the Union forces in Natchez, where he enlisted. Bridget also began to cohabit with another man. Charles never returned to the plantation.

When interviewed by a pension examiner, E. J. Quince remained adamant that neither Susan nor Maria was Charles's wife even though both bore children by him. Quince argued that neither woman had been married to Charles with Quince's consent and thus were not married. Moreover Charles's "lawful wife [Bridget] still being on [Quince's] place" during Charles's cohabitation with the other two women indicated to Quince that Charles and Bridget were still married. Quince's unwittingly ironic use of the word "lawful" indicated his confidence in his authority over the personal lives of slaves. In his mind his word was law.

African Americans previously owned by Quince agreed with their former master's recognition of Charles's first marriage to Bridget. The plantation slave community, however, accepted the demise of the marriage more willingly than Quince. For freedpeople, Charles's refusal to live with Bridget signaled that he considered the marriage to be over. Moreover, Bridget's decision to begin a new cohabitational relationship proved that she considered her marriage to be at an end rather than merely in the midst of a temporary separation. Slaves (and later freedpeople) referred to this practice of non-legal but community recognized divorce as "quitting." Freedman Edward Letcher recalled, "at the time Charlie ran off I was still on the place and Charlie was with Susan about as much as Maria those times and nobody considered either one of them Charlie's wife. Bridget was the only one who could have been called his wife." Letcher added a caveat that once Bridget began a relationship with "Frank Cade . . . of course she was not his [Charles's] wife then." When first questioned about Charles, Susan insisted that she was his wife by stating "I did not consider myself the sweetheart (a term roughly equivalent to lover) of the soldier. I considered myself his wife because I was the last one with him." Although another male slave concurred with her view of her marriage, most of the freedpeople providing testimony did not. When confronted with the testimony of E. J. Quince and others, Susan deferred by admitting, "It is truth as Master Eddy says that Charles Hutchins was married to Bridget and so I did not have Masters permission to marry Charles. . . . All that master Eddy says is exactly true. The slaves just called me Susan—they did not call me Charles wife. They just knew I was his 'sweetheart.'"

Although Charles Hutchins's personal life was more complicated than that of most men, the former slave men and women who knew him recognized the significance of his first and only slave wedding. Most accepted the end of the marriage when Charles and Bridget quit and cohabited with other partners. The slave community might have willingly accepted either Susan or Maria as Charles's second wife, particularly given Bridget's newer liaison, if Charles had established a stable relationship with either one of them.[82] These definitions of "husband and wife" continued after emancipation.[83]

Masters often encouraged slave marriages, believing that the arrangement created a more stable work force by keeping slaves from running away. They also thought that marriage helped to establish a peaceful environment in the slave quarters by regularizing sexual relations. Religious owners who perceived themselves as moral paternalists also espoused the importance of slave marriage. One planter explained, "I did not permit my slaves to go together without formal marriages."[84] As one freedperson recalled, "on our plantation they wouldn't let them live together unless they was married."[85] Malinda Hubbard explained that once her master learned that she was pregnant by George Hubbard, her owner "made us get married."[86] Certain owners also interfered in domestic disputes, in part to protect the integrity of slave marriages and to maintain order on the plantation. Masters such as E. J. Quince tried to enforce the sanctity of slave marriages, in that case by sending away a woman with whom one of his married slaves was being unfaithful.

Although the majority of slaves selected their own spouses, exceptions existed.[87] During slavery, Louisa married her slave husband because "the white folks put us together."[88] As opposed to slave marriages that the slave community accepted as valid, slave men and women viewed this coupling differently, particularly when the spouses failed to love each other over time.[89] Adaline Gordon dismissed her relationship with her slave husband because they were "not regularly married" because they had been "made to go together by the white people who said they had to have 'niggers.'"[90] Mary Allen recalled bitterly that she never married during slavery but her "owners sent a man by the name of John Allen to live with me in order that I might have children."[91]

Sources show many types of African American marriages, varying from those in which partners bore great love and affection for each other to those in which marital discord was the keynote of the relationship. Couples struggled to be together during slavery and the war. Union officials in Holly Springs and Memphis noted that "[T]he greater number [of runaway slaves] have lived together as husband and wife, by mutual consent."[92]

Slave women were workers, wives, and mothers. Their work for their masters continually conflicted with their labor and devotion to their families. The overwhelming economic success of cotton in Mississippi depended on slave labor. These agricultural demands left little time for family life. Yet slave couples married and raised families. They grounded their faith in these informal marriages by judging the quality of the relationship and how long they maintained it. Community reactions also helped establish the perimeters of a "binding" although not legal slave marriage.

With the war came emancipation behind Yankee lines in Mississippi. The war separated women like Lucy Brown, whose story began this book, from their husbands. Freedom profoundly changed both the work and family lives of slave women and men, resulting in labor and marriage contracts. Although the war freed them, Lucy Brown and other freedwomen continued to rely on the agricultural and domestic skills developed during slavery. Freedwomen wanted greater change than emancipation brought. They sought more time for their families and less control of their labor by whites. Liberation from slavery only partially fulfilled the desire of slave women and men for freedom. Moreover, first they had to survive a brutal war.

ONE

THE IMPACT OF THE
WAR OF LIBERATION ON
FAMILIES AND WORK

"So glad I'm free" [1]

On the Fourth of July 1863, Vicksburg finally fell to the Union army. The war had come slowly to Mississippi. Northern troops failed to penetrate much of the state until late in the conflict. Significant fighting in the state began in 1862 with General Ulysses S. Grant's first failed attempt to take Vicksburg, but the heaviest fighting did not begin until 1863.[2] While Grant's forces prepared to capture Vicksburg in the spring of that year, Charles Clark's wife desperately tried to hold on to her most productive slaves, among them Thomas and Lucy Brown. According to Charles Clark's plantation record, Tom Brown was a particularly good worker. Brown picked more cotton than most slaves; he also worked the cotton press and took care of the hogs. In January 1862, sixteen slaves had fled Clark's Doro plantation, so Mrs. Clark had reason to be concerned.[3]

Mrs. Clark began to move her slaves south from the plantation in northwestern Bolivar County to Fayette, Mississippi, close to Natchez in the southern part of the state. Federal troops intercepted them en route and moved them to Grand Gulf, north of Fayette, near Port Gibson and southwest of Vicksburg. At Grand Gulf, Union officials separated the slave men from the slave women. Soon after, "Thomas Brown . . . and other coloured men were enlisted in the US army." The Fifty-third Infantry of the United States Colored Troops (USCT), which included private Thomas Brown in its ranks, was stationed in Vicksburg. Once there, Thomas reunited with Lucy, who had recently arrived in the city. Thomas Brown died while in service.[4]

The war transported the vast majority of African Americans in Mississippi from slavery to freedom and caused profound changes in the family and work lives of African Americans and in race relations in the nation. During and after the war, African Americans struggled to create the private lives that had been barely allowed during slavery. The war broke up families even while it held the promise that families would be unified with emancipation.

Reconstitution of families after the war was a primary objective of African Americans. Former slave men and women wanted to try to mend the damage that had been done to families by slavery and the war. They also fought to maintain the integrity of their definition of family against white employers' need for labor and control.

During the war, slave men and women either remained on plantations or went with or to the Union soldiers. When the Union soldiers penetrated a particular area, slaves fled to them. Raids on food supplies by both armies and the resulting devastation influenced slaves to leave ruined plantations and flee to the Union army. When men either volunteered or were impressed into the army, their families wanted to stay near them within the Union lines. Enslaved people in remote areas far from Union soldiers, however, were far less likely to flee. Slave women with very young children whose husbands left with the Union army also found flight difficult.

The Disruption of Slave Families in Mississippi during the War

Slaves supported the Civil War because, along with other benefits, freedom promised to end the break-up of slave families. But, ironically, the war also disrupted the family life of slaves.[5] Although the fighting did not start in earnest in Mississippi until 1862, the temporary successes and defeats of Union and Confederate troops caused the control of territory to change sides, leaving plantation life in confusion. In 1862, Grant's failed attempt to take Vicksburg created chaos and caused raiding and counter-raiding on plantations. The Union Army won and lost territory along the Mississippi River. By August 1862, the Confederates had recaptured large sections of the Mississippi River. The evacuations of plantations by planters separated members of slave families; masters left some slaves behind and forced others to accompany them. By mid-1863 and the fall of Vicksburg, much more of Mississippi was under Union control, but Confederate raids made life on plantations far from safe.

Once fighting began, slave men were forced to leave their families to accompany their masters into the Confederate army, serving as body guards and personal servants.[6] Beginning in 1862, the Confederate government also impressed slave men to dig trenches and to build bridges and fortifications.[7] Confederate army officials wanted only physically fit slave males, deciding that "old men, women and children will be allowed to remain" on plantations.[8] Initially, white southerners considered the Confederate army to be a secure place for their male slaves. The masters were convinced that military supervision of the men prevented slave insurrections or escape to the Union lines.

As the Confederate government increased its demands for slave men, planters began to resent this policy, particularly when the government failed to care properly for the slaves or to compensate their owners adequately. Planter James Allen raised other objections, "Mr. Hankerson down with requisition for negroes to work on V'burg Fortifications one night, declined sending any—can't walk negroes 25 miles to work 1 night & no overseer to work them when they get there."[9] However, the reluctance of slave owners failed to stop the Confederate military from appropriating male slaves for manual labor.[10]

Impressment caused slave men to have to leave their families, but masters who deserted their plantations also broke up slave families. When they fled from encroaching Union soldiers, planters rarely considered the unity of slave families. To minimize the chance of their slaves running away, Mississippi slave owners moved them to Texas or the interior of Alabama and Georgia.[11] Owners often chose not to move all their slaves, or "furlough" them, as they referred to these involuntary migrations of slaves. Thomas Steward sent one of his female slaves to Arkansas, but he kept her children in Mississippi.[12] One slave owner took his slaves to South Carolina, including a male slave named Anderson, but he left behind Anderson's wife, Minerva, whom he considered to be too sick to travel.[13] Slave masters preferred to relocate individual slaves or groups of enslaved people who were believed to be most likely to escape to the Yankees. According to one freedwoman, "before Vicksburg (long before) surrendered Dr. Phillips took all his young people slaves into Alabama near Demopolis out of the way of the Yankees."[14] When moving his slaves, one owner separated a slave woman from her grandmother. "She am so old 'n feeble," the woman explained. "I hates dat, but don't say nothin' at all."[15]

These evacuations also split up abroad slave marriages, in which husbands and wives lived on different plantations. Amanda Mackie's slave owners moved their slaves to Montgomery, Alabama, while her husband's owners "run theirs off up in the Miss. River somewhere. I never seen my husband after I got back." She later discovered that he had remarried.[16]

Individual slaves protested these forced separations when they threatened slave families. When her slave mistress planned to move her slaves to Alabama, a domestic slave, Emmeline Trott, soon to give birth and unable to travel, pleaded for her young son to remain with her. Her mistress reluctantly agreed.[17] When Hosea Brittain discovered that his wife's owner was going to move his wife, who lived on a different place, to Alabama, he, according to his former owner, "was very much opposed to being sent away from his wife." His wife's owner bought Hosea so that the couple could be together.[18] One woman reported that her brother-in-law and his wife "ran off to Vicksburg to keep from" being furloughed to North Carolina.[19] Slaves resisted these evacuations en masse. One owner complained that planters who moved their slaves to safer territory "lost nearly if not all the men and many of the women and children. . . . I believe every Negro on this place will go to the Yankees before they go to the hills."[20]

The enlistment of thousands of African American men from Mississippi, the majority of whom were slaves, in the Union army caused a greater impact on slave families than either furloughing or impressment to the Confederate army did.[21] Although they were initially reluctant, federal officials finally allowed African American men to become soldiers in 1862, even though they had previously used escaped slave men as army laborers. Almost eighteen thousand men, close to ten percent of the African American male population in Mississippi, formed the core of several segregated regiments of the United States Colored Troops (as they were designated).[22] Although many African American men volunteered enthusiastically, the Union army also coerced slave men when white officers failed to fill their quotas.[23] As white northerners resisted the draft, the military pressured slave men to enlist.

Black soldiers were not treated equally with white soldiers. Throughout most of the war, the government paid African Americans less than white soldiers ($10 as opposed to $13 each month) and refused to promote them to officers. Black soldiers also performed more manual labor than white soldiers such as loading and unloading wagons and building fortifications. They received inferior weapons and less qualified medical care when they needed it.

In addition to the inequitable treatment they received in the army, leaving their families to go to the Union soldiers was emotionally wrenching and sometimes dangerous for slaves. Masters and overseers treated them as runaway slaves. When his father escaped during the war, Levi

McLaurin's son recalled, "I was present when he left and I told him good-bye. He said he would send back after us all." The son "saw men put dogs on his tracks and heard dogs running after my father." Another male slave joined McLaurin but turned back after three miles "because I could not leave my family."[24] Mary E. Johnson remembered her father's departure "very distinctly as it was the last time that I ever saw him."[25]

Families who lived on plantations close to Natchez and Vicksburg where the military was stationed received information about their male relatives through friends or returning servicemen. Eliza Ann Mathey, a domestic slave, was unable to escape to Natchez with her husband James Mathey because "her owners watched her and would not allow her to go, but there were coloured people passing back and forth secretly who conveyed messages" and informed her of her husband's new location.[26] Eliza Ann's husband, a private in Natchez, also sent her soap and a handkerchief.[27]

As southern white men entered the Confederate army, fewer masters or slave patrollers stood in the way of runaways.[28] Pension records of soldiers' wives on plantations close to liberated cities such as Natchez and Vicksburg where United States Colored Troops were stationed give the impression of considerable movement of quasi-free people. A few women even seemed to commute from nearby plantations to the cities. One soldier's wife remained on the plantation until "word came for her to come in town." Immediately, she went to be with her husband, who had managed to send for her.[29]

Women and Children on the Plantation

Many enslaved women and, less often, men remained on plantations during the war.[30] Enslaved women and men stayed on plantations when they lived on places far removed from the presence of Union soldiers. Moreover northern soldiers who encountered slaves more frequently encouraged men rather than women to leave the plantation. The army wanted male laborers and, later in the war, potential African American soldiers. One freedwoman explained that after her husband left for the army, "I staid right at home all the time. Mr. Minnus (last owner) told us that if we got our freedom we could get it there as well as any place and all we women staid right there until peace was declared."[31] Even with the soldiers close by, movement involved a certain amount of risk and the home plantation seemed to provide more safety.

Home had complex meanings for Mississippi slaves.[32] Although slaves did not choose their homes, once they were established, they made them their own. For some, home meant their birthplace, which was sometimes out of state. For others, like the woman on Minnus's plantation, it meant the place where they lived and felt emotional attachment.[33] Many historians have discussed the strength of the community (of which family and kin were crucial components) that slaves created on plantations.

Slaves located themselves by referring to their respective masters. In a more personally meaningful way, they also placed themselves by making connections with other slaves, particularly family members. The slave master and slave family as dual self-identifying points can be seen in a conversation between two USCT soldiers. As one soldier explained, "we were talking about who we belonged to." Although these two strangers began their discussion with the names of their masters, they soon moved to their own families. As soon as one soldier mentioned that his master's name was Nat Kinnison, the other replied that his wife's former owner's surname was also Kinnison and that her master must have been the brother to his master. The first soldier recalled, "I remembered that Nat Kinnison the brother of my owner had a girl named Isabella," who turned out to be the wife of the other soldier. After the first soldier's death, the second soldier contacted Isabella and informed her that he had known her late husband.[34] This complex sense of home, tied to family, in addition to such factors as troop movements, provided reasons why some enslaved people, particularly women, stayed while others fled to the Union soldiers.

Most of all, home meant family. Primary sources such as pension records suggest that the decisions of slave women to go with the Yankees or to remain on plantations often hinged on family concerns. Family ties help explain the reluctance of slaves to leave a particular place during the war even though they might have wanted to rid themselves of a particular master. Slave kinship strengthened a sense of belonging to a given plantation. Although slave masters viewed remaining on the plantations as a sign of devotion, slaves who stayed offered little proof of loyalty or a passive acceptance of slavery.[35] Slave women often stayed to achieve their own goals for freedom, including the goal of keeping their families together. The military pension interviews of widows indicate that women who stayed on plantations when other slaves left were more likely to be mothers with children under the age of ten.[36] As one planter noted in 1863, "71 negroes went to Yanks have 3 old men & a few women & children left."[37] After he became a soldier, Nicholas Thomas told his wife that "he did not want me to come away to see him and leave the children at home alone."[38] When Millie Stewart came with her husband, Horace, to Vicksburg where Horace enlisted, Millie was unable to bring her toddler. Another soldier's wife who shared a residence with Millie in Vicksburg recalled, 'she frequently spoke of having a little girl back at Natchez where she came from. . . . [S]he spoke of her as 'my baby'." Apparently the separation became too painful because a few months later Millie brought her young daughter to Vicksburg.[39] Hannah White felt the pull between residing with her husband and the needs of her children. She recalled that while her husband was stationed in Vicksburg, she "visited him often except for a year when I stayed up the river with my children."[40]

Elsy, a domestic slave woman, was concerned with the security of her child during the turbulence of the war. Some domestics felt caught between the pull of factors such as working in a familiar environment and the safety of their children and the push of leaving. Materially, domestic slaves lost the most by fleeing. On larger plantations, their housing differed from that of field slaves because they lived closer to their owners. On Joseph Montgomery's plantation near Port Gibson, field hands lived in the quarters but domestic servants such as the cook, seamstress, and waiters lived "in the yard near the big house."[41] The accommodations were often roomier and better furnished with more cast-off pieces from whites.[42]

Pressed by her husband and mistress, Elsy stated her preference for living with her man over remaining with her slave mistress. But Elsy refused to forsake familiar surroundings. She did not want to risk giving up a known environment for the perils of freedom without some reassurance that she and her children would have a new home. Security for her family rather than loyalty to her mistress was her first concern, even though her husband wanted to move immediately. Concerned about her children, Elsy refused to move until he found "her a home and a way of earning a living." Meanwhile her mistress, Elizabeth Meade Ingram, offered her $12 a month and provisions for her and her four children if she remained. Ingram explained, "It seems big wages, with four children, making five mouths to feed; but I know her ways and she mine, besides she is strictly honest and true a rare thing in a black."[43]

Elizabeth Meade Ingram saw Elsy's decision to remain on the plantation as evidence of her loyalty, although she was not completely convinced she would stay: ". . . don't feel as I could trust anyone, but Elsy; she feeds and takes care of me. My children must never forget or desert her; and if she should leave us, remember she has tried to do right." Later she wrote, "Elsy still true . . . she is very attentive and kind, and does all she can to make us comfortable. . . . And if not too bothered, I still think she will stay." She found solace in Elsy, who did "not like to see me work" and reminded her of a more protected and, for her, civilized environment. A loyal Confederate (although born in Pennsylvania), she watched Grant's soldiers on their way to Vicksburg and watched her own slaves ransack her beautiful Ashwood plantation home, destroying or looting most of her personal belongings. Afterward, many of the slaves deserted the place.[44]

Although Elsy and her husband disagreed about her service to her mistress, Elsy tried to negotiate the meaning of freedom while working for her slave mistress. According to Ingram, Elsy had "a hard time between her duty to her husband and that to her old mistress. . . . He complains that she waits on me and none of the others do; that she behaves just as if she was not free." Elsy showed signs of appreciating the meaning of freedom to a greater degree than her husband acknowledged. She insisted on setting her own work schedules. She stated her own preference for the benefits of freed labor by her willingness to leave if her husband was able to obtain "a way of getting a living." Her mistress was not convinced that Elsy would stay out of loyalty without wages so Elsy probably had at some point shown interest in free rather than slave labor. Whether she finally left is unclear from the diary excerpts.[45]

As Elsy's story shows, the plantation environment changed with the vicissitudes of war. As soldiers invaded parts of Mississippi, slave homes failed to provide security. The war also disrupted established work patterns. The loss of slave men to either the Confederate or the Union army depleted plantations of needed labor.[46] The presence of fewer men also made plantations more vulnerable to raids from both armies.

Slave women's work changed as the war progressed. Wealthy slave owners moved their domestic town slaves to rural areas in order to restrict their mobility and to increase their own agricultural work force. Although the work of domestic and field hands was rarely completely separate during slavery, the distinctions blurred even more during the war. Victoria Randle Lawson, who had worked in a town in Monroe County, was sent to her master's plantation and recalled, "den, I didn't know nothing 'cept go out dar and chop dat corn and cotton."[47] Similarly, female field hands took on domestic responsibilities in addition to their field work. Before the war, women field hands became cloth makers on rainy winter days, but during the war they were regularly transformed into spinners and weavers by necessity.[48] The Union attempted to blockade the entire Confederate coast and concentrated their ships most heavily off the coasts of the major ports. This effort limited the supplies, including cloth, that were brought to plantations. One freedman remembered, "[M]y mammy was a field hand, but when de war come she had to help spin and weave, cause we couldn't get no cloth." Her owners, who resided near Alabama on the eastern side of the state, had previously bought cloth in Mobile, but because of the Union's blockade they were unable to obtain any.[49] During the war, slave owners made fewer gender distinctions when they assigned work than they previously had. One former slave recalled that after the slave men left a plantation near Athens, Mississippi, "de women and us boys had to finish de crop dat year.[50]

Although many women stayed on plantations to try to best provide for their children, raids by soldiers of both armies made it more difficult for slave women to maintain a safe home for their families. One slave-holding woman complained that "our own soldiers will eat us out of house and home while they are camped so near."[51] The northern army also lived off the land as they marched. The military determined that the North needed to break the will of southern whites to achieve victory, resulting in the destruction of civilian property in the South. As Sherman graphically explained after his army marched west to east from Vicksburg to Meridian, Mississippi, in the early part of 1864, "We lived off the country and made a swath of desolation 50 miles broad across the state of Mississippi which the present generation will not forget."[52] This Union strategy, combined with diminishing supplies of the southern soldiers, led both armies to forage from African Americans and the white population.

Food shortages caused great hardships and even encouraged slave women, when possible, to leave with the Yankees to avoid starvation.[53] As one slave owner complained, "no loyal citizens can obtain permission to purchase needful supplies of food or clothing—for the starving half-naked blacks (women & children) that remain on the plantations . . . "[54] Women and children who stayed on the plantation after the rampages of the soldiers recalled that they "were all hungry many a time" during the war.[55]

The war also complicated race relations for slave women. Their initial contact with Union soldiers who were raiding plantations was sometimes brutal. Northern soldiers were the liberators of the slaves but sometimes also their tormentors.[56] Some soldiers who at first shared plunder from the master with slaves later stole from the slave quarters. Some soldiers saw little distinction between slaves and the property of slave owners. Few of the Union soldiers were committed abolitionists. In fact, many shared the racist views of their countrymen and women.[57]

Women on plantations were unable to protect themselves against as-

saults. Mary Ingraham's diary noted that Yankees tried to "abuse" two
slave women. In a private manuscript, a Confederate captain with a place
near Vicksburg noted that "all the Negro women were ravished, the Yankees held them whilst others were gratifying their hellish desires. This is
the testimony of the old Negroes."[58] Confederate soldiers indulged in the
same activity. According to a secessionist, southern military men "visited
the Negro quarters and subjected the women to their lusts, raising loud
complaints from the men slaves."[59]

Slave women resented the harsh treatment from Union soldiers and
some were not inclined to aid the northerners. Possibly because of the
brutal treatment they received from Union soldiers, some slave women
helped their masters. The recollections of planters as well as 1930s Works
Progress Administration narratives of former slaves sometimes contain
vignettes of the cunning domestic slaves used when they saved the property of their masters during encounters with Yankee soldiers. When Union
soldiers directed one master to surrender his silver, one of his slave wom-
en, undetected by the soldiers, quickly scooped all the flatware into her
apron.[60] Similarly, Bell Kearney, in her memoir *Slaveholder's Daughter*,
tells a similar tale of a slave woman who, when confronted by a Union soldier who demanded to know the location of the silver, responded by explaining that her owners were so cheap they refused to buy anything that
nice. This same slave woman earlier had helped bury the family valuables
near the spot where she spoke to the Yankees.[61]

Such anecdotes about faithful slaves reinforced the self-perceptions
of many plantation owners as paternalists. Slave owners often spoke of
slaves as being part of their families and used the analogy of the family
to explain slavery's hierarchical nature.[62] Slave masters were patriarchal
heads of households that included slaves. They specifically included female domestic slaves in their conception of family.[63] Although they relied
on physical force and state laws to ensure slavery's survival, many nineteenth-century slave owners also tried to foster a sense of personal loyalty
among their slaves. Planters justified their ownership by contending that
they were fatherly guardians who expected the strict obedience (even when
they failed to receive it) of racially inferior slaves.[64]

Planters and their families saw their slaves mainly in the context of
their own lives. For example, slave holding families remembered the birth
dates of their slaves by relating the event to events in the life of a white
family member. (African Americans in the pension record testimony rarely remembered a date in their lives by attaching it to an event significant
to their former masters.) Writing to a freedwoman previously owned by

her father, a former slave mistress reminisced, " . . . your age was said to be 20 years old when you were bought—you nursed my brother George Darden, 58 years ago, so I firmly believe you are 78 years old."[65] Mrs. Lizzie A. Childress recalled the age of one of her father's former slaves because the child was born after her own brother came home from the Confederate army.[66] Another slave owner's daughter recalled that her father's former slave "suckled my nephew A. F. Herring, who was born in Dec. 1870, at the same time she nursed her own child." Thus, she assumed that the two children shared the same birth year, 1870.[67] Because they viewed enslaved men and women only as connected to them, former slave owners did not comprehend the desire of African American women and men for greater independence from white domination in their personal and work lives.

The decisions of slaves to escape caused slave owners to express a great sense of betrayal. Reverend Samuel A. Agnew summed up the feeling of most white slave masters when he concluded that "negroes as a class are faithless."[68] He further commented on the hypocrisy of slaves by noting that "Becky bid Mother and the girls goodbye and they say looked like she hated to leave. But this was only an appearance."[69] Even after the war ended, whites viewed the desire of their former slaves to seek employment elsewhere as personal disloyalty, although vestiges (and in certain instances even expectations by freedwomen) of planter paternalism remained. The inability of former slave holders to comprehend freedom's appeal or to accept the reality of emancipation helped poison race relations after the war.[70]

The Desire for Freedom

Even slaves who remained on the plantations wanted freedom.[71] Dora Franks, a young domestic slave who overheard the whites in the household talking about the war, recounted, she "started prayin' for freedom and all de rest of de women did de same thing."[72] As soon as slaves learned of the war, they assumed that the reason for the war was slave emancipation. They shrewdly realized, earlier than northern leaders, that the North could not achieve victory with slavery intact.[73] Enslaved men and women eagerly anticipated the war, assuming that they would win their freedom.

As the war dragged on, northern leaders began to acknowledge this wisdom. After military orders freed slaves in areas under Union control and, later, Lincoln's more general Emancipation Proclamation, northern soldiers who entered portions of Mississippi informed slaves of their freedom. These scenes could be quite dramatic. One freedman vividly recalled the day that three federal cavalry men rode onto Major Sartin's plantation in Pike's County in the southern part of the state. As they looked for Sartin, they chanced upon a group of slave women hoeing behind a slave man who was harrowing the cotton to loosen the soil. "The soldiers then inquired of him who the negroes were working for and if they had been told that they were free." As soon as the soldiers left the field to find the slave master, the women "rushed to the quarters telling the news to the other women and children." The cavalry men forced Major Sartin to gather his slaves together, and the soldiers announced to them their emancipation.[74]

Enslaved people who were freed by Union soldiers during the war discovered that their emancipation depended on the location of the soldiers.[75] Because the northern armies moved on after they declared emancipation, slaves who remained on plantations learned that, at least in the short term, freedom could be temporary. The problem became acute at different times during the war such as when Sherman collected thirty thousand soldiers to begin his march to the sea. The absence of Sherman's army at various intervals meant that the North gave up vast areas of Mississippi to the Confederates. Once the Union better established itself, thousands of slave men and women resided behind the Union lines for the rest of the war.

The disappointment and distress of African Americans during the war and Reconstruction failed to undermine the genuine love of freedom that both male and female slaves possessed. One story of an elderly slave couple illustrates the point. When Si and his wife Cindy left a plantation near Vicksburg to join the northern soldiers, Cindy died from the arduous trip. When his former slave owner met him later in Union-controlled territory, he demanded "'Uncle Si, why on earth did you so cruelly bring Aunt Cindy here for, through all of such hardship, there by causing her death?" Lifting up his eyes and looking directly at his former master he answered, "I couldn't help it, marster; but then you see, she died free."[76] A significant part of this story is Si's refusal to look down when speaking to a white man. Whites considered an act such as being looked at directly as an affront; freedpeople interpreted it as an assertion of their equality and liberation.

This simple action, with its two different interpretations, symbolized the coming conflict under Reconstruction that started during the war. Clashes occurred both during the war and after as whites contested freedpeople's definitions of freedom. For former slaves, freedom included family unity, mobility, economic opportunity, and autonomous communities. In contrast, whites desired race and economic relations based on subservient African Americans.

Like Cindy and Si, thousands of other slaves gained their freedom by going to the Union soldiers. Slaves' encounters with the Yankees gave them their first taste of freedom, with all of its complexities and contradictions. Federal policies about marriage, the family, and free (nonslave) wage labor that were established during the war had a profound impact on African American women and would ultimately lay the groundwork for Reconstruction after the war.

WITHIN
THE UNION LINES

"The arrival among us of these hordes was like the oncoming of cities"[1]

When her husband Thomas Brown began his military service in 1863, the Union army sent Lucy Brown and other soldiers' wives to what she described as a "corral across the river from Vicksburg" at Youngs Point, Louisiana. She was "kept there for about a year" by the Union army until she managed to move to Vicksburg where her husband was stationed. Living outside her husband's army camp, she "used to visit him and sometimes he would visit me." In Vicksburg, they "were married again by the chaplain of the regiment."[2] The army provided Lucy and Thomas Brown with their first opportunity to be legally married, since their slave marriage had no status in law. Brown used the phrase, "married again" because she considered her slave marriage to be valid.

During the war, freedwomen composed the majority of the workers under the experiment of northern-imposed labor contracts for nonslave labor on plantations in Mississippi. Freedwomen in areas that had been captured by the Union army sometimes spent part of the war in cities and in camps established by the army. Ultimately thousands ended up on plantations that were leased either to white northerners or to southern whites who swore loyalty to the United States. Military officials in the Mississippi Valley established two approaches to African American self-sufficiency: free (nonslave) wage labor developed largely with female workers (although African American men served in the Union military) and land ownership by an elite minority of African American males.[3] After the war, the Freedmen's Bureau continued the labor policies that had been developed under wartime labor contracts.

Northern officials believed that freedwomen should be an integral part of free labor; they easily reconciled their own race- and class-bound views of appropriate gender roles with field labor for African American women. White northerners considered African American women to be similar to immigrant working-class women. Middle-class whites did not apply their bourgeois beliefs about female delicacy to women in these two groups. Therefore, native-born whites believed that, unlike middle-class women, they did not need to be kept from the harshness of the workplace; nor did they believe that they possessed innate female physical weaknesses that made them unsuitable for hard labor. The work that black women did for whites, rather than their efforts to maintain their own private lives, was the concern of whites both before and after the war. Northern whites assumed that black women would continue to labor partly because black women had worked as slaves, partly because they were poor and lacked "proper" breeding or status, and partly because of their race, which whites often conflated with class. Although northern white women worked for wages, the prevailing ideology about race allowed whites to think more easily of white women as temporary workers rather than as workers first and foremost.

Except for a few African American landowners, northerners and southerners defined "work" for African Americans as labor that was performed for whites.[4] Thus free labor did not include the option of working for oneself. Moreover, African American employment, both as it was practiced and as northerners imagined it for the future, remained central to the North's concept of a reconstructed South. In this new South, slaves would be transformed into free laborers; even their character and morals would change. Northern reformers, including many Freedmen's Bureau officials after the war, touted agricultural labor for wages as similar to industrial work in the north. In both cases, honest hard work cultivated the desired characteristics in the workforce, northerners believed.[5] Although they also held biological notions of race, northern reformers blamed the institution of slavery for instilling sloth, dishonesty, thievery, and sexual promiscuity among slaves. As Samuel Thomas, a white officer of an African American regiment argued, "[S]lavery has made them what they are!"[6] In contrast, southern whites traced these supposed traits to innate biological inferiority. Northern free labor arguments rested on the principle that men generally did not want to work and only labored for the things they needed and desired. Slavery artificially kept people from working diligently because it provided for basic needs such as shelter but gave no additional incentives to work harder or more productively within a free labor economy.[7]

Northerners such as military officials and Freedmen's Bureau agents saw wage labor as a counterbalance to the negative impact of slavery that would also keep African Americans from depending economically on the federal government.[8] Northerners, particularly abolitionists but also others in the military, believed that African Americans could become an effective free labor force without direct coercion. As historian Laura Edwards concluded, "this view of African Americans is consonant with the racial ideology held by many white northerners. At its best . . . it took the form of a sense of responsibility to bring the ways of free labor and political democracy to an oppressed people. At its worst, it took the form of a racism that rivaled any southern variety in its virulence."[9]

Officials in the northern military and the Freedmen's Bureau linked African American attitudes toward sex outside of marriage to the ability of freedpeople to become an effective work force.[10] The northern prewar abolitionist literature and speeches emphasized that slavery fostered immorality and influenced conceptions of African American morals.[11] The majority of military officials accepted the same stereotype as southern whites. They believed that African American sexuality was less controlled and more passionate than that of whites.[12] These officials believed that their mission was to reform morals by speeding conformity to middle-class values that would help regularize both the work and personal lives of formerly enslaved men and women. Personal sexual restraint and, most importantly, legalized marriage could foster and reinforce conscientious work habits.

Freedpeople did not agree with the northern or southern conviction that work only meant work for whites. They wanted free labor to be a far greater change from slavery than the situations that northern military officials arranged. They wanted more economic independence from whites. Family concerns also played an important part of African American conceptions of freedom. Although Union officials viewed many relationships between slave men and women as fleeting, many couples took their slave marriages very seriously and wanted to be together after they escaped to the Union lines.

Almost immediately, tensions developed between the desire of African American women to stay close to their families, particularly their men, and desire of the army to make the men into soldiers and have the women work. In order to deal with large numbers of enslaved people, at least temporarily, the army established living areas (usually outside cities) as a way to both keep African American women out of army camps and to organize their labor. As northerners removed women from these areas close to African American regiments to work on plantations, their soldier husbands protested. The attempts of African Americans to establish personal lives were foiled by the war and by Union policies about free wage labor.

The military had not planned to introduce free labor to formerly enslaved women during the war. Federal policy directed toward freedwomen emerged from conditions that the army had not anticipated. Union officers never expected that thousands of slaves would decide to free themselves by following the army.[13] Because of the passionate desire of African Americans for freedom, the Union army was faced with the challenge of dealing with newly freed slave men and women. As Chaplain John Eaton of the 27th Ohio Infantry wrote "[I]magine . . . a slave population, springing from antecedent bondage, forsaking its local traditions and all the associations and attractions of the old plantation life." He explained, "The arrival among us of these hordes was like the oncoming of cities. There was no plan in this exodus. . . . But their interests were identical, they felt, with the objects of our armies."[14]

Military policy toward the runaway slaves changed during the war. Early in the war, before the Emancipation Proclamation, Union General George McClellan's men returned escaped slaves to their masters. Congress outlawed this action when it became increasingly unpopular in the North for the Union army to serve as slavecatchers for the enemy.[15] Strategic concerns also played a part in shifting policy. Many northerners, including some within the military, believed that freeing the slaves would vastly diminish the southern workforce and demoralize Confederates. Therefore, other generals treated escaped slaves as essentially free as early as May of 1861, setting the stage for thousands to enter military lines.

Women Flee to the Union Lines

Slaves believed that they became free when they accompanied Union soldiers who were marching through Mississippi. Their understanding of Lincoln's Emancipation Proclamation reinforced this belief after January 1863. Living within the Union lines either in camps set up by the army or on plantations in Yankee-occupied southern territory gave slaves the opportunity to "break those chains at last," in the words of one of the slave spirituals.[16] By some estimates, one-third to one-half, well over one hundred thousand Mississippi slaves, tasted freedom before the end of the war.[17]

Slave women came under federal control either when they escaped to Union lines or when the Union army seized their owners' land. When Yankee soldiers foraged on southern plantations for provisions, the soldiers encouraged slaves to escape with them. They were particularly interested in male slaves, but when it was possible female slaves followed their men. The Union soldiers knew that runaways meant fewer slaves on plantations to contribute to the production of southern foodstuffs or highly lucrative cotton. Former slave Sally Dixon recalled that when "the Union cavalry came past our plantation [and] told us to quit work, and follow them, we were all too glad to do so."[18]

With each northern victory in Mississippi, starting with the seizure of Corinth, Mississippi, and particularly with the fall of Vicksburg and Natchez in 1863, greater numbers came under Union lines; some estimated that as many as thirty to forty thousand slave women and men came under Union lines.[19] Young African American men quickly enlisted in the army, while the women, both single and married, followed the soldiers in the hope of freedom. During the battle at Corinth, one Illinois soldier wrote on October 7, 1862, "nothing to day worth note only occasionally we see a drove of female negroes fleeing from Bondage."[20] John Eaton, a military chaplain in the Mississippi Valley, saw freedwomen after the fall of Vicksburg "following the army, carrying all their possessions on their heads, great feather beds tied up in sheets and holding their few belongings."[21] In the winter of 1863–1864, William Tecumseh Sherman advanced through the state of Mississippi from Vicksburg across the state east to Meridian to destroy railroads at Grant's request. As he returned to Vicksburg, behind his army were "10 miles of negroes . . . a string of ox wagons, negro women and children behind each brigade that equaled in length the brigade itself."[22] As one freedwoman recalled, "the soldiers came through there [Hinds County] and I came away with them. I did not know one regiment from another; all I knew was that they were Yankee soldiers. I came right here to Vicksburg, Miss. with them."[23] In Natchez, immediately after Vicksburg fell in July 1863, African Americans began to enter "by the thousands about one able-bodied man to six women and children." The men had enlisted, which left the women and children.[24] By November 1863, William Thirds of the American Missionary Association, a northern philanthropic organization established to aid freedpeople, counted approximately six thousand African American people in Natchez: most were women and children.[25] They had to stay in the city because of fear of Confederate guerrilla attacks on plantations in Union-captured territory. In March 1864, northerner Isaac Shoemaker, who operated a plantation in Adams County and had earlier noted Confederate raids, watched five thousand freedpeople entering with the army on vehicles, "all loaded with old men, women, and children. . . . Able-bodied women and elder children thronged the road by the side of the teams, in plantation dress covered with dust and dirt."[26]

When they arrived in cities where African American soldiers were stationed, the women occasionally lived in army tents that the soldiers set aside for them.[27] Gradually, the majority of women found other shelter, although some female family members, if they became army washerwomen and cooks, remained in the barracks.[28] As army widow Elizabeth Kane explained, "I was with him [her husband] in the army. I washed for him during his entire service in the army. . . . The officers let me live in a tent with my husband."[29] The living quarters of African American soldiers stationed in cities must have resembled bustling neighborhoods with all the noise and chaos that children bring. When he was ten years old, Robert Paul, whose father served in the infantry and whose mother worked as a laundrywoman for the army, explained how he "stayed with my father at the barracks a good deal." Another soldier recalled that the boy "was well known by all the Company men."[30]

Women who were not employed by the army settled as close to the African American soldiers as the army officers permitted. The women wanted protection from the enemy and the companionship of family and plantation acquaintances. Rural slaves in Vicksburg and Natchez where African American soldiers were stationed searched for familiar faces as they tried to create a sense of community, often based on kin, in their new environment. Women who resided outside the barracks visited as often as possible to see their husbands or male relatives.[31] According to a former soldier, "there were lots of women hanging around the camps." He was not referring to prostitutes.[32] Even white officers knew the wives of their men when the women were frequent visitors or lived in the camps. Eliza Drake recalled that after her husband's death, "Captain Serrerk sent for me and give me some of his things. He gave me a cup and a spoon and a pair of blankets—what he left in his camp as the captain knew that I was the wife of this said soldier."[33] Most army officers objected to this family atmosphere because they felt that it undermined army discipline.

African American husbands and wives displayed their mutual affection by seeing each other whenever possible, often at night. When their wives resided outside the barracks, soldiers obtained passes to see them. Richard Robert's bunkmate recalled that "whenever [Richard] could get away at night he was with" his wife, Anna, who lived "about a quarter of a mile from the barracks."[34] Benjamin Lee's passion for his new wife propelled him to obtain "a pass to come from home whenever he wanted to and often [he] ran in home without a pass."[35] Immediately after her marriage to a soldier, Anna Taylor found lodging in Natchez "and her husband . . . used to visit her nightly, sometimes (whenever he could) staying all night."[36] Moses Wilson's wife recalled "I was there near my husband in the camps and he came often to see me of nights." Unlike the newlywed couples, the Wilsons had been married nine years before Moses Wilson enlisted.[37] Some African American soldiers temporarily deserted to visit their families before moving out on maneuvers. They often returned to the army after short sojourns to their families, not comprehending that army policy forbade such unauthorized visits.[38]

When former slave women moved to the cities or were sent to the special areas on the edge of cities, their accommodations ranged from boardinghouses to shanties. According to one northerner, the former slaves in Natchez, mainly women and children, "live in a community by themselves in the outskirts of the town, a cabin is built . . . say 12 feet wide with walls, 7 feet in height and divided off into compartments . . . and each one is appropriated to a family."[39]

The desire for family possibly made up for unsatisfactory living conditions in cities where soldiers were located. Comfortable housing during wartime for either soldiers or displaced civilians seemed relative. To an African American soldier even the poorest housing looked better than army accommodations. One soldier recalled that a fellow comrade, when not on duty, stayed with his wife, "who lived but a short distance from the barracks" in a shanty. "This house was covered with boards. . . . I have been in the house. It was a comfortable house. The house was more comfortable than a tent."[40]

When they lived near the army, some of the African American women worked as nurses, cooks, and laundresses.[41] Both African American men and women served as cooks and/or nurses, but the army seemed to hire only women as laundresses.[42] Because they washed and ironed clothes for the same men over a period of months, women kept in close contact with the troops. Alfred Johnson's tentmate recalled that "like most of the boys he had a woman to do his washing & cooking for him." She "washed for several men in the company" while her husband served in the army.[43] Margaret Williams followed the regiment as a laundrywoman and moved with the soldiers on maneuvers after she married one of the soldiers.[44]

As freedwomen continued to flood across the Union lines, the army was unable to employ all of them in domestic work such as washing clothes.

Women who were unable to obtain work directly from the military developed entrepreneurial enterprises.[45] Anna Roberts followed the Union soldiers to Vicksburg. Once there, she moved in with a woman who baked for the soldiers. Roberts later remembered that "the Fifth Heavy Artillery was camped right up on the hill above where we lived and I would go there every morning and sell the pies about all out."[46]

The army in Mississippi discouraged such business activities. In the ordinances they issued, acceptable "work" for African Americans was defined as employment by whites.[47] One military order issued in August 1863, after the Union victory in Vicksburg stated that "all such persons supported by the Government will be employed in every practical way, so as to avoid, as far as possible, their becoming a burden upon the Government." The government suggested that freedpeople "be hired to planters or other citizens . . . employed on any public works, in gathering crops from abandoned plantations, and, generally, in any manner local commanders may deem for the best interests of the Government."[48] "Citizens" was synonymous with "whites". Work was best done on plantations.

Contraband Camps

For the military the challenge of providing for the escaped slaves, particularly women and children, increased as the war progressed and reached Mississippi.[49] By late 1862, freed slaves who had crossed Union lines were known as "contrabands" because, as the property of southerners in rebellion, they represented the spoils of war. The term contrabands also legitimized through the prerogatives of war the Union army's refusal to return slaves to their former masters.[50] The army called areas where they placed runaway slaves "contraband camps." Although these camps signified a change in the military policy of returning slaves to their masters, they ultimately proved unsatisfactory for the military as the numbers of freedpeople swelled. Before coming to Mississippi, General Ulysses S. Grant faced this problem in the Cumberland River area. There, masses of former slaves who followed his army impeded his ability to maneuver in the field.[51] He did not want a repeat of the experience in the Mississippi Valley.

As the army continued to be overrun, northern army officers realized they needed to deal more effectively with escaping slaves, particularly with women and children, who could not serve in or for the Union army. They decided to put them to work. In late fall of 1862, General Grant appointed 33-year-old military chaplain John Eaton, Jr. to help implement a coherent program for the freedpeople who followed the army.[52] Eaton's title was Superintendent of Freedmen for the Mississippi Valley. Born in New Hampshire, Eaton served as chaplain for the Twenty-seventh Ohio under Grant and became a colonel of the Sixty-third United States Colored Troops.[53]

With his superintendent of freedmen in place, Grant immediately sought to rid the army of unwanted African American civilians by having them placed in special areas where they could perform productive agricultural labor. In December 1862, he issued a field order in which he stated that: "Women and children are hereafter to be excluded from the army in the field." Grant told army officials that as they marched they were to send the African American women and children who followed them to northern Mississippi. Once there, army officials were to send these "Negro women and children and unemployed men" to "Chaplain J. Eaton, Jr.," who would "provide for them" by setting up contraband camps for them. The camps were named for the formerly enslaved people who as human property were contraband of war for the Union army. Grant allowed African American women working for soldiers, such as laundresses, hospital nurses, or officers' servants, to remain with the army.[54] Employment, not marital status, was the definitive factor.

In order to supply food and shelter for escaping slaves, Eaton followed Grant's order and established contraband camps at Grand Junction, Tennessee, in Kentucky, and in Mississippi.[55] Eaton also took control of the contraband camp already established by the army at Corinth, Mississippi. The northern troops held Corinth (which had been previously captured in May 1862 by Union soldiers) against a Confederate attack in October of that year in the Battle of Corinth. After the Union victory, freedpeople from all over Mississippi and neighboring states converged on the city of Corinth. The freedpeople at first lived in tents, but later moved to cabins, which they built. The camp soon developed a small-town atmosphere with a school, a hospital, and a church.[56]

Organizing the freedpeople's labor was one of the most important tasks assigned to Eaton. Although Grant instructed Eaton to "provide" for the welfare of the former slaves, Grant also urged that freedpeople entrusted to Eaton's care work in exchange for their provisions. Grant ordered Eaton "to take charge of the contrabands that come into camp in the vicinity of the post, organizing them into suitable companies for working . . . and set them to work picking, ginning and baling all cotton now out and ungathered in the fields."[57]

Compensation for this agricultural labor immediately became a problem. Freedwomen's complaints about nonpayment of wages became a constant theme during and after the war and tempered African American faith in the fairness of the free labor system. Working conditions at the contraband camp at Corinth pointed out the weakness in this labor system. When asked by government officials "What of the work done for individuals or Government, by men, by women?" the response from the Corinth camp in 1863 was "all men, except the infirm, & few for camp, employed. All women, save those having large families or small children; —generally reported industrious & faithful." Significantly, "many have worked for 2 to 12 months, and never received a cent or rag yet as reward —alike as private servant & Government employees."[58]

Contraband camps often did not include intact families, although if the African American soldiers were stationed close by, they visited. Contraband camps contained more women than men because the army absorbed more men, first as laborers and later as soldiers. In March 1863, Eaton counted 3,657 newly liberated freedpeople at Corinth: "658 men, 1440 women, and 1559 children."[59] When the federal government decided to induct African American men into the Union army, the male population of the contraband camp decreased even more dramatically. In the middle of 1863, when African American regiments such as the First Alabama formed, males left to become soldiers. At Corinth, only a few men who were unfit for combat remained with the women and children.[60] The statement of an authority on the camp at Corinth that "the sudden removal of able-bodied men from the camp's work force scarcely seems to have impeded agricultural progress" offers testimony to the agricultural competence of freedwomen and their desire to be free.[61] Corinth proved to be a model contraband camp, cleaner and better-organized than most. But the war threatened the residents. When Sherman needed Union troops elsewhere, the number of Union soldiers in the vicinity decreased. Because of constant rumors of Confederate raids, the federal officers felt unable to protect the camp against attack and disbanded it in early 1864. Many of its residents moved to Memphis.

In August 1863, as the Union soldiers captured more of the state of Mississippi, Grant established other contraband camps at military posts for unemployed freedpeople and directed officers to distribute rations.[62] Grant saw the issuing of rations as a temporary measure until adults could become self-sufficient workers for the army. Later that month, Grant tried again to prohibit unemployed African Americans from entering the army camps. The military located contraband camps on the outskirts of cities where the United States Colored Troops were often garrisoned, including Meridian (in the eastern part of the state) and Vicksburg (almost straight across to the west).

The military also sent African American women, including the spouses and children of soldiers, to Paw Paw Island in Mississippi, and to Goodrich's Landing, Milliken's Bend, and Young's Point in Louisiana. Former slave woman Zelphia Ross summed up the Union army's plan for African Americans. She recalled that after Vicksburg fell, "we were told by the men in blue, who for the first time swarmed our neighborhood, that we must to go to a place or plantation near Vicksburg. Many hundred of the colored people assembled there and after several months there was a call for troops from our camp." She explained, "all the men that were not taken to the army [and] the women and children were sent on to an island called Paw Paw where we were to make as much of our living as we could."[63] Bias Clarke recalled meeting another slave, Henry Patterson, at the camp at Young's Point. Both "had our wives there and we left them there and came over here [Vicksburg] and enlisted the same day." Similarly, "during the war in the spring of 1864 at the time of Sherman's raid through Madison County, Miss" during Sherman's retreat to Vicksburg, Chloe Love and her husband "with their two children followed the army of Gen. Sherman to Vicksburg, where" her husband joined the Fifth Heavy Artillery and she "was sent to a gov't farm near Milliken's Bend." Alternately one slave man "was sick and couldn't enlist with the rest . . . and was put in the corral at Youngs Point with the women."[64]

Officials advocated the removal of African American women from contraband camps onto plantations as wage laborers by continually expressing concern about the large numbers of deaths in federally controlled camps. Colonel Samuel Thomas, a colonel in his early twenties from Ohio who was later appointed Provost Marshall General of Freedmen, found that "the camp at Young's Point (opposite Vicksburg), during the summer of 1863, had been a vast charnel house—thousands of people, dying."[65] An annual report of the New England Freedmen's Aid Society stated that "the most frightful misery and sickness had prevailed at Young's Point and Natchez. In each place as many as seventy-five had at one time died in a day."[66] Pension records of the wives of African American soldiers also discuss such tragedies: Private Benjamin Lee's wife, children, and sister-in-law died of measles, and William Harris's parents both died at Young's Point.[67]

Relations between Women and Soldiers

The plantation solution also removed African American women from what the military perceived to be moral temptation and exploitation. The military justified the placing of women on plantations by arguing that such plans would stop intercourse between African American women and African American and white military personnel.[68] Colonel Samuel Thomas complained "the Regiments are crowded with women of bad character and soldiers' wives and children are living in wretchedness and miserable hovels, when land can be furnished in safe localities where they can build good houses and support themselves by cultivating it."[69]

Intimate relations between the soldiers and African American women were more varied than army officials conceded. White officers, particularly at first before they got to know them individually, viewed African American women as prostitutes. Both white and African American women engaged in sexual relations with Union soldiers. African American women engaged in prostitution for the same reason as white women; they needed money. Although Winnie Lee coyly refused to answer questions about her sexual conduct during the war, she finally explained, "Well, we women had to make a living." She also complained about her poverty during the war: there was "nothing to live on."[70] John Eaton attacked the white soldiers' "licentious connections with the [African American] females." These relationships, he argued, brought about a "serious demoralization." Equally important, the military worried about the soldiers who were "physically disabled by the diseases they receive."[71] In contrast, soldiers who viewed sexual pleasure as their right during war resented any interference by the army in their sexual activities. While in charge of the barracks in Columbus, James Pierce proposed to remove several African American women "out of the yard" because of their "lewd habits." Their partners strongly objected and the soldiers "threatened" Pierce if he "interfered with them."[72]

Because of the racial beliefs of the white soldiers, the quality of the relationships between white soldiers and African American women differed from the intimacies of African American soldiers with African American women. Whites in both the North and the South viewed African American women as more passionate and more sexually experienced than white women.[73] Few of the liaisons between white soldiers and African American women were long-standing nor did they represent a lasting commitment for white men. The majority planned to return North and marry a woman of their own class and race. While in Vicksburg, Frank Johnson's niece enjoyed her status as paramour for Lieutenant Charles Ambrook, a white officer of an African American regiment. Johnson's niece's contentment may have been based, in part, on false hope. After living with the wife of Ambrook's sergeant, Ambrook's companion went to stay in "a kitchen next to his barracks," where ostensibly she worked as his cook. According to her uncle, the true motive for her residing with Ambrook was known since "every man in his company knows well that he had her in his kitchen where she slept." Although her uncle pleaded with her to return to him, his niece refused. Assuming the air of a belle, she explained to her uncle that "she liked it very well in camp where she got the men of the company to wait upon her."[74] Ambrook also promised to take her with him when he moved North. According to Ambrook's pension file, he requested several times to be transferred North from Vicksburg for health reasons. Although it is not possible to know what became of Frank Johnson's niece, Lieutenant Ambrook returned to Michigan after the war and married a white woman.[75] Given prevailing racial views, white army officers did not pressure these men to marry their African American lovers, although they enacted policies to encourage their African American soldiers to legally marry women with whom they were intimate.

Unlike white soldiers, African American soldiers did not view African American women as exotic or innately licentious and did not assume that all African American women were potential prostitutes. Many of the women had become wives of the soldiers during slavery or were involved in a stable romantic relationship. Although those women who visited the African American soldiers' army camps engaged in sexual activity, few of the women were prostitutes.[76] The concern of army officials about the immorality of African American women, however, led them to advocate legalized marriage.

Legalized Marriage and the Army

Because they did not in theory approve of any relationship other than legalized marriage, white officials prohibited any sexual contact between African American soldiers and African American women outside of marriage. Slave marriages were not legal unions. Because abolitionist literature pictured slave life as promiscuous, the majority of northern officers refused to accept slave marriages as legitimate. Such attitudes were expressed in an April 1863 report from the Corinth contraband camp that responded to the question, "What of their marital notions & practices?" The report answered, "All wrong. All entering our camps who have been living or desire to live together as husband and wife are required to be married in the proper manner, and a certificate of the same is given. This regulation has done much to promote the good order of the camp."[77]

Corinth's requirement that freedpeople legally wed before they cohabited together foreshadowed military policy in places such as Vicksburg as well. Army officials argued that legalized marriage and its implicit standard of moral behavior buttressed the discipline necessary to create an organized labor force. The military tied morality to work in order to make former slave men and women into a new southern working class.

Legalized marriage became the first line of defense in the northerners' war against the assumed promiscuity of former slave men and women. Colonel Eaton decided to restrict the entrance of African American women into army camps to tackle the inferred problem of immorality among the soldiers. The connection that northern reformers made between marriage and "good order" (as at Corinth) suggests that they saw legalized marriage as an important component of the establishment of a new society in the South based on free labor among freedpeople. Eaton instituted legalized marriage and a strict pass system for freedpeople who wanted to come into military camps or live in the towns in which the camps were located in order to control women's sexuality and ultimately their labor. As he explained, "untold evils resulted from the presence of lewd women; to meet this, marriage was started on the basis of the laws of the U.S., [and] regular registration [was] established." Eaton elaborated on the greater stability and order that legalized marriage brought: "a rational idea of marriage was urged, so that all the family instincts, which so largely constitute the foundations of society, might come to our aid."[78] Northerners such as Eaton wanted this new freed working class to possess sound middle-class values that included a respect for property and domesticity.

Freedmen and women received their first access to legalized marriage through the military. As supervisor of the freedmen during the war, John Eaton issued an edict in 1864 giving army chaplains authority to perform marriage ceremonies for civilian freedmen and women as well as for soldiers. Such ceremonies validated over fifteen hundred existing marriages, which were performed at the Vicksburg post from March 1864 to the end of that year. Military policy probably spurred such marriages since it forbade female visitors at army camps except for legally married wives.[79] Freedpeople referred to legal marriages, especially marriages that took place after emancipation, as marriages "under the United States flag."[80]

As had been demonstrated earlier at Corinth, the military moved beyond simply urging freedpeople to marry legally to mandating it. Samuel Thomas, a white officer commanding African American troops in Vicksburg who had worked with Eaton, only allowed legally married African American soldiers to cohabit or have sexual relations with their wives and prohibited any other sexual activity. One former soldier, explaining why a widow was eligible to receive her husband's military pension, emphatically stated that, "I have personal knowledge that said parties lived and cohabited as man and wife in the camp and [she was] so treated by the officers and all others, and if she had not been recognized by the officers as his lawful wife she would not have been allowed to remain in the camp as such."[81] The army forcefully "encouraged" couples such as Private Benjamin Lee and Winnie Moore to wed. Moore had known Benjamin Lee before the war, and she moved in with him when she came to Vicksburg. While they were living together, "there was a law passed by the officer that no man should live with a woman unless he married her and then Ben and Winnie went up to [Samuel Thomas' headquarters] . . . and were married or they said they married any how. Most all the boys were living with women and went up and were married."[82] Army officials assumed that marriage would bring order and regularize relations between soldiers and their lovers.

African American couples kept army chaplains busy performing marriage ceremonies. Lucinda Westbrooks recalled being "married by a white man preacher Miller—who came there with the first Yankees and went around marrying the soldiers. He married lots of other soldiers the same day."[83] Chaplains often held weddings for several couples simultaneously. One army wife recalled that "there were about a dozen married at the same time and stood right around in a row."[84] These marriage ceremonies occurred in the quarters of army officers or in local churches.[85] In Natchez, Rev. S. G. Wright, chaplain of the Fifty-eighth United States Colored Infantry, used to teach school and preach at the Wall Street Baptist Church. According to one soldier, Rev. Wright "used to marry coloured people and kept a record of such marriages." Such army weddings were festive occasions. One woman who acted as bridesmaid remembered a soldier's wedding that was officiated by Rev. Wright. After the wedding, the bridesmaid's mother held a wedding reception at her home.[86] One soldier recalled a wedding presided over by "a white soldier preacher" after which the couple "had what we call a 'walking wedding' just passed around cake and wine."[87] Col. Samuel Thomas conducted a group marriage ceremony after which everyone in attendance returned to the army camp for "a wedding feast . . . that night and all the boys of the company were at it."[88]

Although this policy gave freedpeople their first access to legal marriages, it failed to take into account the validity of their preexisting slave marriages. Thomas's orders forced slave couples to remarry whether or not they so desired by refusing to allow couples any intimacy unless they were legally married. Freedpeople did not dismiss their slave marriages as northerners did. They viewed their existing marriages as binding and did not always see the need to legalize them.

The army officers considered these marriages to be a couple's first wedding; freedpeople viewed it as their second if they had married the same spouse during slavery. They counted their slave marriage as binding. Although freedpeople did not object to legally marrying, they did not see the urgency to do so. According to other recruits with Gordon Fulgert, "regiment . . . orders [were] enforced that soldiers should remarry under the laws and flag." Due to the order, "Gordon Fulgert . . . remarr[ied] [Emily] again this being the second marriage once by the owner and once by Provost Marshal Samuel Thomas at Vicksburg."[89] Enslaved Eliza Foreman and Nathaniel Foreman had wedded first in 1858 as slaves, but when Eliza Foreman came to Vicksburg as a domestic servant for a Yankee officer, she "again married" her soldier husband. The Foreman marriage certificate stated that:

This certifies, that I have this day joined in lawful marriage, Nathaniel Forman . . . and Eliza Todd . . . in compliance with the ordinance of God, and by authority of the United States of America, vested in me, in accordance with No. 15, Special Order of the Secretary of War . . . signed Joseph Warren, chaplain 25, Inf. assistant in charge of freedmen."[90]

Colonel Thomas applied the new orders to women living either inside or outside of the barracks and only granted passes to soldiers who were visiting their legal wives. This policy encouraged men "who had been living with women as their wives under old slave customs" to marry; it also encouraged men to marry women they had met while serving in the army.[91] Thomas's rule also led to a certain amount of exaggeration, because, as Jake Morton pointed out, "many of the boys would tell stories about the women because no one but a wife or other relative was allowed to come in the lines to see the soldiers."[92] The statement implies that the policy was not one hundred percent effective. Some soldiers may have resented the military's interference with their private intimacies. The ma-

jority of African American soldiers took army marriages seriously and remained with their spouses after the war. Whites in the South considered
army marriages of African Americans less significant than either northern
reformers such as Samuel Thomas or African Americans did. A pension
examiner commented on one such marriage as "an army alliance and just
one month after his enlistment and while in the service. Such marriages
among a certain class were common and understood 'for during the war'
only; and negroes are not better than whites." Although undoubtedly this
sometimes occurred, testimony in the same pension file contradicted the
examiner's premise. The examiner ignored statements by several freedpeople who stated that they witnessed the soldier's marriage to the same
woman in a slave ceremony almost twenty years prior to their army marriage.[93] It was the legal marriage that had only taken place "one month
after [the soldier's enlistment]."

Marriage to soldiers was only one of several policies designed to control the interactions of African American women with the United States
Colored Troops. The military also viewed as a problem the propensity of
African American soldiers to appropriate military "rations and clothing"
for needy civilian contrabands.[94] The military expected African American
women to become self-supporting as wage earners for whites and expressed
continual concern that they would become financially dependent on the
federal government. These concerns, coupled with concerns about the
supposed immorality of African American women and crowded housing
conditions, informed a policy of ejecting African American civilians, including soldiers' wives and families, from cities. Such forced evacuations
occurred regardless of the turmoil they caused to African American families or of the wishes of African American soldiers.[95] The military enacted
such plans in Mississippi throughout the latter part of the war. Reminiscent of Grant's initial 1862 policy, the military preferred that women pick
cotton for wages on Union-held land.

Forcing Freedwomen onto Plantations

The military's insistence that women be employed by whites and be
legally married pointed to the military's problem with African American
women. The exigencies of wartime caused the military to separate the
families of African American soldiers even after the officers encouraged
marriage. During the war, wage and marriage contracts became the means
of controlling African American women.[96] The attempt to restrain wom-

en's sexuality was linked with the military's greater concern of placing civilian African Americans onto plantations to ensure women's economic productivity. Northern views of the nature of African American female sexuality in part led to two significant changes for African American women: the introduction of free labor and legalized marriage.

A military commander in Natchez provides an excellent example of such thinking, which linked military considerations with the potential of African American women as workers. In 1864, in Natchez, General James M. Tuttle (at the suggestion of chief health officer A. W. Kelley) decided to rid the city of large numbers of civilian African American residents. Tuttle ordered every African American man and woman "to present a paper certifying that he or she was living on the premises of some responsible white person and was *employed* by them." The order ignored those who were self-employed or employed by African Americans; people in both of these categories were classified as unemployed.

Although the army allowed African American women who worked for the military such as laundresses to remain, it began to remove other freedwomen and children from the city. One northerner in Mississippi reported that "an old woman who has lived fifty years in this city, and was never disturbed before, was driven at the point of the bayonet to the camp. Mothers having young infants and attending to lawful business were arrested and were not allowed to see their babes."[97] According to Selig G. Wright of the American Missionary Association, a northern philanthropic organization for the benefit of newly freed slaves, "mothers came running to us weeping, begging us to go & plead their cause." Sympathetic to the freedpeople's plight, northerners informed Tuttle that "the colored soldier hearing that his mother or his wife had been driven from her quiet and comfortable home, simply because she supported herself and was not dependent upon some white person, may feel less inclined to hazard his life in the cause of his country now struggling for its life." Tuttle's order also broke up schools that had been established for freedpeople by the American Missionary Association. The military changed the policy only when African American soldiers insisted to one of the Union officers that "they could no longer endure the trial of seeing their wives and children driven in to the streets and if he would not at once interfere and protect them they should *positively* do it themselves."[98]

Even after General Tuttle was relieved of his command in June 1864, other military officials initiated civilian removal plans. In March 1865, Lieutenant L. W. Brobet grew concerned as great numbers of former slaves arrived in Natchez. Brobet, as with military officers elsewhere, believed that freedwomen should be taken to work on Union-held plantations. Another military commander in Natchez thwarted Brobet by allowing the wives and children of African American soldiers to stay, even though Brobet considered the families of soldiers to be the "main cause" of the crowded conditions in Natchez.[99]

In Vicksburg in early 1865 the commander ordered that unemployed freed slaves, which included many women who lived near the army barracks, be moved. This procedure was not enforced, due, in part, to pressure from a chaplain in the United States Colored Troops. Possibly complaints from African American soldiers prompted the chaplain's attack on the policy. When this plan of forced evacuation failed, a twenty-cent permit was required for all nongovernmental personnel. The permit allowed an African American person to stay in the city for thirty days. The army intended to use the money raised to fund funerals for destitute freedpeople and to provide for orphans. Northern military officials, however, also expected the price of the permit to affect adversely "those who" in their opinion "ought to leave the city," particularly soldiers' wives.[100] The women resisted. According to government officials, they "openly refused to work, on the ground that the recruiting officer promised them the government would take care of them."[101] To the wives, the agreement with the military meant that they could reside near their husbands.

Individual African American soldiers resisted the army's insistence on relocating the soldiers' families. When Samuel Williams's wife was "taken to a government farm . . . he came after her and she came to Vicksburg to her husband."[102] Similarly, when another soldier found his family on federally controlled land, "he hired a wagon and carried [his wife] and the children . . . here to Vicksburg."[103] Because ensuring a stable family life was one of the considerations that prompted slave men to enlist, soldiers were unwilling to tolerate the army's further breakup of their families. As William Tecumseh Sherman pointed out, "[I]f negroes are taken as soldiers by undue influence or force and compelled to leave their women in the uncertainty of their new condition they cannot be relied on." Sherman suggested further, "Put their families in some safe place."[104] Soldiers' wives protested their removal from their husbands by leaving government land as quickly as possible and returning to their husbands.[105] Thus, during the war African American women tried to define their own identity as wives or family members, giving these roles more significance than that of plantation worker. After the war, African American men and women would continue to assert their right to control women's labor.

Free Labor and the Army

In spite of objections of African American soldiers, the army moved large numbers of African American women from cities and contraband camps onto plantations. The job of organizing freedpeople onto Union-held plantations fell, in part, to General Lorenzo Thomas, who Secretary of War Edwin M. Stanton had sent to the Mississippi Valley in the spring of 1863 to recruit African American troops.[106] A West Point graduate, the 59-year-old adjutant general acted on a plan for the Mississippi Valley to alleviate crowding in the cities and contraband camps.[107] He suggested that former slaves (particularly women, men who were not in the army, and children who lived in contraband camps) be removed and compelled to become wage laborers on plantations in Union-held territory. Thomas argued that freedpeople "should be put into a position to make their own living. The men should . . . be mustered into the service as soldiers, and the others with the women and children placed on abandoned plantations to till the ground"[108]

In August 1863, Thomas "advised" African American women and children "desirous of seeking refuge within the line of the United States troops . . . to remain on the plantations" within Union lines.[109] Thomas did not want them to enter the cities. Federal officials leased the plantations under their control to northerners or loyal southerners, referred to as lessees.[110] According to a March 29, 1864, letter from William P. Mellen of the Treasury Department, the number of lessees were 209 in the Vicksburg area and 35 in the Natchez area.[111] Lessees expected large profits from these plantations because cotton prices had jumped from approximately eleven cents a pound in 1860 to more than forty cents a pound during the war.[112] Thomas wanted the planters to pay a tax of one cent per pound of cotton to the federal government, thereby raising additional revenue for the war effort.[113] In return the federal government committed its resources to supplying the lessees with African American labor. Lessees obtained their workers through three commissioners at the contraband camps, which Thomas and Eaton converted to temporary quarters for potential workers.[114] Thomas also suggested that African American troops protect the plantations from Confederate guerrilla attacks.

To prevent freedpeople, particularly women and children, from becoming an expense to the government, Eaton furnished local plantations with mostly female laborers from the camp. Eaton's belief in the virtue of working hard and his fear that the former slaves would become economically dependent on the government reinforced his compliance with the plan.[115] Military officials who administered contraband camps established ties with surrounding plantations and provided them with workers. These arrangements soon raised problems for African American women because they were inadequately compensated and they were separated from their families.

Some northerners and southerners viewed the northern lessees disdainfully. As James Yeatman, the head of the Western Sanitary Commission noted, "the desire of gain alone prompts them; and they care little whether they make it out of the blood of those they employ or from the soil." One official in Natchez, where conditions for workers were worse than in many other places in the South, complained that the lessee's "highest thought is a greenback, whose God is a cotton bale and whose devil is a guerrilla." Obviously making a profit was a chief concern for the leaseholders. Often such men showed little regard for their workers.[116]

The federal military expected the leaseholders to sign labor contracts with their employees, the great majority of whom had been female slaves. Under Thomas's plan, adapted from General Nathaniel Banks's policy in Louisiana, employers calculated wages based on their workers' sex and rating as laborers. Employers were to pay $7 per month to first-class men over the age of fifteen and $5 to first-class females. Male and female children between the ages of twelve and fifteen were to receive half the wages of men and women.[117]

African Americans objected to their placement by the military on leased plantations on several grounds. They disliked being separated from their families. As John Eaton wrote to Senator Henry Wilson, "The able bodied men may become soldiers. That does not take care of the women and children and feeble. Who shall keep up the connection between the colored soldier and his family?"[118] Too often the lessees seemed only interested in profit, and exploited their workers and cheated them out of their wages.[119] Workers received their wages after the harvest rather than monthly, which meant they were without any remuneration for months at a time.

African Americans resisted leaving the camps for the leased plantations. Due in part to the freedpeople's dissatisfaction with the lease system, during 1863 the Treasury and War Departments bickered over control of the federal area in the South.[120] After March 12, 1863, the Treasury Department ostensibly managed the abandoned lands and the War Department supervised freedpeople. The War Department, however, failed to address the problems with the free labor system on leased plantations.

In October 1863 the Treasury Department gained authority over the leasing practices and immediately instituted reforms. In part because of high death rates in contraband camps, officials planned to abolish the camps and replace them with home farms in order to provide former slaves with a way station before placement on plantations.[121]

The Treasury Department revised the wage scale upward, and determined the class of a worker by the individual's age and health. Third-class hands included boys and girls between the ages of 12 and 14 and men and women over the age of 50. Second-class hands consisted of people from 15 to 19 and 41 to 50. Healthy workers from 20 to 40 comprised first-class hands.[122] The new wages required the leaseholders to pay $25 each month to their first-class male laborers, $20 to second-class male laborers, and $15 to third-class male laborers. African American women were to be remunerated with $18 for a first-class hand, $14 for second-class hand, and $10 for a third-class hand. Workers were to be paid at least half the wages per month rather than be forced to wait until the end of the year.[123] By March 1864, after more internal governmental maneuvering, the War Department regained authority over the freedpeople and instituted yet another wage structure, higher than the first one it had proposed but lower than the wage scale of the Treasury Department. Under this plan, first-class male hands were to receive $10 and females were to be compensated $7. "To children, invalids, and aged, half rates were to be paid."[124]

Despite the efforts of both the War and Treasury Departments, the unhealthy and exploitative conditions on the federally controlled plantations helped to explain why freedpeople resisted the army's removal of African American women and children from cities to plantations. One historian concluded that some leased plantations experienced even higher death rates than contraband camps because the planters failed to provide any medical care for their workers.[125] Lessees also did not furnish agreed-upon rations.

In fall of 1864, Chaplain Asa S. Fiske negatively analyzed the new War Department payment structure in terms of the actual net wage of a freedman and freedwoman after the employer deducted certain items. Assuming the rate of $7 per month for ten months of labor, a woman should have received a total of $70 (the new War Department pay scale started in March 1864). Fiske then subtracted for clothing, personal expenses, and days when a woman might miss work and concluded that a woman without children would have $9 at the end of the year. Fiske further speculated, "But suppose she had a child, and black women *do* have children, what then? Suppose the rebels took off the first suit of clothing she bought, suppose fraud to have been practiced toward her, or in sickness her ration charged her, or that she was compelled to pay for the rations her children ate—what then?"[126]

Fiske's litany of concerns foreshadowed freedpeople's complaints against wage labor after the war: freedpeople rarely received full compensation for their work because of deductions and fraud.[127] Laborers also complained of irregular payment, unfairly high deductions for days missed, and even corporal punishment.[128] Furthermore, when freedwomen worked while they lived on the home farms or in contraband camps (which remained in existence), they received only room and board. The military refused to pay any monetary wages as a method of coercing women from camps or home farms onto Union-controlled plantations as laborers.[129] This policy changed in 1865 at Davis Bend's home farm, where officials allowed the inhabitants to keep one-half of their wages.[130] The other half went into a general fund.

In addition to the problem of poor wages, Fiske's quote also points to the problem of Confederate guerrilla attacks (particularly in the Vicksburg and Natchez areas).[131] Union soldiers, often United States Colored Troops who were assigned to the area, were unable to protect the plantations from guerrilla raids by Confederate soldiers. The soldiers were unable to patrol every plantation, and periodically they were called away to fight elsewhere.[132] Such raids also interrupted agricultural production.[133] Throughout 1864, Confederates carried off foodstuffs and kidnapped freed workers.[134] The Natchez area, which was often left unprotected, was particularly dangerous. The lessees sometimes deserted to safety, leaving their workers to fend for themselves against the Confederates. During 1864, guerrillas raided plantations daily and by the end of the year they had captured over a thousand African Americans. Earlier in the spring of 1864, life on the plantation was so dangerous that the army temporarily took women and children back to cities. The military brought Winnie Dorrity and other women, children, and old men to government-controlled land but "they had to move [them] away to save [them] from being killed by rebel bushwhackers."[135] During 1864, less than half of the four hundred and fifty lessees finished the season.[136] One U.S. Treasury agent pleaded for Union troops to ward off Confederate attacks because he had difficulty persuading northerners to lease without a commitment of military strength. "I feel justified in asserting that if I could have given applicants for lands any assurance of protection every Freedman woman and child capable of work in this district would have been employed on these plantations," he insisted, "and been supporting themselves instead of being a burden to the Government or demoralized marauders, living by theft and murder as many of them now are."[137]

Ultimately, the army succeeded in moving freed African Americans out of the cities and contraband camps to plantations. From May 1864 until April 1865, the number of contrabands declined in the Vicksburg area from approximately 13,000 to 405. Of the 8,000 freedpeople in the Natchez area in the winter of 1863, 5,712 worked on plantations by the summer of 1864.[138] In March 1864, in the areas around Skipwith's Landing, 17,000 African Americans worked on leased plantations.

The first large-scale experiments in Mississippi of free (nonslave) African American wage labor began on these leased plantations and relied mainly on a workforce of freedwomen and children.[139] As he congratulated himself on the success of the lease experiment, John Eaton declared, "finally, it should be remembered . . . that after the Negroes began to be enlisted into the United States service, the communities upon which we had to depend for our laboring force were composed largely of men deemed unfit for regular service, together with the women, the children, and those positively disabled." He added, "even with this crippled body of workers, free labor could be compared not unfavorably with slave labor."[140]

Eaton's encouraging if patronizing sentiments reflected that the northern leaseholders considered a labor force of freedwomen inferior to one composed of men. When he investigated conditions of the formerly enslaved people in the Mississippi Valley for the Western Sanitary Commission, James Yeatman complained that the army had taken all the best men, and that the employers on the leased plantations would "have to rely mainly upon the labors of women."[141] Several lessees from the north left their plantations in disgust and grumbled that the workforce was weakened by the lopsided "proportion of able bodied men to women, children, and infirm persons."[142] In the Natchez area, "over fifty percent of the hands were female workers."[143] Such perceptions that women made poorer workers than men helped explain why women received lower wages than men.

A conglomeration of military, economic, humanitarian, and moral concerns motivated federal policies toward African American women during and after the Civil War. Chaplain John Eaton wrote sensitively of the struggles of former slave women with the circumstances of war: "[Y]ou easily see that between the citizens and the conquered and the conquering armies the poor colored woman and child, the able men going with the army, stand a small chance of special attention to their prediction [sic] or comfort at the time of the surrender."[144] Eaton, like many northerners, saw African American women as different from men, but without the idealized characteristics of passivity and purity of a nineteenth-century "true" woman. The federal government consistently advocated that African American women work throughout the war in Mississippi and, under the auspices of the Freedmen's Bureau, after the war ended. The military and the Freedmen's Bureau forced women out of the army and contraband camps to ensure a labor force on plantations that were under Union control. Moreover northerners such as John Eaton and Freedmen's Bureau agents explicitly tied morality to labor. They advocated both marriage and work even as they forced the women away from their soldier husbands, showing what they valued the most.

Ultimately, the government's policy that freedwomen must become field wage laborers for whites undercut the humanitarian impulses of northerners.[145] The military's faith that turning women into free laborers would solve problems, such as food shortages, that were brought on by the war was naïve. Military and federal officials underestimated the impact of the war in Mississippi both in terms of the devastation on some plantations and the continued guerrilla raids. They also underestimated the resistance of southerners to the concept of African American free labor.

The War and Treasury Departments established a labor system on leased plantations by which the women worked under conditions that were reminiscent of slavery; their mobility was restricted and monetary compensation was minimal or nonexistent. Placing women on plantations apparently did not improve the health and safety of freedwomen during wartime. Even though the military officials justified moving the women from contraband camps by pointing to the healthier conditions that were said to exist on the plantations, such was often not the case.

Even wage labor, which is usually associated with giving women more independence, ultimately caused the freedwomen to live in a state of dependency. Policies that forced women onto plantations emphasized northern beliefs that African American women as well as most African American men should be in subordinate relationships, particularly as workers.[146] The federal government never leased directly to the women or involved freedwomen in successful, albeit short-term, land ownership by a small group of freedmen.[147] Although northerners accepted that an elite group of African American men could become small landowners, they saw women, even those without men, as subordinate members of male-headed households who would work as wage laborers in the fields. John Eaton, Jr. continued to see men as head of the household even when women fulfilled that role. Although he acknowledged that men would become soldiers,

Eaton insisted that within the contraband camps there should be "a method of business which keeps families together in responsibility if not in fact [with] the husband and father made responsible for the Support of his family."[148]

The federal government directly leased land that had been confiscated from southern planters to a small number of African American males. Although Eaton and Lorenzo Thomas leased plantations mainly to northerners and loyal southerners, 500 former slave men became farmers. The government set aside small plots of land for African Americans on the Brierfield and Hurricane plantations of Jefferson Davis and his brother Joseph. The criteria that were established for these lessees at what was known as Davis Bend and in other areas guaranteed that very few freedwomen would possess land.[149] African Americans who were judged to be best suited for land leasing or ownership included males who had held leadership positions during slavery, such as slave drivers and heads of households. African American men found it difficult to keep their land at Davis Bend after the war and by 1867 Joseph Davis had regained his land.[150] Although African American men acquired land, particularly during the war, the amnesty policies of President Johnson and the laws of the state of Mississippi made if difficult for men to retain the land they had acquired or to gain new land.

For African American women land ownership was even more difficult during the war. Only two women out of 110 signed petitions as "the colored planters of Davis Bend, Mississippi."[151] Even though they were sympathetic to idea of economic autonomy for freedpeople, northern officials implicitly made land ownership difficult for African American women. Women who arrived from the cities lived on the home farm established on the Bend and then were sent to other plantations as workers; they were not given the opportunity to obtain land.[152]

Congress further restricted land ownership for women when it passed the law that formed the Bureau of Refugees, Freedmen, and Abandoned Lands, popularly known as the Freedmen's Bureau, in March 1865. As the war's end approached, the U. S. Congress decided to open up opportunities to own land to loyal men of both races. The legislation included a section on the leasing of forty acres of confiscated southern territory to freedmen and stated that "the commissioner, under the direction of the President, shall have authority to set apart, for the use of loyal refugees and freedmen, such tracts of land within the insurrectionary states as shall have been abandoned, or to which the United States shall have acquired title by confiscation or sale, or otherwise, and to every male citizen, whether refugee or freedman . . . there shall be assigned not more than forty acres of such land."[153]

Rumors of this law filtered back to southern freedpeople, even if the exact terms were misconstrued into a universal belief that they would obtain forty acres and a mule. President Andrew Johnson dashed any hopes that freedmen would own land under this law when he quickly restored the confiscated property to the original owners.[154]

Land meant far more to African Americans than personal property. Of all material possessions that signified freedom, former slaves considered land to be the most important.[155] Freedpeople viewed the ownership of land as the solution to many problems caused by slavery, particularly because it seemed to promise financial and racial independence. Blacks depended on the federal government to sell or lease land to them because after the war, the Mississippi legislature outlawed rural rental or leasing of land by African Americans. These laws, part of the Black Codes that were passed after the war, made owning land close to impossible. Additionally, freedpeople had few financial resources. Southern whites were concerned that land ownership or rental would give freedmen too much economic independence and would make them less willing to work for whites and more difficult to control.

African American women in Mississippi coped with federal policies that sought to control their mobility, their sexuality, and their labor and also threatened their definition of freedom. Slave women and men ran to the Union lines to gain liberation from such aspects of enslavement. But freed men and women learned that their northern liberators would often play contradictory roles. The desire for autonomy in family and community relations, reinforced by land ownership, did not mesh with white northern or white southern plans for freed African Americans. Northerners wanted African Americans to become wage earners, not landowners. They also wanted legalized marriages that did not interfere with the needs of employers for the labor of women and children. Freedpeople discovered during the war that freedom and even legal marriage failed to remove white interference with African American labor and in their families.

Although the northerners such as Freedmen's Bureau agents argued that racial uplift was best achieved though hard work within the confines of a labor contract and sexual morality within the marriage contract, such traits rarely guaranteed any meaningful access to upward mobility for freedpeople. In Mississippi, the majority remained poor and landless, and family stability under these conditions was difficult to achieve, especially because of the threat that their children might be apprenticed by whites.

Too quickly, former slaves learned that the promise of freedom was not the same as the grim reality of Reconstruction. Postwar suffrage for African American males proved insufficient to secure economic security and personal safety. Julia Stubbs complained, "After de war wuz over we wont give no land nor nothing dat dey promised fo' de war."[156] Similarly, Sally Dixon recalled, "We was told when we got freed we was going to get forty acres of land, and a mule. 'Stead of that, we didn't get nothing."[157]

THREE

LABOR AFTER THE WAR

"A good hand for a woman"[1]

After her husband's death in 1865, Lucy Brown moved around, working on various places. One employer "brought her . . . to work in the crop" for him, on a place about ten miles from Vicksburg, where she also served as his cook. A few years later, she moved to Freetown in Warren County for a year. By the early 1870s, Lucy Brown had settled near Freetown. There Reuben Kelly, a freedman who was leasing land, hired her "as a field hand and [to] do his cooking and washing."[2] After the war, agricultural and domestic work represented the main employment options in Mississippi for the vast majority of freedwomen such as Lucy Brown.

Although most African Americans in Mississippi continued to be agricultural workers, emancipation encouraged them to challenge the conditions under which they worked. Freedwomen performed the same type of work as they had when they were slaves, but freedpeople and former slave owners held conflicting views about the definition of nonslave labor.[3] For African Americans, free labor meant adequate compensation and less white supervision. Blacks contested the insistence of white planters that they make all labor decisions and their continued use of force.

As 1865 ended, freedpeople were reluctant to enter into year-long contracts as wage laborers because they expected to receive their own land. They also concluded that the labor contracts would limit their control over their own labor.[4] They resisted the insistence of northern and southern whites that they become laborers for whites. Blacks wanted to work for themselves. They preferred to set their own work schedules and construct a greater distinction between public and private life, which laboring for whites permitted.

Employers expected their workforce to continue to labor the same number of hours each day and under many of the same restrictions as slavery. Many former slave owners relied on the threat of violence as a means of controlling workers. Whites even found it hard to adjust to new terminology for their employees. The word "slaves" was erased from W. S. Noble's labor contract of July 11, 1865, and "servants" written in its place.[5]

The agricultural and domestic work of blacks set the scene for struggles with employers, but labor disputes must also be viewed in the context of the larger political struggle for race equity. Historian John Hope Franklin refers to this period (1865 and 1866) as Confederate Reconstruction, a particularly apt phrase for Mississippi. In Mississippi, whites elected former Confederates to office, such as Governor Benjamin Humphrey, a general in the Confederate army.[6] In the fall of 1865, the Mississippi legislature passed restrictive legislation collectively known as the Black Codes. The codes were so named because almost all the provisions applied solely to African Americans. The legislation included restrictions on owning or renting rural land in the state by newly freed African Americans.[7]

These laws reflected the attitude of the majority of white planters toward free labor. Although planters accepted the demise of slavery, they rejected the concept of free labor for African Americans by which laborers freely sold their labor and worked without coercion. This lack of faith in free labor, combined with their need for racial domination, led the Mississippi legislature in 1865 to approve strict vagrancy laws as part of the Black Codes in order to force African Americans to work on plantations. These laws were aimed at African Americans who resisted working for former slave masters.

The vagrancy laws defined African Americans solely in terms of laborers and more specifically in terms of their employment to whites.[8] Targeting African American women as well as men, the vagrancy laws ensured that any African American who left an employer for any reason without permission could be arrested as a vagrant. These laws, reinforced by yearlong labor contracts that were strictly enforced, vastly decreased the ability of African Americans to gain higher wages when they signed contracts.[9] Such conditions made African Americans leery of signing labor contracts.

Most freedpeople anticipated that freedwomen would work with their husbands on their own land safe from sexually harassing or violent overseers or employers. The failure to divide and distribute the land of former owners bitterly disappointed freedpeople and forced them to seek employment with former masters.[10] Nevertheless, African Americans continued to petition the government for land "for every man and woman" and they remained reluctant about working for white planters.[11] Mississippi's 1865 laws that restricted African American rental of farm land caused individual African American men and a few women to try to buy land under the Homestead Act.[12] A chart of properties purchased by African Americans in Mississippi under the Homestead Act showed thirteen names of African American women out of thirty-one owners.[13] Although the 1870 Unites States census showed almost no real property ownership by freedmen, a small minority of African Americans had become landowners in Mississippi by 1870.[14]

Congress charged the Freedmen's Bureau with supervising the transition of African Americans from enslavement to free laborers; this was the new status of the majority of African Americans in Mississippi. The Bureau, which was funded through the War Department, continued the functions of John Eaton and the Freedmen's Department.[15] The Bureau's job was made difficult by the expectations of freedpeople of land and by their opposition to working for former slave owners.[16] African American resistance added to the war's disruption of the plantation workforce. The initial refusal of blacks to contract with employers helped create an apparent labor shortage in Mississippi by the end of 1865. According to one Freedmen's Bureau official, freedpeople equated contracting with "signing them[selves] back to their masters."[17] The Freedmen's Bureau broke the stalemate between planters who needed field hands and freedpeople who wanted land.[18]

During Confederate Reconstruction and for a few years after, the federal government through the Freedmen's Bureau government continued to supervise free labor and legal marriages of the former slaves. Although Congress established the Bureau, in part, to oversee the distribution of land taken from the Confederates, this program ended quickly with Johnson's restoration of plantations to southern owners. Bureau agents attempted to dissuade African Americans from the tenaciously held belief that the plantations of former slave owners would be divided by the government and that the former slaves were entitled to it.

Bureau agents encouraged the planters to offer higher wages or a greater share of the crops, while agents grimly informed former slaves that the federal government was not giving them their forty acres. Samuel Thomas, the first Freedmen's Bureau assistant commissioner in Mississippi, wrote a stern letter on January 2, 1866, "To the Colored People of Mississippi." He explained, "some of you have the absurd notion that if you put your hands to a contract you will somehow be made slaves. This is all nonsense, made up by some foolish or wicked person." He added "I hope you are all convinced that you are not to receive property of any kind from the government and that you must labor for what you get, like other people." Additionally he reminded them that "the time has arrived for you to contract for another years labor. I wish to impress upon you the importance of doing this at once. . . . You cannot live without work of some kind. Your houses and lands belong to the white people, and you cannot expect that they will allow you to live on them in idleness." A combination of remonstrations by Freedmen's Bureau officials, strict vagrancy laws, and restrictions on available land pushed reluctant African Americans toward contract labor by early 1866.[19]

Samuel Thomas, like John Eaton, blamed the slavery system for the weak work ethic and morals of African Americans while they were slaves.[20] They both believed in the redemptive power of hard work for freedpeople.[21] As adherents of free labor ideology, many Bureau agents believed that diligent labor would lead to upward social mobility and economic self-sufficiency for freedpeople and that they would be able to progress as far as their innate characteristics permitted.[22] Samuel Thomas even hoped that with decent wages and frugality particularly able freedmen could save enough money to acquire land.[23]

Because Johnson's amnesty programs kept the land firmly under the control of white planters, Thomas's major task became that of convincing freedpeople to work as wage earners for white employers and to abandon, at least temporarily, their aspirations to become landowners.[24] As one of its primary functions, the Bureau promoted free (nonslave) wage labor for African American men and women.[25] Agents encouraged freedpeople to work for former masters.[26] Some Bureau agents shared the belief of southern whites that African Americans were naturally lazy and were sympathetic to the difficulties of employers. They willingly used such disciplinary tactics as refusing to pay workers or dismissing them when their white employers complained about their work performance. Samuel Thomas worried that Bureau agents did not care about the welfare of the freedpeople. In November 1865, he complained that agents "were not qualified for their places and had but little heart in their work."[27]

The cornerstone of the free labor plan of the northerners was the wage labor contract, which required a mutual understanding of obligations between employer and employee.[28] As historian Harold Woodman has explained, "the basic assumption in the free labor ideology was that people would work without physical compulsion because it was in their own interest to do so."[29] The contract allowed freedpeople to choose their own employer but it also enforced the concept that "work" meant hiring with a white employer.[30] Trusting the contract to bind both parties to a fair agreement, Freedmen's Bureau agents assumed that labor contracts would minimize labor conflict. Stymied by Johnson's return of land to planters, Samuel Thomas turned to wage labor as a way of supervising an orderly emancipation process.[31]

Agents under Thomas upheld the "sacredness of contract," promising freed workers protection against physical abuse and economic exploitation by white employers, while guaranteeing white landowners a stable workforce.[32] They were particularly concerned that families stay together and support the children lest they became a burden on the government. To ensure fair treatment for African American laborers, the officials insisted that employers of freedpeople use written contracts that the employees signed and Bureau agents approved.[33] The Bureau printed sample forms for employers, which some employers used in 1865. In each successive year, employers relied less on the printed form, preferring to write their own. The vehemence of Bureau agents in upholding the legality of a year-long contract made it difficult for African Americans to terminate contracts any earlier. Added to this was the illiteracy of the majority of the freedpeople so that they were easy prey to unfair contracts. Meanwhile, planters developed various ploys to remove employees without pay after they had completed their work. The Freedmen's Bureau did not solve the underlying problems in a labor system under which African Americans continued to work for former slave owners.

One part of the conflict involved the refusal of planters to acknowledge the distinctions that freedwomen made between their reproductive and productive activities as mothers and as workers. As African Americans sought to control these aspects of their lives, white employers tried to maintain the work schedules they had mandated under slavery. The attitudes of employers toward the work of women and children did not change radically with the end of slavery. On the other hand, African Americans expected family life to be removed from the workplace to a much greater degree than it had been during slavery. Hostile relations with employers invaded the personal lives of freedwomen and the worlds of work and family often collided.

The Freedmen's Bureau wanted to finish the job begun by the military and get the freedwomen who still remained in cities onto plantations. They were not entirely successful.[34] As military officials had done during the war, Bureau agents as well as local officials tried to prevent freedpeople from traveling around the countryside or wandering into cities. Between 1860 and 1870, Vicksburg gained over 5,000 African Americans and Natchez grew by close to 3,000.[35] The Bureau argued that if freed-people moved about, they were more likely to become destitute and to need aid from the federal government.[36]

African Americans who journeyed to cities for better employment or educational opportunities had to find work immediately. Soon after the war, the Freedmen's Bureau issued passes based on employment: "All Freed-men in and about the different towns and posts of this command must procure passes from this office, and to procure these passes, it must be clearly shown that the person is engaged in some laudable pursuit."[37] In most cases, "laudable" meant working for whites. Freedpeople who lacked passes were subject to incarceration.

The Bureau used the perceived immorality of African American wom-en as a rationale to move women out of cities after the war. Policies that were begun during the war were completed soon after. The freedmen's camp at Meridian was abolished because it was "the harboring place for lewd women, and other disreputable characters."[38] The Bureau easily made such charges given the general perception among whites of the immoral-ity of African American women.

The Bureau's closing of the contraband camps affected African Ameri-can women more than men because of their greater numbers in the camps. For example, in September 1865 the army shut down a camp in Macon, Mississippi, that contained 158 children, 115 women, and 10 men.[39] When the Washington Home Colony was broken up in November 1865, there were 258 children, 150 females, and 25 men.[40] Fearful that the newly freed people would become a burden on the federal government, Bureau of-ficials wanted them to work on plantations. The women who were evicted from such camps faced difficult decisions that required them to balance their ideals of family life and privacy against the harsh labor policies of northerners and southerners alike.

Free Laborers

When Mississippi freedwomen worked on plantations, they labored in the field or provided domestic work. As during slavery, when rural freed-women performed agricultural labor, they hoed more often than plowed.[41] Freedwomen probably switched to plowing when there was a shortage of men on the plantation. Much to the surprise of transplanted New Yorker Henry M. Crydenwise, a former United States Colored Troops officer and a manager on R. B. Elam's plantation in Issequena County, women were "as good ploughers as the men."[42] Employers provided additional incentives by paying more for plowing than for hoeing. Eliza Oliver earned $10 a month when she plowed and only $8 a month for other jobs on the plantation.[43] A division of labor by sex continued after the war on plantations like that of R. B. Elam, where women hoed and cleared brush from new land while the men split rails.[44] On the Ormonde plantation Wilmer Shields divided the plantation's "tools, implements, etc." among the "hands." Of fourteen men, ten received plows, one received a hoe, and three did not obtain either. Of twenty-two women, twenty-one received hoes.[45]

Planters and planters' wives also hired freedwomen to be domestic servants.[46] Caroline agreed in her labor contract "to do cooking, washing, ironing, and general housework and anything about the yard or garden that may be required of her."[47] In addition to these general housekeeping chores, a freedwoman employed by P. F. Howell also served as seamstress for her white employer.[48] As during slavery, women's domestic chores included gardening and caring for livestock. Lucy Davis cooked, milked, washed, and ironed.[49] Charity Riley's employers expected her to be responsible for the dairying (including making the butter), feeding the chickens, cooking, washing, spinning, and weaving cloth. She also raised cotton, potatoes, and other vegetables, which her employer allowed her to sell for her own profit.[50]

Planters continued to assign house servants to the fields when they needed extra hands. Although he hired Venus William as a cook, her employer also required her "to work in the field when necessary."[51] While Margaret Lee cared for Samuel Tyler's deaf brother, she also performed field labor.[52] Amanda Burkey planted potatoes and performed other agricultural duties even though her contract defined her occupation as a "cook, washer, and house servant."[53] Occasionally employers moved female field hands to the house and domestic servants to the fields by the request of the workers, but, as during slavery, planters usually initiated such changes.[54] J. C. Caruthers mentioned in one of his letters that "we were compelled to keep several old women who can not make hands in the field who I think can spin enough to supply the place. I have an understanding with all to go to the field that can . . . when we are in a push and the weather fit." Except for Melinda, Caruthers continued: "[S]he [has] no interest in the crop at all. She is to do the weaving for the place & cook, wash, & garden for me with her two boys. . . . [S]he will be the only one up at the house and I will hold her responsible that everything is kept in order." He added that "the little cooking for me was not enough for Mary to do so I sent her to the quarter."[55]

As freedwomen began to assert their own definition of freed labor, the dynamic between domestics and former slaveholding women altered over time, sometimes subtly, sometimes dramatically.[56] The relationship between domestics and their employers continued in some ways as they had before the war—a combination of ambivalence, occasional affection, white dependency, and white authority.[57] Domestic workers continued to limit their workloads as they had begun to do during the war.

Few southern households employed the same number of house servants as they had possessed during slavery. As a result, former slave owning women performed more domestic work for their families than before the war. The role of these white women in the household shifted from supervision to active participation.[58] This change in the status of white women probably reached its height during the war when slaves fled to Union lines, leaving fewer slaves on plantations. In her diary during Grant's siege of Vicksburg, Elizabeth Ingraham wrote, "The Suggs people are doing their work. Father and son taking the plogh [sic], and mother and daughters the washtub—hurrah for them! better than fretting and sitting down in the dirt."[59] Belle Kearney described former slaveholding women whose "silk dresses were displaced by cotton ones, the parlor was deserted for the kitchen, the piano for the sewing machine. The grind was upon us. We were too pressed in finances to hire anything done but laundry work and wood cutting."[60] One young woman wrote "that my dear father and mother should be deprived of every luxury and almost every necessity of life." She also complained that female relatives "have had to cook for the last day or two!! I think that's coming down to the stern realities of war sure enough."[61] The sense of desertion emanated from James Allen's terse plantation entry for May 6, 1865, which read "wife—sick & no one to wait on her."[62]

The loss of slave women and the increased domestic work for their wives and daughters symbolized a loss of status for former masters. After the war, the women in Samuel Agnew's family began cooking and milking the cows.[63] The sight of his women performing "servant's" work undermined Agnew's sense of his own manhood and emphasized his failure as a provider. Agnew resigned himself to the new domestic scene, as he stated: "I never expected that my wife would have to come to the wash tub, but so it is."[64] Agnew also blamed his inability to hire adequate domestic help on his former slaves who discouraged other freedpeople from working for him.[65] Similarly, planter Dabney Smedes felt demoralized when the women in his family performed domestic work. In defiance of Union General William T. Sherman who, according to Smedes, declared that "he would like to bring every Southern woman to the wash-tub," Smedes decided to do the laundry himself.[66]

Domestics affirmed their emancipation by keeping their personal life removed from white employers in ways that had been impossible during slavery. After the war, physical distance between employee and employer led to more privacy for non-residential domestics. Freedwomen privileged their family life over their labor for whites and fought to keep them separate.[67] It seems likely that the intensity of the old relationships decreased as freedwomen insisted on personal autonomy and white employers lessened their involvement with the lives of their employees outside of work. When Harriet Paul and her husband were slaves, their personal lives intertwined with their owners to the extent that they had to ask for their master's permission to marry. After the war, Harriet Paul, then a widow, went to work for the Shannon family. One of Shannon's daughters explained that "she moved to the country after that and though she frequently came into work for my mother or my sister and myself, I did not know so much" about "her family."[68]

The new attitude of freedwomen toward their work caused many former slave owning women to find dealing with freedwomen difficult. Even after the war, planters continued to expect their domestic servants to behave in a servile manner and felt betrayed when they acted as free men and women. Although white women were terrified by freedmen who refused to play a servile role, white women resented freedwomen who refused to be subservient. Upper-class white women wanted their servants to be docile. Female servants concocted ways to irritate their white employers, a subtle form of resistance that had been practiced during slavery. An efficient laundress, Rosetta Taylor rarely tried to please her employer. According to him, she "neglected 1/2 of her house work." Ignoring racial and class taboos, she purposely infuriated her employer's wife by washing her employer's children's clothes with the clothes of her own grandson and those of "some hireling white laborers."[69] After complaining that freedwomen were "insolent," one potential employer remonstrated, "I would rather have about me the most uncouth Irish girl that ever saw the Green shores of Irin."[70] In spite of their reluctance to do so, most white southerners employed African American women after the war. There were few immigrant women in Mississippi to compete for domestic jobs, and African American women worked for lower wages than white women.[71]

African American women had not envisioned that freedom would mean performing the same type of domestic and agricultural work as they had as slaves. They expected to be working for their own families, prefer-ably on land owned by their husbands. The transition of slave women and men to laborers for white employers who were often former masters re-quired dire economic necessity and on occasion, prodding from the fed-eral government.

Labor Relations

White southerners and northerners valued the contract labor of freedmen over that of freedwomen. When employers hired former slave women for agricultural work, they paid them lower wages than men. The higher wage rates of freedmen also attested to their greater occupational opportunity. Because railroad and mill jobs paid more than field labor, planters in certain areas tried to match the wages.[72] Once they were con-vinced that they would remain landless, the greatest concern of freed-people was payment. In February 1867, A. C. Gillem, the assistant com-missioner of the Mississippi Freedmen's Bureau office, listed the types of compensation, monetary or crops, that were arranged by planters and em-ployers. He enthusiastically wrote that due to the demand for labor, wag-es in Mississippi were very high; they amounted to $15 to $20 per month for men and $8 to $10 for women and children over 12 years of age.[73]

Wages for freed women and men soon declined from the ones Gillem described. Two years of agricultural disaster in Mississippi in 1866 and 1867 caused hardship. The devastation in some areas from the war, bad weather, and an invasion of army worms, a particularly voracious caterpil-lar, contributed to crop failures.[74] Cotton prices declined in 1868 from war-time highs (although not to prewar prices) and interest rates rose as credit for the planters tightened.[75] According to the Freedmen's Bureau agents, in 1868 men received wages between $7 and $10 and women earned be-tween $4.50 and $7 per month.[76] In 1867 and 1868, more freedmen and women began to work for a share of the crop, sometimes known as a share wage, by which the planter supplied everything except for the labor.[77] Gillem explained variations of payment in crops, "the plan is usually for the employee to receive a third or fourth of the crop, the planter furnish-ing rations, charging other supplies to the account of the laborer, to be paid at the end of the year much like share wage." Gillem elaborated about another form of payment by which workers were more involved in the production: "[M]any are working for half the crop, agreeing to supply their own rations and to share equally with the proprietor the cost of stock etc." Even though some freedpeople wanted to work for shares, "others prefer wages, the men receiving from $10 to 15 per month, and the women from $6 to $10.[78]

The Failure of Wage Labor

The factors that influenced the evolution of sharecropping included the failure of land to be distributed, disputes over nonpayment of monetary wages, white supervision and intervention both in labor and in family life, and the fundamental nature of the meaning of freedom. The northern concept of wage labor did not work successfully in the south. Freedpeople and planters defined free labor differently. Slavery shaped the responses of both freedpeople and former masters. Planters expected freedpeople to behave with the deference and obedience of slaves. Former slave owners anticipated that they would rule their laborers with absolute authority and reacted vehemently and sometimes violently to any challenge.[79] In contrast, workers separated their lives from those of their employers whenever they could in ways that had been impossible during slavery.

Labor contracts and vagrancy laws kept freed men and women from using market forces to barter for better wages in spite of the labor shortage.[80] For example, agent John Sunderland reminded freedwomen who worked for Charles Gordon that, under the stringent laws known as the Black Codes passed by Mississippi legislators in 1865, they could be incarcerated as vagrants if they left Gordon without due cause.[81] Bureau agent John Knox dispatched a man to force African American laborers "Betsey and family" to return to their place of employment.[82] Knox believed that workers needed to demonstrate strict obedience to their employers. When workers refused to "obey" a planter's "lawful orders," they failed to live up to "their contract and ought to be discharged," often without payment.[83]

Nonpayment of wages to freedmen and women kept wage labor from becoming the success northerners wanted it to be. According to Freedmen's Bureau documents, including complaint books, the largest area of conflict between African American men and women and plantation owners was the unwillingness of planters to pay wages to their workers.[84] Planters and laborers both expressed dissatisfaction with aspects of contract wage labor. Employers objected to the monetary wage because they often lacked the capital to pay it. Although planters wanted to guarantee themselves a labor force, they did not or could not always pay them. Economic conditions also squeezed employers. After the war, Confederate money was worthless and planters owed money to merchants for supplies.[85] Because planters paid these debts before compensating their workers, the Freedmen's Bureau tried to make planters guarantee that their employees' earnings would constitute the first lien against the employer once crop payments had been received.[86] Such attempts often failed.

To freedpeople, wage labor seemed too reminiscent of slavery. Male and female workers complained that planters found trivial excuses to dismiss workers after the harvest to avoid paying them.[87] This caused hardships for employees both because they failed to receive wages and because employers forced them to leave their homes on the plantations where they worked and lived.[88] Although workers could be forced off plantations, workers could not leave when they wanted to hire for better wages.

Employers countered the complaints of workers. They justified their refusal to pay wages at the end of the year by arguing that they merely withheld accumulated debts from the pay of workers. [89] Restrictive mobility clauses in the labor contracts as well as the inability or refusal of employers to pay in cash often forced freedpeople to buy from their employers and kept laborers from better priced goods available elsewhere. Planters charged at least 20 percent over cost for these products, although some added as much as 50 to 100 percent.[90] Although these are not unreasonable amounts for modern retailers, the prices were expensive for African Americans. For example, a fifty-cent bar of soap became a relatively expensive luxury for a freedwoman who earned a maximum of $10 a month.

Such pricing kept workers in debt to the planters and kept them from receiving wages. An approximation of markup by planters can be determined by comparing prices of J. R. Davis's purchases at J. C. Smith's general store in Crystal Springs, Mississippi, in October 1868, with prices charged to freedpeople in other final account records. These account records show the prices of goods and services charged to freedpeople by the planters who provided them. Although the quality of products J. R. Davis bought may have differed from that sold to freedpeople by other planters, the comparisons suggest the potential profit margin on items that planters sold to freedpeople. Prices on goods for freedpeople almost always equaled or were higher than Smith's prices, and in no case were the prices lower. Davis paid ten cents for a spool of cotton thread while a freedwoman, Margaret Rodger, bought thread for fifteen cents from her employer, a markup of 33 percent.[91] J. C. Smith sold calico at eighteen and twenty cents a yard; several planters sold it to their employees for between twenty-five and thirty-five cents a yard.[92] At Smith's store Davis bought a bar of soap for thirty cents. Accounts in the Alexander K. Farrar papers show that Emily Harris, a freedwoman on Farrar's place, paid fifty cents for soap, a possible 66 percent markup. Plug tobacco, an imprecise quantity, saw the largest profit; Davis paid thirty and fifty cents, but some freed men and women paid as much as seventy-five cents to one dollar.[93]

Additionally, planters specified in some contracts that their employees pay them for such goods and services as provisions for children.[94] Sam and Caroline Anderson paid $36 a year for food and shelter for their three children.[95] Employers also enforced stiff fines, as much as fifty cents or one dollar a day, for missed work, a high rate given the average monthly wage for women. In 1868, E. J. Capell required in his laborers' contracts that "the laborers shall pay one dollar for every day lost, unless such laborer furnish an acceptable substitute."[96]

These deductions suggested a concept of free labor by which the employer paid for a person's labor for an entire year rather than for the amount of labor necessary to perform particular tasks. The planters found it difficult to distinguish between the person and the labor. Northern concepts of labor assumed a difference between labor and laborers, at least in theory. The fundamental difference in thought, if not practice, between southern plantation owners and northerners was a direct legacy of slavery.[97]

In addition to difficulties over the payment of wages, conflicts between freedpeople and planters erupted over what kind of labor would be performed, when, how, and for whom.[98] These disputes pushed both freedpeople and planters toward sharecropping. Former slave owners tried to continue to organize their workers in gangs, having successfully relied on them during slavery.[99] Laborers resisted the supervision of a gang system. They preferred to contract in smaller units on a certain number of acres of land, sometimes with family members working in squads.[100]

In addition to resisting work gangs as a method to organize and control their labor, African American men and women also vigorously protested the use of force. Although labor contracts forbade physical punishment, white Mississippi employers believed that only force made African Americans obey them. Planters occasionally used it as a punitive measure as well as a warning to other workers. Although some whites used violence more readily than others, former slave owners and overseers (after the war referred to as agents) in Mississippi generally considered physical coercion a permissible way to resolve labor disputes with workers.[101]

Employers' rationalizations for the use of force exemplified their refusal or inability to accept the concept of free labor. Free labor by definition should not require physical coercion. The use of force reminded both employer and employee of the slave status. Slave masters had relied on violence to enforce subordinate behavior; their postwar behavior did not manifest significant differences from prewar practices in some cases. Violence against individual workers often illustrated the desire of planters for a workforce reminiscent of slavery and denied the former slaves' assertions of their rights as free workers and freedpeople. The determination of freedpeople to be treated as equals by whites led them into confrontations with former slave owners, who believed that any verbal statements that implied the equality of African Americans were impertinent. They continued to rely on force as a means of labor and racial control.[102] Interracial relations between freedpeople and their former masters became more visibly bitter as tensions that had often been repressed by slaves surfaced.

According to the Freedmen's Bureau complaint records, although freedmen received physical punishment more often than female workers, a woman's sex, as in slavery, failed to protect her from physical abuse.[103] Freedwoman Mary Connor's employer struck her because she "did not know how to plough.[104] Naomi Smith's employer kicked her for "not washing the clothes clean."[105] When her former master ordered her to build a fire, Harriet Kilgore told him that she "had backache and was not in any hurry to get up there." Outraged by her defiance, Kilgore beat her. He later justified his action by explaining, with unconscious irony, that she acted as if she "was free and would do nothing he told [her] to."[106] Another former master beat a woman for attempting to leave his plantation, explaining that he had "a right to beat her for she is his slave."[107] In the first two examples, employers beat freedwomen for incompetence, just as they would have during slavery. In the last two examples, employers physically abused their former slaves for asserting themselves as free laborers: One woman set her own slower work pace and showed, in her employer's mind, disrespect and the other woman decided to exercise her right to leave.

In actions that were reminiscent of slavery, employers hit freedwomen with their fists, kicked them, and whipped them with horsewhips and switches. Southern white gentlemen pistol-whipped freedwomen and struck them with canes.[108] From the violent legacy of slave discipline, whites set dogs on disobedient freedwomen.[109] One employer forced a freedwoman to labor in the fields while wearing a chain.[110] The bodily harm inflicted on freedwomen was sometimes grievous. One woman died from "250 lashes."[111] The records are unclear about the punishment of the men who were accused of the whipping. During these violent episodes, southern men insulted African American women with epithets that were theoretically inapplicable to white women of their own class such as "black bitch."[112] The literal reduction of African American women to animals exemplified the desire of whites to demean African American women. Their race, poverty, and class exempted them from southern male chivalry.

White women also resorted to violence against women workers. When white women physically attacked their female employees, they often used household articles. One woman attacked a freedwoman with a pair of scissors, and another "imprinted a hot flat iron" on a freedwoman's face.[113] When a freedwoman was "insulting" to her white female employer whom she felt had cheated her out of part of her wages, her employer hit her with a fire shovel. African American women retaliated when possible. When her employer, Mrs. Scarborough, hit her with a brush broom, Laura Sloan fought back and tossed "a bucket of water on her."[114] Such actions by employers strengthened the desire of African American women to remove themselves as much as possible from working directly for whites.

Freedmen's Bureau agents were not completely gender neutral in their adjudication of workers' complaints, especially when southern employers continued to rely on physical punishment to ensure obedience from their labor force. As free labor advocates who opposed coercion and as Victorian men with protective feelings about women, they cringed at the corporal punishment of female workers. Although they opposed any physical violence against free workers, agents reacted with particular horror to violence against women workers. One agent wrote that "there can be no excuse for beating a *woman*."[115] The preparations for whippings debased African American women and displayed the sexual overtones prevalent in the violence against African American females. Before their whipping, the women were often "stripped naked." After the male perpetrators undressed them, they tied the women to trees and beat them.[116]

Family and Work

Regardless of whether or not they involved violence, labor disputes were tied to the definitions of former slaves of the concept of freedom in terms of who controlled African American labor, leisure, and time within the family.[117] Freed men and women were interested in the fundamental question of how emancipation would differ from slavery and how freedom was going to change their work. Disagreements between employers and employees developed over the intention of freedpeople to work fewer hours than they had as slaves. After the war, freedpeople strove to minimize the interference of former slave owners in the domestic and family portion of their lives.[118] Although planters opposed any changes from slavery, freedpeople expected that the needs of African American families would be important components in decisions about how much time freedwomen and their children devoted to outside employment. African American parents wanted to send their children to school rather than to the fields. African American women, who assumed most of the domestic responsibility of their own households, needed more time for their families.

Freedwomen wanted their agricultural work to be performed for the benefit of their family and perceived field work, just as much as washing or cooking, to be part of their labor for their family. They did not want to work only for the material betterment of white people but also for their own households. After the war, the link between labor and family strengthened for women as decisions about one had the capacity to influence the other. Ultimately, the desire of freedwomen to set their own schedules for domestic tasks caused men and women alike to resist gang labor and become sharecroppers.

Freedwomen needed more time for their families in part because their private domestic responsibilities increased after the Civil War. Cooking and clothes-making often ceased to be communal activities as they had been under slavery.[119] Clothes production entailed cutting the cloth and hand-sewing it, but rarely making the cloth itself. Because the looms needed for weaving were large and bulky, it was difficult for individual African American women to keep them in the cabins. Most often they bought the cloth locally, although occasionally they obtained spinning wheels, spun cotton thread, and then tried to find a loom for weaving.[120] They dyed handspun or manufactured cloth from colors made from tree bark, berries, or plants such as indigo.[121] After emancipation, freedwomen prepared more meals for themselves and their families. When employers gave their workers patches of land, African American women planted gardens and raised produce, including potatoes, squash, and peas, for sale.[122] Although male farm workers on J. G. Colbert's place received pay of one-third of the crop, Colbert gave their wives "three acres of land" for their own use.[123] African American women also raised animals for their families, such as hogs and chickens for food, while men tended to the draft animals. Pigs proved to have the added advantage of being as loyal and affectionate as dogs. (One freedwoman described a sow that she raised "just like one of her children.")[124] In addition to cooking, washing, sewing and gardening, freedwomen took charge of caring for their own children.[125]

After emancipation, women made their own child care arrangements, including having their older children assist with the younger children. Mothers supervised such sibling care as each family took charge of their own children's daily activities, rather than, as in slavery, having one older woman looking after the children on a plantation. Although often they were only several years older, children helped provide child care for their siblings. Sarah Robinson recalled, "when I got big enough I 'toted' my brother about."[126] Julia Thomas gave birth to three daughters, Louisa, Harriet, and Susan. Lou looked after the other two children for her mother even though she was only four years older than Harriet and six years older than Susan.[127]

Women with children based their desire for a more flexible work schedule than the schedule that gang labor permitted on a realistic appraisal of the amount of domestic work they had to do rather than on an acceptance of cultural norms against women working outside the home.[128] In various societies, including different African cultures, child care and domestic family labor was primarily women's work.[129] After the war, the economic structure of unequal pay for African American men and women by which men received higher wages, as well as cultural attitudes, reinforced the division of labor within the family by which women were expected to perform unpaid household duties. As a result of these multiple responsibilities, freedwomen preferred to limit the number of hours they worked for whites and even tried to cease employment outside the home. Such decisions had less economic impact on families than if men had left the workforce to provide child care. The alternative was for freedwomen to continue to work in the fields during daylight hours and perform familial domestic chores in their limited spare time, as they had during slavery.[130]

Freedwomen's family concerns did not mesh with the desire of white employers to control their labor. For example, the pregnancies and child care needs of freedwomen caused disagreements between freedpeople and employers. [131] Slave masters viewed pregnancies by slave women as a potential increase in their wealth even though they willingly sacrificed some pregnancies to hard work. After the war, employers saw pregnancies only as a nuisance.[132] In contrast, freedwomen wanted more time off for pregnancies and nursing than during slavery.[133] These child-related issues highlighted for African Americans their need for less white interference in their interior lives. Women did not want to risk miscarriages from over-work, and nursing provided special time for bonding with the new baby. Women also wanted to control their nursing schedule both for the health of the child and because an inability to nurse causes the breasts to become uncomfortable and increases the risk of infections such as mastitis.

Freedwomen viewed respite from work during pregnancies and nursing as their right, ignoring the concept of wage labor that no work meant no pay. Nursing and pregnancy issues caused a continual test of wills between William Newton Mercer, a former slave owner in Adams county who moved to New Orleans, his overseer, and his female workers. Mercer's overseer, Wilmer Shields, wrote Mercer that "as soon as one of them conceived or thinks herself pregnant, she gives up work altogether. We have four at B[uckhurst] who have not been in the field the year and probably will not during the balance of 1867."[134] Nursing also posed a problem for white employers. Shields wrote tersely in his journal "*suckler diffi-culty*—arranged by their losing 1/4 their time etc. get 2 hours each day."[135] Mercer lost in a direct confrontation, at least temporarily, when "Harriet and Amelia nursing over 12 months disobeyed order to quit suckling."[136] Labor contracts also indicated that other planters shared Mercer's disputes with women employees. J. W. Field of Lowndes County noted on his labor contract "Martha, 35—pregnant and done no work." Twenty-year-old Julia was "pregnant and will do no work before November."[137] Adeline Anderson's employer complained that "she had a suckling infant which required much of her time."[138] In Yazoo County, a labor contract specified that "should the said Fanny and Julia become pregnant and past the seventh month before the end of the year one third of their wages to be deducted."[139]

Disputes arose when employers wanted to continue, as they had during slavery, to regulate when their African American female employees spent time on their own household tasks. Employers intended to control their labor force to the extent of severely restricting African American women's lives outside of their labor for whites. In his 1867 labor contract, James Gillespie specified "breakfast to be prepared & taken to the fields in the morning" in order to ensure that women and their families would be in the field early.[140] Employers expected women to do their washing and sewing on rainy days, as they had done in slavery.[141]

A few planters even reacted violently against mothers who spent more time with their own families than employers allowed. Her employer and former master William Jenkins whipped freedwoman Annette because she arrived late to work. When Jenkins ordered her to strip off her clothes for the beating, Annette pleaded "Master William I had my children to tend to made me so late." Whereupon Jenkins gave her two hundred lashes with his rawhide whip.[142] Joel Smith whipped his former slave Mary Ann Smith when she surreptitiously fed her children their breakfast rather than feed and water his hogs.[143]

Women's domestic and unpaid labor for their families has rarely been defined as work in the sense of paid labor. For African Americans, this devaluing of domestic work for their families was compounded with the definition of "work" as labor for whites. Most planters used economic leverage to ensure that freedwomen worked for them.[144] Planters in Mississippi raised rents on plantations in order "to prevent the women from remaining idle."[145] "Idle" in this context meant the women's familial domestic tasks. Employers also refused food rations to any unemployed adult member of a worker's family. In his labor contract with his employees, Mercer only agreed to provide "the meat and meal . . . to be the allowance of that laborer while he or she is well or working."[146] Similarly, another planter wrote, "I am only to feed *field* hands they bearing all other expense of themselves and supporting their own 'dead heads.'"[147] Employer G. P. Collins in Tunica County summed up the general consensus when he explained, "I don't feed idlers you know."[148] Employers occasionally sought to have nonworking male and female laborers arrested as vagrants.[149]

African American men ideally wanted to support their families without the help of their wives. Nonworking wives were a symbol of a financially successful man, and the most prosperous African American farmers were proud when their wives and daughters escaped field or domestic work in the homes of southern whites. Providing for their wives and keeping them away from possible sexual exploitation was regarded by freedmen as a symbol of freedom. Freedmen, according to a Freedmen's Bureau agent, possessed "an appreciation of their duty to maintain wife and children."[150] Labor contracts showed African American men's economic support for their nonworking wives or children.[151] When he designated the parental obligations of his employees, employer, R. L. Caruthers "deducted from their portion the expenses of such of their families as d[id] no work or not enough work to support themselves."[152] Thus, Isaac agreed "to furnish rations for his wife," while his food and that of his son and daughter was to be provided by their employer.[153] Tom Tolin's employer charged him $11.27 for his wife's board for one month.[154] Freedman John Fisher promised to "feed his wife and children."[155]

Women between the ages of twenty and forty were more likely to be listed on the contracts as dependents than men of the same age group, and such women were often listed with children.[156] One contract contained the names "John, 48," and "Lucy, 40," and the words, "This dependent Lucy, wife of John to be supported by husband . . . and to receive no part of crop."[157] Contracts listed as "dependents" women who were not employed by the planter. For women with large families of small children employment outside the home was probably not feasible. When Joe Fox signed a contract, the listed dependents were: Jane Fox, twenty-seven; Lucretia Fox, eleven; Alick Fox, ten; Mark Fox, nine; Sallie Fox, eight; Jacob Fox, six; George Fox, three; and Lewis Fox, one. If Jane Fox was the mother of all these children, she may have decided that her domestic responsibilities for her family would make full-time contract employment impossible.[158] For most families such a distribution of labor within the family was an elusive dream.

African American men, when able, supported their wives' desire to spend more time on familial domestic labor.[159] Employer Pickney Vaughn of Lauderdale County contracted with Thomas McArty, his wife Sylvia, and their son Willis. Only McArty signed the contract for his family, which was unusual for the labor contracts from 1865 to 1868. His lone mark suggested that he alone negotiated the terms for his family. The contract stated that Sylvia would be allowed to have "half of each Saturday to wash their clothes."[160] Husbands tried to protect the domestic time of their female relatives from white demands. Peter Dickson made a complaint against his employer Albert Wells because Wells "told Peter's wife to go into the woods & get some rails to put around the cow pen, she objected on grounds she could not leave her baby but said her husband would go, which he offered to do. This response angered Wells and he told them they must leave."[161] After being approached by an employer who wanted to hire Smith's wife, Smith discussed the job with his wife, but "she was not willing to go there." When the employer became angry with Smith for refusing to order his wife to work for him, Smith explained that he "would not try to force her there."[162]

Although the work habits of both African American men and women concerned employers, whites expressed particular pessimism about their ability to exact the continued labor of African American women.[163] Freedmen's Bureau officials argued that the refusal of freedwomen to work for whites led to the poor economic conditions of African Americans. Bureau agent W. Williams grumbled that "many freedpersons are in debt this year, for food, because their wives and families have not worked."[164]

Agents feared that poverty-stricken African Americans might become a burden on the federal government. They also viewed the desire of freedwomen to work either fewer hours or not at all as a corrupting influence on the free labor system.[165] The government's concern turned out to be unwarranted. Even when African American women wanted to withdraw from the workforce, their families were unable to afford the luxury because they depended on the additional income.

Rather than withdrawing from field labor completely, freedwomen settled for adjusting their work schedule to better suit the needs of their families.[166] According to the calculations of Robert L Ransom and Richard Sutch, freedwomen worked for white employers fewer hours per day and fewer days per week than they had as slaves.[167] During the first few years after the Civil War, freedwomen, particularly those with families, probably attempted to shift in and out of the workforce. These women, for example, may have only labored in the fields at certain peak agricultural periods, such as cotton-picking time.[168] Such women as Mary Barton earned $13.50 in ten days for picking cotton.[169] L. H. Sterling paid his cotton pickers a piece rate: fifty cents for every hundred pounds. In two weeks, Bell Body earned $6.00 working for Sterling.[170] Payment varied from fifty cents to one dollar per hundred pounds.[171] Women also found temporary employment as hoers. To have his fields cultivated, David McIver hired women at one dollar a day or seventy-five cents plus food.[172] Some women tried to supplement their income by taking in washing. When she wrote to the American Missionary Association about the conditions of cabins, one white woman outside Columbus, Mississippi, noted "outside is a kettle of clothes boiling over a pile of burning sticks." Almost "every wife takes in washing. She earns nine dollars perhaps" monthly.[173] In addition to the extra income, taking in the washing of white families enabled African American women to work in their own homes, which permitted them some flexibility to watch their children and set their own work schedules.

Freedpeople believed that working in families rather than in gangs led to less white supervision and enabled them to determine their own priorities, which gave them more control over their labor.[174] For women, sharecropping meant that they could decide how to allocate their time between field labor and domestic family labor. Economist Gerald Jaynes has argued that employers accepted sharecropping in part because the system encouraged freedwomen to work in the field.[175] Violence against women added to the resistance of African Americans to free labor as defined by whites. They wanted more control over their labor.

As historian W. E. B. DuBois pointed out, "Mississippi was the place where first and last Negroes were largely deprived of any opportunity for landownership."[176] Because of the inability of freedmen to obtain land and the unwillingness of former slave owners to pay monetary wages, African American women and their men became sharecroppers as a way to support themselves.[177] When a family worked as a labor unit in the fields, rather than as gangs of men and women, it often received a share of the crop. This system, along with factors such as who provided the tools and draft animals, evolved into the sharecropping system. Sharecropping gradually became the fate of freed men and women, although it developed more slowly in some areas of Mississippi than in others. African Americans were sharecropping as early as 1867, when sharecropping coexisted with monetary and share wages.[178]

Ultimately, sharecropping returned African Americans to a new reliance on whites and crippled them economically by keeping them indebted. The federal government's refusal to give land to freedmen had a profound impact on the extent to which African Americans could be self-employed. Because they could not acquire land, freedpeople expected wages; when they became disillusioned with monetary wages, they negotiated for a share of the crop. The failure of employers to pay monetary wages, and the desire of freedpeople for less white supervision in the fields all led to sharecropping. Sharecropping developed as cotton prices declined and white landowners in Mississippi made little effort to shift to mixed agriculture. It emerged despite the political change from Democratic to short-lived moderate Republican control of the state. Even under the civil rights reforms of the late 1860s and early 1870s in Mississippi that outlawed the Black Codes, African Americans continued to work for whites. Freedwoman Rina Brown recalled that "every thing we got we had to buy it on a credit an' den de white man got whut we made."[179]

The inability of Reconstruction to bring about a radical change in the economic lives of the former slaves represented one of the most acute failures of emancipation for African Americans. The lack of economic opportunities ensured that freedpeople remained laborers for whites, unable to achieve upward mobility. To that extent, they felt that freedom had failed them. As one Mississippi woman bitterly stated, "Is I free? Hasn't I got to get up before daylight and go into the field to work?"[180] As the quote points out, formerly enslaved women worked as field hands or domestic workers who performed the same work that they had as slave women. With more resignation, another freedwoman explained, "[D]ere wasn't no difference in freedom cause I went right on working for Miss."[181]

Although sharecropping was far less than African Americans wanted, the labor system did change from slavery. Although sharecropping did not permit economic self-sufficiency and economic mobility, it allowed more flexibility than gang labor. The use of overseers decreased and workers determined more of their own work schedules.

After emancipation the rural African American family became a stronger unit than it had been under slavery. Black women controlled more of their private domestic lives but they had more familial labor to perform as well as the need to work for wages (in money or shares). More domestic familial labor for the family was only one of the new responsibilities which African American families gained after the war.

In one sense work and family were more strongly tied together under sharecropping because families often worked in the fields together. But sharecropping was also part of the separation between family and labor as freedpeople removed their family concerns away from white interference. Women's familial concerns informed the labor choices of freedpeople as they tried to separate reproductive from productive work in their dealings with whites. Although they wanted the end of white supervision of both types of labor, they were never totally successful in their attempts to gain control of these two spheres.

MALE AND FEMALE
INTIMATE RELATIONSHIPS

"I was married to him under the flag"[1]

After her husband's death, Lucy Brown became intimate with Frank Dorsey, a member of the same company and regiment as her late husband. In their narrations of her relationship with Dorsey as well as with her partnership with Robert Owens, Lucy Brown and others defined and described what in their view constituted marriage and what did not. Speaking about Dorsey, Lucy Brown explained, "We were not married and did not claim to be and he just visited me sometimes and never lived in the house with me." Later, when Lucy Brown moved to another place to work, she began a new relationship with Robert Owens. Brown recalled "he had a wife at the time he was visiting me."[2]

Lucy Brown's second husband was Reuben Kelly. At first, Lucy Brown worked for Kelly but soon afterward they married. Andrew Johnson, a preacher, performed the ceremony. Once legally wedded, with a license and a record of her marriage that was kept at the court house, Lucy Brown assumed the surname of Kelly and lived with her second husband for over twenty-five years.

Emancipation made possible the legalization of intimate relationships through the introduction of the marriage contract. Such a contractual agreement was similar to the change from slave labor to wage work that was based on a labor contract. Marital law strengthened African American commitment to having personal lives that were removed from individual whites even though legalized marriage also meant potential interference from the state. For example, once a couple legally married they were obligated to seek a legal divorce if they wanted to end the marriage. Couples who were not legally married could simply agree to end the cohabitational relationship and one partner or the other would leave the household.

Rather than rely exclusively on a strict legal designation of marriage, freedpeople considered the couple's interaction with each other.[3] As during slavery, "marriage" for freedpeople meant a union that was recognized by the community and was based on the intent and commitment of the participants in the relationship.[4] Freedpeople used spousal terms such as husband and wife for both legal and extralegal cohabitational settled unions. Such informal definitions conflicted with legal definitions, as in the areas of extra legal cohabitational relationships known as "took-ups" and extralegal divorce known as "quitting."[5]

Neither the state nor African American communities supported the same male prerogatives over women as white men exercised over their women. The existence of informal, community-recognized divorce, quitting, allowed individual African American women to leave relationships. A woman did not immediately have to remarry to maintain her respectability, and she was not necessarily stigmatized as innately immoral if she engaged in sexual relationships outside of marriage.[6]

The relationship of African American women to their men and the locus of power within the African American family must be examined in the context of white domination of the wider society. As with labor, government policy such as granting military pensions to widows complicated these concepts and definitions and played an often contradictory part in influencing African American family life. White northerners and southerners alike were reluctant to relinquish to African American men access to the labor of African American women. Planters and the Freedmen's Bureau placed more stress on the more restrictive obligations of the marriage contract on women than freedpeople did.

Views of Legalized Marriage

For older freedpeople, the ability to reside with one's family without a master's consent and without the fear of forced separation signified freedom to an even greater extent than did legalized marriage. The attitudes of freedpeople toward legalized marriage were more complex than historians have often suggested. Although historians have argued that state-authorized marriage was a symbol of freedom for former slaves and that couples rushed to validate their slave marriages, evidence from the pension records suggests that they were comfortable with their community-sanctioned slave marriages. All freedpeople did not feel the need to legalize long-term slave marriages.[7] Unlike northern whites, they did not tie legalized marriage to becoming a responsible labor force. The views of freedpeople about the legalization of marriage represented a range of opinions.

On the whole, freedpeople favored legalization. They understood that legalized marriage seemed the surest way to ensure familial stability and protect against white interference. After the war, most African American couples became legally married without renewing their vows under various laws that were passed in Mississippi. Some couples, particularly younger couples or couples without slave ties, married either in religious or civil ceremonies. A minority of African American men and women preferred to live together and not to wed. Couples chose not to marry when they did not equate commitment to legality, in part a legacy of extralegal slave marriages. Some couples actively resisted marriage if they believed that the wife would lose her federal military widow's pension by doing so.

Historians have exaggerated the number of slave couples who remarried each other after the war. It appears that many marriages that were reported to the Freedmen's Bureau after the war were first-time marriages rather than remarriages of slave couples. Freedmen's Bureau data do not indicate whether couples had married each other during slavery and show that a majority of the couples who registered their marriages were fairly young, between the ages of twenty and thirty.[8] Material from marriages registered in Davis Bend, Natchez, and Vicksburg, Mississippi, in 1864 and 1865 show that 57 percent of the women and 39 percent of the men were under thirty when they registered their marriages.[9] Older freedpeople may have been marrying a new spouse rather than remarrying their slave spouses.

Although older freedpeople saw their slave marriages as valid, the next generation born either right before or during the war had a greater understanding of the significance of legalized marriage.[10] Mississippi's African American population was youthful and a large part was of marriageable age.[11] The decisions of young freedpeople to wed under legal auspices after the war showed how quickly they adjusted to the concept of formalized wedlock, although without necessarily accepting the rigidity of nineteenth-century marriage contracts. In some sense, the seemingly new practice of legalized marriage was similar to the commitment of the more enduring slave marriages, although slave marriages could be undermined by slave masters. As one Freedmen's Bureau agent pointed out, "marital relations of the freedmen are in many instances the same as when slaves, but among the younger portion they are legally married and live in accordance with . . . civilization."[12] Freedwoman Josephine Coxe recalled from her childhood that "before the surrender when niggers wanted to git married, Marster told 'em when they was married. But after the war, the Yankees had a bureau." She proudly stated that when she wedded for the first time, "me and Coxe was married by a license."[13] If slave men and women had not taken marriages seriously it is doubtful their children would have adapted to the legalized form so readily.

Most African American couples did not need to remarry in marriage ceremonies because the state constitutions of 1865 and 1870 made remarriage unnecessary. How well freedpeople understood these laws remains unclear. In late 1865, the all-white Democratic Mississippi legislature enacted a special law concerning the marital status of African Americans as part of the Black Codes. The law stated that "all freedmen free negroes and mulattos who do now and have heretofore lived and cohabited together as husband and wife shall be taken and held in law as legally married and the issue shall be taken and held as legitimate for all purposes."[14] In 1868, Freedmen's Bureau official Alvan Gillem complained about the 1865 state constitution's legislation of marriage for all cohabiting freedpeople because "its effect was to enforce matrimony between tens of thousands of freedpeople who were ignorant of the passage of the act. A large proportion of them is today still ignorant of the purport of that law."[15]

Freedpeople who understood the law probably saw little reason to spend their limited resources on a redundant wedding.[16] Paying for a marriage license and for someone to officiate at the ceremony presented a real financial burden. In 1870, George Kelly "paid the preacher $2.00" which represented over a tenth of a man's monthly monetary wage—if he was paid.[17]

Some former slave men and women may have remarried because they did not understand that the 1870 Mississippi constitution made remarriage unnecessary. The 1865 constitution and later the 1870 constitution (passed in Mississippi in 1870 after the United States Congress voided the 1865 constitution) declared as legally married those African American couples (and in the 1870 constitution, whites as well) who were cohabiting together at the time of ratification.[18] Article 12, section 22 of the 1870 constitution stated that "all persons who have not been married, but are now living together, cohabiting as man and wife, shall be taken and held, for all purposes in law, as married: and their children, whether born before or after the ratification of this constitution, shall be legitimate and the Legislature may, by law, punish adultery and concubinage."[19]

Men and women such as Elizabeth and Frank Fletcher completely misinterpreted the law, believing that it actually compelled couples to have a marriage ceremony performed. They misunderstood in part because of the widespread illiteracy of the African American population. Freedpeople also may have felt that the state's arbitrary action regarding their private lives made little intuitive sense because they already regarded their informal marriages as valid. During the late 1860s, Elizabeth Fletcher and her husband, "just went together at first and agreed to live together as husband and wife, and then it was said that everybody who had a husband to whom they had not been married by law, had to have a license and get married, and we did so."[20] Similarly, Elizabeth Kelly Duncan and her partner resided together for a few years after the war and heard plans of "prosecuting people for living that way without being married and then it was that we went into church."[21] In fact, the law prevented couples from being prosecuted if they had lived together before 1870. Jordan Banks and Evaline Bowling started to live together as soon as he returned from the army. According to his brother, "Jordan always intended to marry her by license after the new constitution went into effect but died before he could marry her."[22] If Bowling had comprehended the law, he would not have felt compelled to formally marry. The Works Progress Administration slave narratives also show misunderstanding, as one freedperson suggested: "[D]e slaves dat wuz married all had to git license an' be married over again."[23]

Mississippi marital laws were motivated by several factors. The control of sexuality was in part the goal. Marrying large numbers of freedpeople by fiat kept them from cohabiting without being legally married.[24] More importantly, by stressing legalized marriage, the laws also implicitly made African Americans legally responsible for the economic well-being of their families. These laws sought as well to absolve either slave owners or the state from responsibility for caring for former slaves.

Although the 1865 and 1870 state constitutions and supporting statutes attempted to clarify the marital status of African American men and women, they also complicated them. The constitutions abolished all slave marriages by declaring marriages to be legal only for couples that were cohabiting at the time. This negated the legitimacy of all previous relationships during slavery.[25] The laws adversely affected freedpeople who were forcibly separated from their mates during slavery or by the disruptions of the war if they subsequently lived with someone else. After the war, regardless of the laws that married them to their current live-in lovers, these freedmen and women believed that they had more than one living spouse.[26] Such freedpeople were emotionally torn between their two or sometimes more families, even though with the passage of the 1865 and 1870 constitutions they were only legally wedded to the person with whom they lived at the time the laws went into effect. If people in this situation desired to return to their previous spouse, they needed to obtain a divorce. If they failed to divorce legally and merely left or quit their present spouse to return to a previous family, they broke the law and could be prosecuted for adultery.[27] Even Alvan Gillem, assistant commissioner of the Freedmen's Bureau and a man rarely sympathetic to the problems of freedpeople, wondered if another law should be passed that would allow people who were living together to "voluntarily and without great expense assume the relation of husband and wife and legitimize their children followed by a strict enforcement of the laws relating to chastity." Gillem's suggestion would have allowed couples who were cohabiting at the end of the war to part without violating the law. [28] When their marital problems stemming from the new laws overwhelmed them, freedpeople occasionally appealed to the Freedmen's Bureau or to the Mississippi state courts.[29] Authorities learned of cases of perceived bigamy either from one of the spouses or from the "bigamist" who desired advice.[30] The marital laws also defined children who were born during slavery as illegitimate if their parents were not living together at the time the constitutions specified (a topic that will be discussed in the next chapter).

Ultimately, the 1870 constitutional provision regarding marriages proved too comprehensive, which led to a series of court challenges. Because of appeals over the following decades, the court ruled that couples who were living together in 1870 were married only if their intent in cohabitation was that of a marital relationship. Couples who were casually residing together at that specific time were thus retroactively exempt from the blanket marriage statute.[31]

Black Churches

Black churches became the most significant African American institution to encourage freedpeople to marry and legalize their slave unions. The church explicitly tied de jure marriage to morality.[32] As one Freedmen's Bureau agent explained, "marital relations of the Freedmen [are] improving from their religious association."[33] Many freedpeople who married after the Civil War sought out an African American church because they wanted their marriage to be sanctioned by God as well as by the state. These African Americans preferred to have a religious ceremony rather than a civil one. A Bureau official wrote in 1865 that freedpeople "all manifest a disposition to marry in the church, and prefer a minister of the Gospel to unite them."[34]

Clergymen in cities or small towns performed marriage ceremonies for freed African Americans.[35] On plantations, freedpeople reserved a church house, or cabin, for religious purposes, and preachers came to perform marriage services. Couples delighted in the festivities that accompanied their weddings. They wore special attire and invited their friends.[36]

Clergy frowned on nonmarital cohabitational relationships and, with varying success, tried to deny church membership to couples who lived together without a formal ceremony. Having lived with her companion two years prior to their marriage, one freedwoman recalled that "we got married by license, because the church we joined required every one to be married by license."[37] Maria Demar's son-in-law explained her marriage to soldier James Demar in 1871: "[T]hey had been living together from the time he came out of the army, and she joined the church, and the church would not let them be in the church without being legally married."[38] As one rural preacher pointed out, the clergy paid close attention to the issue of cohabitation. Although speaking of a "devout and zealous Christian" church member, he explained, "I was always very strict on the members of my church, and under no circumstances would I have allowed her to have remained in the church if there had been any such conduct [such as living with a man]. I was always watchful over my members and have often been reproached by some of them for being too strict."[39]

The church expected unmarried women to abstain from sex, which placed pressure on women to legally marry. Pastor Shaw of a Baptist church in Vicksburg vouched that Julia Wells was "a member of said church," and a "widow and respectable." He was positive that if Wells had cohabited with a man, or "had anything of the kind been known or spoken of it would have been brought before the church."[40] Although in some cases, individual clergy may have ignored (or may not have known) the marital status especially when the man and woman were in a stable union, the church occasionally acted against unmarried women who were engaged in what the church considered to be illicit sexual conduct. When interracial marriage became legal for a short time during Reconstruction, one of the African American churches in Yazoo County forced the lovers of white men out of the congregation. The church argued that with the removal of prohibitions against interracial marriage these women needed to gain respectability by becoming married women.[41]

The rationale behind the stand of black churches on legalized marriage consisted of more than its view that moral behavior was best expressed within the context of marriage, nor were the churches simply imitating white middle-class standards. The church also supported legalized marriage as a weapon against white charges of African American promiscuity and uncontrolled sexuality. By insisting on strict codes of sexual conduct, the church hoped to diminish white sexual stereotyping of African Americans. The clergy also hoped that legalized marriage would protect African American women from harassment by white men because whites used such sexual stereotypes to justify even assaults on freedwomen. The church realized it could not directly govern white behavior so it tried to control African American morals in a vain attempt to influence white perceptions and behavior.[42]

The Bureau and Legalized Marriage

The federal government encouraged legalized marriage through the Freedmen's Bureau. Bureau officials argued that the family based on lawful marriage provided stability to southern civil society. The Bureau combined its concern for the economic status of freedmen with the monitoring of more personal aspects of their lives. Just as the Freedmen's Bureau directed many labor initiatives that were begun during the war, they also continued wartime definitions of immorality. Northerners conceived of marriage as providing order and a secure, if subordinate, place for women. According to John Eaton, northerners helped freedpeople to understand that in "the force or inviolability or sacredness of contracts" in regard to their labor "lay at once the foundations of society" similar to "enforcing the laws of marriage . . . accordant with the genius of our free institutions and the spirit of American Christian civilization."[43] In a letter to African American workers, subcommissioner E. E. Platt used the language of contracts to explain the duties and responsibilities of marriage; "[T]he marriage contract is a sacrament and . . . no Law of God or Man is more sacred or binding. . . . You cannot at your pleasure part and take up with another. . . . To have two wives or two husbands is one of the highest and disastrous offenses that can be committed against human or divine law." Marriage required the same diligence as labor. Being free meant being disciplined. "[T]herefore you must be patient, be faithful, be forbearing and forgiving towards each other and serve . . . as to do honor to your freedom and be respectable and happy."[44]

Just as in wartime, views of the sexuality of African Americans informed federal policy. As with military officials during the war, Bureau officials (who were often former soldiers) battled against supposed African

American immorality with a campaign of legalized marriages for freedmen and women.[45] Agents provided clergy with marriage certificates and ministers filed copies of the licenses with the Bureau.[46] If freedpeople were unable to find a clergyman, a "bureau officer was authorized to perform the rite."[47] Uniting African Americans in matrimony, however, only represented one weapon in the Bureau's arsenal. Agents held strict views of the sanctity of matrimony and tried to ensure that freedpeople upheld the marriage contract. When one husband left his wife, a Bureau chief advised husband and wife to "live together as husband and wife, *and sin no more.*"[48] Some agents even invoked the vagrancy laws if a husband left his wife and work by moving in with a woman on another place.

Bureau officials fretted about the marital relations of freedpeople in their monthly reports, duly noting signs of improvement or perceived backsliding. Such statements reflect the personal views of Bureau officials of the proper marital state. It is impossible to know, especially since they contradict each other, how valid their conclusions were. On January 30, 1867, agent George Corliss reported that "the condition of freedmen with regard to their marriage relations appears to improve with marked rapidity."[49] Other agents were much less sanguine, such as the one who wrote, "the condition of the people with reference to their marriage relations 'is bad' [and] though many procure license and are legally united, their ideas of virtue is so low [*sic*] . . ."[50]

Pensions and Marriage

For all the Freedmen's Bureau encouragement of legalized marriage, military pension policy actively discouraged African American widows from remarrying. These women, often in their twenties, could not remarry after their husbands died or cohabit without losing their pension. Based on a prevailing notion of proper sexual conduct for unmarried women, which precluded any sexual relationship outside of marriage, pension law after 1882 prohibited pensions to widows who cohabited or otherwise engaged in sexual activity. The law reflected a belief in the duty of the man to be the sole wage earner, rather than state usurpation of the husband's role by providing a pension to a woman with a husband. Thus the restriction on remarriage.[51]

Pension law, however, also recognized the validity of slave marriages retroactively when southern courts were loathe to do so after the war. Mississippi state law only validated those cohabitational relationships that were in existence at the time of passage of the state constitutions after the war. Originally, pension law only recognized legal marriages and ignored slave marriages. Slaves did not possess legal documentation, such as a marriage certificate, for use as evidence in a widow's pension claim.[52] Aware that slave couples had lived together and raised families, the U. S. Congress authorized guidelines that allowed former slave wives to receive pensions. In 1864, Congress amended the pension bill to allow "that the widows and children of colored soldiers . . . shall be entitled to receive the pensions now provided by law, without other proof of marriage than that the parties had habitually recognized each other as man and wife, and lived together as such for a definite period, not less than two years, to be shown by the affidavits of credible witnesses."[53]

The section of the 1864 act regarding African American marriages was repealed in 1866 and replaced with new provisions. The law eliminated distinctions among states in which black claimants could or could not legally marry because all states by then allowed African Americans to be legally wed. The act of June 6, 1866, required no "other evidence of marriage than proof, satisfactory to the Commissioner of Pensions, that the parties have habitually recognized each other as man and wife, and lived together as such."[54] "Satisfactory" proof of marriage was defined more precisely in legislation passed on June 15, 1873. An African American widow was required to supply evidence that she and her husband "were joined in marriage by some ceremony deemed by them obligatory."[55] The requirement of a ceremony was open to interpretation. In June 1865, J. H. Weber explained why freedwomen Nancy McKay received Willoughby Johnson's pension and why Weber considered her to be Johnson's widow even though she never formally participated in a slave wedding: "[S]he being virtually his wife though not lawfully married, such being the case she is entitled to all of the rights and privileges of a lawful wife."[56] By these laws, the federal government retroactively gave slave marriages legality by deciding on the criteria by which the wives of soldiers of the United States Colored Troops were eligible for military pensions.

The ability of the children of former slaves to receive pensions depended on the sexual fidelity of the parents, particularly the women.[57] Officials at the Treasury Department speculated on the difficulty of verifying claims when legal marriage did not exist and when "under the slave customs, the question of heirship is a difficult one to solve. A man may have 'taken up' with half a dozen women in as many years and each woman with as many men. There can be no true marriage relation established in such cases, nor can the paternity of issue . . . be settled." They suggested that federal personnel investigate claims carefully to elicit "another fact

. . . if possible if these claimants claiming as widow, did not take up with men other than the soldier either before or after 'taking up' with him, the number and ages of children claimant may have had etc." Parents of soldiers needed to be interrogated to find out the length of time the soldier "lived with the parents." Further "brothers and sisters have to prove that parents would be rightful heirs if they were living."[58]

Widows who requested military pensions gave up all rights to privacy. The requirements of credible witnesses sent white federal pension officials traveling to small towns and plantations in Mississippi throughout the latter part of the nineteenth century and even into the early twentieth century. They asked probing questions of employers, former slave owners, neighbors, friends, and relatives of the widows of Union soldiers. Examiners became vigilant when they suspected remarriage or sexual misconduct.[59] The U. S. Pension Bureau assigned special examiners to pursue cases of suspected fraud, which they often anticipated in cases of former slaves who lacked standard documentation such as marriage licenses.[60] Pension examiners gathered testimony and determined the eligibility of a widow to receive a pension, which in the nineteenth century was generally $8 a month for a private's widow and $2 a month for each soldier's child.[61]

Widows believed that the government owed them their pension for the loss of their husbands and the separation from their men while they were soldiers. They saw it as an entitlement for life. Even if they remarried or cohabited with a man, they tried to maintain the pension.

The number of times widows outwitted the pension examiners undercuts the contention by examiners that these women possessed limited intelligence. One examiner exclaimed, "[S]tupidity and persistent untruth make a combination in this claimant difficult to combat." When asked, "[W]hy did you conceal the fact that you lived in Raymond [Mississippi] and the birth of Emily and your living with Vaughn Knowling," one woman responded, "I told you that I lived in Raymond. I didn't tell you the rest because you didn't ask me."[62]

Many women understood the pension laws well enough to devise clever methods to deceive pension examiners about their relationships. After the war these women lied about any remarriages or cohabitational relationships. One pension examiner wrote with disgust, "Here is a woman in good standing in the church deliberately swearing that she has remained a widow ever since the death of her husband," but she had remarried. He added, "It is sickening to think that among this people there is no one that you can trust."[63] Louisa Smith finally confessed to living with Abraham

Speers "since about two years after my husband died." She gave birth to three children by Speers and she explained that "we have never claimed to be married to each other or considered ourselves as married. . . . I have never married Speers because I understood that by marrying I would lose my right to pension."[64]

Informal Marriages: "Took-Ups"

Confused about Mississippi laws regarding marriage, a minority of the widows of Civil War soldiers lived with men instead of marrying in order to maintain their benefits. They did not realize that the passage of the state constitution and state laws meant that living with an unrelated male in 1865 or 1870 became a legal marriage anyway. They believed they could hide their nonmarital cohabitation (took-up relationship) more easily than a formal marriage. These informal relationships did not leave records, a major advantage for widows who were collecting a pension.

After the war, African American and white southerners used the term took-up (the expression originally used to describe slave marriages) to refer to any nonmarital relationship. Took-ups comprised approximately 16 percent of the intimate relationships referred to in the pension files. Given the possible economic repercussions of losing their pensions, military widows may have participated in a larger number of cohabitational, nonlegal relationships than the general African American population.[65] Precisely because took-up relationships left little documentation it is difficult for historians to determine their extent. As one widow explained, "I just lived there with him the same as if we were married but we were not married. We did not make any agreements before any witnesses because I did not think it was anybody's business how we lived." Of course, this possibly referred to snooping pension examiners.[66]

For most couples, a took-up indicated a settled union with a committed, sexually intimate, usually cohabitational relationship between a man and woman. Took-up was in part a legacy from slavery, when the community recognized extralegal unions. Such beliefs stayed alive after slavery, reinforced by federal pension policy. Regardless of their reasons for not legally marrying, many couples took cohabitational relationships as seriously as legalized marriages. When a pension examiner informed James and Sarah Donnegan in 1872 that their took-up relationship was a legal marriage under the 1870 Mississippi constitution, they explained to him that "they have always considered themselves as legally a man and wife since the time they first took each other as such."[67] After explaining that she and Thomas Toller had never married but had "lived together [from 1866 to 1904] until he died" freedwoman Isabella Toller elaborated, "I had the name Carter and was called Isabella Toller and have not been called or known by any other name since. . . . I was a member of the church and was known and received by the members of the church as sister Toller. . . . He went with me and we were known and received as husband and wife." She noted also that when the Tollers' first child was born, "It was his child and he said it was and we agreed, he and I and my mother that we would go together for all time."[68] Similarly Abram Speers began to live with Louisa Smith a year after her husband died. He stated that "I have had three children by her. She bears my name and is known as my wife. I have always considered her my wife and she has always been known as my wife ever since I had her."[69]

Some couples viewed took-up relationships as a precursor to marriage, a trial marriage whose partners planned to wed at a later time.[70] From his examination of slave records, historian Herbert Gutman concluded that enslaved men and women accepted premarital sex as a form of engagement.[71] Such couples such as Alone and Sophie Starkey "lived together as husband and wife for some six years before" their slave wedding ceremony."[72] Such attitudes toward nonmarital sex remained after the war. As Mary Johnson's brother explained, in 1870, "Mary and John Johnson lived in the same house. The understanding John gave me then was that he was going to marry Mary if she would have him and so when [she] began living with him in January 1870, I took that to be an agreement between them that they would be married." Mary's brother felt particularly betrayed when Johnson disregarded his pledge to marry her and humiliated her by bringing his new lover into the same residence.[73] Other couples waited for their wedding night. One freedwoman explained, she "was acquainted with him the 3 years but not well enough acquainted with him to let him bed with me till he married me."[74]

Some African Americans did not see the need for legalized marriage; they felt that cohabitation provided more flexibility and fewer complications if the partners wanted to terminate the relationship. As one Bureau agent explained, "I find the rites of matrimony among them seldom ever solemnize[d] or legalized, but whenever they choose, they call themselves married and live together until they take a notion to separate."[75] Some couples may have seen taking up as equivalent to marriage so that a legal ceremony seemed superfluous. Overall, freedpeople considered these to be private matters that the state and the Freedmen's Bureau should in general leave alone unless specifically asked by one of the partners to in-

terfere. Agents of the Freedmen's Bureau complained that "living together in a state of concubinage they seem to regard as a social right that no
one has permission to interfere with. . . ."[76] One agent blamed local conditions in part for the practice: "[T]his being a river town, men often leave
their wives for months at the time or entirely, and the wives 'take up' with
other men. Great ignorance seems to exist, perhaps is sometimes affected,
concerning the laws on the subject."[77] According to the Freedmen's Bureau, a lack of civil or religious officials to perform weddings in outlying
rural areas created a further rationale for not marrying.[78]

Significantly, although the Freedmen's Bureau saw the distinction between marriage and cohabitation as crucial, African American women who
brought complaints of abandonment to the Freedmen's Bureau did not
distinguish between legal and extralegal unions. The women saw the familial obligations as the same regardless of the legal status of the relationship. The Bureau made a clear distinction between legal and extralegal
marriages. When queried about the "cases where freedmen having lived
for years with women . . . lately have deserted them and taken up with
other women," Alvan Gillem responded firmly that "where the parties are
legally married the civil law provides for such cases. If they are not legally
married this Bureau has no authority to make the people live together."[79]
With such differing views, the Bureau and freedpeople were frequently at
odds over this issue.

Gender Distinctions

Gender distinctions between men and women were the same in both
took-up and legalized relationships. African American men and women
generally agreed on a sexual division of labor and responsibility within the
family. Patterns of cohabitational relationships, legal or extralegal, as well
as marital harmony and conflict indicate how freedpeople defined relationships and roles of men and women. Men held the major economic
responsibility, although women worked for compensation as well. Women
took charge of most of the familial domestic labor. Husbands more often
than wives were in positions to make decisions about familial resources
but in the first three or four years after the war, both husbands and wives
contracted debts in their own names. Husbands alone more often assumed
this responsibility for the family later, possibly with the onset of sharecropping.

Regardless of whether couples legally married or took up, freedpeople defined the nature of their relationships in terms of cohabitation,

commitment, and obligations that were distinguished by gender. Freed-people rooted their conceptualization of the roles of wife and husband in part in their slave experience, but their new free status also modified it.[80] The expanded economic role of men and the enlarged child care respon-sibilities of women reflect those changes. The domestic expectations of the spousal relationship crystallized with freedom. The couple lived to-gether as an economically interdependent unit, the woman adopted her man's surname, they cared about each other's well-being, and they were physically intimate. A clear division of familial labor existed between men and women.[81] Women performed the domestic work of cooking and laun-dry even though they continued some agricultural or outside domestic labor for their families. A few pension applications recorded women per-forming domestic labor for pay and one labor contract noted women re-ceiving special time off from paid labor to wash clothes for their fami-lies.[82]

Both freedmen and women accepted such gender distinctions within marriages or took-ups that entailed different responsibilities for men and women within the family. Such issues were uncontested by the vast major-ity of freedpeople. Women saw these functions not just as duties that they were obligated to perform but as part of their dignity and status as women. They knew from slavery that work outside the family was not necessarily liberating and like their men, they did not define work solely as paid labor for whites.

Emancipation greatly enhanced the economic role of men within the family. Freedmen assumed the major responsibility for the material needs of the African American family. One freed soldier began thinking about his new role while he served in the army: "[H]e had a chance to marry in the service, but could not take care of a wife like he ought to in the army, and did not marry."[83] He wedded four years after the war after finding work. Family, friends, and neighbors evaluated a man by his ability to sup-port his family. Commenting on one married couple, a friend recalled, "O yes they lived together as man and wife and a good living they had too. Isaac was a good provider and made money."[84] One Freedmen's Bureau's agent referred to this transition, although he underestimated slave mar-riage, when he reported that "since the termination of the rebellion . . . the women begin to look upon their husbands as helpmates and not mere bed companions."[85] Daniel Sanders's will shows his economic concern for family. Although such documents were rare given freedpeople's poverty and illiteracy, Daniel Sanders dictated his to his employer. He directed that, "[A]fter my burial expenses are satisfied and all of my just debts are paid which is but few I will all I have to go to my wife Leather as long as she lives, And then to be disposed of as she may see fit." Sanders also made provision for his wife's grandson. Sanders's estate "consist[ed] of one mule, one cow, and some debts due me."[86] After emancipation, African American men sought a greater role as protector of the security and sanctity of the family, roles that had been denied them during slavery. African American women supported this new male role as positive. They wanted protection, long denied them during slavery, for themselves and their children.

The took-up relationships of freedpeople, as well as their legalized marriages, reflected specified gendered roles for husband and wife. Freedwoman Frances Long "took up with Dallas Miles . . . and lived with him" for nine years. She "lived in the house with him, slept in the same bed with him and cooked and washed for him but I was never married to him." As she recalled, "I had three children by him. . . . We were recognized as husband/wife while we lived together by all the people on the place and I was known by the name of Frances Miles during that time."[87] Similarly, former slave Ellen Turner, "'took up' with Peter Hardy and they lived in the same house . . . ate at the same table and slept together and he provided for her the same as if she had been his wife."[88] Frances Brown Knowling explained that while she was sharecropping, "Vaughn Knowling came along and he wanted me to cook for him. He and I had a talk about it and we agreed to go in the house together. . . . From the first, Vaughn Knowling and I slept together. . . . No preacher was called in to marry us but we just went to living together like man and wife. The agreement was that he was to do for me as much as he could." She reported that Knowling fulfilled his part because he "secured the supplies for the family. We lived just like man and wife. I did not do any trading on my own account while I lived with him except what cash or produce trading I did."[89] The last examples shows that although women worked, men and women acknowledged the husband as the primary provider, a role unobtainable during slavery.

Impressionistic evidence, such as the above, suggests that some African American rural wives (either legally married or took-up) worked at least partly independently of their husbands. This employment allowed them to bring additional income into the family. In 1868, Robert Shackleford signed a contract for yearly wages for himself and his sons. The employer also agreed "to let the wife of said Robert Shackleford have for cultivation a certain piece of land . . . for her sole care and benefit" as well as land for a garden.[90]

Even when a couple did not refer to each other as husband and wife, probably to keep pension examiners from claiming remarriage and stopping a widow's pension, they fulfilled the duties of each role. For several years Marshall Powell lived with Celia Wilson and their child; Powell acknowledged that Wilson "cooked for me, mended my clothes," but "she did not pass as my wife, but I kept her in provisions and clothes and worked too. We acted as man and wife." Celia concluded, "I did not call myself his wife, but I ate and slept with him and did his cooking, washing, and acted as his wife. . . . Before our separation, Marshall Powell supported me and his boy Henry Powell."[91]

Differences in roles were reinforced by gender distinctions in the age at marriage, just as with whites. Men were almost always older.[92] Such a differentiation possibly reflected the view that maturity was stressed more for men than for women, while potential fertility may have been a factor in the ages of younger wives. African Americans may have also believed that older men would be more stable and responsible in providing for families. Freedpeople commented on exceptions outside the norm. Recalling the marriage of Robert and Harriet Caswell, one freedman declared, "She was a heap older than Robert Caswell but she had him any how."[93]

Purchases from the plantation store reflected the differences in the gender division of labor, functions within the family, and style of dress. On the Oakwood plantation near Vicksburg in January 1868, most men and women kept separate tallies. Men's accounts included such items as pants, caps, shirts, boots, fishing line, powder, shot, hooks, and buckets. Women purchased cloth such as cotton plaid, but no pants or shirts. Such accounts imply that men assumed responsibility for hunting and fishing equipment while women bought materials for clothes-making. Men and women both purchased whiskey, tobacco, lamp oil, and thread.[94]

In addition to differences in age and familial roles, personal appearance reinforced distinctions. Even though white society excluded them from the dominant ideal of womanhood in Victorian America, African American women possessed their own view of womanliness. They expressed their desire to define themselves as womanly through their appearance.[95] African American women wore dresses or skirts and blouses for field labor, while African American men wore pants and shirts. Women also decorated their outfits by adding ribbons.[96] When they could afford it, African American women wore jewelry, often buying earrings.[97] They willingly spent part of their pay on their attire. When Hattie Jefferson received her first wages for picking cotton she bought a dress.[98] Women elaborately styled their hair, particularly on special occasions. As one historian has pointed out, "the custom of wearing handkerchiefs . . . reflected continuity with African tradition and expressed a high degree of personal pride."[99]

Such gendered differences in appearance also signified freedom for freedwomen. As much as possible, former slave women and men wanted to avoid looking poor in their attire. They tried to enter a material world unconnected with the identifying marks of slave status. For freedpeople new clothes meant literally "taking back the body": from being property as slaves to owning their own labor; from lowering their eyes when they talked to whites to meeting the gaze of former slave owners; and from wearing clothes provided by their masters to dressing as they wanted to, particularly during leisure time.[100]

Women translated this latter desire by changing their appearance, usually by buying cloth to make dresses for special occasions. "Since gaining their freedom, the negro women's natural love of dress had developed inordinately," one planter's daughter wrote. "Those about us bought brilliant hued stuffs and had them made with most bizarre effects—a favorite being bright yellow calico trimmed with blue."[101] Change as seemingly insignificant as a new hairstyle reflected a wish, not to look "white" but to look like something other than slaves or laborers. One little girl who, upon learning she was free, "run de cards an comb my hair just like de white girls."[102] (A card was like a brush.)

On a deeper level, former slave owners understood that the acquisitions of former slave women of goods and different styles of dress, some of which had been reserved for whites, upset established social norms. From these changes freedpeople derived a sense of equality that the whites believed was undeserved. After complaining that freed African American women became "noisy" and "insolent" on one occasion when they were given special finery brought through the blockade during the war by northerners, one white woman concluded: "[H]ow disgusted it makes one feel to see these creatures so set, out of their place."[103]

Assumed differences in male and female sexuality also shaped how freedpeople defined themselves as men and women. Much has been written about the way whites viewed African American sexuality, but very little on how freedpeople perceived their own sexual identities.[104] The pension records provide historians with a valuable record of sexual attitudes of African Americans who had been enslaved. Although some statements in the pension records fail to reflect the reality of an individual's situation (because statements were clearly for the special examiner's consumption), the pension records, nevertheless, give clues about the thoughts of freed-people about sex and male-female relationships.

Freedpeople formed their own opinions about responsible sexual behavior for men and women and established their own codes of prescribed sexual behavior.[105] Although some individuals violated these standards, these values continued to exist and to reinforce existing norms for African Americans. Freed African Americans acknowledged both male and female sexuality. Their understanding of differences between male and female sexual behavior was quite nuanced. Although it is difficult to determine the extent to which African Americans accepted the concept of female sexual pleasure, the pension records offer some insights into this private world. The somewhat defensive explanation given by a former slave woman to a pension examiner for her nonmarital sexual activity that "I was a young woman then and in my prime" can be seen as an affirmation of female sexuality.[106] Romantic love and passion are found in statements such as those of Anna Roberts, who described her late husband as "black and slim and fine looking and I just naturally loved him."[107]

Although both women and men discussed their lovers when asked to do so by pension examiners, freedpeople articulated distinctions between the conduct of men and that of women when speaking of male and female sexual intimacy.[108] African Americans almost never spoke of women as the initiator of sexual relations; mutual intimacy was suggested by the preposition "with." One freedwoman used the expression "bed with me."[109] Another woman "knocked about then with" men.[110] Men and women spoke of both genders mutually seeking one another or of men as initiators. The preposition "after" was used only in terms of men. Discussing his intimate relationship with his lover, a married man explained, "I slipped and dodged round after her just like other men do after other women."[111] One man's bold statement suggests the prowess that some men felt about their role as sexual initiator: [H]e bragged that he "wasn't married. I was just hitting every woman I could get."[112] A man would "run after" or "run about" women, while women would "run about" or "run with," but they would never "run after."[113] For example, one man "was a great [one] to run after women but not so much inclined to stick to them."[114] A freedwoman described another woman as "running with Reynolds who she said was her husband."[115] The statement "[h]e was running two women at the same time" describes the man as the controller of the relationships.[116]

Both men and women used gender-distinct expressions in the same way to discuss differences between women and men. The word "have"

was given different meanings according to which gender was being referred to. When they discussed men, men and women more often used
the verb "have" to imply sexual intercourse. When they explained wom-
en's behavior toward men, the word "have" implied a relationship rather
than only sexual relations. Freedwoman Jane Williams recalled that Lucy
Brown's former lover, Frank Dorsey, mentioned he "had" Lucy. He was
curious about Brown's present lover Robert Owens "having" her.[117] The
following sentence shows the man clearly as the initiator and the verb
"have" as equivalent to sex: "[A]s I had no wife, and had not 'had any' for
a year from any woman I asked the question and I 'laid her clean' in a
fence corner and she gave it up to me."[118] In contrast, when George Washington, a former slave, discussed women he stated that "All the culled wom-
en you know has men and sometimes they marries him and again they
don't," or in discussions of Robert Caswell's marriage to his wife, "she was
a heap older than Robert Caswell, but she had him any how," meaning she
married him.[119] One freedwoman explained, "I knew Bias only 3 yrs. before I got him. I met him at church one Sunday and would see him only
on Sundays until we were married."[120] In these instances that applied to
women, "has," "had," and "got" implied sexual content but when a woman
"had" a man it also meant involvement in a relationship.

This consistent gendered use of vocabulary allowed women to view
their sexual activities as initiated by men. These narrations occasionally
took on romantic overtones. Men "courted" women, women never "courted" men.[121] The only exception in the pension records to this differenti-
ated language was when a woman spoke of a particular rival, and possibly
jealousy prompted her description of the other woman's bold action. She
stated, "Richard courted me after his wife died but sister Sled caught
him."[122]

African Americans expressed decided views of what conduct constituted illicit sexual relations as distinct from permissible nonmarital intimacy. Such behavior included chronic infidelity on the part of men, frequent partner changes on the part of women or infidelity by women who
were in a committed relationship, and prostitution. Single women who
caused discord by sleeping with another woman's spouse also engaged in
unacceptable behavior. When freedpeople referred to Lucy Brown seeing
the married Robert Owen "on the sly," they implied a moral judgment.
Because of Owen's marital state, their secretive liaison was considered illicit. "On the sly" meant that the relationship was supposed to be kept
hidden even though it was actually not clandestine. In a sentence that
says multitudes about the African American plantation community's col-

lective knowledge of individual activity, one freedperson recalled, "they were meeting on the sly. It was known on the place that they were doing that way."[123]

Lizzie Jones engaged in affairs with at least two married men, Talbert Royal and Jim Spears, and according to the wife of one of the men, caused "turmoil among all the men and their wives in the neighborhood." Mrs. Royal angrily explained that Jones "had the reputation of being a very bad character and she deserved it all." Royal's half brother Luke Matthews assessed Jones unsympathetically. He remarked that "like any other loose woman" Lizzie Jones "would claim a man that she has children by." Explaining the term "loose," he stated that "the reason I call her a loose woman is because she had several children, and had no husband. She laid the children to Talbert Royal." The children born outside a cohabitational settled union may have made her conduct reprehensible in Matthew's eyes. Possibly, the fact that she bore those children by a married man or claimed Royal as the father and caused internal familial tension was what influenced Matthew's judgment.[124] Friends and neighbors discouraged adulterous relationships. Two sisters ceased to visit each other, according to one woman, because one sister slept with "another woman's husband."[125]

In addition to adultery, a woman's conduct was considered less acceptable if she had intercourse with several men over a relatively short period of time, usually without living with them. Men rarely received criticism for the same behavior. Such sexual behavior can be seen in the ways in which a woman referred to her children: children "by chance," "picked up" or "on the run" were usually conceived with different men, including white men, without co-residence. "By chance," "picked up" or "on the run" was considered a less respectable way of conceiving than in the context of a settled union. Such conduct, however, was rarely condemned unless it happened frequently.[126]

With the possible exception of paid prostitutes, the evaluation of respectability, or lack of it, seems to have been situational. Women were not forever stigmatized for sexual activity outside of the institution of marriage. Usually the behavior rather than the person was condemned unless such actions were often repeated. When women such as Lucy Brown married or entered into a committed cohabitational relationship, the community accepted them as a respectable member in spite of past conduct such as sleeping with a married man. Only one freedman restated in the pension records the traditional double standard—"I would not marry any woman that would let me sleep with her without being legally married"—although this attitude failed to keep him from taking up for four years

with a woman, providing for her and acting "as man and wife." His statement reflected one of very few from African Americans that denigrated
the settled, cohabitational, took-up relationship, and one of the only statements that used legalized marriage as the measure of morality.[127]

A subtle double sexual standard existed between African American
men and women. Although in most societies a double standard provides a
way in which women's sexuality may be controlled, the double standard
among freed African Americans allowed women some sexual latitude.
Nonmarital sex by women was tolerated and, in most cases, women were
allowed to quit their spouses for another man without community sanc-
tion. The lack of a strong sexual double standard among freedpeople was
also due in part to their lack of property. Part of the rationale for the
double standard stemmed from a father's need to know the paternity of a
child to whom he would leave his property. In contrast to women's sexual
liaisons, men's illicit relationships in Western societies did not interfere
much, if at all, with the distribution of property within the family.[128]

Even so, African Americans distinguished between permissible behavior for men and women.[129] Infidelity for married or settled women was
considered more serious than men's unfaithfulness. A single woman's sexual behavior was judged more harshly than a single man's behavior when
the conduct involved several serial partners over a relatively short period
of time. A man's sexual misconduct was almost always defined as chronic
infidelity to his cohabitational partner. Although a few freedpeople viewed
male promiscuity as a natural characteristic, they more often blamed the
institution of slavery. When he described his sister's first husband, one
former slave commented, "Ishman was a big vigorous man and the master
would influence him to go to different women."[130] Arguing that slavery
encouraged her husband's baser instincts, one woman said that "men are
running, running after something fresh all the time and leaving their wives
at home. The owners did not care. The more children were born the more
niggers they had."[131]

In the nineteenth century, African Americans used the word "sweetheart" as an equivalent of the modern word "lover." An unfaithful man
was said to have both a wife and a sweetheart.[132] In this context, according
to the pension records, men took sweethearts more often than women.
Allen Burell's relationships with Elvira and Rose, whom he saw simultaneously, help to clarify the use of sweetheart: Elvira was considered "his
only legal wife," even though they had never been legally married. "This
woman here [Rose] in Jackson was simply his 'sweetheart' as the col'd folk
called it."[133] Sweetheart also referred to a lover who rarely shared a resi-

dence, but to whom one had an emotional commitment. As Minerva Wilson explained when she discussed her brother Levi: "Ena 'took-in' with Levi as a sweetheart—they did not pretend to be husband and wife and [were] never so looked upon as husband and wife by the colored people."[134] As one freedperson described Burrell Bass's complex love affairs, "no one called Elvira Burrell [his] wife that I know of, but it was generally understood that he was living in open adultery with both Elvira and Vina at the same time. He was not legally married to either one of them but just went from one to the other as the notion took him." Bass concurred, "I was keeping two women as 'sweethearts' at the same time—Elvira and Vina. Neither of them was considered my wife. I had no house of m[y] own and I stayed at the house of first one and then the other. . . . She was never called Elvira Bass."[135] Sweethearting involved more than just a casual relationship. As one man explained, "I won't say I never was in bed with her for I was but I was not 'sweethearting' with her. I had another at that time."[136] Similarly, Rose Ann Wallace explained "I just knocked about then with the men but never had any regular sweetheart until my marriage to the soldier."[137] As a verb, "to sweetheart with" was roughly equivalent "to make love with" as in Emma Caston's assertion that she and her husband "never did 'sweetheart' together until we was married."[138]

In a few instances men brought their wives and sweethearts together under the same roof, with disruptive consequences.[139] When Robert Young's father returned home from the war, his new companion accompanied him. Young's first wife refused to accept this addition to the family and "run him an' de gal off."[140] Another woman, Mary Johnson, bitterly resigned herself to the same type of arrangement by living under the same roof with her partner and his new sweetheart. After living for over a year with John Johnson, Mary Johnson discovered that he "had been going to see this Mary Francis." When Johnson brought Mary Francis into the Johnson's household, she recalled that "all he wanted of me was my work." Mary Johnson remained in the house for three years: "[A]ll that time he slept with Mary Francis Brooks and she had three children by him; people still called me his wife, but during all that time I had nothing to do with him; he, John, abused me terribly, but I had no place to go to and could not get away."[141]

Unlike Mary Johnson, who seemed to have been completely victimized, wives of unfaithful husbands often protested the adulterous liaisons of their mates.[142] Women complained about male unfaithfulness although freedpeople tolerated male infidelity to a greater degree than they did the infidelity of females. When Edna's husband Gilbert "took up with another woman, Edna and he had a good deal of 'cutting up' about it."[143] Wives' nagging, however, rarely had much impact on their husbands' affairs, except that it sometimes prompted their mates to become more discreet.[144] As one woman explained, "I quarreled with him about it but that done no good. A woman can't help what a man does."[145]

Although couples quarreled over male fidelity there are no recorded cases, either in the Freedmen's Bureau or the pension records, of a woman divorcing or "quitting" (as leaving a spouse was commonly called) over the issue of male infidelity. Freedwomen rarely complained formally to the Freedmen's Bureau about male adultery on their own behalf. Usually the complaint involved infidelity and lack of financial provision for the children. In one of the few cases involving a husband's adultery, the Freedmen's Bureau brought in the sweetheart to discuss the situation with the wife. According to the Freedmen's Bureau officer, the wife became "satisfied after fair promises and the case was dismissed."[146] In another case, the Bureau blamed the husband's lover for "making trouble between" the spouses. The husband received "a severe reprimand" and the officer ordered the lover "to seek employment elsewhere."[147]

A woman's infidelity caused a greater reaction on the part of her spouse than a man's infidelity affected a wife because female infidelity indicated a man's loss of control. The pension records showed only three examples of a wife's discovered infidelity. In one example, Benjamin Lee immediately divorced his wife Winnie, although it is unclear whether the infidelity itself or her unfaithfulness combined with his public humiliation caused him to file immediately for divorce. While Benjamin served in the army, his wife was unfaithful and several of the husband's army compatriots knew of his wife's infidelity before he discovered it. One of the other soldiers, while on leave, discovered the adulterous relationship between Winnie Lee and Jim Shoot. Later, when Lee obtained a pass "to see his family," he caught Shoot at his home with his wife. Lee returned to camp "cussing and swearing," while the other men "all laughed at him and told him they had known it for two months." Immediately, Lee went to Colonel Samuel Thomas for a divorce.[148] Richard Bryant had a similar reaction when he returned after running away to the Union army and discovered that his spouse Louisa "had *had* a child since he left." He "could not stand such as that" and said "that he was not going to support other people's children and did not intend to have anything more to do with her."[149] In the third case, rather than divorce his wife, George Hubbard "threatened to shoot" his wife's lover, Jeffrey Manning. Manning quickly retreated from the plantation where they lived, but Hubbard's wife soon followed him.[150]

A woman's infidelity made a clear record of descent difficult to determine for a child, and knowing one's family history was of great significance to African Americans. Sources such as pension records show that mothers, grandfathers, and even stepfathers talked to their children about their birth father and made clear the pride in lineage within African American culture.[151] Naming patterns also showed gender differences.

Enslaved and freedpeople acknowledged their family lineage through the names they gave their children even though slavery and the war broke up families.[152] Part of this bond was maintained by giving children first names of older family members. Occasionally, children shared their first name with one of their biological parents or parents sometimes bestowed a variant of their own names. Thus, Jane Charleston Turner "was called after my mother" whose name was Rebecca Jane.[153] Although difficult to determine from the United States census, the name of girls seemed to skip a generation, and were more frequently identical to the names of their grandmothers.[154]

Boys received their father's name much more often than girls were given their mother's name. This naming pattern may have been a result of slavery when children were more often sold away from their fathers than their mothers and by the disruption of slave families caused by the war. Families feared the loss of connection between children and their fathers. As one woman who bore a child after her husband went to war explained, "I named him Leonard after his father because his 'daddy' didn't see him."[155] Because paternity is always harder to establish than maternity, naming sons after fathers was an acknowledgment of the tie.

Children learned their lineage, and in the majority of cases could correctly identify their biological father even if he died or left their mother when the children were quite young. Mothers conveyed such family information to their children. Harriet Branch's mother taught her "that her father's name was Archie Branch, and that he was a soldier and died in the US service."[156] According to Alex Henderson, "my father was Levi McLaurin I suppose. . . . I was too young to know whether my father and mother lived as husband and wife but I was always told so by my mother and grandmother."[157] Mothers candidly admitted the circumstances of their children's birth. Children accurately recited descent on their paternal side regardless of the convolutions of a family history. Melder Allen Williams "never saw my father. Mother told me that his name was Allen, and that he died before I was born. She also told me that she was never married to my father."[158] Roxy Rudd impressively recalled family information, "I always understood that George Sanders was my father, but he never lived with mother that I know of." About her "brother or half-brother William," she explained, "His father I understood to be a white man named William Hinton, and Outlaw, my mother's youngest. . . . His father is the same man as my father George Sanders." This statement corroborated her mother's story. Both testimonies refuted arguments in favor of her mother's ability to retain her pension, so they were probably true.[159] Sarah Robinson knew her father was Leonard Barnes, although she did "not remember my father." When asked if her mother gave birth to children after her father's death, Sarah Robinson replied, "One named Lizzie: her father was Uncle Peter Hardy."[160] Although his parents never married, and he "never saw my Father," Dock Bowie retained his father's name, Zadock Bowie.[161] Even children with white fathers often learned about their paternity. Stella Robinson's mother "told me that my father's name was James Reynolds, her master before the war."[162] This precision in delineation of lineage continued even when single women remarried or took up. Such concerns may have stemmed from the fragility of family ties during slavery and continued after the war.

"Quitting" and Marital Discord

In addition to the impact on children's knowledge of their lineage, there were other complications when spousal infidelity led to the breakup of the household. Desertion brought about more serious consequences for women than for men. Abandonment was often accompanied by adultery and lack of economic support, particularly for children. One such case involved Nathan Williams who, after nine years of marriage to his wife Louisa, left her and "married again leaving her with one child without means of support."[163] Similarly, Matilda Stafford accused Thomas Lee of abandoning her, stating that she was "compelled to labor to support herself and her child," which Lee fathered. He failed "to give her assistance."[164] Such abandonments could be emotionally painful for the remaining spouse. When a northerner inquired of a freedwoman, "You have no husband?" the woman responded, "I had one chile but he ran away one day with another woman. . . . Feel like it most killed me at first. I get over it now."[165]

Freedmen complained to the Bureau about a spouse's desertion less frequently than freedwoman did. Either abandonment of men occurred less frequently or, because the children most often stayed with their mother, the men did not need the Bureau to arrange a financial settlement. Even so, according to the Freedmen's Bureau records, wives occasionally abandoned their husbands. John Taylor reported that "his wife Martha has left his 'bread and board' and taken away his child with her, and is now living in adultery with Peter Clark."[166] When women left, they felt entitled to take certain household property, including their clothing, cooking utensils, and bedding, that they perceived as their own.[167]

The instances of marital discord in the pension records and the Freedmen's Bureau papers offer clues about expectations of male and female responsibilities and also showed how freedpeople dealt with familial conflict. When freed African Americans stopped cohabiting, it sometimes involved a failure of one of the spouses to fulfill anticipated roles. Freedwoman Margaret Spencer complained that her husband refused to live up to his responsibilities as a husband and became physically abusive, although he had "promised to protect and provide for her."[168] Peter Holmes thought that his wife left him because he was not able to work, and other couples fought over the man's inability to support his family.[169] Husbands wanted to free themselves from spouses who failed to fulfill their domestic role or conform to their idea of a good wife. Tom Jones was adamant about wanting a divorce from his wife Judy because she was "lazy and dirty."[170]

Legalized marriage imposed legalized divorce on couples who wanted to dissolve their marriage. When freedpeople on plantations desired to terminate marriages they usually did so through extralegal separation rather than through the courts.[171] African Americans on plantations often failed to understand why legalized divorce was necessary, especially because African Americans wanted to shield their private lives from white interference. [172] As one former slave explained pragmatically, "We colored folk don't waste time and money on lawyers and divorce courts no more than we can help."[173] As they had done during slavery, freedpeople simply moved out of the residence. Freedman Peter Gregory explained that after living with Viney and having two children, "they wish to part." The Freedman's Bureau agent reported that "Peter does not love Viney and Viney has no affection for Peter. They have agreed to separate. Peter cares for the children—and both are satisfied."[174] The Freedmen's Bureau agent willingly agreed with this solution because the couple had never married.

Northern and southern whites usually interpreted the dissolution of these unions by "quitting" as an act of African American irresponsibility and immorality. As one southerner wrote scornfully, "They 'marry' and '*un*marry' as it pleases one or both parties."[175] A pension examiner contemptuously explained, "I have yet to find an instance where a negro of this plantation cotton-field type has ever expended time or money on a divorce. They divorce themselves at will."[176] The Freedmen's Bureau agents considered took-up and quitting immoral behavior because both constituted extralegal sexual behavior. One agent stated in disgust that "there had been several cases reported of husbands quitting their wives and taking up with other women, and wives quitting their husbands and taking up with other men."[177] The apparent assertiveness of African American women in leaving unsatisfactory relationships exasperated a Bureau agent who wrote that "freedwomen seem to have less regard for 'marriage vows' and for themselves and families than the men."[178] There is no evidence to support this contention in the pension or Freedmen's Bureau records.

Marital disagreements occasionally led to domestic violence.[179] Domestic violence is a more accurate description than wife-beating, a term that implies that women failed to fight back. Little evidence exists to indicate that these women experienced the social isolation or helpless sense of victimization usually associated with battered wives.[180] Rarely displaying passivity in other contexts in relation to their men, many of the women involved in these instances fought back when their spouses hit them.[181] Performing physical labor as field hands may have helped to enforce women's belief in their strength vis-à-vis their men and made them less willing to accept a beating. When Charity complained that her husband Louis abused her, Louis protested that not only did she start most of the fights, but that she "would give blow for blow."[182] Women felt justified in leaving an abusive spouse. Amanda Fay's slave husband used to "whip her and treat her roughly," so "she quit him because he treated her badly, and because she thought she had a perfect right to [do] so."[183]

Extended family members interfered in marriages when violence against a woman became a problem.[184] Assuming that an employer's power equaled that of a slave owner, one mother asked her employer to separate her daughter and her son-in-law because he beat her daughter.[185] Having been assaulted by her husband, one wife complained to her father about the beating. Her father and brother threatened the husband to keep him from inflicting any further abuse. The three men began quarreling and when the offending son-in-law grabbed his gun, his brother-in-law shot him in the leg.[186]

Victims of domestic violence complained to the Freedmen's Bureau.[187] Five percent of the complaints brought by freedwomen to the Freedmen's Bureau in Mississippi involved physical abuse by their spouses. In most

cases, husbands who hit their wives had already abrogated their familial responsibilities but wanted the right to control the behavior of their
wives in some form.[188] Women often disagreed with this interpretation of
the husband's prerogative. In one case, according to a Freedmen's Bureau
agent, a freedman "whips her [his wife] and tries to make her behave which
she won't—then he whips her again and goes off and does the same deed
himself that he whips her for. He caught her in bed with another man . . .
but then he was himself caught."[189] In complaints brought to the Freedmen's Bureau by freedwomen, violent husbands also cheated on their wives
or refused to provide for their children. Occasionally when a woman criti-
cized her husband for these actions, thus challenging his conduct, violence followed. Harriet Buchanan's husband beat her when she accused
him of sleeping with another woman and Delpha Bolen's husband struck
her whenever she complained about his infidelity.[190] Husbands and wives
resorted to physical violence over infidelity during slavery, but certain
other domestic issues such as lack of support of children came to the fore
after emancipation.

Freedom may have exacerbated conflict as husbands and wives negotiated gender roles after the war. It is difficult for historians to know to
what degree the incidents of domestic life recorded in Freedmen's Bureau
records are representative of household patterns among freedpeople. Bureau agents dealt with the problems of domestic violence either by threatening the husband with jail if he refused to cease or by suggesting that
the couple try to reconcile their disputes without resorting to violence.[191]
One Freedmen's Bureau agent suggested that the husband and wife "love
one another." The official felt that the couple would "live happily together
in future" after talking with him.[192]

The Bureau's interest in keeping couples from quitting stemmed both
from the moral issues and from the possibility that deserted spouses, particularly women with small children, would become dependent on the government.[193] Alvan Gillem of the Freedmen's Bureau saw legalized marriage
as the source of morality and stability, and he also felt that the law better
protected women and children from abandonment than if they merely
relied on community standards. He explained, "[T]he universal custom
among the sexes of 'taking up' with each other at pleasure gives a license
to men to leave their companions as soon as there is a prospect of additional mouths to feed."[194] These concerns caused the Bureau to remind
Jack Thompson that even though he had left his family, he was required
to provide for his blind wife and their five children.[195] It is unclear that the
breakup of legalized marriage actually protected children more than sepa-

rations in took-up relationships. It also is not a certainty that quitting occurred less often in legalized marriages than in informal marriages.

Bureau officials encouraged the local sheriffs to arrest African Americans on the charge of adultery and imprison them for a few days as examples to dissuade other potential adulterers from breaking their marriage vows.[196] The agents suggested that the local authorities rectify the perceived problem of immorality by incarcerating freedpeople who indulged in unlawful fornication, defined as any form of nonmarital sex.[197] Both southern whites and African Americans opposed, although for different reasons, the practice of using jail as an instrument of moral reform for freedpeople. White employers quite practically resisted incarceration of their workers on morals charges because it interfered with their workforce. Because Bureau agents thought adultery also disrupted work by undermining moral discipline, they encouraged white employers to at least punish their workers for infidelity if the employers were reluctant about sending them to jail.[198] Planters, however, resisted constant involvement in the marital relationships of their laborers when they did not stand to benefit from such interference.[199]

Newly freed slaves opposed unsolicited interference with their family life, particularly because slave owners had forced them to endure such intrusions during slavery. Employers who tried to keep an unhappy couple from dissolving their marriage complained that husbands sabotaged the work schedules. Employers "affirmed that if the Freedmen are admonished they are very sure to offer impudence and refuse to work as much time as they might and consequently they are allowed to suit their own pleasure about taking to themselves wives and leaving them at their choice."[200]

When, however, family disputes disrupted the work performance of individual workers, planters asked the Freedmen's Bureau to settle marital disagreements. One employer complained that the abandonment of African American women by their husbands was "causing great dissatisfaction and trouble" on his plantation.[201] White employers also expressed concern when they lost workers due to marital conflicts.[202] If a husband deserted his wife to move in with a woman on a different plantation, he violated his labor contract.[203] The Bureau advised these men that if they failed to finish their contracts, they risked arrest as vagrants. By threatening men who left marriages with incarceration either as vagrants or adulterers, the Bureau hoped to keep couples together and the labor force stable.[204] Freedmen were incarcerated more frequently than freedwomen on these charges. Even so, women received punishment for participating in illicit sexual affairs.[205] If the Freedmen's Bureau felt that a woman had stolen a married man away from his wife, the "seductress" was thrown off the plantation without being paid.[206]

Bureau officials failed to recognize that enforcement of their concept of morality allowed southern whites to jail African American men on the pretense of combating immorality. In reality, whites used jail to punish African Americans for other conduct. Solomon Grant represented such a case. Grant failed to marry his cohabitational spouse, having been correctly assured that legalized marriage was unnecessary. The couple had lived together since the end of the war and thus the Mississippi 1865 constitution legalized their relationship. When Grant became involved in a disagreement with a white neighbor in 1869, the local law enforcement officer arrested him for adultery and threatened to imprison him. Vindictive behavior on the part of local whites was the motivating factor in Grant's arrest.[207]

Southern whites used perceived moral violations as weapons against any African American who was not (in their minds) sufficiently subservient to whites. Thus, Mississippi whites only prosecuted domestic violence when they could use the issue as a pretext for harsh dealings with those African American men who they considered to be a threat to the white community. In contrast to the responses of the victim's family or the Freedmen's Bureau, local Mississippi officials often ignored domestic complaints from African American women.[208] These white officials showed little interest in protecting the wives.[209] Local authorities incarcerated Barry Harper for assaulting his wife, but Harper's activism in the Republican party probably prompted his arrest.[210] The Klan also manipulated the issue of marital violence. In 1871, twenty members of the Ku Klux Klan killed Abe Womble, an African American preacher, ostensibly because he beat his wife. Because the welfare of African American women was never a main concern of the Klan, the reason for the killing must remain suspect.[211]

Interracial Sex and Relationships

The above incidents attest to the complications involved when whites interfered in the personal lives of African Americans. Complex sexual tensions as well as the power relationships between the two races during and after slavery made freedpeople wary of southern white intentions. Sexual liaisons between white men and African American women also complicated race relations. Sexual intimacy between white men and African American women ran the gamut from sexual assault to mutually affectionate relationships.

Because of the realities of past enslavement, economic dependence, and racial oppression, the threat of forced interracial sexual relationships often loomed large[212] One of the threats to the private lives of African American women was sexual abuse by white men. During slavery the rape of a slave woman by a white man was not generally considered a crime because the women's bodies belonged as property to white men.[213] Evidence exists of molestation of women by slave traders, overseers, and slave owners. Sexual abuse of slave women by overseers occurred frequently enough that one slave owner, when specifying his qualifications for an overseer, wrote that he did not want to "be troubled with their running after negro women."[214]

Intimate relations between slave women and their masters sometimes continued after the war, especially when the woman worked for her former master. Three painful examples suffice. After the war, Mary Brooks gave birth to two children by her former owner Thomas Williams. According to Brooks, he "was a single man and he and his father (with whom he lived) owned several negro women with whom he had sexual intercourse during slave times whenever he wished, said women being entirely under his control." As she explained, "[S]he never lived in the house with him and never slept with him a night in her life but had occasional acts of intercourse with him when he required it. Said Williams had as much to do with other slaves of his and with other women of the neighborhood." Her owner even engaged in intercourse with her during her slave marriage (which began with a wedding ceremony in the slave master's parlor). According to the pension examiner, "after emancipation . . . having no other home, [she] remained with her master as before for several years after the surrender. She was in fact no more free than before. She continued to work the same as before and was entirely under the control of her master until after the birth of said children, as much so as she ever was." According to Brooks, Williams supported their children, one of whom she named Mary Magdalene, possibly as a symbol of Brooks's own suffering.[215] Similarly, Albert Talmon Morgan, a transplanted northern lawyer who lived in Yazoo described an African American woman who had two children by her master and remained on the plantation after the war. Although she worked in the cotton and corn fields, he had not paid her except with "some little things fur de chilluns." She began a fight with her former master's newest African American lover and her former master promptly beat her with a rawhide whip and threw her out. After protesting to Morgan, who advised her to inform her former master that he owed her wages, she returned and remained on his place.[216] Freedwoman Angeline Johns complained to a Freedmen's Bureau agent that "Mr. Humphrey beats her nearly every day," although she was pregnant by him and continuing to do his "cooking, washing, and ironing."[217]

Unlike many abused women in relationships with African American men, the inability of these women to break out of such destructive relationships was probably caused in part by their economic dependence on their employers. Employers could have a worker arrested as a vagrant if he or she left without permission. As in the case of Mary Brooks, such women perceived that they had no place to go and no other options. They exhibited the psychological and emotional isolation of battered women. Their apparent disconnection from other African Americans was atypical and not true of all women who had relations with white men.

When freedwomen complained to the Freedmen's Bureau about sexual assaults, they most often accused their employers of making unwarranted advances or attempting rape. Ann Woodson accused both her employer and his son of pursuing her.[218] Women and their men both protested such attacks. They pleaded for the release of the women from their labor contracts with pay and without penalty.

Although sexual harassment by white men often occurred in a work context, freedwomen were subject to assault from white men other than their employers. White violence toward African American men and women enforced racial domination.[219] Vigilante groups such as the Ku Klux Klan that were formed to repress black equality used gang rape as an instrument of terror and racial control.[220] Although these groups murdered more African American men than women, freedwomen were vulnerable to sexual assault.[221] While in disguise "with their faces blackened," white men whipped an African American man and his wife and then raped her "three times after they beat her."[222]

Such events acted as powerful reminders of the continuation of southern white domination after the war and the fragility of African American women's protection from white assault. Freedwoman Laura Sanders stated that six white men "broke into her house" and three "ravished her and otherwise mistreated her."[223] The attackers picked some of their victims because of their links to political activists. Ellen Parton testified in the early 1870s before the United States Congress Joint Select Committee to investigate the Ku Klux Klan that eight men broke into her home looking for Republican activists, and one "committed rape upon me." She explained, "I yielded to him because he had a pistol drawn, when he took me down he hurt me of course."[224] In addition to being devastating for women, rape served as a surrogate attack on African American manhood, because it reinforced an image of the powerless African American man. Men could not protect their women in spite of emancipation and the women could not protect themselves.[225] In cases such as Ellen Parton's, the assaults also reminded African American men that their support of the Republican party endangered the entire community.

African Americans who complained to the Freedmen's Bureau and the United States Congress during the Klan hearings about sexual assaults defied southern silence and denial of the issue. White men were rarely convicted in Mississippi for raping African American women. In many instances, African Americans were reluctant to discuss interracial sex with whites, possibly because they feared economic retribution or more violent retaliation, particularly if such relationships involved prominent local planters. One freedwoman gave birth to two children by a white man, but she claimed to the pension examiner that she only knew his first name.[226] Emily Ellis emphatically refused to talk about the father of her children, who "was a white man," declaring, "I do not want to tell his name." She later admitted that the father was her former slave owner.[227] In the case of Mary Brooks's sexual relations with her former master, the pension examiner found that people who knew Mary Brooks "professed to know nothing of the father of said daughter nor could I learn any particulars by ordinary inquiries in the neighborhood."[228]

Although they professed ignorance, the reticence of freedpeople to talk about such affairs rarely stemmed from their lack of knowledge of the circumstances. Certainly the woman who denied knowing the last name of the white father of her two children is not credible. After slave owner James Reynolds bought a mulatto girl named Millie, he kept her in the house as a domestic slave. When Millie gave birth to a daughter, Stella, the other slaves guessed the identity of the child's father. According to one former slave, "It was the common report among the colored people on the plantation that Stella was James Reynolds' child." They based their opinion on several factors, including the color of the child and the mother's insistence that James Reynolds was the father. Although her mother was only half white, "Stella was almost white and had straight hair." After he married, Reynolds converted Millie from a house slave to a field hand, but he kept the baby Stella in the house with his new wife.[229] This housing situation reinforced the contention of the African American community that Reynolds was the father.

Some white men and African American women formed long-term liaisons based on mutual affection. Interracial marriage was forbidden during slavery. In 1865, when the all-white Mississippi legislature legalized marriages between African Americans, it continued to prohibit marriage between the races. Under the Black Codes "any person who shall so intermarry shall be deemed guilty of felony, and on conviction thereof, shall be confined in the State Penitentiary for life."[230]

The Federal Civil Rights Act of 1867 prohibited discrimination by race, which made the ban on interracial marriages questionable, and gave African American women the right to sue white men for paternity.[231] African American Republican delegates and a few sympathetic white delegates who attended the 1868 Mississippi Constitutional Convention called for a lifting of the ban on racial intermarriage.[232] They also introduced a provision that "the Legislature shall provide by law for the punishment of adultery and concubinage." The law would have made interracial relations outside marriage serious offenses. The final approved wording contained "may provide" rather than the more forceful "shall provide," in order to protect the access of white males to African American women.[233] "May" provided for optional rather than mandatory enforcement. In 1870, Mississippi formally repealed the restriction against interracial marriage.[234]

For the majority of Mississippi whites, marriage between white men and African American women threatened to raise the status of African American women to that of white women. Even more threatening, the possibility of legalized liaisons between white women and African American men heightened the worst fears of many whites about the sexual prowess and power of African American men. Such marriages completely contradicted the concept of racial subordination by challenging the sole dominance of white men over white women and by placing African American men in positions of power within the family over white women.[235] White southern ideology regarded any access of African American men to white women as a threat to white manhood.[236] White women who had relations with African American men were pictured dichotomously as either innocent victims if they resisted or "depraved" if they showed any signs of consent.[237]

The legalization of intermarriage empowered African American women who were involved with white men. Former slave mistresses became interested in legitimizing their relationships and in gaining more control over their sexuality. The legality of mixed marriages raised immediate concerns for planters who were involved with African American women.

When a church in Yazoo County excommunicated freedwomen for co-habiting with white men, the women insisted that their lovers marry them. According to northerner Albert Morgan, when the men resisted, these women refused to have intercourse with them and "not only kicked against pricks, they actually began to wear armor against them." One of the men yielded to the demands of his mistress and secretly married her. While one "began the erection of an elegant new residence" for his lover, "another gave money to his," and "another satisfied his with promises." A few of the men gave up the relationships "while the great mass 'bided their time.'" Most of the other men complained that emancipation had ruined their paramours by encouraging them to become assertive.[238] Their companions, according to Morgan, "perceiving their advantage, became stronger supporters than ever of Republican principles," including civil rights and equity. Relatively egalitarian cohabitational relationships be-tween white men and their African American mistresses became more of a problem for white southern men with the end of slavery.[239] Such relation-ships embarrassed the white family and threatened the legacies of white children. N. W. Lee's own white children, as well as the local courts, ha-rassed him when he tried to provide for his African American lover and their children. Juda McLaurin had become N. W. Lee's mistress while she was his slave. After the war, middle-aged and widowed Lee lived openly with McLaurin and their children. Realizing that his legitimate sons were hostile to his relationship with McLaurin, Lee tried to allay the fears his white heirs expressed about his second family by dividing his wealth. In the latter part of 1866, he gave a large part of his property to his sons. On the remaining parcel of land, he built a home for himself, McLaurin, and their children. One night while the couple were out, their house was set on fire. Lee believed that his sons were responsible. Later, Lee and Mc-Laurin were brought before the grand jury "for living together in an un-lawful way."[240] Lee believed that they would be convicted because the community resented their cohabitational arrangement. A Freedmen's Bu-reau official suggested that Lee either reside separately from McLaurin or marry her, but the latter solution would have displeased his sons and the local white community even more.

The content of the interracial relationship often helped determine how the white community judged these couples. White southerners charged partners who were involved in an interracial relationship with a crime when, as in the case of N. W. Lee, the African American woman's status within the relationship was close to that of a white woman. This couple came too close to negating the race and class distinctions of a Mississippi household. In the case of Lee and McLaurin, an African American woman who was living as white planter's wife broke too many societal rules. Similarly, one householder complained that the Mississippi courts seized his land because he lived with a mulatto woman.[241] According to another southerner, when a transplanted northerner fell in love with an African American woman, "a committee of white citizens" informed him "that the relationship was intolerable and that if he visited the Negress he would do so at the risk of his life."[242] One of the missions of the Ku Klux Klan was to punish freedwomen who were involved in committed interracial relationships.[243] Although the Ku Klux Klan occasionally beat the white men involved, more often the Klan only punished the African American women.[244] The Ku Klux Klan savagely whipped black mistresses of three white southern men.[245] A white southerner explained that one of the women was beaten for "messing with" a white man.[246] The three men were all unmarried, and the women had been residing with them for several years. One man had cohabited with his mistress before the Civil War and they had had children together.[247]

White southern men tolerated their male neighbors' practice of engaging in casual affairs with African American women because such liaisons appeared to reinforce white male superiority over African Americans. Freedmen's Bureau officials argued that white southern tolerance of extralegal interracial sex between white men and African American women demeaned African American women and threatened the African American family.[248] In contrast, southern white men blamed the northern concept of racial equality for racial mingling and intermarriage after the war. White southerners pointed to the few transported white northerners who intermarried, such as A. T. Morgan who moved to Yazoo City with his younger brother to practice law. Morgan's support for civil rights for African Americans and his marriage to Lillian Higate, an African American teacher from Jackson, Mississippi, raised the ire of his southern white neighbors.[249]

According to white southern men, Union soldiers and northerners such as Morgan were responsible for the introduction of racial equality and interracial relations to the south. One southern author wrote, "[T]he negro men seeing and having a knowledge of the intimate relations between white Federal soldiers and officers with negro women and openly taught equality, led them to desire an equal opportunity with white women."[250] A few white southern men in one small town decided to teach one northern soldier the consequences of emancipation and northern meddling in southern race relations. In the fall of 1865, they played a particularly vicious joke on a white soldier from the Second New Jersey Cavalry that was stationed in Mississippi. When the soldier became inebriated at a local tavern, several local white men forced an African American woman to join him in the bar for a marriage ceremony. Then they stripped the soldier, put him in the woman's bed, and locked the soldier and the woman in the bedroom. The next morning the soldier's superior officer found them, borrowed some clothes for the soldier to wear, and searched for the men who had victimized the couple. They were gone, but the woman identified them, and the military left the civil authorities to deal with them. It is unclear if local officials pursued the matter.

In addition to demonstrating their own contempt for U.S. military forces in the South after the war, these men also threatened and humiliated the African American woman they forced to participate in their farce. First they tried to convince the woman that if she agreed to participate and marry the soldier, she would be entitled to his property. When she resisted they tried to bribe her with their own money. When she refused again the men dragged her into the bar. The men also tried to elicit names of African American women who were suffering from venereal disease to serve as sexual companions for northern soldiers.[251] They assumed that all African American women would serve as sexual companions for white men, particularly for money. One southern author argued that sexual relations between federal soldiers and African American women forced the rise of the Ku Klux Klan. This explanation is a historically inaccurate description of the genesis of the Klan, but it does demonstrate the lengths to which most white southerners would go to deflect attention away from their own interracial sexual practices.[252]

When southerners accused northerners of introducing interracial intercourse to the South, northern soldiers quickly pointed out its true origins. While he was a prisoner temporarily housed in the slave quarters on one plantation, a Yankee soldier was asked by the slave owner, "Now, I suppose you would just as soon marry a nigger wench as to marry a white woman." The soldier answered, "I wouldn't like to marry any nigger wench that I have seen around here, for fear that I would have some of you rebels for a daddy-in-law." As the soldier turned to stare at the light-skinned female slave who was serving him dinner, the slaveholder raged at him.[253] The persistent assumption that racial equity would lead to intermarriage was a constant and ultimately devastating theme in southern white discourse.

In blaming northern soldiers for interracial sex, white southerners absolved themselves of any culpability in the practice. Moreover, white men never publicly recognized that they coerced African American women into sexual intercourse. They argued that African American women by their nature were always accessible and thus always willing.[254] During congressional hearings, a white southerner expressed a typical southern attitude toward the sexuality of African American women. When asked why southern men dismissed the concept of African American equality even though they engaged in intercourse with African American women, he responded: "upon the same principle on which I account for the fact that a man at the North will go to a house where lewd women hold themselves out for sale, and have intercourse with them, and yet refuse to introduce the women into his family."[255] The comparison served both as an attack on perceived northern sexual hypocrisy based on class and as a description of African American women as whores.[256]

Such racial beliefs informed military pension decisions relating to African American widows. Pension examiners assumed that all African American widows lied because they were by nature immoral, incapable either of truth or sexual morality.[257] Pension law did not sympathize with women in their twenties who would remain poor even if they remarried. Such women tried to keep their eight dollars a month without being forced into lifelong celibacy. In their correspondence, the examiners never acknowledged that African American women may have lied because they were poor women who needed to keep the additional revenue of their pension in order to survive economically.

Although poor white women also lied about remarriage or cohabitational relationships, pension examiners saw African American women as fundamentally different from white women.[258] Because pension examiners viewed African Americans as morally deficient and sexually promiscuous by nature, the examiners were automatically suspicious. As historian Evelyn Brooks Higginbotham explained, "[T]he categories of class and racial groups according to culturally constituted sexual identities facilitated blacks' subordination within a stratified society and rendered them powerless against the intrusion of the state into their innermost private lives."[259] One agent noted about one widow, "I closely questioned her as to her history and mode of life during her long widowhood feeling assured from my experience with negro 'widows' that she had not lived alone all these years."[260]

Pension examiners cited took-up relationships as examples of the lowest form of illicit sexual behavior and general moral depravity of African American women. An examiner defined one African American woman as "a handsome woman of the class above 'take up.'" She "*may* have dodged in a sly corner with a white man, heard no such intimation, but no 'nigger take up in hers,' and no tell-tale . . . baby." This quote trivialized and sexualized the expression "take up" by graphically adding "in hers."[261] African Americans rarely used the expression "took-up" to describe sexual intercourse only. Rather, took-up most often provided a context for a male-female relationship on a more holistic level although it implied that sex was part of a nonmarital cohabitational relationship. The examiner's quote also elevated the status of women who engaged in interracial sex above that of a woman who took up. The quote also degraded African American men. There is no evidence to support the contention that African American women considered casual sex with white men to be more acceptable than a settled nonmarital cohabitational union with African American men.

Although white women concurred with the widely held view that African American women were sexually promiscuous, gender ideology about sexual difference between white men and women trapped white women.[262] Southern men's exploitation of African American women as a sexual outlet linked southern white and African American women in a highly sexualized matrix.[263] The southern white perception of African American women made it possible for white women to be viewed, in contrast, as "pure."[264] Inculcated with a belief that respectable white women possessed a more limited capacity for sexual passion and desire than African American women, elite southern whites believed that the innate purity of white women gave them a responsibility to raise the moral standards of men. When white southern men became involved in illicit liaisons with African American women, white women, particularly of the planter class, were tacitly accused of and even blamed themselves for failing in their mission to uplift their men. White southern women were not in actuality passionless but the prevailing ideology gave conflicting messages about a woman's desire for sexual pleasure and to some extent released men from responsibility for male infidelity by implicitly blaming their wives.[265] As historian Caroll Smith-Rosenberg explained, the middle-class woman's appearance of "lack of desire, that is her sexual purity, symbolized her class respectability."[266]

Given the rigid sexual double standard of southern whites before and after slavery, white women continued to be relatively powerless both by custom and by law to stop relations between white men and African American women.[267] For white women these relations became even more painful after the war in cases where they felt usurped by their husband's African American lovers. At least during slavery white women received a modicum of comfort in the knowledge that marriage between interracial couples was impossible. With the Civil Rights law and the change in Mississippi law in 1870, white wives whose husbands cheated on them with African American women feared for their marriages and their right and their children's right to their husbands' property.[268] After John K. Anderson deserted his wife, he lived with an African American woman, Polly. Following his death, Anderson's widow learned that Polly claimed his estate. During her husband's lifetime, Mrs. Anderson argued, he wasted much of the property she brought to the marriage. Polly contended that her claim rested on the domestic chores that she performed for her lover; she even supervised his cotton acreage.[269] The Freedmen's Bureau ruled that Polly was entitled to the property but whether she received it remains unclear from the records.

White women blamed interracial relationships for providing African American women who performed domestic labor for them with another rationale for disrespectful behavior toward them. One southern white woman complained that her husband's business associate, who shared their house, slept with his own servant. According to the white woman, the servant's constant impertinence was due in part to her status as a white man's lover.[270] White women directed their frustration and anger over interracial intercourse toward African American women, further straining the relationship between African American women and their female employers after the war.

Because of racial stereotypes about the sexuality of African American women, the concept of African American women's respectability became an area of contested terrain between southern whites and African Americans during Reconstruction.[271] Control over African American women's sexuality heightened struggles against racial oppression. Whites viewed African American sexuality as different from their own, and whites perceived interracial marriage as a direct threat to white men's domination over African American women. The white stereotype of the sexuality of African American women placed them outside the boundaries of respectable womanhood.

Unlike whites such as pension examiners, African Americans considered women who were involved in steady cohabitational took-up relationships to be respectable. Freedpeople did not confuse an expression of sexuality outside of legalized marriage under certain prescribed conditions with immoral behavior. Even though officially the church frowned on unmarried couples who lived together in committed relationships, women such as Isabella Toller and Julia Wells became members of the church.[272]

Mary Harrington understood the white definition of "wife" even as she indicated that freed African Americans held a different view. Although she was unmarried to John Johnson, Mary Harrington "was generally called John's wife." She "let it go so. I was rather glad to feel that I had a protector." She further explained, "I conducted my self toward John Johnson . . . just as I would [have] done if I had been his lawful wife, but cannot exactly say that I was his wife because we were not legally married but we had sexual intercourse with each other the same as man and wife." The sentence states that she was considered to be his wife, she was his wife, but she wasn't his wife, perfectly summing up the linguistic and conceptual misunderstandings between plantation African Americans and whites.[273]

The general agreement among African American men and women that African American men initiated romantic encounters also supported a view of African American women as respectable. By and large, African American women and men saw African American women as partners in sexual relationships but not as enticers and seducers, as white stereotypes characterized them. When defending the women they slept with against the pension examiner's assumption of immorality, a few freedmen recalled that these women had taxed their persuasive powers by behaving modestly rather than boldly or aggressively. One freedman explained, "I do not know or believe that she has had sexual intercourse with any man since the death of her husband except myself. I had long and persistent work in getting her consent to begin."[274]

In contrast, male pride in sexual expertise was heightened by the racist context of the patronizing conduct of white men toward African American men. One freedman explained, "[I]n my courtin' days I wuz a *man* [my emphasis] among women." His boast left unstated that as an African American man, whites called him "boy." Demeaned by whites, his relationship with African American women reinforced his manhood.[275] Describing African American men's prowess with women was part of a complex view of manhood that began to be constructed during slavery and that African Americans continued to define with freedom. This conceptualization included the new economic responsibilities of men and their status as protectors of their families.[276]

Just as views of the sexuality of African American women were contested after emancipation between whites and African Americans, so also were attitudes about African American men. Although African Americans saw freedmen as initiators of romantic and sexual relationships, whites frequently portrayed African American men as sexual aggressors and rapists. Whites associated African Americans with uncontrolled passion. Southern whites tied African American sexual and immoral conduct to their inability to govern. Thus, African American sexuality became a rationale for not granting African American men the vote.[277]

Whites often conflated definitions of the desire of African Americans to vote with their desire for miscegenation.[278] Immediately after the war, whites in Mississippi connected the image of rapacious African American men with African American soldiers probably because these men posed the greatest threat to their view of a docile slave man.[279] One southern author proclaimed that "there was a barrier that stood between them [African American soldiers] and the white women, and they knew it. It was a gun and a Southern white man behind it."[280] Although Mississippi whites constantly protested against their "occupation" by African American soldiers, there were only 8,784 African American troops in Mississippi in January of 1866.[281] By May 1866, the troops were gone by order of President Johnson. During Presidential Reconstruction in Mississippi, white southerners relied on both violence and a justice system that was sympathetic to their own interests to control African American male sexuality. One of the earliest lynchings after the war occurred in Mississippi when an African American man was alleged to have raped a white woman.[282] Southern whites quickly arrested an African American former soldier for cohabiting with "a white woman, who [was] indicted with him." The couple had been legally married during the man's military service before white southerners regained control of the Mississippi government in 1865, but they were arrested anyway as an example.[283]

With emancipation, whites exaggerated African American women's immorality to justify controlling their labor, private lives, and, in the case of men, access to political participation. Only romanticized asexual "mammies" were seen as respectable. As African Americans demanded political power for their men, whites more often portrayed African Americans as sexual aggressors and rapists. Meanwhile, whites limited the ability of African Americans to redress any wrongs done to them during slavery. During Presidential Reconstruction, white men passed laws in their own interests about African American marriage that precluded most African American women from suing white men for support of children born to white men and slave women.

Emancipation provided freedpeople with an opportunity to bring new meanings to gender roles, marriage, and sexuality. Although freedom significantly changed aspects of the labor and families of emancipated slave men and women, freed African Americans grounded their attitudes toward marriage in their slave experience. The slave experience influenced African American definitions of male and female and husband and wife, but freedpeople also explored fundamental questions about how free men and women should relate to each other. They integrated certain aspects of slave culture that stressed distinctions in gender roles.

After the war, familial relationships were not totally egalitarian between husband and wife. Husbands held economic and social prerogatives that were denied to women even though white society greatly restrained the familial rights of African American men.

FIVE
FAMILIES

"They reared a family of children"[1]

In late summer 1859, "on a dark rainy night," Lucy Brown gave birth to a daughter, Clara. According to a former slave of Charles Clark, Clara "favor[ed] her father very much." Tom and Lucy Brown knew the pain of high infant mortality that many slave families suffered. Two other children who were born before Clara died before the fall of Vicksburg. A few years later, another little girl, Rachel, was born to Lucy and Thomas. Clara and Rachel accompanied their parents to Vicksburg. Neighbors remembered Clara as a lively child who could "run and play about" at the time they left the plantation. For a while, the girls stayed with their mother on a government camp in Louisiana, where Rachel died.

Lucy's insistence that Clara learn about her slave father provides another example of the depths of feeling that were developed within slave families. Clara did not "remember her father," but she was "taught that her father was a soldier named Thomas Brown." After the war, Clara lived with her mother on the various places where Lucy Brown worked and when she became old enough she labored with her. Lucy Brown's experiences after the war were like those of many freedpeople who combined raising a family with working.[2] When children became old enough, they worked with other family members to contribute to the family's economic survival.

Recent scholarship in African American history has stressed how "family" in its many manifestations helped slaves construct and maintain an identity and culture.[3] Together families sustained each other during the day-to-day rigors of slavery. After the war, relationships within African American families developed a different immediacy.[4] Under slavery, the slave master had been the final authority over slave families; after the war, freedpeople undertook these familial duties and responsibilities for themselves.

After the war, African American households, whether nuclear or extended, were male-headed but not patriarchal. African American men became legal heads of their household, a concept that was uncontested by
the majority of African American women unless the man abused his power, particularly with physical violence. For decades, historians have argued over the roles of fathers and mothers within the African American
family. Although this debate has focused mainly on whether or not the
slave family was matriarchal, and therefore deviant, the arguments have
also addressed the post-emancipation African American family. These discussions were often tinged with the sense that women who exercised power and authority over the family emasculated African American men and
threatened the natural order.[5]

To refute the matriarchal theory of the African American family, many
historians concentrated on the ways in which fathers maintained their
dominance both within the slave family and within the family of newly
emancipated freedpeople.[6] They argued that slave men asserted themselves as slave drivers, preachers, and skilled artisans and that the slave
community respected their leadership.[7] After the war, freedmen obtained
leadership roles on plantations. African American agricultural workers
elected men to head the squads and divide the crop.[8] For example, on
C. N. Brown's plantation the employees consented to "select from their
number a foreman or leader to be governed and controlled by him as to
hours for working or the time to come in from the field."[9]

The Fourteenth and Fifteenth Amendments, which gave African
American males all the legal rights of citizenship, including the right to
vote, to serve on juries, and to hold public office, further extended the
man's position in the public within African American communities. The
entrance of African American men into politics caused more distinctions
between the public sphere of men and the private realm of women than
had existed during slavery. Even though they could not vote, women conveyed their interest in national and local politics and with their men supported the Republican party.

Although the fact that some African American men rose to socially
and publicly prominent positions in freed families and communities suggests the existence of a postwar patriarchal African American family, the
word patriarchy does not realistically describe the African American family.[10] Patriarchy implies that law, culture, and custom entitled the father to
sole authority and power within a household. It assumes the ability to keep
women under African American male rule even when they wanted to leave.
The debates about African American patriarchy have focused only on re-

lations between men and women within families. These discussions need to be held in the context of class and race positions in the larger society that also influenced men and women. After the war, African American men exercised more power in relation to African American women than during slavery, but they held much less power than white men did over white women, African American males, and African American female laborers. In reality, the power of men within any individual African American family was much more fragile than in a legal "patriarchy."[11]

The benefits and costs of the absence of an African American patriarchy raise complex issues about the place of African American within the African American family and within the wider southern white patriarchy. Within the African American family, the lack of legally supported patriarchy meant that a woman encountered little financial, social, or legal pressure to stay in an unsatisfying relationship. The practice of quitting, as opposed to time- and money-consuming legal divorce, gave women more latitude to leave. They could often move back with kin in male-headed households. Although women received lower wages than men, unattached African American women with older children found employment. Women also maintained the option of quitting and establishing a new relationship with another man without, in most cases, incurring family or community sanctions.

The ease with which African American women quit relationships resulted in part because of the economic marginality of African American men. Thus the fear of economic hardship rarely kept a woman from terminating a relationship that she no longer wanted. The legacy of slavery, racial oppression, and the low rate of payment (either wages or shares) received by African American men, however, caused continued poverty for African American society as a whole. Moreover, the ability of African American women to quit and maintain a certain degree of independence from individual African American men left them more vulnerable to sexual harassment and assault from white men. As historian Suzanne Lebsock has quipped, "It was all enough to give autonomy a very bad name."[12]

A male-headed household rested on different roles for husbands and wives. Men and women achieved adult status within their communities in different ways. During slavery and after the war, motherhood, which signified the end of childhood and passage into adulthood, raised a woman's status within African American communities.[13] In contrast, marriage, rather than the birth of a child, signified adulthood for the freed male. At marriage, a man's status changed from that of son to that of head of his own household. A son within his parents' household contributed to the economic livelihood of his family, but after taking a wife a man assumed new familial obligations.

Male-Headed Families

Because fatherhood during slavery held no legal status, biological and non-biological fathers needed to publicly acknowledge their children to tie them to their paternal family heritage within slave communities. Thus, Robert Graves "claimed all the children born to his wife, and they all favor[ed] him."[14] According to Susan Dabney Smedes (whose father and husband were slaveowners), the annual distribution of the blankets to the head of slave households gave slave fathers the opportunity to acknowledge their offspring. As Smedes wrote, on that day, even "the babies that had been in their cradles more than a few days . . . were remembered and mentioned in due turn."[15]

At times, fathers refused to recognize certain children who were born outside of slave marriages. In these instances lineage became contested, raising questions within the community as to the birth father. Commenting on Charles Hutchins's complicated intimacies with his wife Bridget and "sweethearts" Susan and Maria, fellow slave Edmund Letcher felt "certain" that "Bridget's child and Susan's child were Charlie's because they favored him and he claimed them as his. There was some doubt about Maria's child being Charlie's . . . he never took much interest in it and I don't know that he acknowledged it as his."[16] Similarly, although people speculated that Benjamin Lee fathered children such as Andrew Lee outside his slave marriage, and Harriet Povard also "charged a[nother] child on him," Lee vehemently and publicly "denied all of them." In such cases, the community speculated about the paternity. People on the plantation offered their own interpretation. Benjamin Lee's son Willie, "the only living child . . . acknowledged as his," recalled that he had "heard people say that Andrew was laid to my father." Andrew Lee insisted that Benjamin Lee was his father, but Andrew's mother made no such assertion. Such public discussion infuriated the suspected father. Lee's brother recalled, "If I wanted to make him really mad, I told him about these children."[17]

Even when slave fathers willingly acknowledged their family, slave masters kept them from performing much of the role associated with a nonslave husband and father. During slavery the master fulfilled the economic functions of the head of the household, providing most of the food, clothing, and shelter, although slave families supplemented their diet through gardening and hunting.[18] Exercising their ultimate authority in family disputes, masters interfered in family quarrels to minimize conflict among their workers and to reinforce their role as paternalists.[19] They arbitrated cases of wife-beating and disciplined slave children.

In minor symbolic ways, slave owners recognized slave fathers as heads of individual slave families. When masters distributed rations to the "head" of the household, the father of the family, if he lived on the same plantation, received them.[20] The masters considered the mother-child tie to take primacy over the relationship to the father, a reversal over the legal status of white families. Legally, slave children took the mother's slave status even when their fathers were free. Masters often kept small children with their mothers but were less concerned with keeping fathers together with their children.[21]

As husband and father, a freedman assumed the role of legal head of the family and maintained guardianship of his children.[22] Symbolic of the transfer of family power from slaveholder to father was the universal acceptance of the father's paternal surname by former slave wives and children.[23] Widowed Jane Kendrick explained that "the reason I changed my name to Jane Reece was my husband's father was named Reece and directly after the war every slave had the privilege of choosing their sir names and I chose the name of my husband's father who had chosen the name of Reece."[24]

After emancipation, as freedmen gained the responsibilities of citizens, the male head of household became the family's legal representative and protector.[25] When necessary, African American men went to court on behalf of their families, acting for their wives and siblings as well as their extended kin.[26] When employers refused to pay both husband and wife their wages, or drove families off their plantations, the husband spoke for the family before the Freedmen's Bureau agent.[27] African American men such as Elisha, "representing the interests of himself, mother, two brothers and sister" applied for help "in effecting a settlement and division of crop."[28]

African American men attempted to act as intermediaries between their families and employers. They tried to protect their families against violence. When Richard Bryant's wife's employer severely whipped her, Bryant demanded an explanation. For his efforts, Richard Bryant barely escaped death from an attack with an iron bar.[29] Peter Robinson complained to the Bureau that Gill Gordon struck Robinson's wife to the ground and then kicked her.[30] When J. Monroe Palmer beat Abner Abraham's wife, Abraham protested. In retaliation, Palmer "beat him."[31] Men also objected to other injustices, such as when whites insulted their wives.[32]

When a white Justice of the Peace called William Davis's wife a "damn black bitch," Davis threatened to report him to the federal military officer stationed in the town.[33] African American husbands also resorted to violence to protect their wives. One African American man defended his shooting of a white man, explaining that the man had "abused [his] wife."[34]

Wives rarely voiced complaints on behalf of their husbands in a public forum such as the Freedmen's Bureau.[35] African American women represented their husbands only when circumstances kept men from speaking for themselves, for example in cases when their men were unfairly jailed or very infirm. Instead, women defended their husbands in more informal ways. When necessary, wives refused to reveal the hiding places of their husbands, thereby shielding their men from the Ku Klux Klan. Fearing death at the hands of the Klan, men ran for safety, leaving their wives because, as one man explained, the Klan "don't hurt women unless some of the women is sassy to some of their wives, or speak like a white woman, and they call that sass; then they go and whip them nearly to death." This man felt comfortable leaving his wife because he knew she "wouldn't say nothing; she says nothing, or only so little that you can't take no offense at it—can't get mad."[36] Such loyalty incurred risks. A Klansman hit Ann Burris with his gun when she refused to divulge where her husband had fled, and Klansmen threatened to kill Hester Ann Buford for withholding her husband's location from them.[37] Women left behind were also vulnerable to rape.

In addition to assuming responsibilities as head of the family, African American men exercised certain familial prerogatives. White employers and Freedmen's Bureau agents encouraged freedmen to control freedwomen's labor when such behavior reinforced the sanctity of the labor contract or ensured the women's continual participation in the labor force. Thus, employers and the Freedmen's Bureau supported a dominant role for African American males when it promoted their own interests.

Legally, any married woman's signature (regardless of the race of the woman) on labor contracts was invalid unless her husband approved it.[38] As one Freedmen's Bureau agent explained, "I have the honor to inform you that a contract made with [a woman] without her husband's consentis illegal and good for nothing."[39] In accordance with the law, S. L. Bishop required his employee's husband to agree to allow his wife to work for him.[40] One such contract specified "Albert freedman acting for himself his wife his children."[41] Andrew Jones signed such an assurance for Bishop, certifying "that I give my full consent for my wife Frances Jones to enter into this contract." African American husbands sometimes both signed labor contracts for their wives and guaranteed their wives' work performance in writing.[42] George Brown promised his wife's employer that he would "see that his wife, the aforesaid Melissa works faithfully, that she is respectful in her manners, and obeys all reasonable orders that she may receive from her employers."[43] Similarly, a Freedmen's Bureau agent "admonished" a freedman "to work faithfully and see that his wife does the same."[44] Some planters involved African American husbands in any labor difficulties with their wives. Leer Austin, angered by one employee's poor work performance and insolence toward him, demanded that her husband whip her. When the husband refused, Austin assaulted the woman himself and threw them both off his place without paying them.[45]

Some African American men exercised their legal authority over other family members by collecting their wages. Freedmen sometimes received the compensation for the work of the entire family.[46] Charles Boone permitted his white employer B. P. Perry to hire his wife and daughter as domestic servants and his son as a field hand. He also promised to become "a good and faithful hand . . . and to cause my wife to perform her duty and her children also." For performing these duties, Boocher was to be paid "for the services of his [Boocher's] wife Sharloat and her two children, Mariah and Allen."[47] C. H. Jones, another employer, agreed to pay William Pimpleton a yearly wage for both his and his family's labor.[48] James Hayes hired Squire Brook's wife to work for him. He expected her "to work the time each day she was accustomed to work before freed" and pay her own medical expenses and taxes, but it was her husband who was "to receive for wife's services" the amount of fifty-five dollars.[49] In such cases, the African American men came closer to white families in legal status by gaining control of their wives' property.

Although only a few contracts indicate that men signed for their wives from 1865–1869, there is not one example of women marking contracts for their husbands. Women lacked legal authority to sign for their husband in contrast to their husbands, who were able to endorse contracts for them. On D. D. Jackson's plantation in 1867, several men signed for the "proceeds of the cotton" for women with the same surname. Next to "Angelina Clark, $17.60" was Richard X (his mark) Clark. Out of twenty women's names, twelve of the women's entries were signed by men, indicating that they had received the proper amount. It is unlikely that these were names of children because the document specified when a parent signed for a child.[50]

When families were in conflict, women resented this exercise of male authority. When Daniel Bell tried to receive payment of his wife's wages, his wife protested, "my wages were my own. My husband had nothing to do with them."[51] Given how many freedmen and women received little compensation or were in debt at the end of a work year, the right of men in certain instances to gain their wives' wages seems often to have been more theoretical than real. Moreover, when they acted in their own racial or economic interest whites willingly ignored or contested the prerogatives of freedmen as heads of households.

The sources intimate that some male household heads decided certain familial matters. In some families, the husband decided where a family worked and lived. Mary Jane Royal and her husband Talbert Royal lived on different plantations as slaves. Once freed, Talbert joined his wife on her plantation. The next year, according to Mary Jane Royal, "he moved me over into Wilkerson County where we lived one year . . . then we went to Fairbank place which we rented from Mr. Dixon" for a year. Mary Jane Royal's expression, "he moved me" may indicate a reluctance to leave her home plantation, or that her husband decided for her.[52] Similarly, Melinda Edwards recalled that her slave mistress wanted her and her husband "to continue living with her." A few years later, according to her Works Progress Administration slave narrative, "Melinda's husband decided to move," so the couple relocated and Melinda Edwards found new employment.[53]

Purchases from plantation stores may have been joint decisions. The plantation accounts of employers sometimes listed husbands and wives together, and sometimes employers kept separate accounts for spouses. Although W. T. Williams contracted with both Washington Williams and his wife Caroline, the accounts only appeared in Washington Williams's name. The purchases, however, indicate that couples made joint decisions about household expenditures. Although Williams might possibly have decided to buy pork and bacon and whiskey on his own, Caroline Williams probably decided on the four purchases of flour. Most often women did the baking and so probably helped with the list of food provisions to be bought.[54] With monetary or share wages immediately after the war, the planters often kept separate accounts for husbands and wives because they paid them as individual wage laborers.[55] Joint accounts or accounts in only the husband's name probably became more prevalent after the family sharecropping system became established.

Although the male head of the African American family maintained legal rights such as custody and right of contract over other family members, his power was less than the law implied. The legacy of the slave experience and racial animosity from whites undermined the authority of

the father within the family. Southern whites generally refused to acknowledge the African American man's newly acquired legal privileges over
members of his family, especially when the father's rights interfered with
the labor supply of white employers or with white male sexual access to
African American women. As Thomas C. Holt has argued "there was a
blatant contradiction between the notion that workers would imitate the
bourgeois private sphere and the planters' demand that they control the
labor of whole families."[56]

The Black Codes that were passed in 1865 in Mississippi in part denied African American men privileges associated with manhood, including land ownership, possession of a weapon, and "civil responsibilities and
rights."[57] These policies helped to keep African Americans in an economically and racially subordinate status to white men. Southern whites refused to defer to African American men regarding their families. White
expectations of African American subservience also included a concept of
work which required African Americans to labor for whites. White belief
in African American inferiority ill-prepared whites to accept the creation
of an African American patriarchy. According to one Freedmen's Bureau
agent, Mississippi whites wanted "to establish some relation which evades
the simple recognition of the freedom and manhood of the negro."[58]

The ability of white southern employers to dictate labor terms, and,
by extension, the structure of the family, to freedpeople was a prominent
feature of the postwar labor economy. It was inconceivable to white employers that any African American father or husband would challenge their
will. As one Freedmen's Bureau agent noted, "The marital relations of the
freedpeople is anything but pleasing. Nothing is more surprising than the
disregard . . . by the whites in their dealings with them." He elaborated "If
it suits the white man's or woman's convenience to discharge the husband
. . . and retain the wife . . . they will."[59] A perplexed Mississippi planter
requested that the Freedmen's Bureau help him regain a freedwoman employee who left once her husband brought an order from a Bureau agent
that authorized the husband to remove her without penalty from the plantation. The employer expressed puzzlement about the freedwoman's action in joining her husband because the woman never "expressed a desire
to leave."[60] Similarly, A. F. Mount pleaded with the Bureau to force the
spouse of a former hand to return to his place. Mount stated simply, "I do
not want him. I only want his wife and children."[61] He saw no inherent
problem even though his request if granted, separated the wife and children from their husband and father.

One complicated complaint to the Freedmen's Bureau reveals the means by which white employers fought the attempts of freedmen to head their own households. In 1866, freedman Orange Gully tried to retrieve his wife, Emily, and their children from his former slave owner, Philoman Gully, before their labor contact expired. Philoman Gully denied his right to take them. Philoman, a deputy sheriff in Kemper County, arrested Orange for "threatening to kill his former master, Mr. P. Gully," and for making threats against other whites and "a number of negroes in the neighborhood." Orange escaped from jail but authorities rearrested him when he attempted to retrieve his children from Philoman. Philoman explained to the probate judge that Orange engaged in an incestuous relationship with his oldest daughter. Philoman argued that he was protecting the child from her father by refusing to release her to her father's custody. Philoman also insisted that the children were legally bound to him. The probate court agreed with him, relying mainly on his own evidence. The court also heard the children's half-sister, who stated that Emily was not the mother of the children, although she did not deny that Orange was the children's biological father. She also testified that Orange had never married the children's mother and that in any event, Orange had abandoned them. The abandonment charge implied that Orange had willingly relinquished the children.

Orange disputed this accusation, arguing that the threat of violence kept him away from his family. Emily explained that after she left Philoman because he refused to pay her, Philoman dispatched men to take her from her husband's house on another plantation and return her to work. She testified that these men "went after her, blindfolded her and after going two miles through the water and wood . . . they tied her hand and foot—her clothes over her head and they all whipped her." Orange also accused Philoman of trying to "seduce my daughter and also made the like attention up on my wife." Emily concurred that "Gully tried often to have intercourse with her and by reason of her obstinacy he became enraged." When Emily told her husband about Philoman's sexual advances, Philoman "turned her cloths over her head & paddled her with a green fence paleing." Orange's threat to kill Philoman for beating Emily prompted his arrest. [62]

One Freedmen's Bureau agent was unconvinced that Orange could gain justice in the local civil courts or that Philoman would comply with a judgment against him if Orange succeeded. Ultimately in June 1866, he suggested that Orange obtain a writ of habeas corpus through the civil probate courts. Unimpressed by the testimony presented at the probate court, the agent annulled the contract that bound the children to Philoman on the grounds that the parents were able to support the children. He sent two guards to ensure Philoman's compliance with the order that he permit Emily to leave as well.

Orange's experiences are instructive because they show how southern whites restricted African American men's power within their families. White desire to control African American women's sexuality and African American labor, including that of women and children, motivated such measures. They relied on the indenture of children, labor contracts, the courts, law enforcement, and violence to maintain their control over African American families. The case also indicated the tenacity of African American men's attempts to protect their families against white southern employers and the local courts and their ultimate reliance during Reconstruction on federal authority in the form of the Freedmen's Bureau.

As with Orange, when husbands claimed their families from white employers, they often met with strong resistance.[63] In 1867, Bill Price's wife's employer shot at him when he attempted to reunite with his family. The local courts ignored Price's complaints of violence and the forced separation of his family. The Freedmen's Bureau threatened military intervention to bring the family together after the local court's inaction and ruled that the original contract was invalid because the woman's husband had not consented to the signing.[64] Freedman Abram Munice charged Andrew J. Donaldson with "the unlawful detention of his wife and four children." Munice wanted his family to join him in Memphis, Tennessee. When he went to visit his family during the Christmas holidays in 1866, "he was driven off the place by Donaldson." Donaldson's overseer caught Munice and broke his arms to remind him of the consequences of trying to reunite with his family.[65]

Torn between the wants and needs of their own families and the danger that awaited them if they attempted to assert themselves as heads of their families, African American men sorted through the conflicting messages of their families and white society. Immediately after the war, freedman Adam Smart received both a threat from his wife's employer and a letter from his wife, Fanny. She explained that she believed he had died and therefore she had contracted with a white employer, R. M. Cready. "I now have eight children, all dependent on me for support," she explained, "only one large enough to work for herself, the rest I could not hire for their victuals and clothes. I think you might have sent the children something or some money. Joe can walk and talk. Neat is a great big boy bad as ever. My baby I call her Cassinda. The children all send howda to you. They all want to see you." Enclosed was also a note from her employer.

Cready warned Smart to wait until his wife's contract had expired before he attempted to see her.[66] Such cases caused one Freedmen's Bureau agent plaintively to inquire of a federal military commander if former slave owners had the power to "part man and wife and bid defiance of God and man."[67] Clearly, southern whites intended to keep this authority over the labor of African American families just as they had during slavery.

African American soldiers who tried to rejoin their families immediately after the war encountered great hostility from white employers both because they fought against the Confederacy and because of their interference with the labor of women and children. Allen Burrell's young son served in the army with his father as a water boy. Although his father sent him home to his mother, the boy explained that "after father was mustered out he was afraid to go home for nearly a year because he heard that the white folks were going to kill all col'd soldiers." Even though Burrell's reasons for staying in Vicksburg included the company of a young woman, his fears about vindictive southern whites reflected a prevalent and justifiable belief.[68] One former slave owner in Mississippi observed that "Colonel Thomas, assistant commissioner of the [Freedmen's] bureau for this state, tells us that there is now a daily average of two or three black men killed in Mississippi; the sable patriots in blue as they return are the objects of especial spite."[69]

As Chapter 3 discussed, individual Freedmen's Bureau officials, particularly Alvan Gillem (the assistant commissioner of the Mississippi Freedmen's Bureau) upheld the sanctity of labor contracts over the authority of African American men. Such was the case of Jackson Irving, who forbade his wife to help other female hands on the plantation "in weighing down the lever to raise the Gin House." A gin house contained equipment that removed seed out of cotton, which was usually two stories tall. Irving went to the head of his wife's squad to find another task for his wife. Meanwhile their employer, G. S. Wilson, demanded that Irving's wife return to work with the other women. Asserting his role as protector and representative for his wife, "Irving ordered her not to obey him, saying to Wilson if you have anything to say I am the man to talk to." Irving later explained that "he was afraid his wife might get injured." Irving's employer complained to the Bureau that Irving kept his wife from working. The Bureau agent insisted that Irving agree not to "interfere hereafter with the work assigned to his wife" and "that he will himself work steadily during the remainder of the year." Irving quickly learned the limits of his authority over his family.[70] Irving's statement that "I am the man to talk to" assumed a short-lived equality with his wife's white employer. The Bureau agent stripped him of his illusions by reminding him of his own social and racial status.

Although the law prohibited African American women from signing contracts without the consent of their husbands, white southerners willingly violated the ordinances and hired women without their husbands' permission. Although employers were much more reluctant about hiring single and pregnant women or nursing mothers or mothers of small children than other workers, other women who quit their husbands could obtain work. When George Sheppey went to the Bureau agent to complain that his wife contracted without his consent, she revealed that she had found employment on another place and did not live with him.[71] When Ann Griffin refused to follow her husband, a farm laborer, to a rural area because she preferred to work in the city as a domestic, she easily found work.[72] Similarly, Charlotte Small told a Bureau officer that she intended to remain with her present employer rather than live with her husband.[73]

Once a wife signed a labor contract, the husband had very little legal recourse to retrieve his wife against her wishes. African American husbands had far less recourse, in reality, than white middle-class husbands if their wives decided to become independent from them. The Waddington family provides an apt example. Because of Albert Waddington's frequent intoxication and abuse of family, his employer, H. F. McWilliams, forced Waddington off the plantation, but the rest of the family chose to remain. McWilliams paid Albert's wife, Ann Waddington, her own wages. After Albert's departure, she gained full charge of all the family wages as well.[74] McWilliams gave the balance of credit of the younger children's earnings to Ann Waddington; "they being her children and not Albert's." The inability of fathers to control the income or the actions of their older children also undermined the development of African American patriarchy. Albert Waddington's older daughter, Julia Adair, gained control over her own wages and her own account at the plantation store as well. Because of Waddington's cruelty, Adair refused to reside with him. She "took her business into her own hands." Adair secured her complete independence from her father and she insisted "that he was to have nothing to do with her business."[75] Freedmen also found their right to the custody of their children challenged.

Custody and the Apprenticing of Children

When freedmen and women separated or quit, they sometimes argued over custody of the children.[76] Neither parent was automatically granted custody by virtue of their gender. Couples occasionally brought their custody fights before the Freedmen's Bureau. Olly Coalman wrote to the Bureau: "I being in trouble. I want your advice. I have bin married. My husband has lef me. We had but one child. [H]e being married again wants to take the child from me to aggravate me. He cares nothing for the child and has never don anything for it since we parted." Coalman emphasized her ability to provide for the child. "I am not willing to give it up. I am able to support the child. I want to no how long I can ceek [*sic*] it or whether i can ceek it at all or not."[77]

As this letter indicates, parents used economic arguments to convince Freedmen's Bureau officials to allow them to retain custody of their children.[78] The Bureau refused to uphold the legal rights of African American fathers in custody cases as mid-nineteenth century law often dictated. The Bureau's concern that children receive financial support from their guardian guided its decisions. Mothers who demonstrated an ability to provide for their children often managed to keep them. Celia Ratliff supported her son for seven years prior to the boy's father's request for his son, and as a result, she retained custody.[79] Similarly, because Eliza Banyon "had raised the boy [her son] at her own expense and had always had him with her," the case was decided in her favor.[80] Although the sympathy of Freedmen's Bureau lay with the claims of the parent who supported or promised to provide for the child in the future, it considered other grounds as well. If one parent proved that the former spouse had committed a crime, the complainant gained custody; custom barred criminals from guardianship. Therefore, the crime of adultery caused either a man or a woman to lose a custody fight. For women, engaging in prostitution produced the same result.[81]

Because they desired autonomy for their families, freedpeople tried to keep whites and particularly their employers from interfering in their personal lives. African American parents anticipated disciplining their own children, educating them, inculcating their own values and culture, obtaining their wages if they worked and, most importantly, living with them without the fear of separation that reigned in slavery.[82] Such views of family were a hallmark of freedom. In reality, the African American family remained somewhat fragile because of the ability of whites to gain the right to raise African American children by apprenticing them.

The legacy of slavery, under which slave fathers had no legal rights to their children, undermined an African American father's right to custody after emancipation. The lack of previous legal status automatically raised questions about the validity of the father's claim. While she was enslaved,

Ellen Riley married Ben Copeland and they had three children. After a forced separation during slavery and Copeland's subsequent remarriage, the three children stayed with Riley. After emancipation, she supported them "until they were large enough to be useful, and . . . then he took them." The Freedmen's Bureau agent, William S. Tidball, reasoned that the children belonged with Riley because slave children, like illegitimate children, went "with their mother."[83] Were Tidball's logic to have been applied uniformly, it would have prohibited any former slave father from ever gaining custody of his children unless he legally married the children's mother after the war, either by ceremony or by state statute.[84]

African American parents also argued over custody without the intervention of the Freedmen's Bureau. Accompanied by his new wife Harriet, freedman David Austin went to claim his children from his former wife Mary. Having often fought while married, Dave and Mary literally began a custody fight, with Mary and Dave armed with axes and Harriet with a "broken rail." Mary's employer stopped the battle and enforced a temporary cease-fire.[85] African American women also used weapons subtler than axes in their struggles for their children. When Peter Irwin took her eighteen-month-old child away from her, Ella told the Freedmen's Bureau that she would swear that "Peter is not the father."[86]

African American parents wanted their children with them for several reasons: In addition to their emotional ties to their children, parents also benefited from their children's future earnings. Because some of the quarreling involved financial remuneration, the partners occasionally resolved custody questions with economic settlements. Margaret and her former husband, Edward Wolf, agreed to an arrangement whereby he kept the two oldest children; the youngest three remained with her, and Edward promised to give Mary $20.00 [probably a year] as child support.[87] Joe, whose son worked for him, disputed his first wife's right to the boy. Finally they agreed that Joe would pay his son's wages to his mother, and Joe would "keep the boy in subjection" until he reached his twenty-first birthday. The Freedmen's Bureau agent noted that this compromise left "all parties satisfied."[88]

Fathers' relationships with their children when their mothers gained custody of them depended on various factors. These ranged from physical proximity of the non-residential parent to the age of children when they left their father's household. Some fathers remained close to their children even after both parents remarried. Oliver Braxon's "girls lived with their mother, but they would very often come to [his] house. [He] sent them all to school after they got here, they were just young girls."[89] After the war John Matthews's parents quit each other and Matthews recalled, "Sometimes I stayed wid my pappy an' some times I wus wid mammy."[90]

After the war, one of the greatest threats to the African American family and African American parental authority over their own children was the apprenticing of African American children by white planters. The majority of disputes concerning children that freedpeople reported to the Freedmen's Bureau involved attempts by southern whites to retain or apprentice African American children. These conflicts combined the issues of African American control over their families and the labor of freedpeople. Special laws passed in 1865 as part of the Black Codes authorized Mississippi officials, which included "sheriffs, [and] justices of the peace" to report African American (defined as "freedmen, free negroes and mulattos") orphans and impoverished children to local authorities so that the probate court could apprentice them. The law also specified "that the former owner of said minors shall have the preference when, in the opinion of the court, he or she shall be a suitable person for that purpose."[91] Former slave owners paid a bond in probate court for the child after following legal procedures that required "due notice" to the parents (if living) "by posting notices in five public places, and by calling [the parent's name] three times at the court house door." Such legal gestures did not protect African Americans from losing their children, especially given the high rate of illiteracy among freedpeople and their unfamiliarity with the law.[92] One woman who swore that she could support her daughter lost her case because she "was ignorant of the requirement of law regarding witnesses" that she needed to fulfill to prove that she could support her child.[93] Apprenticed children remained with the white family until they reached 21 years of age, if male, or 18 years, if female. Immediately after the war if the court declared African American parents destitute or vagrants, it apprenticed the children without parental consent.[94] The courts justified their decisions on the grounds that unapprenticed, orphaned, or destitute children needed private support to prevent them from becoming a financial burden to the local government.[95] Children were apprenticed in significant numbers during Presidential Reconstruction. According to one historian, "the probate court at Calhoun City apprenticed two hundred and twenty at one term."[96]

In disputed cases between parents and former owners, the Mississippi local courts usually gave the children to whites. In 1865 and 1866, the local government, controlled by Democrats and still sympathetic to the interests of planters, supported the apprentice system as a form of race

and labor control. In contrast, the federal government, usually represented by Freedmen's Bureau agents in Mississippi, generally sided with freed
families who were trying to regain their children if the families could support them. Although it was committed to keeping former slave families
together, the Bureau also wanted to prevent African American children
from becoming financially dependent on the federal government. Because
the apprentice law allowed whites to break up families and gave them the
virtual slave labor of children, Freedmen's Bureau agents protested the
widespread abuse. As Samuel Thomas wrote the head of the Freedmen's
Bureau, Oliver Otis Howard, the apprentice law "is capable of being made
an instrument of oppression to the colored people and is being so used."[97]
Former slave masters swore that children who were bonded to them were
orphans and tried to convince the courts that the parents who claimed
them were frauds.[98] Others falsely accused parents of destitution even in
those cases where such claims proved highly questionable.[99] J. H. Grace
testified in civil court that the mother of the children he wanted to apprentice, all of whom were his former slaves, was mentally deficient and
incapable of caring for her children. The court granted him the apprenticeship. When the mother sought aid from a Freedmen's Bureau agent,
he found her completely competent and bitterly complained to his superior, "better would it have been for them to remain in slavery if they are to
be dragged up and apprenticed in violation of law, and against their will
and common sense."[100]

Apprenticeship laws raised questions about the rights of single African American parents to custody. Freedman Henry Cannon was separated
from his wife during slavery. When his wife died, his children were "declared illegitimate by the law" and apprenticed to a white man.[101] Cannon
objected but to no avail. The Mississippi probate court ruled that because
of the 1865 Mississippi constitutional provision concerning freedpeople's
marriages, a slave father held no legal right to his children. The postwar
marriage legislation failed to recognize families that were formed before
1865 unless they met the requirements of the new law. Therefore, if a
slave man and woman had children and the woman died before their marriage was legalized after the war, the law considered the offspring to be
fatherless. Even if the father were living and providing custodial care, by
this ruling the children were considered illegitimate and became orphans
and wards of the state. In such cases, judges ruled that they could not
legalize slave marriages retroactively. One Mississippi judge explained as
he patronizingly refused to acknowledge slave marriages, "they should

not, when free, be held bound by their acts or manner of life, when slaves, when they had no care for the future, no sense of responsibility, no choice, often but the indication of circumstances and the necessities of the condition."[102] Because they were outside of the law, slave marriages were outside the notion of the respectable bourgeois family that buttressed a stable workforce.

When apprenticeships were contested, some officials also questioned whether stepfathers possessed any legal claim. In October 1866, a Bureau agent inquired whether children with a mother and stepfather where considered orphans by the state of Mississippi. He shared his personal view that because "the stepfather is able to support the children and wants them . . . it is simply an outrage to deprive the parents."[103] Although children often accepted their new fathers, laws limited the legal rights of stepfathers over their stepchildren. A Bureau official informed one stepfather that because his wife apprenticed her son before marrying him, he lacked any authority to terminate the apprenticeship against the wishes of the mother.[104]

Mississippi Democrats even raised doubts about women's rights to their children who were born in slavery. At one point, the Mississippi governor, a former slave owner, questioned the right of unmarried African American women to child custody. His query hinged on the universal use of the word "freedmen" for both men and women. In March 1866, the governor of Mississippi asked his attorney general to clarify if the "mother of a fatherless child, under 21 years of age, [is] entitled to its custody and service?" He raised the issue because the statute on apprenticing only specified that a "freedman, free negro or mulatto" could gain certain custody rights over children. The use of the word "freedmen" confused the governor because it implied that only men could exercise those rights. The attorney general responded that a single African American mother in fact possessed guardianship over her child. He explained that "the use of the general terms employed in the title of the act 'freedman,' 'free negro,' or 'mulatto' must be construed to embrace either parent."[105] As one Freedmen's Bureau agent explained, southern whites "have the labor of a hand for five or six years and it costs them comparatively nothing, it is a very sharp practice—and according to their plan—they can deprive a mother of the labor of a child that would be nearly if not quite able to support her."[106]

To counteract laws such as the apprenticeship legislation that discriminated against African Americans, the United States Congress passed the Civil Rights Act in 1866 over Andrew Johnson's presidential veto. The act stated that "citizens, of every race and color, without regard to any previous condition of slavery or involuntary servitude . . . shall have the same right . . . as is enjoyed by white citizens." Because the special apprentice laws passed in Mississippi as part of the Black Codes applied only to African American children, the Civil Rights Act effectively nullified the law.[107] Some Bureau agents interpreted the Civil Rights Act as requiring parental consent prior to the apprenticing of their children. To regain custody of their children under the Civil Rights Act, African American parents needed to obtain a writ of habeas corpus in Circuit Court and file it with the probate court.[108] Even with a writ, the courts required parents to prove their ability to support their children. Although the use of habeas corpus expanded after the Civil War, African American parents found gaining habeas corpus difficult.[109] Poor African Americans discovered that the legal system was expensive, slow, and governed by incomprehensible court procedures.[110]

Occasionally the current employers of the parents aided them in their attempts to regain custody of their children from their former slave owners.[111] Because the parents' employers reasoned that children would work for them if the parents recovered them, they anticipated winning both more labor from older children and the loyalty of the parents. Ironically, this situation forced African American parents to rely on the paternalism of a new employer to combat the former slave owner's apprenticing of their children. In such cases, the attempts to end the apprenticeship ensnared African Americans in a new dependent relationship with whites. Ironically, freedpeople had intended to avoid such involvement with whites by leaving their former masters to seek employment elsewhere.[112]

The Freedmen's Bureau negotiated some apprenticeships with the permission of the families. An analysis of three months of the Freedmen's Bureau's apprenticeship records from Macon County involved thirty-nine children in twenty-seven families. This examination shows that in cases where parents were incapable of supporting their children, single female-headed households apprenticed their children more often than two-parent households. More boys (twenty-five) were apprenticed than girls (fifteen) and the average age of the children was 9 years of age; the person apprenticing them would gain many years of productive labor from these children. These records show that almost half of the children were apprenticed because of the death of the parents and about another third of the families gave permission for the apprenticeships. In a small number of cases, the Freedmen's Bureau agent stated abandonment by the parents as the reason for apprenticeship. Of the six families who were incapable of supporting their children, single mothers headed five of the families.[113]

According to Freedmen's Bureau complaints, some whites, even with the advantage of laws that gave former slave owners preference in apprenticing their former slaves, used their position as employers to coerce single female parents into apprenticing their children. Thomas Smith told Harriet Goodwin that unless she relinquished her children to him, he would "punish her."[114] One employer threatened to send illiterate Mary White to jail unless she placed her mark on an apprenticeship contract. White later swore that she misunderstood the contents of the paper that she felt pressured to sign.[115] Another employer refused to pay his female worker until she apprenticed her child to him.[116] Even when it was signed under these circumstances, the apprentice contract proved difficult to break.[117] Parents who regained their children were occasionally confronted by whites who demanded payment that was not required by law as compensation for providing for the apprenticed children.

Southern whites felt justified in taking African American children away from their parents and based their arguments on the paternalistic practices that had developed during slavery. Underlining the apprenticeships was the belief that African Americans were essentially workers or potential workers. White apprenticers protested that they wanted to keep the children because they were "attached to" them.[118] They argued that their status as former masters obliged them to support children whose freed parents remained too poor to provide for them.[119] They also contended that the children reciprocated feelings of affection. Isaac Bennett quoted a boy whom he was retaining against the wishes of the boy's mother as saying "[I]f they carry me off I will run away and come back to Master again."[120] In 1869, one former slave owner wrote the commander of the United States military district of Jackson about a child who was separated during slavery from its mother and raised practically from birth by his family. After the war the mother came to claim her son. During that time the family legally apprenticed the child while continuing to educate him. According to the planter, "the boy was sorely averse to going with the mother—an almost total stranger," but the white family persuaded the boy to leave. Two weeks later, the child returned, "alleging that he had been unkindly used, ill fed, and no provision probable for his further education."[121] The former master received a favorable ruling from a probate judge that allowed him to keep the boy. One Freedmen's Bureau agent countered such assertions of the children's devotion by arguing, "I am much opposed to this system of slavery, as I am not aware of any minor apprenticed under the state laws who are not able to support themselves—and I have yet to see the first one thus apprenticed who had . . . learned . . . ABC."[122]

Some former masters illegally withheld African American children from their families without the inconvenience of a formal apprenticeship. Planters defended themselves before the Freedmen's Bureau agents after African Americans brought complaints by arguing that the formerly enslaved children, although free, belonged to them. Even though she objected, Ellen Lowe's former owner continued to keep her child after the war.[123] Her former master barred Rachel Johnson from taking her son George with her when she decided to leave his place. She tried to obtain the child, but attempts proved unsuccessful.[124] A former slave woman complained that a white man contrived her arrest on false charges when she threatened to take him to court for illegally detaining her child.[125] When parents tried to reclaim their children, whites occasionally greeted them with violence. As he aimed his gun at her, Mr. Woodson told Polly Reaves that he would "blow her brains out" if she attempted to take her children.[126] Ennis Scarver told one mother he would kill her if she ever came for her child.[127]

Even when their African American laborers maintained custody of their own children, white employers occasionally punished these employees for exercising parental authority. One Freedmen's Bureau agent reported "that on or about the 18th. day of August, 1865, Matilda, a colored woman, was murdered by one J. H. Riley and son, in Newton County, in this state for simply remonstrating against whipping her son."[128] Doctor Calhoun swore at Phyllis Johnson when she demanded that Calhoun pay her daughter or forfeit her labor. Calhoun argued with Johnson and "threatened to have her arrested and sent to jail."[129] Ann Johnson's employer, William Brown, "discharged" her when she prevented her daughter from continuing her work as a nurse for him. Johnson contended that he abused her daughter.[130]

Other planters simply ignored the parental rights of African Americans. They based intervention on their fundamental right as employers. They also believed that white interference was needed to keep African American families stable by working for whites. P. L. Criglin obtained Ellis's mark on a labor contract although he noted that "Ellis' mother belongs to another person and is opposed to it on the grounds that compensation is not sufficient."[131] The word "belongs" indicated how little this employer had adjusted to free labor.

Employers limited the visits between parents and children who were working as domestic servants. Lizzie Benson contracted her daughter for a year "to do all necessary house work, cooking, washing, serving and all things that is necessary." The daughter, Cate, was not able "to leave the mansion and go to the quarter to remain any time without . . . permission." As a live-in domestic, the child was expected "to remain in the mansion of nights and in the event the said Cate stays away from the mansion any night without permission her wages is to be docked $1.00 for each offense."[132]

Relying on tactics reminiscent of slavery, employers tried to influence how their workers raised their own children. They sometimes specified in their labor contracts that they held the right to discipline the offspring of their employees even when the children were not listed as workers.[133] As one contract stated, "laborers having children under (14) fourteen years of age agree that their children shall be governed and corrected in a kind and humane manner" by the employer [a woman], "her agent or nurse."[134] Some employers penalized parents for failing to discipline their children according to their dictates. Charlotte Ross's employer pressured her to punish her child for any behavior he found inappropriate, telling her "that if she did not whip her son that she must leave."[135] Some parents signed labor contracts that permitted whites to punish their children. Phyllis Ann John allowed her former owner, John H. Collins, Jr. "to correct" her daughter Harriet "when she needed" it.[136]

Other African American parents, however, resisted white attempts to punish their children by protesting to the Freedmen's Bureau. Edie Glover complained that John Glover, her former slave owner, beat her children with a walking stick. In defending himself, Glover pointed out that "the woman and her family have always lived with him, and that he has always controlled the children." Edie Glover later agreed to continue working for Glover after he pledged that he would not "strike her children, but let her punish them."[137] Such families were trying to maintain private family relations, but that goal was difficult to realize. Former slave owners were quite relentless in finding means, including the power of local and state law, to control aspects of African American family life. The apprentice laws were a case in point. Employers were particularly unwilling to concede the concept of a private life for freedpeople if they believed that they would lose control of the labor of their employees.

This conflict with whites was an important reason why African American families became male-headed, but not patriarchal, after the war. Slave customs, race relations, the access of African American women to wage work and their ability to rely on an extended family all conspired to undermine (for better or for worse) a reality of an African American patriarchy. One of the most serious threats to the autonomy of the African American family was the apprentice law, which showed the weakness and potential instability of both male- and female-headed households.

KIN NETWORKS

*"The coloured people on the . . . estate
are generally friends of claimant, a
number of them being relatives"*[1]

Almost thirty years after the fact, Robert Owens's sister Jane Williams described her brother's relationship with Lucy. Like many extended kin, Williams knew all about her brother, even those activities he did "on the sly." "My brother Robert Owens used to visit Lucy and sweetheart with her on the sly but they did not claim to be husband and wife. . . . Robert never did stay openly with Lucy." Owens was also unfaithful to his wife with women other than Lucy, but he remained married until his death in 1894. Jane Williams was certain that Lucy kept the "name of Lucy Brown and was never called Lucy Dorsey or Lucy Owens." Williams added that since that time, "she has told me that she married again but I do not know her present husband."[2]

Although the majority of African American families were headed by males, other family forms existed. A minority of families were headed by women although these women often depended on other family members. Extended families were significant, particularly to women, regardless of whether members were part of the household or lived close by. After emancipation, families, which sometimes included single pregnant women or aged parents, took on new economic functions for its members. Such commitments began with a search for missing family members.

Once the war ended, freedom meant an opportunity to reunite or reconstitute families and gain the autonomy to keep members of the family together.[3] Lucy Galloway recalled that as her master stood on his slave block, he told his slaves that "Dis block has parted many a mother and chile, husband and wife—brother and sister—but, now you is all free as I am."[4] Husbands from abroad marriages were finally able to reside with their families.

Freedpeople sought information about the location of their nuclear or extended kin. Such inquiries poignantly testified to the strength of the slave family. Moses Norman wanted "information of the whereabouts of" his sister because he was "anxious to have her come and live with him."[5] Frances Bell wanted to know about her children, who had been slaves in North Carolina, because she had "great anxiety regarding their welfare."[6] Years after being sold away from her family, Peggy Kelly wrote to her former slave owner asking for information about her parents and siblings. She pleaded, "any information given if any or the whereabouts of them will be thankfully rec'd. Let me know if they are dead or alive. My name was Peggie one of the children of Prince and Rose."[7]

Extended Kin

After the war, African American families contained people outside of the current narrow definition of nuclear family.[8] Sometimes extended families included three generations in the same household. Freedmen's Bureau documents indicate many different family and household arrangements. A chart that listed the former slaves on Garland's plantation in Hinds County one month after the war shows such variety.

The list from Hinds County also makes clear the economic transition kin groups had to make from enslavement to freedom. Even before sharecropping developed, African American families began to function as economic units whose concern was the well-being of their members. The chart identifies five distinct families who were living on the plantation. With four of the families, the list used the father's name as an appropriate nomenclature for designating the family, calling them "Robert's family," "Wm. Minors' family," "Telghman's family," and "Washington's family." Ramsy, a 42-year-old woman, and her family comprised the fifth family, listed as "Ramsy's family." In Robert's family, Robert, 49, Emeline, 36, Richard, 16, and Jam, 14, were listed as work hands. Robert was "a pretty good shoe maker and has all the profits of his trade" probably in addition to agricultural labor. The family raised hogs, tended a garden and a potato and melon patch, and had "the use of 2 cows for milk and butter." The employer noted that "meal [was] furnished regularly every week." A similar situation existed for Teighman's family, and for Washington, who was a carpenter, and his family. In each case, the female and male children over 12 in these families were identified as work hands.

Unlike Robert's family, William Minor's family included extended family. William Minor was "a blacksmith and has all the profits of the shop for the uses of his family." Minor's family consisted of himself and several children including Nelson, 16, marked "idiot." The family probably supported Nelson. Parents tried to aid handicapped or any offspring who were physically unable to work regardless of their age. Minor's daughter Grace Ann Minor and her "infant child," also lived in William Minor's two-room house. Additionally William Minor's son Tom Minor and his two toddlers resided "with [his] father's family having separated from his wife about two years ago." Although the chart listed Tom Minor as a work hand, Grace Ann was not distinguished in the same manner. Possibly Grace Ann performed domestic labor for the Minor family and cared for her baby and her brother's toddlers. No woman close to William Minor's age who might have been his wife was listed.

The one woman designated as head of her own household, Ramsy, was also not listed as a work hand but she was "a good cook, washer, and ironer, and can support herself and family." Her employer furnished her with meal weekly, "the use of a first rate cow for milk and butter, vegetables and fruits from plantation garden and orchard." Ramsy did not have her own melon and potato patch like the other families, presumably because she was a domestic and was not given the time to work on one. Ramsy lived with her four children, which included a three-year-old. Other freedpeople on the plantation who were not bracketed under one family included 20-year-old Stephen, recently married, and Old Aunt Rose, a 60-year-old midwife, who lived in a "comfortable house . . . and has all she wants." Claiborne, a tanner by trade, and his son Douglas were also listed separately without a family title.[9]

A few contracts and other documents indicate that women without husbands, either young women with small children or older women who were possibly unable to work, relied on kin. African American women and men interacted with extended families from both the mother's and the father's side when possible.[10] Although the vast majority of labor contracts do not specify family relations, a few contain examples of extended family relationships on plantations. In Lowndes County in August 1865, 70-year-old Suzy resided on the Drummond place with her three married daughters. Matilda, 45, and her husband, Sampson, lived with their son, Alfred. Matilda's sisters, Nancy and Sarah Ann, also resided on the same place with their spouses and children.[11] On J. A. Nixon's plantation, freed-man Bram, 75, lived with his 65-year-old wife, Fanny, and his two daughters, Judy and Silvy. J. A. Nixon counted Bram's granddaughter Della, the daughter of Silvy, as part of Bram's family. There was no mention of Silvy's spouse. Nixon also listed John's family, which consisted of Bram's son-in-law John and John's wife, Nelly, who was also Bram's daughter. Bram's son, Jim, his wife, and their baby also lived on the place although Nixon counted them as a separate family.

Such enumeration showed a large extended family with designated male heads.[12] Even sources that describe an attack by the Ku Klux Klan indicate the closeness of the extended family. Henrietta Murray's family resided in a double cabin. When she, her mother, and father fled the cabin under orders from the Ku Klux Klan, Murray indicated who lived in the other section of the house. "Uncle Jim reached fo' his gun an' they struck him 'cross de hand. Out de doo' he went an' Auntie right behind him. Grandma followed 'em."[13]

On these plantations, African American children grew up in close proximity to their grandparents, aunts, and uncles, with their siblings and cousins as playmates. Extended family stayed together long after the war ended. Carroll Russell's paternal aunt "knew him all his life."[14] As late as 1886, a pension examiner discovered that most of the people who lived with Charlotte Branch on a plantation in Adams County were her "friends" and "relatives."[15]

Interfamilial marriages further strengthened extended families as sisters, sisters-in-law, brothers, and brothers-in-law all merged and extended family distinctions blurred. Family trees occasionally shared more than one branch of another family tree when more than one member of one family intermarried with another family. While they were enslaved, Benjamin and Robert Lee both married sisters. Cyrus Macklin described a similar situation: "I had [married] Bouncer Hardaway's sister and Bouncer is now married to my sister Rebecca."[16] Henry Sims married his first wife's sister after his wife died.[17] One person who recalled the slave couple George and Malinda Hubbard explained, "I am a cousin of George Hubbard and my wife Amy Watson is a cousin to Malinda."[18] Extended family kept track of relatives even when the immediate family connection ceased. Once part of a particular family a person stayed in the network of kin. Monroe Walker remained keenly interested in the activities of his late brother's wife. Living three miles from her, he knew when his sister-in-law remarried and to whom.[19]

Stepfamilies became one more branch of the elaborate extended family upon which African American women relied. Although Charlotte Brady was the daughter of Archie Branch's first wife, Branch's widowed second wife, "sent word" to her stepdaughter "that she was suffering" after the war. Brady arranged for her employer to send for her stepmother so that she could reside on the same place as Brady.[20] Half-siblings within these families became close. Emily Benton, who shared a birth mother with William Harris, "reared him" after the death of their mother. While Harris served in the army, his wife resided with Benton "many nights while William was soldiering."[21]

Family members became involved in each others' lives. Nisey Horton's brother-in-law struck up a friendship with George Clark, a fellow brakeman on the railroad. Nisey's sister considered him a suitable suitor for her sister. Nisey's family ensured that she met Clark when she spent the summer with them. Nisey recalled, "it was not long 'till he courted" her. Nisey and George held their marriage ceremony in the home of her sister and brother-in-law.[22]

Of course stepfamilies and biological families endured their share of stress and unhappiness. One girl complained to the Freedmen's Bureau of having "been most cruelly treated by her mother and stepfather."[23] When dealings with extended families became unpleasant, the close proximity exacerbated existing problems. One freedwoman reported to the Freedmen's Bureau that her mother-in-law physically abused her.[24] Such complaints were rare, probably because most African Americans tried to work family tensions out for themselves without relying on an agency of the federal government.

Women and Extended Kin

Even with occasional stresses, women depended on kin in times of crisis. After the war solders sometimes failed to return because of death, difficulty in traveling, or new intimate relationships. The women they left tried a variety of strategies to gain the emotional support and economic help that they needed. The disruption caused by the war increased the numbers of women and children who lived in families without men. As one federal assistant inspector general explained, "[F]amilies are disunited very much, and they have suffered greatly during the Rebellion. Husbands have been conscripted or have joined the army leaving their families in extreme poverty."[25] Single women who were pregnant or were supporting small children needed help from their extended families. Army widows became part of extended families by joining the households of other family members. Less often, they lived with other widows. After staying with friends or family for awhile, these women, even if they were not widows in the strictest sense, often formed new relationships with men. Widowed women often chose not to marry (although they might cohabit) because their remarriage would jeopardize their widow's pension from the U.S. government. For these women, extended family became a way station between relationships.

The ability of freedwomen to rely on kin and their work experience gave them the option of leaving a spouse or partner. After leaving their husbands women often lived with or relied on male kin or female kin who resided in male-headed households.[26] As the 1870 census showed, rural African American women rarely lived completely on their own as single women.[27] Rather they chose to reside with family members. Although life was more difficult without a hardworking man at a woman's side, men who drank or became abusive were much less of a loss. When women chose to quit these men, they depended on their kin. Within the restrictions of family and work, women practiced a limited form of autonomy.[28] Nettie Cooper left her alcoholic and "very abusive" husband and worked as a nursemaid for a white family. When her husband took their 12-year-old girl, Nettie's father helped her regain the child from her husband. Nettie argued that her ability to support the child meant that she should keep her.[29] When George Nelson left the employ of John Barkley, he expected his wife to go with him. She refused to join him, preferring to stay with her siblings on the place where she was reared.[30]

When necessary, extended family replaced the emotional and financial support women and children had received from husbands or fathers. Although usually connected in some way with their extended families, women became physically closer or more distant to their kin depending on their needs and romantic circumstances. Single women, including widows, relied on parents or siblings when they were not engaged in a cohabitational or stable relationship. Parents willingly aided their single daughters. After the death of her husband, Helen Thomas Shaw lived with her mother and father and recalled that her "father helped support me till he died."[31] When her cohabitational relationship broke up, Celia Wilson "went to live with [her] father."[32] Civil War widow Anne Patterson moved in with her sister and brother-in-law for three years before she remarried.[33] After living together for a while Cinthy Barnes's took-up husband, in a move uncharacteristic of stepfathers, refused to support all her children from her first marriage. She, in turn, decided that she "would not support him." Barnes accepted her brother's offer to move to Louisiana, where he "would care for me and my children as his wife was dead." In this case, Barnes probably repaid her sibling by attending to the domestic labor for the extended family.[34] The relationship between Barnes's children and their uncle grew so strong that when Barnes returned to Mississippi, her two oldest sons stayed on with their uncle.

Women discovered that they lost their privacy when they reentered the households of their families. When women moved back in with their parents, siblings, or other extended kin, the families gained knowledge of the women's intimate activities. Emmanuel Middleton's widowed daughter lived with him after her husband, a soldier, died. Middleton knew that his daughter engaged in intimacies with John Douglass "as his sweetheart" and that "he often . . . visited her at my house and at other times at places where she was working."[35]

Extended family members, particularly siblings, did not seem to exercise authority over their grown-up sisters. They rarely kept a woman from her chosen man, although in several instances the family's critical evaluation of a suitor proved accurate. Family resistance to Joe Duncan's desire to wed Rose failed to keep the couple from marrying. According to Rose's sister-in-law, "the family opposed him and he took Rose over to Nathan Coff's and married her over there."[36] Because of Duncan's chronic adultery, Rose's marriage to him was an unhappy one. Mary Johnson's brother intensely disliked his sister's choice of her new partner, but her brother's displeasure failed to prevent Mary from entering an extremely abusive relationship.[37] Victoria Johnson's sister and guardian opposed Johnson's marriage, but to no avail: "[S]he was a small young girl, not fit to get married, and I did not want her to, but she did."[38]

The reliance of freedwomen on extended kin decreased when they entered into these new committed relationships. Freedman George Brooks described his sister-in law's closeness to her extended family. Elizabeth Fletcher lived with her sister and brother-in-law after the war until, according to Brooks, her sweetheart "came there and took her out of the house and they said they were going to marry."[39] After leaving Vicksburg, Frances Brown "moved in the house with William Adams; my brother and I work[ed] on the Hal Smith place with him for one year." Then Brown decided to work "for myself on the same place for one or two years. After that I rented a house from my brother." Brown explained the agreement, "I was working with him in his crop and he had to furnish me a house . . . [that was] in the same yard and had one room in it." Brown's quotes suggest that she may have found working on her own difficult and had therefore returned to receive assistance such as housing from her brother. Even when she took up with Vaughn Knowling, she "continued to work on my brother's crop the first year and Knowling working round [at different places] for wages." After continuing this arrangement for two years, she and Knowling "moved on to the Wardell place and rented land."[40]

As a rule, men needed lodging from their relatives less than women did. Men had somewhat better employment opportunities and pay and less concern for personal safety when they lived alone. Single men rarely had to care for children. An exception, Peter Holmes, sick and deserted by his wife, "lived with one of my cousins until I got well."[41]

Single pregnant women found supporting themselves difficult. Employers either docked wages from pregnant workers or threw them off the plantation. These women often chose to move within close proximity of their birth family, sometimes reentering the household. Freedwoman Page requested transportation funds from Howard Hospital to return to her mother and father in Alabama, even though Page assured the Freedmen's Bureau that she planned to remain financially independent from her parents.[42] Rosanna's employer forced her off the place where she was working and tossed all her belongings "out in the rain."[43] When the father of the child refused to acknowledge paternity or support the child, Rosanna turned to her own parents for aid.[44] Elias vehemently denied fathering Mary's child, arguing that Mary could not be certain who impregnated her. Mary's father "agreed to care for her and the child" on the condition that Mary would "behave herself."[45] This proviso seemed less an indictment of the pregnancy and more a condemnation of perceived questionable sexual behavior; possibly Mary had engaged in sexual relations without sustaining a committed relationship.

Women also had problems making a living after their babies were born. Planters often considered single women with young children a burden because of the expense of wage labor, particularly because children were no longer the property of planters. They based this assumption on their perception that women's labor was much less valuable than men's labor in the context of the sexual division of labor on plantations. In 1865, a Bureau official in Woodville, Mississippi, noted in a monthly report that "A great many planters say they can't support so many women and children next year and are going to send them off when the time comes."[46] Similarly, a report from Grenada stated that "single men and women are more successful in obtaining work than those having families to support, and women speak openly of their children as encumbrances and hindrances in their search for places."[47] Planters such as W. H. Offitt near

Greenville in the Delta argued that their reluctance to hire these women stemmed from rational economic thinking. Offitt complained, "I have hands here women with small children on whom I know I am losing money every day." Offitt paid his women workers half the crop, from which he deducted their clothes, food, and tobacco. Offitt understood, as did "all sensible persons," that he lost money because a woman's earnings could not cover her debt to him for provisions for her and her children.[48]

Planters solved their problem by only paying room and board. Such an arrangement was reminiscent of slavery but it furnished food and shelter for women with children. In August 1865, H. Cox contracted with both "colored women and children" for only sustenance as payment. The contract did not indicate the presence of any men and included Emeline, 40 years old and her children, Sarah Jane, 18; Steve, 16; Eli, 14; Isabella, 12; Clara, 10; Wilson, 8; Rose, 5; Jessie, 4; Sydney, 2; and Rosetta, 5 months. Sarah, aged 47, also lived with several children.[49] When their children were too young to work, their mothers provided for them when possible.[50] Because of the labor shortage after the war, some former slave owners reluctantly hired freedwomen with families without husbands, such as widowed Emily Ragland, whose children, 8-year-old India, 11-year-old Penina, and 5-year-old Maris, were "supported by her" work.[51]

The labor of older children proved especially valuable to single freedwomen, who depended on their children's added compensation. As Amanda Mackie explained, she and her "children have been hired to white people ever since they was big enough."[52] Widowed Sophia Simon "has hired with her children on the Sharley place most of the time and has supported herself by working on the farm."[53] Freedwoman Mary Ann Ellsey attempted to gain release for her apprenticed children, pleading that "with their aid now I could make head way and get a start in the world."[54] Although the women preferred to keep their children within their own family and work as a family unit, when financially pressed, parents hired out their children to employers on different places.

Extended Families and Child Custody

When African Americans were unable to care for their younger children, other kin raised them. When the Black Codes were passed in Mississippi right after the war, extended family tried to prevent orphaned children from being apprenticed to whites. Children benefited from residing with their relations, receiving food, clothing, and shelter. When grandmothers were able to provide for their grandchildren, the Freedmen's Bureau granted custody to them.[55] Freedwoman Viley Rodenheimer raised her grandson, John Long, after his mother died and his father abandoned him.[56] Another grandmother cared for her granddaughter after the death of the child's mother. The grandmother "ha[d] to work hard to take keer of it" because the child's father, a "respectable white man" residing in the nearby town, failed to help financially.[57]

Parents who supported adult daughters and their children felt that they were entitled to authority over the children. When Martha Johnson became ill, her father apprenticed her children to a white family.[58] Occasionally, poverty precluded the option of grandparents caring for both their own immediate family and their daughter's children. Harvey Whitehead asked the government to care for his wife's grandchildren because their mother was unable to raise them.[59]

Aunts and uncles also provided for their sibling's children when necessary. When Susan Washington deserted her baby, the child's uncle cared for the infant and became the child's legal guardian.[60] Aunts and uncles tried to gain custody of their orphaned nieces and nephews in order to end their apprenticeships to whites.[61] Laventa Leadbetter promised to provide for her niece, Polly, to ensure Polly's release from apprenticeship.[62] Success depended on intervention by the Freedmen's Bureau.

Aunts and uncles played a central part in the life of William Lee. While Lee's father and uncle served in the army, William, his siblings, his mother, his mother's sister Jackie Ann, his father's sister Ellen, and other relatives stayed at a government farm across the river from Vicksburg. When his mother and brothers died of measles, his aunts brought him to Vicksburg to be with his father, Benjamin Lee. In Vicksburg, he lived with his father and very soon acquired a stepmother, Winnie. William bitterly remembered his stepmother, who "would not feed me and beat me," a situation which worsened when his father went on maneuvers for three months. When his father returned and discovered his wife's flagrant adultery, he divorced her, retaining custody of his son. Upon Benjamin Lee's death, William Lee's aunt, Jackie Lee (who remained in Vicksburg after bringing William to his father), cared for him. Meanwhile, his uncle, Robert Lee, mustered out of the army. He left Vicksburg and returned to the plantation where the family had lived as slaves. When Robert Lee learned about the death of his brother in 1867, he sent for Jackie and William Lee to come live with him. According to William's statement in 1879, he "returned to the vicinity of his old home in Scott Co., Miss. and he has lived in said vicinity ever since."[63]

When sisters and brothers were old enough, they applied for guardianship of their younger orphaned siblings.[64] When her stepmother moved out to remarry, Caroline Cory recalled that she had "nothing more to do with us children and my older sister . . . came in and took charge of us."[65] Virginia Posey's sister raised her and when John Posey wanted to marry Virginia, he asked her sister for Virginia's hand in marriage.[66] In addition to providing a residence, brothers and sisters acted as protectors, protesting cruel treatment of their siblings by white employers.[67]

Most children lived with their kin through informal agreements rather than through any legal process. The courts only became involved in cases of apprenticing or pension rights. If the children's father had served in the army during the Civil War, their new guardian obtained the military pension for children of deceased military personnel. Louis Gardner and his wife, Laura, gained custody of Laura's brother and sister after their parents died. Because the children's father served as a private in the Union army, the government granted the military pension for minor children to Louis.[68] In the case of apprenticeships, siblings obtained legal custody for an apprenticed child only after they could prove family connection, often a difficult task because of the absence of legal records among slave families.[69] As with parents, kin also had to demonstrate financial ability to provide for the children. One Freedmen's Bureau agent reported that one sister wanted her siblings to stay with her, and that her husband "expressed a willingness to do for the children."[70]

Although extended kin ties involved blood relatives, close family friends (called "fictitious" kin by sociologists) also raised children.[71] African American parents who were unable to care for their own children sometimes entrusted them to a friend, rarely formalizing the arrangement through the courts. Minnia Jenkins cared for an orphan child from its infancy only to discover that the Mississippi probate court refused to recognize her as its guardian. The court seized the child and apprenticed it to a white man. Although Jenkins possessed little legal claim to the child, she explained that she loved it as much as a birth mother.[72] A white man threatened Emily McCrane and her husband with a "concealed revolver" because they refused to give him custody of an orphaned child that they were raising. The McCranes proved successful in their fight to retain the child.[73]

Care of the Elderly

Families tried to support the elderly. After emancipation, when older people ceased to be a productive part of the labor force, they expected their children to help support them. Parents perceived their children as social security because their own long years of work had failed to provide adequately for them in their old age.[74] Adult freedpeople bore responsibilities toward two generations: the generation following them and the one preceding them.[75] Adults accepted the double burden of providing for the welfare of both their parents and their children.[76]

Labor contracts listed African American over 60 years of age as dependents, indicating that other employed adult workers paid for their room and board. Usually, the employer deducted the expenses of maintaining nonworking kin from the payment of those who worked. Charles Eagley's mother "was very feeble and her said son furnished her all she required in food and clothing."[77] Adult men supported their own parents and occasionally their in-laws as well. One freedman was the main support of his five children, his wife (whose health prevented her from working for wages) and his mother-in-law, Ginny, who was too old to find "hire."[78]

After the war, the concern for economic security of elderly former slave men and women overshadowed their desire for economic opportunities as the harsh reality of wage labor without any provision for old age became apparent. Letters to the Freedmen's Bureau gave many examples of former masters who were unable or unwilling to even marginally support older former slaves. Planters abandoned them and forced them off their plantations.[79] The extended family tried to provide for this population. Freedmen's Bureau agents found a "general desire manifested by the Freedmen to care for their own relatives" but "when positive starvation threaten[ed] even the young and strong, they look[ed] to the Bureau for an asylum and relief for their former charges."[80] Such asylum occasionally meant institutionalization in a hospital for elderly or destitute African Americans, although such a drastic measure remained the exception.

Elderly African American women needed more governmental services than men. African Americans depended on the federal government for social services because the local governments in Mississippi refused to help. The Bureau established a new medical complex that included a hospital and orphanage in Lauderdale Springs for African Americans. By August 31, 1866, hospitals in Mississippi treated more adult African American women than men: 2,152 women to 1,742 men. Freedmen constantly requested that the Bureau provide transportation to these facilities for destitute or ailing freedpersons in Mississippi.[81]

In Mississippi the county boards of police held the responsibility of caring for poor people, but officials rarely spent money on African Americans, in part because the war depleted the funds of such boards. Whenever possible, state authorities tried to force the federal government to care for indigent African Americans, but the Freedmen's Bureau increasingly refused to help. Instead the Bureau insisted that the state of Mississippi should assume responsibility for their poor, sick, and destitute, regardless of color. Federal officials began to limit admission of African Americans into Freedmen's Bureau hospitals on the grounds that local Mississippi institutions ought to care for them.[82]

The situation of one ailing freedwoman who was taken to the board of police serves as an example of the problems of destitute African American women. The board promptly sent her to Lauderdale Hospital. Soon after, the board received a curt message from the Bureau ordering it to remove the woman from Lauderdale and assume her support. The Bureau expected the police board to "care for her in the same manner as white paupers." The county explained that it lacked a poorhouse in which to keep this woman, although probably the county wanted to keep their facility all white. Rather than continue the debate, the Freedmen's Bureau decided to compromise. They allowed the woman to remain at the Lauderdale hospital, but the board of police had to reimburse the hospital for her board.[83]

Race relations complicated the duties of freedpeople toward extended family. Mississippi whites did not want to use state funds to support destitute and elderly African Americans. Black families ultimately had to shoulder the burden. Family responsibilities included the support of unmarried pregnant daughters and physically or mentally handicapped children regardless of age. Families also took in orphaned children.

Maintenance of sick and destitute family members was only one of the profound changes within the family life of freedpeople. African Americans called on family in times of economic or emotional crisis and expected assistance. Such demands led to economic strains for struggling adult freedmen and women who were negotiating the new experience of free labor. The vast majority of freedmen and women were poor after the war and caring for other adults who were unable to work was difficult. On occasion, they tried to call upon the state for assistance but often found that solution unsatisfactory. Mostly they coped as well as they could while fulfilling their own obligations.

Family meant more than the nuclear family both in slavery and after the war. Extended kin were considered members of the family. The definition of family was fluid enough to include relatives on fairly distant branches of the family tree. Family members knew that they could count on support by becoming "family" even when that claim was quite tenuous. As with marriage, legality was not the only consideration; other informal ties were also included in the definition of family.

Family ties became the center of freed African American community life, which stretched out in increasingly wide concentric circles, ultimately supporting religious, political, and educational activities.

SEVEN

COMMUNITIES

"I lived within talking reach of them"[1]

Henry Young, a slave of Governor Charles Clark of Bolivar County, witnessed the wedding of Lucy and Thomas Brown. He and Thomas Brown left the plantation in 1863 to enlist in the army together; they served in Company B of the Fifty-third Infantry regiment of the United States Colored Troops in Vicksburg. Young kept in contact with Lucy Brown after the death of her husband, following her movements to different places and her acquaintance with a "man by the name of Reuben." He was unclear, or so he indicated to the pension examiner, about the exact nature of the relationship that existed between Lucy Brown and Reuben Kelly. Lewis Baker, another former slave of Governor Clark and also a member of the same company, also saw the wedding of Lucy and Thomas Brown while Thomas was still serving in the army. Baker also stayed in contact with Lucy after Thomas's death and reported that she lived with Reuben for several years after the end of the war. Such was the strength of the slave community that even the war could not completely destroy it. Lucy Brown's friends and neighbors shared many experiences with her, including slavery, the war, and their postwar attempts to protect each other in threatening interracial situations.

In 1879, Lucy Brown Kelly, her husband Reuben Kelly, and her daughter Clara Brown Hill lied to the special pension examiner about Lucy's marriage to Reuben. Fearing the loss of her military widow's pension for remarrying after the death of her husband Thomas Brown, they all claimed that Lucy Brown merely worked for Reuben Kelly as his live-in housekeeper and occasional field hand. The neighbors joined the conspiracy by obfuscating their testimony as much as possible without outright falsehoods. Those who knew that the couple were legally married but had not attended the ceremony cunningly told the examiner that they had not seen Lucy Brown married to Reuben Kelly. They also testified that they did not consider Brown and Kelly to be husband and wife. Lucy Brown lived her life within various communities of African Americans. Never isolated, she always resided in close proximity to friends and neighbors who knew about her and made up part of her world. When called upon, they commented on her "private" life with knowledge and precision.[2]

Communities in Slavery and Wartime

The world of African Americans on plantations expanded with the war. Local slave communities gradually changed into wider African American communities. On plantations during slavery, daily interactions with extended family members and fellow laborers helped to create a feeling of commonality among slaves. Relatives and friends shared the precious little private time that they had. Enslaved men and women developed a strong sense of identity apart from their white masters. After the war, common interests and goals strengthened collective efforts in religion and politics, widening the vision of freedpeople through contact with other African Americans. African Americans relied on collective activity, including political action, to preserve their freedom.

Before emancipation, slave plantations, particularly larger ones in Mississippi, evolved into places where a strong sense of community developed and where neighbors were sometimes also kin. Slave men and women worked together, spent the brief available leisure time with each other, and knew each others' lives intimately. Much current historical work explores "the world the slaves made."[3] African Americans who were raised on the same plantation shared both joyful and sad times. Former slave Andrew Walker lived on the same place as James Brown and his wife Martha. Although a small boy at the time, he recalled their marriage: "I was a dining room servant on the Edmond Randall plantation . . . and they were married in the white folks house by our marster Edmond Randall." Later Walker married their daughter and witnessed James Brown's "burying. He was buried right on the Randall plantation."[4]

The most immediate development of community occurred on individual plantations. Most slaves, however, often knew other slaves on neighboring plantations even though the need for passes from slave owners made travel difficult. The pension records indicate interplantation contact that was usually an outgrowth of abroad slave marriages but also occurred because of friendships. Lewis Allen lived approximately four miles from the plantation where Henry and Ann Patterson lived. Allen was "well acquainted with [Henry]. I used to visit the place and I know they lived together as man and wife."[5]

One historian has argued that the slave community may have been less cohesive than historians have portrayed because of slave marriages in which spouses lived on different plantations.[6] These marriages actually broadened the sense of commonality. These arrangements allowed glimpses of other plantations and of their African American residents. One former slave described a slave husband's visits to his wife on another plantation as "just the same as one of the people on the place."[7] A cross-plantation husband became part of two slave communities: his wife's and his own. When a husband visited his wife once or twice a week and stayed over on weekends, he brought information about his own plantation. Through these men, residents of different plantations exchanged news.

Ironically, even familial connections between planters fostered wider slave communities. As a former slave explained, "I know Elizabeth Fletcher. . . . She was a slave of Mr. Sam Duncan, and I was a slave of his brother Steven Duncan. They lived about five miles from each other, but we colored people visited each other on Sundays."[8] When extended members of the same family owned neighboring plantations, visiting between families included bringing at least a slave carriage driver and possibly a domestic slave onto the plantation. Former slave Minerva Weeks knew fellow slave Louisa Williams because Weeks provided child care for her mistress, Mrs. Baldwin, and Louisa worked as a domestic slave for Mrs. Baldwin's sister. When Mrs. Baldwin "visited her sister," Weeks accompanied her and the two house slaves became friendly.[9] When Richard Cordell married the widow Barrett's daughter, he administered his mother-in-law's plantation. Thus, according to one freedperson, "the Cordell and Barrett plantations joined and there was an acquaintance kept up by the people servants of both places." Peter Dorsey "live[d] on the Cordell place, but he sometimes visited the Barrett place." Because of cross-plantation slave marriages and the visits of domestic slaves when their masters and mistresses socialized, slave men and women developed networks that continued after emancipation. While living on the Cordell place, Dorsey became acquainted with Minerva and Anderson Martin who resided as slaves at the Barrett place. During his army service, Dorsey saw Minerva in Jackson, Mississippi. He renewed his friendship, saw her "daily," and met her new spouse.[10]

Those friendships formed during slavery sometimes lasted a lifetime. African American men continued their plantation relationships when they ran away together to the Union lines. Thomas Richardson recalled that many slave men and women "left the plantation at the same time and went to Vicksburg, Mississippi."[11] Men from the same plantations or vicinity enlisted in the United States Colored Troops, sometimes in the same company within a regiment. While enslaved, Samuel Wilkins and Nathaniel Foreman lived on the same plantation, and even courted the same woman (who eventually married Wilkins). Later, Wilkins and Foreman served together as privates in the same company and Wilkins attended Foreman's marriage. [12] As one freedman explained, "Ever since I can remember I have known James Gray. Before the war we both belonged to the same man and we enlisted together in Co. M, USCHA [United States Colored Heavy Artillery] and were mustered out at the same time and all the time after the war up to his death I saw him every month and sometimes two or three times a month."[13] Although different masters owned Bias Clarke and Henry Patterson, Clarke knew Patterson during slavery. Placed together in a contraband camp with their families, the two men decided to join the Union army. They left their wives and "came on over here [to Vicksburg] and enlisted the same day and were placed in the same company and regiment."[14] Pension records show the length of relationships. James Williams, who served in the fifth regiment of the United States Heavy Artillery with Hapless Nash, swore on a pension request that he had known Nash's wife, Violet, for twenty-five years, essentially all his life. Williams's mother acted as midwife to Violet Nash.[15]

Kinship bonds also linked soldiers together. Archie Hunt left with his brothers to follow the Union soldiers. John J. Johnson and his uncle "served together and tented and messed together till we were mustered out." Johnson claimed knowledge of his uncle's intimate relationships, as he explained: "I was right with him all the time, and would have known it if he had married while in the army or lived with any woman."[16]

New friendships between men also developed in the army, strengthened by sharing common military experiences. Frank Jackson met James Johnson in the army—"I knew him all through our term of service," stated Jackson. "My association with him was of such a character that I knew most if not all of his business matters." The two men continued to live close to each other after the war, as did their regimental comrade Richmond Pipes. After mustering out, Pipes and Johnson "both came to Coahoma Co., Miss." to the same plantation. Pipes attended Johnson's marriage ceremony in 1867.[17] Similarly, Cales Hamilton and Henry Turner served together in the army and became reunited when Hamilton moved to the same plantation. They resided with their families "under the same roof" because their "houses were adjoining." In 1870, both couples moved to the same plantation and again "lived in adjoining houses" for several years.[18] Such closeness in the army led Louis Caston to make an intimate request of his comrade Henry Kinnehue, who was in the same regiment and company. According to Caston's wife Annie Caston, her late husband had asked Kinnehue to "take care of [her]" after his death "and make [her] his wife and do by [her] as he had until death parted [them]." Eventually, the couple married.[19]

Just as their husbands formed new relationships in the army, freed-women also made new acquaintances when they moved to cities or con-traband camps from plantations. Although their war experiences afforded African American women who fled plantations fewer opportunities for close contact with plantation friends and family than those maintained by their military husbands, female slave friendships also existed during the war. Friends Dora Hinton and Harriet Innis witnessed Frances Innis's slave marriage to Gadby Innis, visited Gadby when he became sick while in the army, and attended his burial.[20] When slave women accompanied other slaves who left the plantations, the groups of women tended to stay in closer proximity to each other than did women who left on their own.[21]

Women's war experiences introduced them to new female acquain-tances. Josephine Wilson met Margaret Williams when they "were both corralled . . . by the federal soldiers and taken up to Youngs Point," Loui-siana. They both moved to Vicksburg and Wilson attended Williams's marriage to a soldier in the Fifty-third Infantry. A laundress for the Fifty-third, Wilson kept close contact with Williams during the war by remain-ing "with the regiment pretty much until it was mustered out." After the death of Williams's husband, she and Wilson moved to Louisiana, where they still lived at the turn of the century.[22] After "they had all fled from the plantation and the men had gone to the army," Laura West moved to Sarah Harris's boardinghouse in Natchez. After her soldier husband's death, West "hired out to sew . . . but always continued to come back" to Harris's house. When Laura West married Henry Clay, she held the cer-emony in Harris's father-in-law's house "when the minister stopped."[23] Regardless of whether the army wives and soldiers stayed in the cities or returned to plantations after the war, their wartime contacts with other African Americans considerably widened their social landscape.

Postwar Plantation Communities

Although the housing patterns of freedpeople revealed the breakup of the slave communities, they also demonstrate that the transition was

gradual rather than abrupt. As with the demise of the gang system in labor, such a shift in housing represented a movement away from close
physical proximity to other African Americans in the quarters and from
whites.[24] Interactions between freedpeople continued on plantations after
the Civil War, although they changed as the housing patterns of freedpeople began to change from slave quarters to more separate tenant cabins. Because few African Americans owned their own land, they either
rented housing from whites or obtained lodging as partial payment for
plantation labor.[25] During and immediately after the war, newly freed people lived in existing housing if it survived the devastation of the war, even
though freedmen preferred not to reside in the old slave quarters. As one
Freedmen's Bureau agent reported, the freedpeople lived in a "comfortable frame cabin, of one room. . . . The quarters are the same that were
occupied before the war, and are, for the most part, well shaded and laid
out."[26] Former slaves used the term "quarters" to describe their housing,
which referred to "a row of house[s] where the colored people lived."[27]
The quarters sometimes consisted of attached houses. As late as 1889,
pension examiner A. F. Posey wrote that "for years after the war, and at
the present, many plantations, especially the smaller ones, are rented to
negro men who carry on the farming by hired labor, and occupy with
different families the double cabins used in 'slavery times.'"[28] Because they
were familiar with double houses, freed families and their friends continued to build and occupy this style of housing. When federal troops placed
former Mississippi slaves on Paw Paw Island, freedman Albert Dickson
built a cabin for Maria Clark and her grown daughter. Dickson designed
the cabin "to be occupied by the two families jointly."[29]

For women who were without kin or a man, life in joint cabins may
have seemed more inviting than to men. According to historians, family
men demanded individual cabins and an end to the communal quarters.
In contrast, Julia McCaskell, a freedwoman who managed to acquire her
own land, recalled that she "did not feel secure living alone with my daughter in the woods without some man person about the place." McCaskell
ultimately solved her isolation by adding a shed to her cabin and having
an older male worker reside there.[30] With the spread of sharecropping
and the demise of gang labor, individual cabins spaced farther apart became more common, although some cabins continued to be in close proximity or actually attached.[31]

After the war, African Americans became more mobile than they had
been as slaves. They frequently visited other plantations, although white
employers tried to restrict these journeys, particularly during working

hours. Employer John Simmons specified in his contract that "the employees will receive no visitors during working hours."[32] Employers also wanted to maintain some control over the leisure time of their employees. Gatherings of African Americans concerned whites because such assemblies might lead to collective labor actions or political activity. Freedmen's Bureau agents accused employers of "discharging men and women for attending public meetings."[33] Most freedpeople visited other local plantations on Sundays to attend church, and on holidays.[34] Maggy Gilman was unusual in obtaining an annual vacation with wages. Her employer agreed to give her "two weeks time to herself during the year for the purposes of visiting her friends."[35]

As in other close-knit communities, calling at a person's home allowed friends to check on the health of a sick friend, bring food, examine any new household purchases, and investigate any changes in the household. The pension file of Julia McCaskill showed the degree of intimacy that could be gained through regular visiting. Albert Duvall knew Julia McCaskill before the war and rented land from her in the late 1860s. He dropped by for social calls and he knew the layout of the rooms, even the placement of her beds. Through this knowledge and other information, he deduced that she was not cohabiting with a man.[36] Very little remained safe from the scrutiny of observant eyes. Harvey Dear knew personal details of the life of his friend Henry Smith. Dear "was living in the quarters on the Offutt Buck place in Jan. 1867 when Millie came then, and lived with Henry Smith." Dear was emphatic about the nature of Smith's relationship with Millie, "I know they slept together, for I saw them in bed together many a time; many a time I would go there to call him in the morning, and he would tell me to come in, and I would go in, and saw them in bed together."[37]

Plantation networks continued to operate after the war, and its members continued to share information. Weddings brought people together and provided topics for months afterwards because they involved gossipy details about clothing, food, decoration, who attended and, equally important, who did not attend and why. Two workers on Somerset Place in Copiah County recalled the day that fellow workers Martha McLaurin and Madison Washington married in 1869. Although they "were not exactly at the marriage ceremony, they were invited to attend and were within a short distance from the place and saw the guests going and coming from the wedding. They saw the preacher Ned Johnson go to perform the marriage ceremony and saw almost as much as if they had been actual eye witnesses to the ceremony."[38] When James Johnson married Martha Johnson who lived on a neighboring plantation, "40 or 50 person" attended, including Johnson's close army buddy Richmond Pipes and the wife of his other comrade, Frank Jackson. The wedding was memorable. The African American preacher that was hired to officiate was prevented from performing the ceremony when "high water and loss of his skiff cut him off from crossing the creek." Another freedwoman recalled the story even though she did not attend; because the flood kept the minister from coming, she "heard all about it. They were married by Squire Champion, a white man. It was generally talked of on the plantation."[39]

Hiring a white preacher to conduct a wedding ceremony for an African American couple, much more common before the war than after, was only one of an infinite number of topics such as love affairs, births, and deaths that were fair game for discussion among plantation workers. Talking was the most popular form of entertainment during slavery and afterward.[40] People knew each other's business, particularly details of a person's romantic attachments even when one could not personally visit the parties in question. As in the case of freedwoman Lucy Brown, the community even knew when couples were trying to be secretive about their relationship. During slavery, Julia Thomas's affair with a man from another plantation received quite a lot of attention. A freedwoman who resided on the same plantation as Julia recalled, "[I]t was the talk among the people on the place that Nick was slipping to see Julia and staying with her as much as he could."[41] After the war, such discussions continued, as freedman Albert Duvall stated, "such things are generally known when a woman lives with a man and is not married."[42] Talking about sexual conduct also provided a way for African Americans to try to control what they considered to be undesirable behavior. Talbert Royal's wife learned about her husband's infidelity "through the neighbors," who kept a watchful eye out for wrongdoing and informed spouses in order to stop philandering.[43]

Within the comfortable web of communities, African American women depended on other women for support and comfort as well as information and conversation. Female bonds during slavery grew stronger as women worked together in gangs, particularly the trash gangs, where pregnant women performed lighter duties.[44] After the war, African American women helped each other in the fields when they could and even protected each other from their employers if necessary. When Mary Neill spanked her child, her employer Thomas Purcell ordered her away from the house because of the noise of the child's cries. Purcell called Neill a "bitch" and while holding his pistol, threatened to shoot her. To prevent any injury to Neill, "other women interfered [and] she got away."[45]

As the pension records show, freedwomen established long-lasting relationships with each other. Women served as witnesses for each other when they tried to obtain their husbands' pensions from the government. In order to act as witnesses, a person must have known the claimant for ten years.[46] Louisa Cummings testified that Sarah T. Foster was the widow of W. W. Foster and entitled to his bounty. Cummings's husband served in the same army unit as Foster's spouse. Cummings "had known [the] claimant since she was quite young." Moreover, Cummings attended Foster's wedding.[47] Caroline Christian knew Mary Brown "from childhood." She attended Brown's slave wedding in the late 1850s and came to the nuptials with her second husband. Additionally, Brown lived near other close female friends whom she had known during slavery.[48]

Women's ties with each other became most significant during specific female gender-related experiences, such as pregnancies. A few labor contracts indicate that at any given time on larger plantations several women were pregnant or nursing their babies. In August 1865, on Alex Hamilton's plantation in Lowndes County, five women were breastfeeding their children.[49] On James Banks's place, five women, ranging in ages from 20 to 40, were "suckling" their babies, and five women, the youngest of whom was 17, were pregnant. While she was living on Banks's place, pregnant 17-year-old Rosetta knew women she was able to confide in, and they probably helped her feel less apprehensive about the changes in her body and her psychological state.[50]

When the babies began to arrive, midwives cared for both the babies and the mothers. Among women, midwives possessed a special status because they aided women during the life-threatening and life-giving experience of childbirth.[51] The pension records and Works Progress Administration slave narratives provide many examples of African American women helping each other during childbirth.[52] Although some African American women healers treated both men and women with roots and herbs, other African American women specialized in midwifery.[53] During slavery, midwives worked in other capacities on the plantation. Peggy Fisher cooked for her owners while acting as a slave midwife.[54] At age 15, Rena Clarke began midwifery, concentrating on healing "women troubles." She knew very little about the sicknesses that afflicted men, and besides she argued, "it always looked lak dey could take care of dyselves anyhow."[55] African American women trusted midwives both for their technical skills and their knowledge of the spiritual world. Midwives oversaw the health of the babies, in body and in soul. After Rena Clarke washed and dressed a baby, she "would tie a mole's right foot around his neck" in order to ensure "good health . . . and good luck." Clarke recommended "a mixture of soot and sugar from the tenth brick of the chimney" for colic. A small pouch of asafetida worn around the neck prevented measles, mumps, and other childhood illnesses.[56]

If a midwife was unavailable, other women served as attendants at the delivery so that the woman would have company and be provided with encouragement or assistance. While Elizabeth Ellison testified on her pension application that she was unable to furnish evidence of a midwife to testify to the birth of her children, (to prove that the children deserved a military pension), she could give "the testimony of the nurse who attended her on the occasion." The nurse was a fellow slave, Matilda Guy, who swore that she "was at the birth of said child, and assisted in nursing the mother and child during the sickness of the mother." The relationship between Guy and Ellison evidently continued after the war, because Guy also stated that she spent time with the family after the birth of the child.[57] Jane Porter and Alethe Smith witnessed the marriage of Harriet Johnson and were "present at [the] birth" of her children. No midwife is mentioned in the pension file.[58] The same situation appeared in the file of Matilda Jones; Eliza Lee and Laura Jones "were present at the birth of the child" and midwife testimony was said to be absent. Thus, even without a midwife, women relied on female companionship during labor.[59] Just as women aided each other during childbirth, they also tended to each other at the end of life. One freedwoman recalled, "I was present when Rhoda was on her death bed and waited on her."[60]

Women confided in each other, especially about their relationships with men. When Nathaniel Foreman reassured the young Eliza Jones that he was unattached and able to marry her, he also confessed to her that "the woman he used to have" was Marinda Wilkins. He implied that the liaison with Wilkins had ended. Jones immediately sought out Wilkins, who confirmed Foreman's assurances by explaining, "she was the wife of Saml Wilkins and had been for years. That Foreman courted her before the war but they were never married." Reassured, Eliza Jones married Foreman and lived with him until his death.[61] Mary Jordan recalled that Rosa Duncan, upset by her husband's Joe's infidelity "talked to me many times about how Joe Duncan had treated her."[62]

Except in gender-specific circumstances, such as childbirth, pension records suggest that women were not as close with their female network of unrelated individuals as they were with male or female kin. Freedwomen lived in a highly heterosexual world of family, kin, and work. Close female friendships coexisted with male-female relationships and to some extent substituted when there was no specific man or kin in women's lives. For example, Peggy Anderson remained in Vicksburg after the war and after the death of her soldier husband, she resided in Rachel McNeill's house. Anderson found employment in other places, but "she left her things at [McNeill's] house and when not too far away came there to stay over Sunday." McNeill testified that there was no man in Anderson's life at that time, and further, "when at my house she was always slept in the same bed with me and there was no man in it at any time." Although no evidence exists that these women engaged in sexual activity, they enjoyed a close friendship that afforded Anderson a haven from work and a family-like environment.[63] Similarly, Malvina Bird lived with and testified to sharing a bed for four years with Julia McCaskell in rural Mississippi after McCaskell's husband died.[64]

Married women or women who were cohabiting with a man acted as intermediaries between the private female world and men. With their spouses acting as conduits, men became privy to knowledge about other women that they were unlikely to gain directly. Thus, Lewis Plummer knew that Helen Thomas "had some private internal female disease" because his wife told him. Helen Thomas would generally not have discussed her condition with an unrelated male with whom she was not intimate.[65] Men probably shared this type of information with other men. Men chatted with each other and, just as women talked about men, men speculated on the lives of certain women. Arthur Jackson recalled a group of males speculating about why the widow Martha Johnson never remarried.[66]

African American women saw their lives inextricably linked to those of African American men, and they felt connected to wider communities. Race intensified this sense of shared identity between men and women. Freedwomen also shared work experiences, physical space, and close kin ties to men. After the war, African American women conceptualized the implications of gender difference in certain areas (such as being more reticent about being seen as sexually aggressive) even when they shared some similar experiences with men. This is not to say that gender was not an important distinction, but it did not always play out in contested ways or influence all areas of life.

Because both men and women performed field labor after emancipation, the sphere of work outside the home included both men and women, rather than being confined to only men. The houses of freedpeople were too small to allow separation of physical space between men and women. Rural African Americans lived in a cabin consisting of only one or two rooms, sometimes attached to another cabin. Household activities were done in full view of all the family rather than relegated to a closed-off place such as a kitchen or laundry room. Such openness precluded a romanticized view of women's domestic labor or gender differences. Private female or male space within the home was nonexistent for freedpeople who lived on plantations.

The absence of gendered vocabulary in the testimony in the pension files when individuals discussed events and concepts of time suggests that freedmen and freedwomen held similar views of the world of work. Shared slave culture and common ties strengthened their perceptions but also, as with other rural peoples, their agricultural labor was integral to their lives. Men and women noted an important event in the same ways; they used the Civil War as a point of reference or related an event's proximity to natural disasters. Alice Brown assisted at the births of Rosanna Hines's children, and connected each birth: "Lucy was born shortly after the soldiers was discharged from the army and come home. That Robert was born shortly after Big [probably Tombigbee River] over flow of all the bottom land was cover[ed] with water."[67] To remember children's ages, men and women both used work as a reference point.

Such commonality failed to prevent occasional discord between individual African Americans. Although women and men argued about some of the same issues, other concerns were gender specific. White employers tried to minimize arguments between workers in order to ensure a well-disciplined work force. One contract specified that, "No Negroes shall enter the house of another without the consent of the occupant. No quarreling, contention, or fighting allowed among the laborers."[68] Just as tensions had existed between slaves, disagreements surfaced among freedpeople after the war. Although they most often complained to Freedmen's Bureau agents about white injustices, African Americans occasionally brought grievances against each other. Generally freedpeople may have preferred to work out such grievances themselves without outside interference.

The Freedmen's Bureau records contain complaints about damage caused by livestock, which freedpeople grazed openly rather than inside fences. Rebecca Flournoy and Anderson Forrister quarreled because Flournoy continually allowed her mule to run through Forrister's crops. One day Forrister kicked the mule, which made Flournoy furious. She told Forrister he was "a low lived dirty dog." According to Forrister, Flournoy struck him over the head with a stick. Flournoy retaliated by accusing Forrister of hitting her with an axe handle.[69] New economic relationships produced new tensions, including the lack of payment by African American employers or subcontractors.[70] When freedman Bob Harrison accused Celia Harrison of not working, he called her a "bitch" and she called him "a red eyed scoundrel."[71]

A more serious conflict in the Freedmen Bureau's records concerned the one complaint of rape against an African American man brought by an African American woman. The charge brought by Catherine Harkins against Sam Hughes helps explain why freedwomen might have been reluctant to bring complaints of rape against African American men. Although Hughes was convicted and sentenced to life in prison, the trial turned into a humiliating experience for Harkins. The defendant's lawyer tried to prove that Harkins was an immoral woman and asked her "if it felt good." Harkins "replied that it could not feel good when she was forced."[72] African American women may have preferred to depend on the African American community to deal with rape or attempted rape by African American men rather than on the legal system.

African American women fought with each other over family concerns. Quarrels between women sometimes started over their children. Sexual competition and friction between women also caused conflict. Mary Jane Royal argued with both her husband and Lizzie Jones over his affair with Jones. When Jones "laid two of her children to my husband," Mary Royal "told her she was such a whore that she could not tell what briar had scratched her."[73] Lea Wilson was accused of assaulting another woman and having an affair with the woman's husband.[74] As these examples suggest, when passions overheated, fights between women became physical.[75] Freedwomen were both the victims of violence and, sometimes, the perpetrators. Like men, they occasionally resorted to physical methods to resolve conflict, fighting with their fists and inflicting wounds with sticks and knives.[76]

Widening Communities: Religion and Politics

Sporadic conflict between plantation freedpeople failed to hamper African Americans from meeting together for religious services and political events. Such occasions sometimes crossed plantations and gave newly freed people a chance to socialize more broadly with neighbors. After the war, African Americans established their own places of worship, most often Baptist- or Methodist-influenced.[77] They attended church services in a cabin or held outside prayer meetings separate from the services of their former masters and other whites. Such places became havens for political activities that freedpeople wanted to keep private.

Religion played a significant part in the lives of African Americans; it provided individuals with a means of coping with a frequently harsh world while it strengthened community ties. Religion offered an emotional release and a view of the world that gave solace and strength. Slaves created a religious creed that differed from that of their masters. With the encouragement of owners, white ministers preached a hierarchical theology that exhorted slaves to be obedient to their owners just as masters needed to be subservient to God. In spite of these teachings, slaves worshipped together privately, led by African American preachers. In discussing Christianity, historian Eugene Genovese concluded, "when the black slaves of the New World made it their own, they transformed it into a religion of resistance—not often of revolutionary defiance, but of a spiritual resistance that accepted the limits of the politically possible."[78]

Although African American women participated in religious activities, they almost never became ministers.[79] Descriptions of religious services implied that African American women often became more fervent than men. When the preacher started speaking, the audience, especially the women, would often begin "stamping their feet, accompanied by a swaying of their bodies and a humming sound proceeding from their closed lips," with freedwomen "jumping and pitching and hollering and the men holding them."[80]

The entire community encouraged and celebrated an individual's salvation. One girl informed her white teacher that "Ann's come through. An' she's shouted for three days, an' she can't hold her baby she's dat full o' glory, she don' eat a bite." When the teacher visited Ann, who was still repeating "glory, glory", the teacher, impressed by the placid look on Ann's face, interpreted it as a sign of inner peace with God. The teacher reported that "from the quarters came a shout of 'Hallelujah. Ann's cum through.'"[81]

Religious services forged vital links within the freed African American community.[82] Ministers read letters during services from former enslaved men and women wanting to know about family members who had been separated during slavery.[83] Religious services gave women an opportunity to wear their prettier dresses and to sit a while without worrying about field or domestic chores. Social life often centered around the church. Laura Ford met her future husband "at a meetin' one Sunday."[84]

As with religion, political activity involved and strengthened community life. During Reconstruction, freedpeople used the church, the African American institution least controlled by whites, to promote political activism. Loyal Leagues that were formed to support the Republican party held "social gathering[s]" with dancing and socializing in churches and schools.[85] In at least one Mississippi community, freedpeople gathered at a church and walked to the local polling place.[86]

Women and children marched with men in these parades. They provided moral support and some protection for the freedmen who were planning to vote. African American men discovered that voting Republican was a dangerous task in Mississippi because it represented the most potent example of emancipation. Although many whites resented it when freedpeople acted outside the confines of their control and even tried to keep them from praying or attending schools, they most fiercely resisted the access of African American men to political power. The Ku Klux Klan and other vigilante groups targeted politically active Republican African Americans and whites who favored equal rights. Political activity, including office holding, political leadership, and voting, reinforced gender differences along more conventional middle-class lines.

Historians have argued that the military service of African American troops became the main justification for African American male suffrage.[87] Southern and northern African Americans, including such notables as abolitionist Frederick Douglass, agitated for the enfranchisement of African American men and for equal rights for freedpeople. Frederick Douglass argued, "Once let the black man get upon his person the brass letters, U.S.; let him get an eagle on his button, and a musket on his shoulder and bullets in his pocket, and there is no power on earth which can deny that he has earned the right to citizenship in the United States."[88] Acting as a source of pride to African Americans for decades to come, the role of African American soldiers in the Civil War encouraged Abraham Lincoln and other white Republicans to support at least limited African American male suffrage. As Secretary of the Treasury Salmon P. Chase stated, "I find that almost all who are willing to have colored men fight are willing to have them vote." Lincoln favored African American male "suffrage on the basis of intelligence and military service."[89]

The argument, a common one in Western societies, that rationalized granting suffrage for military service automatically excluded African American women from suffrage consideration. Exclusion of women from the vote seemed logical to both political parties. Neither party wanted to give the vote to women, African American or white. It is likely that Republican lawmakers anticipated that although African American women would have voted Republican, southern and many northern white women would cast their ballots for Democrats. Even northern radical Republicans could not justify giving the vote to both African American men and women while excluding white women. Moreover, the failure of women's suffrage to win state referenda across the country also influenced the decision of Congress. Democratic candidates tied women's suffrage to miscegenation by arguing that voting raised the possibility that white women would intermingle with African American men at polling places and other public places.[90]

African American loyalty to the party of Lincoln gave the Republican-controlled U. S. Congress sufficient incentive to enact African American male suffrage through the Fourteenth and Fifteenth Amendments.[91] Ultimately Congress forced former Confederate states to accept African American male suffrage by requiring ratification of the amendments to the Constitution as a condition for gaining readmittance into the Union. Some supporters of women's suffrage such as Susan B. Anthony and Elizabeth Cady Stanton opposed the Fourteenth and Fifteenth Amendments because, for the first time, the amendments explicitly tied suffrage to gender in the Constitution. Although the federal government forced whites to accept African American male suffrage, most white Democrats in Mississippi resisted this change in the political landscape.[92]

Despite the opposition African American men and women faced when they became politically active in Mississippi, they aligned themselves with the Republican party. Blacks and whites established a biracial Republican party in September of 1867. Blacks registered to vote for the constitutional convention to be held in the fall. According to historian Vernon Wharton, in 1869 in Mississippi "the Republican party included . . . ninety percent of the more than one hundred thousand registered Negro voters."[93] Support for the Republicans empowered African Americans in their quest for autonomy from whites, an issue of particular importance because of their former slave status. Through activity in the Republican party, African Americans repudiated their former masters and their status as slaves and asserted their equality with whites by advocating civil rights.

African Americans believed that their affiliation with the Republican party would help them achieve land ownership and an independent financial base, education to enable their children to better themselves, and the establishment of a government that could destroy the barriers of race that southern whites in Mississippi had reestablished with the Black Codes after the war.[94] Advocacy of the Republican party rested on much more than a sentimentalized view of the political party that had supported their freedom. Republicans in the U. S. Congress passed the Thirteenth Amendment that freed the slaves, sponsored legislation that permitted African American men to lease forty acres of land, guaranteed African American male suffrage through the Fourteenth and Fifteenth Amendments, protected civil rights, and overturned the Black Codes with the passage of the Civil Rights Act of 1866.[95]

In contrast, when the Mississippi Democrats controlled the Mississippi legislature immediately after the war, they tried to ensure that the economic, political, and social status of African Americans remained as close to their status under slavery as possible. In 1865 the legislators, fearful of the African American population, which outnumbered whites, passed some of the most harsh post-emancipation laws of any southern state. These laws set the context for a number of African American political struggles within the state. The laws prohibited African Americans from most forms of land ownership or rental (particularly in rural areas), granted former masters preference in apprenticing African American children, opposed the establishment of schools for former slaves, and supported strict enforcement of vagrancy laws.

Such policies by the Democrats helped cement African American loyalty to the Republican Party, and there was no gender gap in that loyalty. Sensing that under the Republicans the political situation for African Americans would improve and there would be far less legal threat to their families, African American women in Mississippi endorsed the Republicanism of their men. As one northerner noted, "The colored women formed a line of one hundred or more, and ran up and down near the line of voters, saying 'Now Sandy, if you don't vote de radical ticket I won't live wid ye.' 'Now Jack, ef you don' vote for Lincum's men I'll leave ye.'" According to one northern woman in Mississippi after the war, "[T]he democrats declared they would have gained the day, if it hadn't been for the women."[96] Although this statement underestimated the support of African American men for the Republican party, it demonstrated the fervor with which freedwomen supported the Republicans.[97] African Americans in Yazoo County supported the Grand Old Party in the 1868 presidential election by wearing badges picturing Ulysses S. Grant and his running mate. According to northerner Albert Morgan, who lived in the county, African American men occasionally became wary about displaying the badges in front of their white employers. In those cases, their wives donned them, and "if . . . the husband refused to surrender it," the wife would "buy, beg, or borrow one, and . . . wear it openly, in defiance of husband, master, mistress, or overseer." These buttons acted as a constant reminder to whites of the political independence of former slaves because "the white man's concubine, the mistress' maid, and their cook were liable to appear in the family circle any day with 'Grant's picture' upon their breasts."[98] The caution African American men exercised about flashing a Grant button stemmed from a painfully realistic assessment of the physical risk of being too politically outspoken. Because southern whites viewed them as much less of a threat, especially because they did not vote, African American women could afford to be more politically assertive in the workplace.

Historian Elsa Barkley Brown argues that women's insistence on the Republican party activism of their men was based on a shared vision of "collective autonomy" that rejected the liberal ideal of individual achievement. According to Barkley Brown, freedpeople "claimed black men's enfranchisement as a new freedom which they had all won and operated on the assumption that it belonged not to individual men but to the community and as such they had and took a stake in determining how it would be cast."[99] Similarly, Gerald Jaynes argues "that the freedmen's notion of a *right* to the land was communal, based upon a history of group exploitation" even though the land would not be communally owned. Thus African Americans saw land ownership in a political rather than in a solely private context.[100] Such a belief reinforced their support of the Republican party.

Denial of the vote to women probably reinforced the belief of freedwomen that their newly won freedoms were best sustained through African American communities. In a world with no direct access to political or economic power, the institutions of family and community, regardless of their imperfections, became a major outlet for political concerns for Mississippi's African American women. Yet the lack of suffrage also curbed the formation of freedwomen's own relationships to the nation-state as citizens. African American women saw themselves aided by the strengthening of the African American male position that gave men the possibility of offering more legal protection to women. On the local level, when African American men sat on juries and became sheriffs, they were in a better position to ensure justice for African American men and women.

Conclusion

Their support for the Republican party should not suggest that freedwomen blindly followed their men or that concerns stemming from race were larger factors than gender issues. Gender and race were interconnected in the lives of African American women and were influenced by a myriad of social, economic, and political conditions. Such variables played out differently for men and women even if the resulting actions such as getting out the vote for the Republicans were the same. African American women formulated their problems and the political and economic solutions in terms of their former status as slave women. The context of their desire for change stemmed from a need for a clear delineation from slavery, but this desire was also gendered.

Although women shared the same political aspirations as their men, they emphasized different factors. Their political goals summarize the main topics and themes discussed in this work. Political action helped clarify what African American women and their families expected from their emancipation. The meanings of freedom included economic security and a more distinct personal and family life removed from white interference.

Although African American women gained fewer legal rights than men from the policies of the Republican party, they obtained much that had been previously denied them during slavery. Like their men, they believed that land ownership would lead to economic independence. Both men and women believed that farming would provide sufficient income to allow men to support their wives. For newly freed women gaining more time for their families was a more pressing concern than it was for the men. Ideally, land ownership would enable African American women to schedule their own familial domestic chores and agricultural labor rather than whites determining those decisions. Land ownership would also lessen the contact of freedwomen with white men and therefore decrease African American women's chances of sexual assault or harassment by white employers.[101] After emancipation, resistance to an overseer in the fields resulted, in part, in a desire to keep him away from African American women. Thus even the political fight for land touched issues of sexual autonomy.[102]

Moving from one's slave plantation also symbolized freedom because the mobility of slaves had been quite restricted. After the war, mobility, family, and work became increasingly interrelated. Mobility was tied to making choices for the family and to autonomy from individual white employers. The ability to travel allowed both the reunification of slave families and the possibility of finding a job with higher wages. This movement was a political issue; whites tried to legislate against it by passing vagrancy laws. Many African American men and women moved yearly or every couple of years to find employment or better opportunities. According to historian Gavin Wright, "[A] study of four Mississippi plantations during the years 1871 to 1874 shows that between 27 and 56 percent of the labor force was new in each year."[103] After the war, women typically moved with male partners, kin, or friends to different places.

Issues of public and private life were never far from the surface when African Americans considered what changes emancipation could bring. The tension between what was considered public and what was private belied an ambivalence in women's attitude toward the state regardless of African American enthusiasm for the Republican party. Freedpeople supported the state when it promoted their meanings of freedom. Although they supported state intervention on behalf of racial equity, freedpeople tried to keep certain aspects of their lives private. Unwanted interference in intimate relations—first by the military and later by pension examiners —led to an uneasiness about certain aspects of white-controlled law. Only rarely did African American women and men resort to the Freedmen's Bureau and state intervention in cases of marital discord. They preferred to keep aspects of their private lives removed from federal interference and especially from whites. Given their experiences during slavery, freedpeople held few illusions about the paternalism of whites. They understood the extent to which paternalism and control were interconnected.

Within the overlapping spaces of public and private, freedom became defined in gendered terms. The surnames of freedpeople symbolized freedom but they also reflected the new legal status given to freedmen. The state made African American men the legal head of their families. Freedwomen and children adopted the surname of the male member of the family. Although African American men had responsibility for their families they could not exercise the authority that white men of privilege had over their families. White employers did not allow freedmen to interfere in the labor conditions of their wives.

The discussions of the morality of African Americans exemplified the gendered nature of the meanings of freedom as well a struggle for the private sphere that entered the political realm. Freedom became contested as African Americans entered the white-coded definitions of marriage and morality. After the war Mississippi whites tried to use their power to negate African American definitions of emancipation. Whites exaggerated the immorality of African American women in order to justify their efforts to control their labor and private lives. As African Americans demanded political power for their men, whites more often portrayed African American men as sexually aggressive rapists to undercut their political influence. Reconstruction marked the first time that white perceptions of

African American sexuality informed public policy. Discussions by white pension examiners of African American widows foreshadowed late–twentieth-century welfare debates.

Traditionally, historians debate the successes and failures of Reconstruction in male terms. The successes include the ability of African American males to vote and hold office and their ascendancy to the head of the household. Failures include the inability of African Americans to own land, which made a solid economic base impossible. When we also look at women, we see that the victories for African Americans included the ability to establish greater boundaries between what Thomas C. Holt called the "interiors and exteriors" of people's lives. For the newly freed people, wrenching control away from whites meant making decisions about work, families, and communities that women as well as men helped make. Although the successes were incomplete in the end, African American women and men gained more independence in the workplace and within their families than they managed to obtain during slavery.

NOTES

Preface

1. Introduction by Thomas C. Holt in *The State of Afro-American History: Past, Present, and Future*, ed. Darlene Clark Hine (Baton Rouge: Louisiana State University Press, 1986), 6.

2. Ada Hurtado, "Relating to Privilege: Seduction and Rejection in the Subordination of White Women and Women of Color," *Signs* 14 (Summer 1989): 849.

3. During the antebellum period, white workers began to form their own concepts of free men by contrasting themselves to slaves. They began to view African Americans as different and "other." David R. Roediger, *The Wages of Whiteness: Race and the Making of the American Working-Class* (New York: Verso, 1991), 13–14, 24, 27, 56, 119; Leslie A. Schwalm, *A Hard Fight for We: Women's Transition from Slavery to Freedom in South Carolina* (Urbana: University of Illinois Press, 1997), 119.

4. George P. Rawick, *The American Slave: A Composite Autobiography*, Supplement, Series 1, Vol. 6, *Mississippi Narratives*, pt. 1 (Westport, Conn.: Greenwood Press, 1974): 277–78; Eric Foner, *Reconstruction: America's Unfinished Revolution, 1863–1877* (New York: Harper and Row, 1988): 77–123; Rebecca J. Scott, "Defining the Boundaries of Freedom in the World of Cane: Cuba, Brazil, and Louisiana after Emancipation," *American Historical Review* 99 (February 1994): 90.

5. Armstead L. Robinson, "'Worser dan Jeff Davis': The Coming of Free Labor During the Civil War, 1861–1865," in *Essays on the Postbellum Southern Economy*, ed. Thavolia Glymph and John J. Kushma (College Station: Texas A & M University Press, 1985), 37; John K. Bettersworth, *Confederate Mississippi: The People and Policies of a Cotton State in War Time* (Baton Rouge: Louisiana University Press, 1943), 163.

6. Foner, *Reconstruction*, 78; Leon F. Litwack, *Been in the Storm So Long: The Aftermath of Slavery* (New York: Alfred A. Knopf, 1979), 186–87; Nell Irvin Painter, *Exodusters: Black Migration to Kansas after Reconstruction* (New York: Alfred A. Knopf, 1977), 5.

7. Northerners tied the concept of free labor by contract to the concept of contract marriage. Charles Sumner claimed that freedom meant "rights of family and rights of contract." Amy Dru Stanley, "Conjugal Bonds and Wage Labor:

Rights of Contract in the Age of Emancipation," *Journal of American History* 75 (September 1988): 471.

8. Pension file of Thomas Brown, 147.977, 53rd Regiment, Record Group 15, National Archives and Records Administration, Washington, D.C.

9. For a general discussion of the pension records, see Noralee Frankel, "From Slave Women to Free Women: The National Archives and Black Women's History in the Civil War Era," *Prologue: Quarterly of the National Archives and Records Administration* 29 (Summer 1997), 100–104.

10. Annie E. Jacobs, "The Master of Doro Plantation—An Epic of the Old South," 61, 62, 90, 157. Unpublished ms., Mississippi Department of Archives and History, Jackson, Mississippi.

Introduction

1. Pension File of Bannister Bowman, 408.241 J 413.202, 5th Regiment, Record Group 15 (hereafter RG 15), National Archives and Records Administration (hereafter NARA), Washington, D.C.

2. Pension File of Thomas Brown, 147.977, 53rd Regiment, RG 15, NARA; Annie E. Jacobs, "The Master of Doro Plantation—An Epic of the Old South," unpublished ms., Mississippi Department of Archives and History, Jackson, Mississippi, 16, 61, 62, 90.

3. James C. Cobb, *The Most Southern Place on Earth: The Mississippi Delta and the Roots of Regional Identity* (New York: Oxford University Press, 1992), 23.

4. W. E. B. DuBois, *Black Reconstruction in America,1860–1880* (Kingsport, Tenn.: Atheneum Publishers, 1962), 431.

5. Thomas Holt, "Reflections on Race-Making and Racist Practice: Toward a Working Hypothesis" (paper presented to the Newberry Seminar in American Social History, May 30, 1991), 9–10.

6. Richard Sutch, "The Breeding of Slaves for Sale and the Westward Expansion of Slavery, 1850–1860," in *Race and Slavery in the Western Hemisphere: Quantitative Studies,* ed. Stanley Engerman and Eugene D. Genovese (Princeton, N.J.: Princeton University Press, 1975), 178.

7. Charles Sackett Sydnor, *Slavery in Mississippi* (New York: D. Appleton-Century, 1933), 15; John Hebron Moore, *Agriculture in Ante-Bellum Mississippi* (New York: Bookman Associates, 1958), 33.

8. Vernon Lane Wharton, *The Negro in Mississippi, 1865–1890* (New York: Harper and Row, 1965), 12–13.

9. James C. Cobb, *The Most Southern Place on Earth,* 31; James W. Loewen and Charles Sallis, eds., *Mississippi: Conflict and Change* (New York: Pantheon Books, 1974), 15–24.

10. Paul A. David, Herbert G. Gutman, Richard Sutch, Peter Temin, and Gavin Wright, *Reckoning with Slavery: A Critical Study in the Quantitative History of American Negro Slavery* (New York: Oxford University Press, 1976), 100.

11. Sutch, "The Breeding of Slaves for Sale and the Westward Expansion of Slavery," 178, 181; Robert William Fogel and Stanley L. Engerman, *Time on the Cross: The Economics of American Negro Slavery* (Boston: Little, Brown, and Co., 1974), 69.

12. Allan Kulikoff, "Uprooted People: Black Migrants in the Age of the American Revolution, 1790–1820" in *Slavery and Freedom in the Age of the American Revolution*, ed. Ira Berlin and Ronald Hoffman (Charlottesville, Virginia: University Press of Virginia, 1983), 155.

13. Pension File of Tod Welcome, 397.384, 440.081, 5th Regiment, RG 15, NARA.

14. Herbert G. Gutman, *The Black Family in Slavery and Freedom, 1750–1925* (New York: Vintage Books, 1977), 154.

15. See Chapter 6 for more about extended families.

16. Fogel and Engerman, *Time on the Cross*, 39.

17. David L. Cohn, *The Life and Times of King Cotton* (New York: Oxford University Press, 1956), 90.

18. Fogel and Engerman, *Time on the Cross*, 15–106; Joan M. Jensen, *With These Hands: Women Working on the Land* (Old Westbury, N.Y.: The Feminist Press, 1981), 67.

19. Eugene D. Genovese, *Roll, Jordan, Roll: The World the Slaves Made* (New York: Vintage Books, 1976), 495; Leslie A. Schwalm, *A Hard Fight for We: Women's Transition from Slavery to Freedom in South Carolina* (Urbana: University of Illinois Press, 1997), 21; Fogel and Engerman, *Time on the Cross*, 141.

20. Sydnor, *Slavery in Mississippi* 10; Jacqueline Jones, *Labor of Love, Labor of Sorrow: Black Women, Work, and the Family, From Slavery to the Present* (New York: Vintage Books, 1985), 17.

21. Sydnor, *Slavery in Mississippi*, 21; Elizabeth Fox-Genovese, *Within the Plantation Household: Black and White Women of the Old South* (Chapel Hill: University of North Carolina Press, 1988), 141, 173.

22. Frederick Law Olmsted, *Back Country* (New York: Burt Franklin, 1970), 14–15; Fox-Genovese, *Within the Plantation Household*, 172–73.

23. Ulrich Bonnell Phillips, *American Negro Slavery* (New York: D. Appleton-Century, 1933), 208–209.

24. Moore, *Agriculture in Ante-Bellum Mississippi*, 42.

25. Moore, *Agriculture in Ante-Bellum Mississippi*, 43; Fox-Genovese, *Within the Plantation Household*, 174.

26. James Allen Plantation Book, Mississippi Department of Archives and History, Jackson, Mississippi, 54, 56.

27. Entries of the Overseer of "Fonsylvania" Plantation, Fonsylvania Plantation Book, April 21, 1863 and May 13, 1863, Mississippi Department of Archives and History, Jackson, Mississippi.

28. Sydnor, *Slavery in Mississippi*, 9.

29. Sydnor, *Slavery in Mississippi*, 15.

30. Robert W. Fogel and Stanley L. Engerman, "Explaining the Relative Efficiency of Slave Agriculture in the Antebellum South," *American Economic Review* 67 (June 1977): 292; Ralph Shlomowitz, "The Origins of Southern Sharecropping," *Agricultural History* 53 (July 1979): 568.

31. Evernand Green Baker Diary, Vol. II, 4 September 1862, 158, Southern Historical Collection, University of North Carolina, Chapel Hill.

32. John Campbell, "Beyond Slavery: Market Activities of Female Slaves in the Cotton South," paper presented at the conference "Women and the Transi-

tion to Capitalism in Rural America, 1760–1841," Northern Illinois University, DeKalb, Illinois, March 30–April 2, 1989.

33. Sydnor, *Slavery in Mississippi*, 15; Cohn, *The Life and Times of King Cotton*, 16.

34. Pension File of Anderson Lee, 590.330, 405.169, 5th Regiment, RG 15, NARA.

35. Pension File of Washington Webb, 165.531, 3rd Regiment, RG 15, NARA.

36. Pension File of Leonard Barnes, 315.847, 250.920, 53rd Regiment, RG 15, NARA. Mechal Sobel argues that this is a different, "older" way of reckoning time—a nonlinear, nonrationalist system that was used by both Africans and Europeans at various times. Sobel, *The World They Made Together: Black and White Values in Eighteenth-Century Virginia* (Princeton, N.J.: Princeton University Press, 1987), 26.

37. Cobb, *The Most Southern Place on Earth*, 22.

38. Fox-Genovese, *Within the Plantation Household*, 167.

39. Genovese, *Roll, Jordan, Roll*, 338–39.

40. Fogel and Engerman, *Time on the Cross*, 75.

41. Francis Terry Leake Diary, 2 January 1862, Francis Terry Leake Papers, Southern Historical Collection, University of North Carolina, Chapel Hill. As Patrick Manning points out, Africans paid higher prices for women. "Contours of Slavery and Social Change in Africa," *American Historical Review* 88 (October 1983): 841. See also Fogel and Engerman, *Time on the Cross*, 77.

42. Stanley L. Engerman, Manuel Moreno Fraginals, and Herbert S. Klein, "The Level and Structure of Slave Prices on Cuban Plantations in Mid-Nineteenth Century: Some Comparative Perspectives," *The American Historical Review* 88 (December 1983): 1216.

43. Kenneth Stampp, *The Peculiar Institution: Slavery in the Ante-Bellum South* (New York: Vintage Books, 1956), 57. See Fogel and Engerman, *Time on the Cross*, 75, 120 for examples of the use of older women slaves.

44. Pension File of George Johnson, 165.386, J. 347.073, 3rd Regiment, RG 15, NARA.

45. Genovese, *Roll, Jordan, Roll*, 551; Jones, *Labor of Love, Labor of Sorrow*, 30.

46. James Allen Plantation Book, Mississippi Department of Archives and History, Jackson, Mississippi, 24, 55.

47. Evernand Green Baker Diary, Vol. II, 1 June 1864; Ira Berlin, Thavolia Glymph, Steven F. Miller, Joseph P. Reidy, Leslie S. Rowland, and Julie Saville, *The Wartime Genesis of Free Labor: The Lower South*, Series I, Vol. III of *Freedom: A Documentary History of Emancipation, 1861–1867* (Cambridge: Cambridge University Press, 1990), 858; Stuart Bruchey, ed., *Cotton and the Growth of the American Economy, 1790–1860: Sources and Readings* (New York: Harcourt, Brace and World, 1967), 184–85.

48. Sutch, "The Breeding of Slaves for Sale," 176, 182–85.

49. George P. Rawick, ed., *The American Slave: A Composite Autobiography*, Supplement, Series 1, Vol. 6: *Mississippi Narratives*, pt. 1 (Westport, Conn.: Greenwood Press, 1974), 248.

50. Fox-Genovese, *Within the Plantation Household*, 148; Sydnor, *Slavery in Mississippi*, 64; Phillips, *American Negro Slavery*, 45–54.

51. Pension of Moses Wilson, 315.778, 273.769, 5th Regiment, RG 15, NARA.

52. Sydnor, *Slavery in Mississippi*, 64; Jones, *Labor of Love, Labor of Sorrow*, 29–30.

53. Pension File of Hapless Nash, 335.410, 235.274, 5th Regiment, RG 15, NARA.

54. Schwalm, *A Hard Fight For We*, 29.

55. Pension File of Henry Ellison, 151.986, 194.705, 5th Regiment, RG 15, NARA.

56. Pension File of Albert Johnson, 182.941, 222.782, 3rd Regiment, RG 15, NARA; Pension File of Sandy Green, 671.278, 921.493, 3rd Regiment, RG 15, NARA; Sobel, *The World They Made Together*, 35.

57. Sydnor, *Slavery in Mississippi*, 62–63; Fogel and Engerman, *Time on the Cross*, 128; Jo Ann Manfra and Robert R. Dykstra, "Serial Marriage and the Origins of the Black Stepfamily: The Rowanty Evidence," *The Journal of American History* 72 (June 1985): 44; Schwalm, *A Hard Fight For We*, 52.

58. Richard H. Steckel, "Slave Marriage and the Family," *Journal of Family History* 5 (Winter 1980): 407, 411.

59. Pension File of Job Paul, 181.700, 434.267, 51st Regiment, RG 15, NARA.

60. Pension File of Allen Alexander, 145.205, 97.533, 58th Regiment, RG 15, NARA.

61. Pension File of Frank Fletcher, 782.007, 599.542, 5th Regiment, RG 15, NARA.

62. Pension File of Henry Ellison, 151.986, 194.705, 5th Regiment, RG 15, NARA.

63. Pension File of George Hubbard, 145.205, 97.533, 51st Regiment, RG 15, NARA.

64. Pension File of Promise Daniels, 322.713 J. 348.591, 3rd Regiment, RG 15, NARA.

65. Pension File of Richard Sled, 394.755, 389.853, 5th Regiment, RG 15, NARA; Pension File of Charles Jones, 166.524, 5th Regiment, RG 15, NARA; Pension File of Moses Wilson, 315.778, 273.769, 5th Regiment, RG 15, NARA.

66. Pension File of Charles Drance, 219.074, 174.551, 51st Regiment, RG 15, NARA; Joseph Edmonds, 229.762, 5th Regiment, RG 15, NARA; Genovese, *Roll, Jordan, Roll*, 475–77.

67. Fogel and Engerman, *Time on the Cross*, 128.

68. Pension File of David Anderson, 3rd Regiment; Genovese, *Roll, Jordan, Roll*, 476; Richard H. Steckel, "Slave Marriage and the Family," 407, 412.

69. Pension File of Lewis North, 225.221, 5th Regiment, RG 15, NARA; Fox-Genovese, *Within the Plantation Household*, 302, 327.

70. Pension File of Solomon Ratliff, 254.238, WO 570.752, 5th Regiment, RG 15, NARA.

71. Pension File of Charles Wabbs, 240.644, 5th Regiment, RG 15, NARA.

72. Genovese, *Roll, Jordan, Roll*, 474.

73. Pension File of Nicholas Thomas, 197.568 J. 626.450, 5th Regiment, RG 15, NARA.

74. Pension File of James Jones, 346.290, 53rd Regiment, RG 15, NARA.

75. Pension File of James Jones, 346.290, 53rd Regiment, RG 15, NARA; Pension File of Charles Drane, 219.074, 174.551, 51st Regiment, RG 15, NARA; Pension File of Moses West, 164.065, 5th Regiment, RG 15, NARA; Pension File of Archie Branch, 168.398, 187.861, 58th Regiment, RG 15, NARA.

76. Pension File of Lewis Carroll, 248.276 J. 226.913, 3rd Regiment, RG 15, NARA; Anthony S. Parent, Jr. and Susan Brown Wallace, "Childhood and Sexual Identity under Slavery," in *American Sexual Politics: Sex, Gender, and Race*, ed. John C. Fout and Maura Shaw Tantillo (Chicago: University of Chicago Press, 1993), 30.

77. Pension File of Squire House, 399.352, 5th Regiment, RG 15, NARA.

78. Gutman, *The Black Family in Slavery and Freedom*, 146–47.

79. John W. Blassingame, *The Slave Community: Plantation Life in the Antebellum South* (New York, 1979) 176, 361; Elaine C. Everly, "Marriage Registers of Freedmen," *Prologue: The Journal of the National Archives* 5 (Fall 1973): 152; Wharton, *The Negro in Mississippi*, 44; Benjamin Quarles, *The Negro in the Civil War* (Boston: Little, Brown, and Co., 1969), 289; Manfra and Dykstra, "Serial Marriage and Origins of the Black Stepfamily," 19; Ann Patton Malone, *Sweet Chariot: Slave Family and Household Structure in Nineteenth-Century Louisiana* (Chapel Hill: University of North Carolina Press, 1992), 228.

80. Gutman, *The Black Family in Slavery and Freedom*, 273; Schwalm, *A Hard Fight For We*, 52; Parent and Wallace, "Childhood and Sexual Identity Under Slavery," 34.

81. Pension File of Lewis North, 225.221, 5th Regiment, RG 15, NARA; Pension File of Moses Sharkey, 168.890, 258.968, 3rd Regiment, RG 15, NARA.

82. Pension File of Charles Hutchins, 178.142, 346.916, 457.840 cert. 457.840, 5th Regiment, RG 15, NARA.

83. Niara Sudarkasa argues that African societies had even more complex definitions of wife and husband. "The Status of Women in Indigenous African Societies," *Feminist Studies* 12 (Spring 1986): 97.

84. Pension File of Jacob Horton, 627.635, 493.946, 3rd Regiment, RG 15, NARA.

85. Pension File of Louis Caston, 388.190, 384.190, 5th Regiment, RG 15, NARA.

86. Pension File of George Hubbard, 145.205, 97.533, 51st Regiment, RG 15, NARA.

87. Genovese, *Roll, Jordan, Roll*, 464.

88. Pension File of John Smith, 348.310 J. 469.269, 5th Regiment, RG 15, NARA.

89. Paul D. Escott, *Slavery Remembered: A Record of Twentieth-Century Slave Narratives* (Chapel Hill: University of North Carolina Press, 1979), 44.

90. Pension File of Riley Gordon, 267.797 J. 410.900, 5th Regiment, RG 15, NARA. See also Jones, *Labor of Love, Labor of Sorrow*, 35.

91. Pension File of Frederick Caldwell, 409.810 J., 3rd Regiment, RG 15, NARA.

92. Berlin, et. al., *The Wartime Genesis of Free Labor*, 696.

1. The Impact of the War of Liberation on Families and Work

1. George P. Rawick, ed., *The American Slave: A Composite Autobiography*, Supplement, Series 1, Vol. 8: *Mississippi Narratives*, pt. 2 (Westport, Conn.: Greenwood Press, 1974), 1039; Leon F. Litwack, *Been in the Storm So Long: The Aftermath of Slavery* (New York: Alfred A. Knopf, 1979), 65.

2. James M. McPherson, *Battle Cry of Freedom: The Civil War Era* (New York: Oxford University Press, 1988), 626–38.

3. James C. Cobb, *The Most Southern Place on Earth: The Mississippi Delta and the Roots of Regional Identity* (New York: Oxford University Press, 1992), 39.

4. Pension File of Thomas Brown, 147.977, 53rd Regiment, Record Group 15 (hereafter RG 15), National Archives and Record Administration, Washington, D.C. (hereafter NARA); Annie E. Jacobs, "The Master of Doro Plantation—An Epic of the Old South," unpublished manuscript, Mississippi Department of Archives and History, Jackson, Mississippi, 16, 61, 62, 90.

5. Leslie A. Schwalm, *A Hard Fight for We: Women's Transition from Slavery to Freedom in South Carolina* (Urbana: University of Illinois Press, 1997), 75.

6. Bell Irvin Wiley, *Southern Negroes, 1861–1865* (New Haven, Conn.: Yale University Press, 1969), 134–45.

7. Vernon Lane Wharton, *The Negro in Mississippi, 1865–1890* (New York: Harper and Row, 1965), 14; Schwalm, *A Hard Fight for We*, 81–86; Litwack, *Been in the Storm So Long*, 36–37.

8. Benjamin S. Ewell to General Chambers, 20 October 1863, in *The War of the Rebellion: A Compilation of the Official Records of the Union and Confederate Armies*, Series I, Vol. 56 (Washington, D.C.: Government Printing Office, 1880–1901), 572.

9. James Allen Plantation Book, Thursday, 15 May 1862, 72. Mississippi Department of Archives and History, Jackson, Mississippi.

10. Benjamin Quarles, *The Negro in the Civil War* (Boston: Little, Brown and Company), 274; Edwina and Betha Burnley, Burnley Family Memoir, Southern Historical Collection, University of North Carolina, Chapel Hill; John K. Bettersworth, *Confederate Mississippi: The People and Policies of a Cotton State in War Time* (Baton Rouge: Louisiana University Press, 1943), 81, 169; Schwalm, *A Hard Fight For We*, 108–114; Wiley, *Southern Negroes 1861–1865*, 110–33.

11. Bettersworth, *Confederate Mississippi*, 172; Wiley, *Southern Negroes 1861–1865*, 4, 6–8; Wharton, *The Negro in Mississippi*, 18–19.

12. George Corliss to A. W. Preston, January 17, 1867. Jackson, Mississippi: Unregistered Letters Received, January 1866–December 1868. Bureau of Refugees, Freedmen, and Abandoned Lands (hereafter BRFAL), Record Group 105 (hereafter RG 105), NARA; Quarles, *The Negro in the Civil War*, 46; Litwack, *Been in the Storm So Long*, 30–33; Peter C. Ripley, "The Black Family in Transition: Louisiana, 1860–1865," *Journal of Southern History* XLI (August 1975): 373.

13. Pension File of Moses West, 164.065, 5th Regiment, RG 15, NARA.

14. Pension File of Moses West, 164.065, 5th Regiment, RG 15, NARA.

15. James C. Cobb, *The Most Southern Place on Earth*, 41.

16. Pension File of Isaac Mackie, 322.326 J. 366.345, 5th Regiment, RG 15, NARA.

17. George P. Rawick, ed., *The American Slave: A Composite Autobiography*, Supplement, Series 1, Vol. 10: *Mississippi Narratives*, pt. 5 (Westport, Conn.: Greenwood Press, 1974), 2129.

18. Pension File of Hosea Brittain (Thompson), 250.551, 242.244, 3rd Regiment, RG 15, NARA.

19. Pension File of Edmund Whitfield, 397.320, 3rd Regiment, RG 15, NARA.

20. Cobb, *The Most Southern Place on Earth*, 41.

21. Ronald L. F. Davis, *Good and Faithful Labor: From Slavery to Sharecropping in the Natchez District, 1868–1890* (Westport, Conn.: Greenwood Press, 1982), 172; Peter Bardaglio, "The Children of Jubilee: African American Childhood in Wartime," in *Divided Houses: Gender and the Civil War*, ed. Catherine Clinton and Nina Silber (New York: Oxford University Press, 1992), 224; Ripley, "The Black Family in Transition," 374.

22. Wharton, *The Negro in Mississippi*, 30–31.

23. Wiley, *Southern Negroes 1861–1865*, 343–44, 24; Pension File of Levi McLauren, 213.748, J., 58th Regiment, RG 15, NARA.

25. Pension File of Hosea Brittain (Thompson), 250.551, 242.244, 3rd Regiment, RG 15, NARA.

26. Pension File of James Mathey, 227.825, J, 268.203, 58th Regiment, RG 15, NARA.

27. Pension File of James Mathey, 227.825, J, 268.203, 58th Regiment, RG 15, NARA.

28. Quarles, *The Negro in the Civil War*, 44.

29. Pension File of Allen Alexander, 145.205, 58th Regiment, RG 15, NARA.

30. Ira Berlin, Thavolia Glymph, Steven F. Miller, Joseph P. Reidy, Leslie S. Rowland, and Julie Saville, *The Wartime Genesis of Free Labor: The Lower South*, Series I, Vol. III of *Freedom: A Documentary History of Emancipation, 1861–1867* (New York: Cambridge University Press, 1990), 50; Clarence L. Mohr, *On the Threshold of Freedom: Masters and Slaves in Civil War Georgia* (Athens: University of Georgia Press, 1986), 83, 89.

31. Pension File of Reuben Caston, 197.609 J. 282.181, 5th Regiment, RG 15, NARA.

32. Litwack, *Been in the Storm So Long*, 8, 134.

33. Litwack, *Been in the Storm So Long*, 307; Mechal Sobel, *The World They Made Together: Black and White Values in Eighteenth-Century Virginia* (Princeton, N.J.: Princeton University Press, 1987), 95; Elizabeth Fox-Genovese and Eugene D. Genovese, *Fruits of Merchant Capital: Slavery and Bourgeois Property in the Rise and Expansion of Capitalism* (New York: Oxford University Press, 1983), 124.

34. Pension File of Henry Carter, 178.418, 256.137, 58th Regiment, RG 15, NARA.

35. Quarles, *The Negro in the Civil War*, 51.

36. Herbert G. Gutman, *The Black Family in Slavery and Freedom, 1750–1925* (New York: Vintage Books, 1977), 265; Jones, *Labor of Love, Labor of Sorrow*, 47; Elizabeth Fox-Genovese, *Within the Plantation Household: Black and White Women of the Old South* (Chapel Hill: University of North Carolina Press, 1988), 304.

37. Robert B. Alexander, Journal Entry, 12 February 1863, Mississippi De-

partment of Archives and History, Jackson, Mississippi; W. F. Smith, ed., "The Yankees in New Albany: Letter of Elizabeth Jane Beach, July 29, 1864," *Journal of Mississippi History* II (January1940): 46.

38. Pension File of Nicholas Thomas, 197.568 J. 626.450, 5th Regiment, RG 15, NARA.

39. Pension File of Horace Stewart, 187.331, 518.689, 5th Regiment; Jones, *Labor of Love, Labor of Sorrow*, 47.

40. Pension File of Samuel White, 382.722, 5th Regiment, RG 15, NARA.

41. Pension File of James Jones, 346.290, 53rd Regiment, RG 15, NARA.

42. Eugene D. Genovese, *Roll, Jordan, Roll: The World the Slaves Made* (New York: Vintage Books, 1974), 331.

43. W. Maury Darst, ed. "The Vicksburg Diary of Mrs. Alfred Ingraham (May 2–June 13, 1863)," *Journal of Mississippi History* XLIV (May 1982): 174.

44. Darst, "The Vicksburg Diary of Mrs. Alfred Ingraham," 144, 166, 167, 171.

45. Darst, "The Vicksburg Diary of Mrs. Alfred Ingraham," 173.

46. Cobb, *The Most Southern Place on Earth*, 41.

47. George P. Rawick, ed., *The American Slave: A Composite Autobiography*, Supplement, Series 1, Vol. 8: *Mississippi Narratives*, pt. 3 (Westport, Conn.: Greenwood Press, 1974), 1303; Bettersworth, *Confederate Mississippi*, 161.

48. David L. Cohn, *The Life and Times of King Cotton* (New York: Oxford University Press, 1956), 59; Fox-Genovese, *Within the Plantation Household*, 121; Wiley, *Southern Negroes 1861–1865*, 54–55.

49. George P. Rawick, ed., *The American Slave: A Composite Autobiography*, Supplement, Series 1, Vol. 8: *Mississippi Narratives*, pt. 3 (Westport, Conn.: Greenwood Press, 1974), 818.

50. George P. Rawick, ed., *The American Slave: A Composite Autobiography*, Supplement, Series 1, Vol. 7: *Mississippi Narratives*, pt. 2 (Westport, Conn.: Greenwood Press, 1974), 596.

51. Cobb, *The Most Southern Place on Earth*, 34.

52. W. T. Sherman to Major General Halleck, 29 February 1864, in *The War of the Rebellion*, Series I, Vol. 58, 498.

53. Armstead L. Robinson, "'Worser dan Jeff Davis': The Coming of Free Labor During the Civil War, 1861–1865," in *Essays on the Postbellum Southern Economy*, ed. Thavolia Glymph and John J. Kushma (College Station: Texas A & M University Press, 1985), 32.

54. Berlin et al., *The Wartime Genesis of Free Labor*, 708.

55. George P. Rawick, ed., *The American Slave: A Composite Autobiography*, Supplement, Series 1, Vol. 8: *Mississippi Narratives*, pt. 3 (Westport, Conn.: Greenwood Press, 1974), 1155.

56. Leon F. Litwack, *Been in the Storm So Long*, 124, 127; Genovese, *Roll, Jordan, Roll*, 152–53; George P. Rawick, ed., *The American Slave: A Composite Autobiography*, Supplement, Series 1, Vol. 8: *Mississippi Narratives*, pt. 3 (Westport, Conn.: Greenwood Press, 1974), 1155.

57. Joseph T. Glatthaar, *Forged in Battle: The Civil War Alliance of Black Soldiers and White Officers* (New York: The Free Press, 1990), 90.

58. Darst, "The Vicksburg Diary of Mrs. Alfred Ingraham," 160; Bell Irvin Wiley, *Confederate Women* (Westport, Conn.: Greenwood Press, 1975), 164.

59. James Gibson Alverson, ed., *Memoirs of J. M. Gibson: Terrors of the Civil War and Reconstruction Days* (San Gabriel, California: James Gibson Alverson, 1966), 22; Schwalm, *A Hard Fight for We*, 102.

60. George P. Rawick, ed., *The American Slave: A Composite Autobiography*, Supplement, Series 1, Vol. 7: *Mississippi Narratives*, pt. 2 (Westport, Conn.: Greenwood Press, 1974), 659.

61. Belle Kearney, *A Slaveholder's Daughter* (New York: Negro Universities Press, 1969), 113; Litwack, *Been in the Storm So Long*, 349; Schwalm, *A Hard Fight For We*, 119.

62. Eugene D. Genovese, *The World the Slaveholders Made: Two Essays in Interpretation* (New York: Vintage Books, 1969), 196, 200.

63. Fox-Genovese, *Within the Plantation Household*, 100–101, 131.

64. Genovese, *Roll, Jordan, Roll*, 5, 6, 70–75.

65. Pension File of Adam Fry, 357.679, 250.690, 5th Regiment, RG 15, NARA. Former slave mistresses recalled information about their former slaves, including the birth dates and names of children; sometimes they even remembered the name of the slave woman's midwife. Such knowledge showed the concern of slaveholding women for slave women both in a paternalistic sense and as property. Slave owners kept track of slave births in the way they noted new livestock. See, for example, Pension File of Isaac Mackie, 322.326 J. 366.345, 5th Regiment, RG 15, NARA.

66. Pension File of Joseph Edmonds, 229.762, 5th Regiment, RG 15, NARA.

67. Pension File of Leonard Barnes, 315.847, 250.920, 53rd Regiment, RG 15, NARA.

68. Samuel Andrew Agnew Diary, January 8, 1866, Southern Historical Collection, University of North Carolina, Chapel Hill; George C. Rable, *Civil Wars: Women and the Crisis of Southern Nationalism* (Urbana: University of Illinois Press, 1991), 254; Lawrence J. Friedman, *The White Savage: Racial Fantasies in the Postbellum South* (Englewood Cliffs, N.J.: Prentice Hall, 1970), 9; Genovese, *Roll, Jordan, Roll*, 109.

69. Samuel Andrew Agnew Diary, December 28, 1865, Southern Historical Collection, Chapel Hill, North Carolina.

70. James L. Roark, *Masters Without Slaves: Southern Planters in the Civil War and Reconstruction* (New York: Norton Press, 1977), 83, 144, 146, 199.

71. Benjamin Quarles, *The Negro in the Civil War*, 51.

72. George P. Rawick, ed., *The American Slave: A Composite Autobiography*, Supplement, Series 1, Vol. 7: *Mississippi Narratives*, pt. 2 (Westport, Conn.: Greenwood Press, 1974), 785..

73. Barbara J. Fields, *Slavery and Freedom on the Middle Ground: Maryland During the Nineteenth Century* (New Haven, Conn.: Yale University Press, 1985), 43, 93.

74. George P. Rawick, ed., *The American Slave: A Composite Autobiography*, Supplement, Series 1, Vol. 6: *Mississippi Narratives*, pt. 1 (Westport, Conn.: Greenwood Press, 1974), 210–11.

75. Litwack, *Been in the Storm So Long*, 119, 173–74.

76. Octavia V. Albert, *The House of Bondage* (Freeport, N.Y.: Books for Libraries Press, 1972), 134; Litwack, *Been in the Storm So Long*, 59.

2. Within the Union Lines

1. Vernon Lane Wharton, *The Negro in Mississippi, 1865–1890* (New York: Harper and Row, 1965), 28.

2. Pension File of Thomas Brown, 147.977, 53rd Regiment, Record Group 15 (hereafter RG 15), National Archives and Records Administration, Washington, D.C. (hereafter NARA).

3. Steven Joseph Ross, "Freed Soil, Freed Labor, Freed Men: John Eaton and the Davis Bend Experiment," *Journal of Southern History* XLIV (May 1978): 217; Ronald L. F. Davis, "The U.S. Army and the Origins of Sharecropping in the Natchez District: A Case Study," *The Journal of Negro History* LXII (January 1977): 68.

4. Thomas C. Holt, *The Problem of Freedom: Race, Labor, and Politics in Jamaica and Britain, 1832–1938* (Baltimore: Johns Hopkins University Press, 1992), 148, 174, 176; Thomas C. Holt, "'An Empire Over the Mind': Emancipation, Race, and Ideology in the British West Indies and the American South," in *Region, Race, and Reconstruction: Essays in Honor of C. Vann Woodward*, ed. J. Morgan Kousser and James M. McPherson (New York: Oxford University Press, 1982), 288.

5. Joe Martin Richardson, *Christian Reconstruction: The American Missionary Association and Southern Blacks, 1861–1890* (Athens: University of Georgia Press, 1986), 41; Leslie A. Schwalm, *A Hard Fight for We: Women's Transition from Slavery to Freedom in South Carolina* (Urbana: University of Illinois Press, 1997), 75.

6. Donald G. Nieman, *To Set the Law in Motion: The Freedmen's Bureau and the Legal Rights of Blacks, 1865–1868* (Millwood, N.Y.: KTO Press, 1979), 54; Robert William Fogel and Stanley L. Engerman, *Time on the Cross: The Economics of American Negro Slavery* (Boston: Little, Brown and Co., 1974), 216–17; Holt, "'An Empire Over the Mind,'" 297.

7. Holt, "'An Empire Over the Mind'," 287.

8. Eric Foner, *Free Soil, Free Labor, Free Men: The Ideology of the Republican Party Before the Civil War* (New York: Oxford University Press, 1970), 12–13, 16–17, 50; Leon F. Litwack, *Been in the Storm So Long: The Aftermath of Slavery* (New York: Alfred A. Knopf, 1979), 403.

9. Laura F. Edwards, *Gendered Strife and Confusion: The Political Culture of Reconstruction* (Urbana: University of Illinois Press, 1997), 12. For a discussion of racist beliefs in the North, see Forrest G. Wood, *Black Scare: The Racist Response to Emancipation* (Los Angeles: University of California Press, 1970), 14–15.

10. Schwalm, *A Hard Fight For We*, 250, 257.

11. Eugene D. Genovese, *The World the Slaveholders Made: Two Essays in Interpretation* (New York: Vintage Books, 1967), 201.

12. Ira Berlin, Joseph P. Reidy, and Leslie S. Rowland, *The Wartime Genesis of Free Labor: The Lower South*, Series I, Vol. III of *Freedom: A Documentary History of Emancipation, 1861–1867* (New York: Cambridge University Press, 1990), 859.

13. Berlin et al., *The Wartime Genesis of Free Labor*, 624; Wharton, *The Negro in Mississippi*, 24.

14. Wharton, *The Negro in Mississippi*, 27–28.

15. James M. McPherson, *Battle Cry of Freedom: The Civil War Era* (New York: Oxford University Press, 1988), 497.

16. Wharton, *The Negro in Mississippi*, 47.

17. Wharton, *The Negro in Mississippi*, 27.

18. Pension File of Henry Clark, 289.087, J 305.330, 3rd Regiment, RG 15, NARA.

19. Martha Mitchell Bigelow, "Freedmen of the Mississippi Valley, 1862–1865," *Civil War History* VIII (March 1962): 44. W. E. B. DuBois described this flight in terms of a strike: "They wanted to stop the economy of the plantation systems, and to do that they left the plantations." DuBois, *Black Reconstruction in America, 1860–1880* (Kingsport, Tennessee: Atheneum Publishers, 1962), 67. Eugene D. Genovese, *Roll, Jordan, Roll: The World the Slaves Made* (New York: Vintage Books, 1974), 151; Berlin et al., *The Wartime Genesis of Free Labor,* 636, 715; Clifton Lloyd Ganus, Jr., "The Freedmen's Bureau in Mississippi," (Ph.D. diss., Tulane University, 1953), 5; Rebecca J. Scott, "Defining the Boundaries of Freedom in the World of Cane: Cuba, Brazil, and Louisiana after Emancipation," *The American Historical Review* 99 (February 1994): 73.

20. J. V. Frederick, "An Illinois Soldier in North Mississippi: Diary of John Wilson, February 15–December 30, 1862," *Journal of Mississippi History* I (July 1939): 192.

21. John Eaton, *Grant, Lincoln, and the Freedmen: Reminiscences of the Civil War* (New York: Longmans, Green, and Co., 1907), 83.

22. W. T. Sherman to Major General Halleck, 29 February 1864, in United States War Department, *The War of the Rebellion: A Compilation of the Official Records of the Union and Confederate Armies*, Series I, Vol. 58 (Washington, D.C.: Government Printing Office, 1880–1901), 498.

23. Pension File of John Brown, 387.412, 5th Regiment, RG 15, NARA.

24. General Thomas E. G. Ransom to Col. W. T. Clark, in *The War of the Rebellion*, Series I, vol. 24, 681. See also Davis, "The U.S. Army and the Origins of Sharecropping," 62.

25. William Thirds to Mr. Whipple, 19 November 1863, American Missionary Association Papers, Mississippi, Amistad Research Center, Dillard University, New Orleans, Louisiana, Microfilm Reel 71567.

26. Isaac Shoemaker Diary, 3 March 1864, William R. Perkins Library, Duke University, Durham, North Carolina; Dan T. Carter, *When the War Was Over: The Failure of Self-Reconstruction in the South, 1865–1867* (Baton Rouge: Louisiana State University Press, 1985), 151–52; James L. Roark, *Masters without Slaves: Southern Planters in the Civil War and Reconstruction* (New York: Norton Press, 1977), 118.

27. Pension File of Richard Roberts, 317.426, J 519.390, 5th Regiment, RG 15, NARA; Pension File of Allen Alexander, 145.205, 97.533, 58th Regiment, RG 15, NARA. Units in Vicksburg included the 3rd Cavalry, the 5th Heavy Artillery, and the 47th, 48th, 50th, 52nd, and 64th Regiments. Units in Natchez were the 6th Heavy Artillery and the 58th, 63rd, 70th, and 71st Regiments.

28. James T. Currie, *Enclave: Vicksburg and Her Plantations, 1863–1870* (Jackson: University Press of Mississippi, 1980), 45; Pension File of Riley Gordon, 267.797, 5th Regiment, RG 15, NARA.

29. Pension File of Charles Kane, 562.118 J. 386.877, 53rd Regiment, RG 15, NARA.

30. Pension File of Job Paul, 181.700, 434.267, 51st Regiment; Ira Berlin, Joseph P. Reidy, and Leslie S. Rowland, *The Black Military Experience*, Series II, Volume II of *Freedom: A Documentary History of Emancipation, 1861–1867* (New York: Cambridge University Press, 1982), 658.

31. Pension File of Hubbard Reynolds, 163.950, 741.430, 5th Regiment and Pension File of James Billington, 383.061, 5th Regiment, RG 15, NARA.

32. Pension File of Alfred Johnson, 649.922 J. 566.335, 5th Regiment, RG 15, NARA.

33. Pension File of Robert Drake, 143.055, 5th Regiment, RG 15, NARA.

34. Pension File of Richard Roberts, 317.426, J 519.390, 5th Regiment, RG 15, NARA.

35. Pension File of Benjamin Lee, 380.960, 5th Regiment, RG 15, NARA.

36. Pension File of Samuel Taylor, 210.144 J, 5th Regiment, RG 15, NARA.

37. Pension File of Moses Wilson, 315.778, 273.769, 5th Regiment, RG 15, NARA.

38. Thomas Wallace Knox, *Camp-Fire and Cotton Field: Southern Adventure in Time of War, Life with Union Armies, and Residence on a Louisiana Plantation* (New York: Da Capo Press, 1969), 432–33.

39. William Thirds to Mr. Whipple, 19 November 1863.

40. Pension File of Richard Sled, 394.755, 289.853, 5th Regiment, RG 15, NARA.

41. DuBois, *Black Reconstruction in America*, 69; Benjamin Quarles, *The Negro in the Civil War* (Boston: Little, Brown and Co., 1969), 94. Black soldiers became army workers as well as soldiers.

42. Berlin et al., *The Wartime Genesis of Free Labor*, 25, 648.

43. Pension File of Alfred Johnson, 649.922 J. 566.335, 5th Regiment, RG 15, NARA.

44. Pension File of William Harris, 695.684 J. 538.313, 53rd Regiment, RG 15, NARA.

45. Nancy Bercaw, "Politics of Household during the Transition from Slavery to Freedom in the Yazoo-Mississippi Delta, 1861–1876," (Ph.D. diss. University of Pennsylvania, 1996), 91, 150–51.

46. Pension File of Richard Roberts, 317.426, J 519.390, 5th Regiment, RG 15, NARA.

47. Berlin et al., *The Wartime Genesis of Free Labor*, 73. Berlin notes that independent farming on abandoned plantations was discouraged (p. 633).

48. *The War of the Rebellion*, Series I, Vol. XXIV, Part 4, 585.

49. Berlin et al., *The Wartime Genesis of Free Labor*, 27, 32, 627; Quarles, *The Negro in the Civil War*, 64.

50. McPherson, *Battle Cry of Freedom: The Civil War Era*, 355, 500; For background, see Berlin et al., *The Wartime Genesis of Free Labor*, 1–83; Wharton, *The Negro in Mississippi*, 24–25, 27; Louis S. Gerteis, *From Contraband to Freedman: Federal Policy toward Southern Blacks, 1861–1865* (Westport, Conn.: Greenwood Press, 1973), 136.

51. Davis, "The U.S. Army and the Origins of Sharecropping," 62–63.

52. Bigelow, "Freedmen of the Mississippi Valley," 39; Gerteis, *From Contraband to Freedman*, 120; W. E. B. DuBois, *Black Reconstruction in America*, 69; Wharton, *The Negro in Mississippi*, 28; Bell Irvin Wiley, *Southern Negroes 1861–1865* (New Haven: Yale University Press, 1969), 184.

53. Stewart Sifakis, *Who Was Who In the Civil War* (Oxford: Facts on File, 1988), 199; John Cimprich, *Slavery's End in Tennessee, 1861–1865* (University: University of Alabama Press, 1985), 48; Elaine Cutler Everly, "The Freedmen's Bureau in the National Capital," (Ph.D. diss., The George Washington University, 1972), 9.

54. Headquarters Army in the Field, Special Field Orders, 9 December 1862, *War of the Rebellion*, Series I, Vol. XVII, 396. DuBois, *Black Reconstruction in America*, 69. Black leaders in Boston had an additional strategy. A resolution affirmed that "Colored women could go as nurses, seamstresses and warriors if need be." Quarles, *The Negro in the Civil War*, 27.

55. Wharton, *The Negro in Mississippi*, 29.

56. Cam Walker, "Corinth: The Story of a Contraband Camp," *Civil War History* XX (March 1974): 7–8.

57. John Eaton, *Grant, Lincoln, and the Freedmen*, 5.

58. For example, see Berlin et al., *The Wartime Genesis of Free Labor*, 691.

59. Walker, "Corinth: The Story of a Contraband Camp," 8, 10; Berlin et al., *The Wartime Genesis of Free Labor*, 686.

60. Walker, "Corinth: The Story of a Contraband Camp," 9.

61. Walker, "Corinth: The Story of a Contraband Camp," 17.

62. Headquarters, Department of Tennessee, General Orders, No. 51, 10 August 1863, in *The War of the Rebellion*, Series I, Vol. XXIV, part III, 585.

63. Pension File of Henry Clark, 289.087, J. 305.330, 3rd Regiment, RG 15, NARA.

64. Pension File of Henry Patterson, 156.614, cert. 500.651, 5th Regiment, RG 15, NARA; Pension File of Bannister Bowman, 408.241 J. 413.262, 5th Regiment, RG 15, NARA; Pension File of Hubbard Reynolds, 163.950, 741.430, 5th Regiment, RG 15, NARA.

65. Bigelow, "Freedmen of the Mississippi Valley," 45; Litwack, *Been in the Storm So Long*, 133; Jacqueline Jones, *Labor of Love, Labor of Sorrow: Black Women, Work and the Family, from Slavery to the Present* (New York: Vintage Books, 1985), 50.

66. Alfred H. Stone, Vol. 34, #1, Second Annual Report of the New England Freedmen's Aid Society (Educational Commission): Presented to the Society, April 21, 1864 (Boston, 1864). Alfred H. Stone Collection, Department of Archives and History, Jackson, Mississippi.

67. Pension File of Benjamin Lee, 380.960, 5th Regiment, RG 15, NARA; Pension File, William Harris, 695.684 J. 538.313, 53rd Regiment, RG 15, NARA; Berlin et al., *The Wartime Genesis of Free Labor*, 848, 854.

68. Schwalm, *A Hard Fight for We*, 101–103.

69. Samuel Thomas, Letter, January 21, 1865. Office of the General Superintendent of Freedmen, Register of Letters Received, Bureau of Refugees, Freedmen, and Abandoned Lands (hereafter BRFAL), Mississippi, Record Group 105 (hereafter RG 105), NARA.

70. Pension File of Benjamin Lee, 380.960, 5th Regiment, RG 15, NARA.

71. John Eaton to Hon. Henry Wilson, no date. Office of the General Superintendent of Freedmen: Letters Sent, BRFAL, RG 105, NARA; Wharton, *The Negro in Mississippi*, 43.

72. James W. Pierce to Captain Williams, August 8, 1865. Columbus, Mississippi, Registered Letters Received, BRFAL, RG 105, NARA.

73. Schwalm, *A Hard Fight for We*, 102–103.

74. Frank Johnson, letter, 12 May 1866. Office of the Assistant Commissioner, Registered Letters Received, June 1865–May 1869. BRFAL, RG 105, NARA, M826-14.

75. Pension File of Charles Ambrook, 229.409 J. 507.515, 971.161 A., 5th Regiment, RG 15, NARA.

76. Quarles, *The Negro in the Civil War*, 321.

77. Berlin et al., *The Wartime Genesis of Free Labor*, 695.

78. Berlin et al., *The Wartime Genesis of Free Labor*, 845. For a delineation of the connection between concepts of free labor and legalized marriage, see Thomas C. Holt, "'The Essence of the Contract': The Articulation of Race, Gender, and Political Economy in British Emancipation Policy, 1838–1866," (draft paper, University of Chicago, Chicago, Illinois).

79. Wharton, *The Negro in Mississippi*, 44; Herbert G. Gutman, *The Black Family in Slavery and Freedom, 1750–1925* (New York: Vintage Books, 1977), 18.

80. Pension File of Ted Welcome, 397.384, 440.081, 5th Regiment, RG 15, NARA.

81. Pension File of Hannibal Wallace, 375.899, 5th Regiment, RG 15, NARA.

82. Pension File of Benjamin Lee, 380.960, 5th Regiment, RG 15, NARA.

83. Pension File of Elick Westbrooks, 171.128, 309.238, 5th Regiment, RG 15, NARA.

84. Pension File of Richard Sled, 394.755, 389.853, 5th Regiment, RG 15, NARA.

85. Pension File of George Washington, 156.961, 119.224, 5th Regiment; Pension File of Milton Compton, 165.573, 159.306, 58th Regiment, RG 15, NARA.

86. Pension File of Samuel Taylor, 210.144 J., 5th Regiment, RG 15, NARA.

87. Pension File of Calvin Gaden, 266.613, 5th Regiment, RG 15, NARA.

88. Pension File of John Posey, 374.985, 5th Regiment, RG 15, NARA.

89. Pension File of Gordan Fulgert, 320.012, 266.793, 53rd Regiment, RG 15, NARA.

90. Pension File of Nathaniel Foreman, 121.340, 177.645, 5th Regiment, RG 15, NARA.

91. Pension File of Daniel Carter, 395.505, 367.340, 5th Regiment, RG 15, NARA.

92. Pension File of William Washington, 687.674 J. 512.928, 5th Regiment, RG 15, NARA.

93. Pension File of Harvey Jackson, 122.560, OJ, 142.785, 3rd Regiment, RG 15, NARA.

94. Berlin et al., *The Wartime Genesis of Free Labor*, 844.

95. Berlin et al., *The Wartime Genesis of Free Labor*, 648.

96. Nancy Bercaw, "Politics of Household during the Transition from Slavery to Freedom in the Yazoo-Mississippi Delta, 1861–1876," (Ph.D. diss. University of Pennsylvania, 1996), 104–105, 118, 122, 133.

97. S. G. Wright to Rev. George Whipple, 7 April 1864, American Missionary Association, Mississippi, Microfilm Reel 71635. Amistad Research Center, Tulane University Library, New Orleans, Louisiana; Alfred H. Stone, vol. 42, Alfred H. Stone Collection, Department of Archives and History, Jackson, Mississippi; Berlin et al., *The Wartime Genesis of Free Labor*, 814–19; Litwack, *Been in the Storm So Long*, 319, 320; Richardson, *Christian Reconstruction*, 29–30.

98. Gutman, *The Black Family in Slavery and Freedom*, 23–24; Randy J. Sparks, "'The White People's Arms Are Longer Than Ours':" Blacks, Education, and the American Missionary Association in Reconstruction History," *The Journal of Mississippi History* LIV (February1992): 6–7; Berlin et al., *The Wartime Genesis of Free Labor*, 649, 814–18.

99. A. W. Brobet to A. S. Mitchell, March 18, 1865. Natchez, Mississippi: Unregistered Letters Received, March 1865–January 1866. Office of the Assistant Commissioner, BRFAL, RG 105, NARA.

100. Samuel Thomas, Endorsement Returned, Register of Letters Received, Office of the General Superintendent of Freedmen, BRFAL, RG 105, NARA.

101. Berlin et al., *The Wartime Genesis of Free Labor*, 810.

102. Pension File of Samuel Williams, 168.903, 175.358, 5th Regiment, RG 15, NARA.

103. Pension File of Gordan Fulgert, 320.012, 266.793, 53rd Regiment, RG 15, NARA.

104. Joseph T. Glatthaar, *Forged in Battle: The Civil War Alliance of Black Soldiers and White Officers* (New York: The Free Press, 1990), 5, 75.

105. Pension File of Love Green, 207.061, 174.498, 5th Regiment, RG 15, NARA.

106. Wiley, *Southern Negroes*, 185–86; DuBois, *Black Reconstruction in America*, 75; Quarles, *The Negro in the Civil War*, 194; Nancy Bercaw, "Politics of Household," 122.

107. Sifakis, *Who Was Who in the Civil War*, 650; Dudley Taylor Cornish, *The Sable Arm: Negro Troops in the Union Army, 1861–1865* (New York: W.W. Norton and Co., 1966), 112–14, 125; James M. McPherson, *The Negro's Civil War: How American Negroes Felt and Acted during the War for the Union* (New York: Vintage Books, 1965), 170; Cimprich, *Slavery's End in Tennessee*, 39; Wharton, *The Negro in Mississippi*, 32–33.

108. Armstead L. Robinson, "'Worser dan Jeff Davis': The Coming of Free Labor during the Civil War, 1861–1865," in *Essays on the Postbellum Southern Economy*, ed. Thavolia Glymph and John J. Kushma (College Station: Texas A & M University Press, 1985), 29. Gerteis, *From Contraband to Freedman*, 123; Wharton, *The Negro in Mississippi*, 33; Berlin et al., *The Wartime Genesis of Free Labor*, 637.

109. Berlin et al., *The Wartime Genesis of Free Labor*, 38–39, 719–20.

110. Lawrence N. Powell, *New Masters: Northern Planters during the Civil War and Reconstruction* (New Haven: Yale University Press, 1980), 3; Quarles, *The Negro in the Civil War*, 127.

111. Berlin et al., *The Wartime Genesis of Free Labor*, 799.

112. Ross H. Moore, "Social and Economic Conditions in Mississippi during Reconstruction" (Ph.D. diss., Duke University, 1937), 71; Robert L. Ransom and Richard Sutch, *One Kind of Freedom: The Economic Consequences of Emancipation* (Cambridge: Cambridge University Press, 1977), 326.

113. Gerteis, *From Contraband to Freedman*, 141; Eaton, *Grant, Lincoln, and the Freedmen*, 59.

114. Gerteis, *From Contraband to Freedman*, 124; Wharton, *The Negro in Mississippi*, 32–33; DuBois, *Black Reconstruction in America*, 75–76.

115. Ross, "Freed Soil, Freed Labor, Freed Men," 215, 217.

116. Wiley, *Southern Negroes*, 238–39; Gerteis, *From Contraband to Freedman*, 127.

117. Eaton, *Grant, Lincoln, and the Freedmen*, 59–60; Gerteis, *From Contraband to Freedman*, 124.

118. John Eaton to Hon. Henry Wilson, no date, Office of the General Superintendent of Freedmen, Letters Sent, BRFAL, RG 105, NARA.

119. Gerteis, *From Contraband to Freedman*, 127.

120. Wharton, *The Negro in Mississippi*, 35–36; Wiley, *Southern Negroes*, 223–24; Gerteis, *From Contraband to Freedman*, 135–36.

121. Gerteis, *From Contraband to Freedman*, 143.

122. Gerteis, *From Contraband to Freedman*, 140–41; for a comparison with 1870 wages, see Stanley Lebergott, *Manpower in Economic Growth: The American Record since 1800* (New York: McGraw-Hill Book Co., 1964), 539.

123. James E. Yeatman, *Report to the Western Sanitary Commission* (St. Louis: Western Sanitary Commission, 1864), 13; Gerteis, *From Contraband to Freedman*, 141–42.

124. Eaton, *Grant, Lincoln, and the Freedmen*, 154; Wharton, *The Negro in Mississippi*, 37; Berlin et al., *The Wartime Genesis of Free Labor*, 802–808.

125. Wharton, *The Negro in Mississippi*, 43.

126. Eaton, *Grant, Lincoln, and the Freedmen*, 160; Gerteis, *From Contraband to Freedman*, 164–65.

127. Wiley, *Southern Negroes*, 231.

128. Wiley, "Vicissitudes of Early Reconstruction Farming in the Lower Mississippi Valley," *Journal of Southern History* III (November1937): 448.

129. Gerteis, *From Contraband to Freedman*, 140.

130. Ross, "Freed Soil, Freed Labor, Freed Men," 223.

131. Wiley, *Southern Negroes*, 231, 242.

132. Wharton, *The Negro in Mississippi*, 37, 38; Wiley, *Southern Negroes*, 321; Berlin et al., *The Wartime Genesis of Free Labor*, 631; Davis, "The U.S. Army and the Origins of Sharecropping," 66, 69; Bigelow, "Freedmen of the Mississippi Valley," 43.

133. Wiley, *Southern Negroes*, 238.

134. Berlin et al., *The Wartime Genesis of Free Labor*, 835; Wiley, *Southern Negroes*, 242; Gerteis, *From Contraband to Freedman*, 126.

135. Pension File of Benjamin Lee, 380.960, 5th Regiment, RG 15, NARA.

136. Gerteis, *From Contraband to Freedman*, 158.

137. Berlin et al., *The Wartime Genesis of Free Labor*, 795.

138. Gerteis, *From Contraband to Freedman*, 157.

139. Berlin et al., *The Wartime Genesis of Free Labor,* 41, 644; Bercaw, "Politics of Household," 122.

140. Eaton, *Grant, Lincoln, and the Freedmen*, 217.

141. Gerteis, *From Contraband to Freedman*, 143.

142. Gerteis, *From Contraband to Freedman*, 145.

143. Powell, *New Masters*, 109. Gerteis notes that because "female workers" could not be punished by forced labor on government works," they were a less disciplined workforce. Gerteis, *From Contraband to Freedman*, 166.

144. John Eaton, Jr. letter, 11 September 1863, American Missionary Association, Microfilm Reel 71541. Amistad Research Center, Tulane University Library, New Orleans, Louisiana.

145. Gerteis, *From Contraband to Freedman*, 154–56, 183–84.

146. Jones, *Labor of Love, Labor of Sorrow*, 45. Gerteis, *From Contraband to Freedman*, 169.

147. Leslie Ann Schwalm, "The Meaning of Freedom: African-American Women and Their Transition from Slavery to Freedom in Lowcountry South Carolina" (Ph.D. diss., University of Wisconsin, 1991), 186.

148. Berlin et al., *The Wartime Genesis of Free Labor,* 679.

149. Samuel Thomas to O. O. Howard, December 22, 1865. Letters Received, D–G, October 1865–February 1866, Letters to the Commissioner, BRFAL, RG 105, NARA. M752-20; Ross, "Freed Soil, Freed Labor, Freed Men," 217; Wharton, *The Negro in Mississippi*, 39–42; Quarles, *The Negro in the Civil War*, 285–86.

150. Gerteis, *From Contraband to Freedman*, 181; Wharton, *The Negro in Mississippi*, 41; Ross, "Freed Soil, Freed Labor, Freed Men" 227.

151. Samuel Thomas to O. O. Howard.

152. James T. Currie, *Enclave: Vicksburg and Her Plantations*, 97–98.

153. Robert Cruden, *The Negro in Reconstruction* (Englewood Cliffs, N.J.: Prentice Hall, 1969), 12; DuBois, *Black Reconstruction in America*, 220–21, 310–11; James M. McPherson, *Battle Cry of Freedom*, 842; Gerteis, *From Contraband to Freedman*, 186–87; June Axinn and Herman Levin, *Social Welfare: A History of the American Response to Need* (New York: Longman Publishing Group, 1992), 110–13.

154. Wharton, *The Negro in Mississippi*, 58.

155. John Hope Franklin, *Reconstruction: After the Civil War* (Chicago: University of Chicago Press, 1961), 114.

156. George P. Rawick, ed., *The American Slave: A Composite Autobiography*, Supplement, Series 1, Vol. 10: *Mississippi Narratives*, pt. 5 (Westport, Conn.: Greenwood Press, 1974), 2070.

157. George P. Rawick, ed., *The American Slave: A Composite Autobiography*, Supplement, Series 1, Vol. 7: *Mississippi Narratives*, pt. 2 (Westport, Conn.: Greenwood Press, 1974), 628.

Appendix

Although the Freedmen's Bureau expected freedwomen and freedmen to seek employment, it reluctantly provided temporary assistance in the form of food to unemployed, destitute African American people. African American women and children received more rations than African American men. The Bureau issued fewer rations to freedmen in part because of the ability of men to find employment more readily than could unmarried women with small children. P. Whitney, a subassistant commissioner in Winchester, reported on September 28, 1867, that 39 freedmen, 120 freedwomen, and 152 freed children received provisions. In Grenada in the same month, 30 freedmen, 80 freedwomen, and 190 freed children obtained pork and corn from the Freedmen's Bureau.

Table 1: Number of Freedmen Who Received Rations, Clothing, or Medicines in the North District of Mississippi, 1865 and 1866 (Jackson, Corinth, Raymond, Grenada, and Meridian)

	Men	Women
September 1865	87	150
October 1865	39	72
November 1865	20	33
December 1865	4	8
January 1866	29	79
February 1866	11	49
Total	190	391

3. Labor after the War

1. James R. Randle, contract, Okitabbeha County, August 28, 1865. Office of the Assistant Commissioner, Labor Contracts, June 1865–June 1868, Mississippi, Bureau of Refugees, Freedmen, and Abandoned Lands (hereafter BRFAL), Record Group 105 (hereafter RG 105), National Archives and Records Administration, Washington, D.C. (hereafter NARA), M826-45.

2. Pension File of Thomas Brown, 147.977, 53rd Regiment, RG 15, NARA.

3. Gerald David Jaynes, *Branches without Roots: Genesis of the Black Working Class in the American South, 1862–1882* (New York: Oxford University Press, 1986); Leon F. Litwack, *Been in the Storm So Long: The Aftermath of Slavery* (New York: Alfred A. Knopf, 1979), 336–86; Thomas C. Holt, *The Problem of Freedom: Race, Labor, and Politics of Jamaica and Britain, 1832–1938* (Baltimore: Johns Hopkins University Press, 1992); Leslie A. Schwalm, *A Hard Fight for We: Women's Transition from Slavery to Freedom in South Carolina* (Urbana: University of Illinois Press, 1997), 187–88, 232; Eric Foner, *Reconstruction: America's Unfinished Revolution, 1863–1877* (New York: Harper and Row, 1988), 124–75.

4. James Wilford Garner, *Reconstruction in Mississippi* (Gloucester, Mass.: Peter Smith, 1964), 134; Armstead L. Robinson, "'Worser dan Jeff Davis':" The Coming of Free Labor during the Civil War, 1861–1865," in *Essays on the Post-bellum Southern Economy*, ed. Thavolia Glymph and John J. Kushma (College Station: Texas A & M University Press, 1985), 31, 33, 41, 42; Vernon Lane Wharton, *The Negro in Mississippi, 1865–1890* (New York: Harper and Row, 1965), 65; Jonathan M. Weiner, *Social Origins of the New South: Alabama, 1860–1885* (Baton Rouge: Louisiana State University Press, 1978), 43.

5. W. S. Noble, Labor Contract, July 11, 1865. Office of the Assistant Commissioner, Labor Contracts, June 1865–June 1868. BRFAL, RG 105, NARA, 826–45; Jay B. Mandle, *The Roots of Black Poverty: The Southern Plantation Economy after the Civil War* (Durham, North Carolina: Duke University Press, 1978), 33; James L. Roark, *Masters without Slaves: Southern Planters in the Civil War and Reconstruction* (New York: Norton, 1977), 144, 146, 147, 197–99.

6. John Hope Franklin, *Reconstruction: After the Civil War* (Chicago: University of Chicago Press, 1961), 44–45.

7. Wharton, *The Negro in Mississippi*, 80–91; Rebecca J. Scott, "Comparing Emancipations," *Journal of Social History* (Spring 1987): 576.

8. Convict labor was used extensively in Mississippi in the 1870s. Jaynes, *Branches without Roots*, 306.

9. Wharton, *The Negro in Mississippi*, 85.

10. Wharton, *The Negro in Mississippi*, 59. Mandle, *The Roots of Black Poverty*, 106.

11. M. Howard to O. O. Howard, April 7, 1866. Mississippi: Letters to the Commissioner, F–H, March–May 1866. BRFAL, RG 105, NARA, M752-27-34.

12. John Hope Franklin, *Reconstruction: After the Civil War*, 37.

13. J. F. H. Claiborne, Letter, September 10, 1866. Mississippi: Office of the Assistant Commissioner, Registered Letters Received, June 1865–May 1869, BRFAL, RG 105, NARA, M826-13.

14. I used a random sample from the 1870 Washington and Wilkerson census of 400 African American households in two Mississippi counties to demonstrate that less than ten percent indicated that they had real property. United States Bureau of Census, *Ninth Census of the United States* (Washington, D.C.: Government Printing Office, 1872), Microfilm Reels 752 and 753.

15. Herman Belz, "The Freedmen's Bureau Act of 1865 and the Principle of No Discrimination According to Color," *Civil War History* XXI (September 1975): 198–99; Gutman, *The Black Family in Slavery and Freedom*, 226. Belz notes the tension between "paternalistic supervision or guardianship and genuine civil liberty." See also Donald G. Nieman, *To Set the Law in Motion: The Freedmen's Bureau and the Legal Rights of Blacks, 1865–1868* (Millwood, N.Y.: KTO Press, 1979), 12.

16. Robert L. Ransom and Richard Sutch, *One Kind of Freedom: The Economic Consequences of Emancipation* (Cambridge: Cambridge University Press, 1977), 46.

17. A. M. Brobst to Captain B. F. Morey, August 9, 1865. Natchez, Mississippi: Unregistered Letters Received, October 1865–March 1866, BRFAL, RG 105, NARA.

18. Ronald L. F. Davis, "The U.S. Army and the Origins of Sharecropping in the Natchez District—A Case Study," *Journal of Negro History* LXII (January 1977): 73, 75, 80.

19. Samuel Thomas to the Colored People of Mississippi, Letters Received by the Commissioner, October 1865–February 1866. Office of the Commissioner, BRFAL, RG 105, NARA, M752-22; Jaynes, *Branches Without Roots*, 66; W. E. B. DuBois, *Black Reconstruction in America, 1860–1880* (New York: Atheneum, 1969), 173.

20. Eric Foner, *Free Soil, Free Labor, Free Men: The Ideology of the Republican*

Party before the Civil War (New York: Oxford University Press, 1970), 45; Jaynes, *Branches without Roots*, 71.

21. Foner, *Free Soil, Free Labor, Free Men*,12; John Cimprich, *Slavery's End in Tennessee, 1861–1865* (University: University of Alabama Press, 1985), 61, 63. Cimprich sees John Eaton as a paternalist and Asa Fiske (see Chapter 2) as laissez-faire. These represent the two approaches toward the freedpeople. Louis S. Gerteis also argued that Eaton was paternalist but stressed Eaton's connection with the economic interests of planters as well. Gerteis, *From Contraband to Freedman: Federal Policy toward Southern Blacks, 1861–1865* (Westport, Conn.: Greenwood Press, 1973), 153–54.

22. Foner, *Free Soil, Free Labor, Free Men*, 23–24; Lawrence N. Powell, "The American Land Company and Agency," *Civil War History* XXI (December 1975): 295.

23. Foner, *Free Soil, Free Labor, Free Men*, 18; George M. Fredrickson, *The Black Image in the White Mind: The Debate on Afro-American Character and Destiny, 1817–1914* (New York: Harper Torchbooks, 1971), 181.

24. Davis, "The U.S. Army and the Origins of Sharecropping," 74.

25. Wharton, *The Negro in Mississippi*, 75; Ransom and Sutch, *One Kind of Freedom*, 61; Jonathan M. Weiner, *Social Origins of the New South: Alabama, 1860–1885* (Baton Rouge: Louisiana State University Press, 1975), 57–58.

26. Gerteis, *From Contraband to Freedman*, 190–91.

27. Nieman, *To Set the Law in Motion*, 16.

28. Litwack, *Been in the Storm So Long*, 408, 419–20; Pete Daniel, "Commentary: The Metamorphosis of Slavery, 1865–1900," *Journal of American History* 66 (June 1979): 96.

29. Harold D. Woodman, "The Reconstruction of the Cotton Plantation in the New South," in *Essays on the Postbellum Southern Economy*, ed. Thavolia Glymph and John J. Kushma (College Station: Texas A & M University Press, 1985), 105.

30. Jaynes, *Branches Without Roots*, 303.

31. Davis, "The U.S. Army and the Origins of Sharecropping," 73.

32. John Williams to Lieut. Barber, Monthly Report, March 2, 1868. Office of the Assistant Commissioner, Narrative Reports from Subordinate Officers, August 1865–December 1868, BRFAL, RG 105, NARA, M826-32.

33. Warren Peck, General Order, August 2, 1865. Natchez, Mississippi, Unregistered Letters Received, March 1865—January 1866, BRFAL, RG 105, NARA; J. Scott Ewing, General Order, August 4, 1865, Vicksburg, Mississippi, Unregistered Letters Received, June 1865–February 1866, BRFAL, RG 105, NARA.

34. Litwack, *Been in the Storm So Long*, 317–19.

35. Even with these procedures, the African American population in Vicksburg between 1860 and 1870 tripled; in Natchez it "more than doubled." Litwack, *Been in the Storm So Long*, 313.

36. Samuel Thomas to Col. R. S. Donaldson, July 3, 1865. Jackson, Mississippi, Unregistered Letters Received, July 1865–February 1866, BRFAL, RG 105, NARA.

37. M. W. Smith and J. H Mathews, July 29, 1865. Natchez, Mississippi,

Unregistered Letters Received, March 1865–January 1866, BRFAL, RG 105, NARA; Clifton Lloyd Ganus, Jr., "The Freedmen's Bureau in Mississippi," (Ph.D. diss., Tulane University, 1953), 199.

38. M. W. Smith and J. H Mathews, July 29, 1865. Natchez, Mississippi. Unregistered Letters Received, March 1865–January 1866, BRFAL, RG 105, NARA.

39. E. L. Buckwalter to Col. Donaldson, July 29, 1965, Jackson, Mississippi. Telegrams Received, July 1865–March 1866, BRFAL, RG 105, NARA.

40. Ganus, "The Freedmen's Bureau in Mississippi," 126.

41. Pierce Butler Papers, Howard Tilton Memorial Library, Tulane University, New Orleans, Louisiana.

42. Henry M. Crydenwise to parents, March 3, 1866, Henry M. Crydenwise Papers, Duke University, Durham, North Carolina; Lawrence N. Powell, *New Masters: The Civil War and Reconstruction* (New Haven: Yale University Press, 1980), 28–29.

43. Eliza Oliver, Account, no date. Starkville, Mississippi, Freedmen's Accounts, February 1866–March 1868, BRFAL, RG 105, NARA.

44. Henry M. Crydenwise to parents.

45. Ormonde Plantation, 1866. Tools, Implements Given to Working Hands. Pierce Butler Papers, Howard Tilton Memorial Library, Tulane University, New Orleans, Louisiana.

46. W. P Gailand to J. B. Holt, May 13, 1868. Jackson, Mississippi, Sub-assistant Commissioner, Unregistered Letters Received, January 1866–December 1868, BRFAL, RG 105, NARA; J. R. Dixon to Henry, January 25, 1869, Harry St. John Dixon Papers, Duke University, Durham, North Carolina.

47. James Shipman, Labor Contract, January 12, 1867, Mississippi, Office of the Assistant Commissioner, Labor Contracts, June 1865–June 1868, M826-50, BRFAL, RG 105, NARA.

48. P. F. Howell to Alfred E. Ellet, February 9, 1866, Alfred Wass Ellet Papers, Duke University, Durham, North Carolina.

49. Lucy Davis, Complaint, November 13, 1867, Office of the Assistant Commissioner, Narrative Reports from Subordinate Officers, August 1865–December 1868, M826-31, BRFAL, RG 105, NARA.

50. Charity Riley, Complaint, September 26, 1868, Canton, Mississippi, Miscellaneous Records, 1865 and 1868, BRFAL, RG 105, NARA.

51. Venus William, Account, January 7, 1867. Starkville, Mississippi, Freedmen's Accounts, February 1866–March 1868, BRFAL, RG 105, NARA.

52. William Tidball to Captain J. W. Sunderland, September 27, 1867. Office of the Assistant Commissioner, Narrative Report from Subordinate Officers, August 1865–December 1868, M826-30, BRFAL, RG 105, NARA.

53. Robert P. Gardner to J. M. Buckley, May 1, 1866. Brookhaven, Mississippi, Letters Sent, March 1866–December 1868, BRFAL, RG 105, NARA.

54. J. W. J Niles to Thomas Wood, June 13, 1866. Office of the Assistant Commissioner, Registered Letters Received, June 1865–May 1869, BRFAL, RG 105, NARA, M826-15; G.P Collins to Anne Collins, December 16, 1866. Southern Historical Collection, University of North Carolina, Chapel Hill.

55. J. C. Caruthers to his uncle, Benton, Yazoo Co., January 2, 1866, Robert L. Caruthers Papers, Southern Historical Collection, University of North Carolina, Chapel Hill.

56. Schwalm, *A Hard Fight For We*, 208–11.

57. Fox-Genovese, *Within the Plantation Household*, 97, 128, 135–38, 155, 164, 315.

58. Litwack, *Been in the Storm So Long*, 354–58; George C. Rable, *Civil Wars: Women and the Crisis of Southern Nationalism* (Urbana: University of Illinois Press, 1991), 118–19.

59. W. Maury Darst, ed. "The Vicksburg Diary of Mrs. Alfred Ingraham (May 2–June 13, 1863)," *Journal of Mississippi History* XLIV (May 1982): 170.

60. Belle Kearney, *A Slaveholder's Daughter* (New York: Negro Universities Press, 1966), 23.

61. James C. Cobb, *The Most Southern Place on Earth: The Mississippi Delta and the Roots of Regional Identity* (New York: Oxford University Press, 1992), 39.

62. James Allen Plantation Book, Mississippi Department of Archives and History, Jackson, Mississippi, 121.

63. Samuel Andrew Agnew Diary, January 1, 1866, Southern Historical Collection, University of North Carolina, Chapel Hill; Roark, *Masters without Slaves*, 149.

64. Samuel Andrew Agnew Diary, January 5, 1866.

65. Samuel Andrew Agnew Diary, January 29, 1865.

66. Susan Dabney Smedes, *Memorials of a Southern Planter* (Baltimore: Cushings and Barkley, 1887), 234.

67. Hortense Powdermaker, *After Freedom: A Cultural Study in the Deep South* (New York: Atheneum, 1969), 119.

68. Pension File of Job Paul, 181.700, 434.267, 51st Regiment, RG 15, NARA.

69. Edward Fontaine to General Gillem, October 14, 1867. Office of the Assistant Commissioner, Registered Letters Received, June 1865–May 1869, BRFAL, RG 105, NARA, M826-21.

70. Mrs. Joseph Lowell to Capt. Joseph Lowell, February 26, 1867, Quitman Family Papers, Southern Historical Collection, Chapel Hill, North Carolina.

71. Amelia Symie to Joseph Addison Montgomery, August 13, 1866, Joseph Addison Montgomery and Family, Louisiana State University, Baton Rouge, Louisiana.

72. B. K. Johnston to R. S. Donaldson, October 3, 1865. Jackson, Mississippi, Acting Assistant Commissioner, Unregistered Letters Received, July 1865–March 1866, BRFAL, RG 105, NARA.

73. Alvan C. Gillem to O. O Howard, February 15, 1867. Letters Received by the Commissioner, M–R, January–May 1867, BRFAL, RG 105, NARA, M752-43. In *Manpower in Economic Growth: The American Record Since 1800* (New York: McGraw-Hill Book Co., 1964), 539, Stanley Lebergott recorded that in 1870 the average monthly earnings (including board) for farm laborers in New England was $19.84. Northern wages for agricultural work were far higher in the North than in the South.

74. Wharton, *The Negro in Mississippi*, 61, 69, 122–23; Jaynes, *Branches Without Roots*, 141; James T. Currie, *Enclave: Vicksburg and Her Plantations, 1863–1870* (Jackson: University Press of Mississippi, 1980), 66–67; Ransom and Sutch, *One Kind of Freedom*, 65.

75. Ross H. Moore, "Social and Economic Conditions in Mississippi during Reconstruction," (Ph. D. diss., Duke University, 1937), 71.

76. J. R. Webster, Report, February 1, 1868. Office of the Assistant Commissioner, Narrative Reports from Subordinate Officers, August 1865–December 1868, BRFAL, RG 105, NARA, M826-32.

77. Robert P. Gardner to Merritt Barber, January 31, 1868; J. R. Webster to S. C. Greene, June 1, 1868; John D. Moore to S. C. Greene, May 31, 1868. All in Office of the Assistant Commissioner, Narrative Reports from Subordinate Officers, August 1865–December 1868, BRFAL, RG 105, NARA, M826-32; Lyle Chandler, Contract, August 20, 1865. Office of the Assistant Commissioner, Labor Contracts, June 1865–June 1868, BRFAL, RG 105, NARA, M826-45; Richard Sutch and Robert L. Ransom, "Sharecropping: Market Response or Mechanism of Race Control?" in *What Was Freedom's Price*, edited by David S. Sansing (Jackson: University Press of Mississippi, 1978), 57; Thavolia Glymph, "Freedpeople and Ex-Masters: Shaping a New Order in the Postbellum South, 1865–1868," in *Essays on the Postbellum Southern Economy*, ed. Thavolia Glymph and John J. Kushma (College Station: Texas A & M University Press, 1985), 55–72; Ransom and Sutch, *One Kind of Freedom*, 61; Wharton, *The Negro in Mississippi*, 64.

78. General Gillem's Report, Report of the Commissioner of the Bureau of Refugees, Freedmen and Abandoned Lands, December 2, 1867, BRFAL, RG 105, NARA. Alfred H. Stone Collection, Mississippi Department of Archives and History, Jackson, Mississippi. For a variety of wages and wage rates, see Ransom and Sutch, *One Kind of Freedom*, 60; Jaynes, *Branches without Roots*, 52, 343; Wharton, *The Negro in Mississippi*, 65.

79. Mandle, *The Roots of Black Poverty*, 31–32; DuBois, *Black Reconstruction in America*, 171. For accounts of arrests of freedpeople in Mississippi under the Black Codes, see Glymph, "Freedpeople and Ex-Masters," 56–59; Edward Royce, *The Origins of Southern Sharecropping* (Philadelphia: Temple University Press, 1993), 26.

80. George Reynolds, Circular #1, Southern District of Mississippi, January 12, 1866. Natchez, Mississippi: Letters Sent, June 1865–March 1866, BRFAL, RG 105, NARA; Wharton, *The Negro in Mississippi*, 117.

81. John Sunderland to Leathy, Jane, and Ester, April 4, 1866. Meridian, Mississippi, Letters Sent, January 1866–February 1867, BRFAL, RG 105, NARA.

82. John J. Knox to J. J. Moore, April 16, 1866. Meridian, Mississippi, Letters Sent, January 1866–February 1867, BRFAL, RG 105, NARA.

83. John J. Knox to J. J. Moore, July 10, 1866. Meridian, Mississippi, Letters Sent, January 1866–February 1867, BRFAL, RG 105, NARA.

84. Jacqueline Jones, *Labor of Love, Labor of Sorrow: Black Women, Work and the Family, from Slavery to the Present* (New York: Vintage Books, 1985), 332; Wharton, *The Negro in Mississippi*, 68; Jaynes, *Branches without Roots*, 142, 145; Gavin Wright, *Old South, New South: Revolutions in the Southern Economy since the Civil War* (New York: Basic Books, 1986), 89, 94.

85. Ransom and Sutch, *One Kind of Freedom*, 60.

86. Daniel A. Novack, *The Wheel of Servitude: Black Forced Labor after Slavery* (Lexington: University Press of Kentucky, 1978), 24.

87. Ralph Shlomowitz, "The Origins of Southern Sharecropping," *Agricultural History* 53 (July 1979): 559.

88. S. S. Sumner to H. W. Smith, Vicksburg, September 4, 1867. Jackson,

Mississippi, Letters Sent, BRFAL, RG 105, NARA; Mandle, *The Roots of Black Poverty*, 47.

89. Wharton, *The Negro in Mississippi*, 72–73.

90. Michael Wayne, *The Reshaping of Plantation Society: The Natchez District, 1860–1880* (Baton Rouge: Louisiana State University Press, 1883), 156.

91. Freedmen's Account, no date, Starkville, Mississippi, Freedmen's Accounts, February 1866–March 1868, BRFAL, RG 105, NARA; Ransom and Sutch, *One Kind of Freedom*, 120.

92. Freedmen's Account, no date, Starkville, BRFAL, RG 105, NARA; C. L. C. Cass to Elizabeth Haines, no date, Macon, Mississippi, Miscellaneous Records, 1865–1867, BRFAL, RG 105, NARA; Accounts with Freedpeople, Alexander K. Farrar Papers, Department of Archives and Manuscripts, Louisiana State University, Baton Rouge, Louisiana.

93. Freedmen's Account, no date, Starkville, BRFAL, RG 105, NARA; Accounts with Freedpeople, Alexander K. Farrar Papers, Department of Archives and Manuscripts, Louisiana State University, Baton Rouge, Louisiana.

94. Amelia Williams, Complaint, September 6, 1867. Greenville, Mississippi, Register of Complaints, September–December 1867, BRFAL, RG 105, NARA.

95. Sam Anderson and Caroline, Labor Contract, Madison County, November 16, 1865. Office of the Assistant Commissioner, Labor Contracts, June 1865–June 1868, BRFAL, RG 105, NARA, M826-48.

96. E. J. Capell Contract, January 21, 1868, Amite County, Mississippi, Eli Capell Papers, Department of Archives and Manuscripts, Louisiana State University, Baton Rouge, Louisiana.

97. Wayne, *The Reshaping of Plantation Society*, 120.

98. Ransom and Sutch, *One Kind of Freedom*, 65–67.

99. Ransom and Sutch, *One Kind of Freedom*, 57; Jaynes, *Branches without Roots*, 44, 83.

100. Jaynes, *Branches without Roots*, 169, 171, 182; Wright, *Old South, New South*, 86–87; Ronald L. F. Davis, *Good and Faithful Labor: From Slavery to Sharecropping in the Natchez District, 1860–1890* (Westport, Conn.: Greenwood Press, 1982), 175.

101. E. Bamberger to Critchfield, October 10, 1865, Canton, Mississippi. Letters Received, July–December 1865, BRFAL, RG 105, NARA; Julia Caldwell to Mr. White, 9 September 1867. Jackson, Mississippi. Subassistant Commissioner, Unregistered Letters Received, January 1866–December 1868, BRFAL, RG 105, NARA.

102. Hannah Arendt, *On Violence* (New York: Harcourt, Brace and World, 1970), 64, 79; Litwack, *Been in the Storm So Long*, 275, 278, 371; DuBois, *Black Reconstruction in America*, 672; Pete Daniel, "Commentary: The Metamorphosis of Slavery," 88–99; Bertram Wyatt-Brown, *Southern Honor: Ethics and Behavior in the Old South* (New York: Oxford University Press, 1982), 153.

103. Paul A. David, Herbert G. Gutman, Richard Sutch, Peter Temin, and Gavin Wright, *Reckoning with Slavery: A Critical Study in the Quantitative History of American Negro Slavery* (New York: Oxford University Press, 1976), 59.

104. Mary Conner, Complaint, April 20, 1867. Grenada, Mississippi, Registers of Complaints, July 1866–December 1868, BRFAL, RG 105, NARA.

105. George Haller, Report, July 1868. Office of the Assistant Commissioner, Narrative Reports from Subordinate Officers, August 1865–December 1868, BRFAL, RG 105, NARA, M826-33.

106. W. F. DuBois to E. Bamberger, December 5, 1865, Affidavit of Harriet Kane, December 5, 1865 (included in DuBois's letter). Jackson, Mississippi, Acting Assistant Commissioner, Registered Letters Received, July 1865–March 1866, BRFAL, RG 105, NARA.

107. Captain Griffin to Stuart Eldridge, August 21, 1865. Office of the Assistant Commissioner, Narrative Reports from Subordinate Officers, August 1865–December 1868, BRFAL, RG 105, NARA, M826-30.

108. Robert P. Gardner to F. B. Hern, July 14, 1866. Pass Christian, Mississippi, Letters Sent, April 1866–September 1867, BRFAL, RG 105, NARA; P. P. Bergeoni, Report, November 1868. Office of the Assistant Commissioner, Narrative Reports from Subordinate Officers, August 1865–December 1868, BRFAL, RG 105, NARA, M826-33; Lloyd Wheaton to S. C. Greene, July 31, 1868. Office of the Assistant Commissioner, Narrative Reports from Subordinate Officers, BRFAL, RG 105, NARA, M826-33; E. W. Wallin [to Alvan C. Gillem], May 23, 1867. Office of the Assistant Commissioner, Registers of Letters Received, BRFAL, RG 105, NARA, M826-6; Bob Eldridge [to Alvan C. Gillem], July 5, 1867. Office of the Assistant Commissioner, Register of Letters Received, BRFAL, RG 105, NARA, M826-6; W. S. Sharkey to Col. Samuel Thomas, October 4, 1866. Office of the Assistant Commissioner, Registered Letters Received, June 1865–May 1869, BRFAL, RG 105, NARA, M826-11; Nancy Emaline, Complaint, September 28, 1865. Hernando, Mississippi, Register of Complaints and Trials, September–October 1865, BRFAL, RG 105, NARA; Lloyd Wheaton to William Shinault, 17 October 1867. Corinth, Mississippi, Letters Sent, March 1867–December 1868, BRFAL, RG 105, NARA; P. P. Bergeoni, Report, October 31, 1868. Office of the Assistant Commissioner, Narrative Reports from Subordinate Officers, August 1865–December 1868, BRFAL, RG 105, NARA, M826-33; John W. Sunderland to Berry Bandy, June 29, 1866. Meridian, Mississippi, Letters Sent, January 1866–February 1867, BRFAL, RG 105, NARA; Jack McDonald, Complaint, September 18, 1867, DeKalb, Mississippi. Register of Complaints, September 1867–February 1868, BRFAL, RG 105, NARA; Viney and Julia, Complaint, 30 July 1866. Grenada, Mississippi, Registers of Complaints, July 1866–December 1868, BRFAL, RG 105, NARA; E. E. Platt to Judge Bagetter, April 25, 1868. Brookhaven, Mississippi, Letters Sent, March 1866–December 1868, BRFAL, RG 105, NARA; Martha Randolf, Complaint, May 11, 1868. Magnolia, Mississippi, Register of Complaints, August 1867–December 1868, BRFAL, RG 105, NARA; Mary Ann, Complaint, December 3, 1868. Grenada, Mississippi, Registers of Complaints, July 1866–December 1868, BRFAL, RG 105, NARA; Lloyd Wheaton to S. C. Greene, June 30, 1868. Office of the Assistant Commissioner, Narrative Reports from Subordinate Officers, August 1865–December 1868, BRFAL, RG 105, NARA, M826-33.

109. Major George D. Reynolds, Endorsement Returned, January 8, 1866, Office of the Assistant Commissioner, Endorsements Sent and Received, June 1865–December 1868, BRFAL, RG 105, NARA, M826-4; E. E. Platt to Stewart Eldridge, June 5, 1866, Registered Letters Received, June 1865–May 1869,

BRFAL, RG 105, NARA, M826-15; Leon C. Duchesne, Court Record, October 29, 1865, Natchez, Mississippi, Miscellaneous Records, August 1864–October 1865, BRFAL, RG 105, NARA.

110. John Rowland to General Ord, June 21, 1867. Office of the Assistant Commissioner, Registered Letters Received, June 1865–May 1869, M826-19, BRFAL, RG 105, NARA.

111. Lieut. H. R. Williams, Endorsement, October 10, 1867. Office of the Assistant Commissioner, Endorsements Sent and Received, June 1865–December 1868, BRFAL, RG 105, NARA, M826-4.

112. Virginia Stewart, Complaint, August 12, 1867, Vicksburg, Mississippi. Letters Sent Relating to Complaints, BRFAL, RG 105, NARA; Captain E. E. Platt, Report, August 1867. Office of the Assistant Commissioner, Narrative Reports from Subordinate Officers, August 1865–December 1868, BRFAL, RG 105, NARA, M826-30.

113. Lina, Complaint, August 30, 1865. Brookhaven, Mississippi, Miscellaneous Records, August 1865–November 1868, BRFAL, RG 105, NARA; E. G. Gilbreath to J. W. Sunderland, September 30, 1867. Office of the Assistant Commissioner, Narrative Reports from Subordinate Officers, August 1865–December 1868, BRFAL, RG 105, NARA, M826-30.

114. O. D. Greene, Letter, August 17, 1867. Office of the Assistant Commissioner, Registers of Letters Received, June 1865–May 1869, BRFAL, RG 105, NARA, M826-7.

115. S. S. Sumner to Thomas Schokleford, September 12, 1867. Jackson, Mississippi, Subassistant Commissioner, Letters Sent, March 1866–December 1868, BRFAL, RG 105, NARA.

116. R. S. Donaldson to W. A. Gordon, September 28, 1865. Jackson, Mississippi, Acting Assistant Commissioner, Letters Sent, July 1865–March 1866, BRFAL, RG 105, NARA; Harriet Murray, Complaint, no date, Sardis, Mississippi. Letters Sent; D. S. Harriman to General Gillem, November 26, 1867. Office of the Assistant Commissioner, Registered Letters Received, June 1865–May 1869, BRFAL, RG 105, NARA, M826-21.

117. Richard Sutch and Robert L. Ransom, "Sharecropping: Market Response or Mechanism of Race Control?," 57; Holt, *The Problem of Freedom*, 152–54.

118. Jaynes, *Branches without Roots*, 87.

119. Joan M. Jensen, *With These Hands: Women Working on the Land*, 73; Susan A. Mann, "Slavery, Sharecropping, and Sexual Inequality," *Signs* 14 (Summer 1989): 782.

120. Newton Ford, Contract, January 16, 1866, M826-49; J. C. Croker, Contract, 13 January 1866. M826-49; W. M. Leigh, Contract, October 8, 1865, M826-48; Mary F. King, Contract, August 10, 1865, M826-47, all in Office of the Assistant Commissioner, Labor Contracts, June 1865–June 1868, BRFAL, RG 105, NARA; Francis Houston, Complaint, 8 December 1867. De Kalb, Mississippi, Register of Complaints, September 1867–February 1868, BRFAL, RG 105, NARA.

121. Cretia Evans, Account, December 11, 1867. Starkville, Mississippi, Freedmen's Accounts, February, 1866–March 1868, BRFAL, RG 105, NARA.

122. Thomas Norton to S. C. Greene, June 30, 1868. Office of the Assistant Commissioner, Narrative Reports from Subordinate Officers, August 1865–December 1868, BRFAL, RG 105, NARA, M826-33; Jones & Boyd (employers), Contract, January 1, 1865, Labor Contracts of Freedmen, January–June 1865, M826-43, BRFAL, RG 105, NARA; Joseph E. Wilson, Settlement, November 16, 1868. Jackson, Mississippi, Subassistant Commissioner, Miscellaneous Records, 1865–1868, BRFAL, RG 105, NARA.

123. J. G. Colbert, Contract, January 1, 1867, Office of the Assistant Commissioner, Labor Contracts, June 1865–June 1868, BRFAL, M826-50, RG 105, NARA.

124. J. Williams, February 1868, Durant, Mississippi. Narrative Reports from Subordinate Officers, Report of Complaints and Investigations, M826-32, BRFAL, RG 105, NARA.

125. Robin D. G. Kelley, *Hammer and Hoe: Alabama Communists during the Great Depression* (Chapel Hill: University of North Carolina Press, 1990), 36.

126. Pension File of Leonard Barnes, 315.847, 250.920, 53rd Regiment, RG 15, NARA.

127. Pension File of Nicholas Thomas, 197.568, J. 626.450, 5th Regiment, RG 15, NARA.

128. Edmund L. Drago, "Militancy and Black Women in Reconstruction Georgia," *Journal of American Culture* 1 (Winter 1978): 842. See also David L. Cohen, *The Life and Times of King Cotton* (New York: Oxford University Press, 1956), 157; Litwack, *Been in the Storm So Long*, 244, 341; Foner, *Reconstruction*, 85; Eugene D. Genovese, *Roll, Jordan, Roll: The World the Slaves Made* (New York: Vintage Books, 1974), 490; Jones, *Labor of Love, Labor of Sorrow*, 58–59, 60; Powell, *New Masters: The Civil War and Reconstruction*, 108, 109; Stanley Engerman, "Some Considerations Relating to Property Rights in Man," *Journal of Economic History* 33 (March 1973): 50; Gutman, *The Black Family in Slavery and Freedom*, 167–68; Moore, "Social and Economic Conditions in Mississippi during Reconstruction," 34; Weiner, *Social Origins of the New South*, 47; Ira Berlin, Thavolia Glymph, Steven F. Miller, Joseph P. Reidy, Leslie S. Rowland, and Julie Saville, *The Wartime Genesis of Free Labor: The Lower South*, Series I, Volume III of *Freedom: A Documentary History of Emancipation, 1861–1867* (New York: Cambridge University Press, 1990), 69; bell hooks, *Ain't I a Woman: Black Women and Feminism* (Boston: South End Press, 1983), 48–49; In *Old South, New South: Revolutions in the Southern Economy since the Civil War*, Gavin Wright raises questions about whether withdrawal of women was voluntary (p. 36); See also Jaynes, *Branches without Roots*, 228–32, 235, 241, 322.

Evelyn Higginbotham argues that the discussion of the decision of African American women to continue to work for whites after the Civil War was very complex. "[T]he interplay of the race-class conflation with gender evoked very different social perceptions of black and white women's work roles. . . . In contrast to the domestic ideal for white women of all classes, the larger society deemed it 'unnatural,' in fact an 'evil' for black married women to play the lady while their husbands supported them." Evelyn Brooks Higginbotham, "African-American Women's History and the Metalanguage of Race," *Signs* 17 (Winter 1992): 259–60. See also Schwalm, *A Hard Fight for We*, 211–14.

129. James Oliver Horton, "Freedom's Yoke: Gender Conventions among Antebellum Free Blacks," *Feminist Studies* 12 (Spring 1986): 52.

130. Powell, *New Masters: the Civil War and Reconstruction*, 108.

131. Schwalm, *A Hard Fight for We*, 38.

132. Schwalm, *A Hard Fight for We*, 38.

133. Laura Edwards, "The Illusion of Freedom: Economic Development in Granville County, North Carolina, 1865–1900," paper presented at the Newberry Seminar, Newberry Library, Chicago, Illinois, February 23, 1991, 2.

134. Wilmer Shields to William Newton Mercer, March 27, 1867, William N. Mercer Papers, Department of Archives and Manuscripts, Louisiana State University, Baton Rouge; Davis, *Good and Faithful Labor*, 170–71.

135. William Newton Mercer, Diary, February 23, 1866, Pierce Butler Papers, Manuscripts Section, Howard Tilton Memorial Library, Tulane University, New Orleans, Louisiana.

136. Mercer Diary, February 23, 1866. See also Kenneth S. Greenberg, "The Civil War and the Redistribution of Land: Adams County, Mississippi, 1860–1870," *Agricultural History* 52 (April 1978): 299.

137. J. W. Fields, Contract, July 1, 1865. Office of the Assistant Commissioner, Labor Contracts, June 1865–June 1868, M826-44, BRFAL, RG 105, NARA.

138. William L. Tidball, Report, September 1867. Office of the Assistant Commissioner, Narrative Reports from Subordinate Officers, August 1865–December 1868, M826-30, BRFAL, RG 105, NARA; Litwack, *Been in the Storm So Long*, 136–37.

139. J. B. G. Reilly, Yazoo, Labor Contract with Fanny & July, January 1, 1866. Office of the Assistant Commissioner, Labor Contracts, June 1865–June 1868, M826-49, BRFAL, RG 105, NARA.

140. James Gillespie, Contract, Adams Co., Hollywood Plantation, January 4, 1867, Department of Archives and Manuscripts, Louisiana State University, Baton Rouge, Louisiana; Davis, *Good and Faithful Labor*, 103.

141. J.C. Caruthers to R. L. Caruthers, Caruthers Papers, Benton, Yazoo Co., Mississippi, January 2, 1866, Southern Historical Collection, University of North Carolina, Chapel Hill; Jaynes, *Branches without Roots*, 112.

142. B. K. Johnston to E. Bamberger, November 22, 1865. Jackson, Mississippi, Acting Assistant Commissioner, Registered Letters Received, July 1865–March 1866, BRFAL, RG 105, NARA.

143. W. F. DuBois to E. Bamberger, Okolona, December 5, 1865. Jackson, Mississippi, Acting Assistant Commissioner, Registered Letters Received, July 1865–March 1866, BRFAL, RG 105, NARA.

144. Jaynes, *Branches Without Roots*, 44.

145. Moore, "Social and Economic Conditions in Mississippi During Reconstruction," 59.

146. Contract, January 1866, William Newton Mercer, Adams County, Pierce Butler Papers, Manuscripts Section, Howard Tilton Memorial Library, Tulane University, New Orleans, Louisiana.

147. J.C. Caruthers to R. L. Caruthers, Caruthers Papers, Benton, Yazoo Co., Mississippi, January 9, 1867, Southern Historical Collection, University of North Carolina, Chapel Hill; for another example, see Robert H. Hord, Labor Contract, Washington County, 9 September 1868. BRFAL, RG 105, NARA, M826-50.

148. G. P. Collins to Anne Collins, December 16, 1866, Tunica County, Box 1, Southern Historical Collection, University of North Carolina, Chapel Hill.

149. R. S. Donaldson to W. A. Gordon, September 28, 1865. Jackson, Mississippi, Acting Assistant Commissioner, Letters Sent, July 1865–March 1866, BRFAL, RG 105, NARA; Harriet Murray, Complaint, no date, Sardis, Mississippi. Letters Sent, July and September–October 1868, BRFAL, RG 105, NARA; D. S. Harriman to General Gillem, 26 November 1867. Office of the Assistant Commissioner, Registered Letters Received, June 1865–May 1869, BRFAL, RG 105, NARA, M826-21.

150. A. W. Manner, Report, December 31, 1868. Narrative Reports from Subordinate Officers, August 1865–December 1868, BRFAL, RG 105, NARA, M826-31.

151. James Moore, Contract, December 27, 1865. Office of the Assistant Commissioner, Labor Contracts, June 1865–June 1868, BRFAL, RG 105, NARA, M826-49.

152. R. L. Caruthers, Contract, January 1, 1866. Office of the Assistant Commissioner, Labor Contracts, June 1865–June 1868, BRFAL, RG 105, NARA, M826-49.

153. M. V. Hamilton, Contract, January 4, 1867. Office of the Assistant Commissioner, Labor Contracts, June 1865–June 1868, BRFAL, RG 105, NARA, M826-50.

154. N. B. Forrest to General Wood, October 10, 1866. Vicksburg, Mississippi, Unregistered Letters Received, April 1866–October 1868, BRFAL, RG 105, NARA. See also Allan Crosby, Complaint, December 28, 1867. Louisville, Mississippi, Register of Complaints, September 1867–November 1868, BRFAL, RG 105, NARA.

155. J. W. Robertson, Contract, January 5, 1866. Office of the Assistant Commissioner, Labor Contracts, June 1865–June 1868, BRFAL, RG 105, NARA, M826-49.

156. William A. Cross, Contract, August 27, 1865; W. P. Love, Contract, August 11, 1865; Samuel Muson, Contract, August 12, 1865; Henry Johnson, Contract, August 10, 1865; A. J. Brown, Contract, August 1, 1865; J. A. Valentine, Contract, September 18, 1865. All in Office of the Assistant Commissioner, Labor Contracts, June 1865–June 1868, BRFAL, RG 105, NARA, M826-45.

157. P. L. Howe, near Okolona, Chickasaw County, August 18, 1865. Office of the Assistant Commissioner, Labor Contracts, June 1865–June 1868, BRFAL, RG 105, NARA, M826-45.

158. William Fox, Contract, August 11, 1865. Office of the Assistant Commissioner, Labor Contracts, June 1865–June 1868, BRFAL, RG 105, NARA, M826-45.

159. Ransom and Sutch, *One Kind of Freedom*, 55; Jaynes, *Branches Without Roots*, 68–69, 229.

160. Pickney Vaughn, Contract, February 1866. Office of the Assistant Commissioner, Labor Contracts, June 1865–June 1868, BRFAL, RG 105, NARA, M826-50.

161. Peter Dickson against Albert Wells, 12 August 1864, Columbus, Mis-

sissippi, Register of Complaints, August 1867–May 1868, Vol. 112, BRFAL, RG 105, NARA.

162. United States Congress, 42nd Congress, Senate Report, No. 41, Pt. 11, *Testimony Taken by the U.S. Congress Joint Select Committee on Conditions of Affairs in the Late Insurrectionary States* (Washington, D.C.: Government Printing Office, 1872), 570.

163. Guston Hearney to Provost Marshall, Vernon, September 23, 1865. Jackson, Mississippi, Acting Assistant Commissioner, Registered Letters Received, July 1865–March 1866, BRFAL, RG 105, NARA; Jaynes, *Branches without Roots*, 88.

164. John Williams to Capt. Sunderland, November 1, 1867, Louisville, Mississippi. Letters Sent, BRFAL, RG 105, NARA.

165. Jaynes, *Branches without Roots*, 187. The census designation of housekeeper ignored women's seasonal employment.

166. Wayne, *The Reshaping of Plantation Society*, 122.

167. Ransom and Sutch, *One Kind of Freedom*, 232–36.

168. Ralph Shlomowitz, "Plantations and Smallholding: Comparative Perspectives from the World Cotton and Sugar Cane Economics, 1865–1939," *Agricultural History* 58 (January 1984): 6; in *Reconstruction*, Eric Foner writes that "This was the pattern at Davis Bend, Mississippi, where most black women listed their occupation as 'keeping house' or 'at home' in 1870, but labored in the fields, often with their children at cotton-picking time" (p. 86). See also Ransom and Sutch, *One Kind of Freedom*, 370; Wharton, *The Negro in Mississippi*, 66.

169. No author, Report, no day October 1868. Office of the Assistant Commissioner, Narrative Reports from Subordinate Officers, August 1865–December 1868, BRFAL, RG 105, NARA, M826-33.

170. George Corliss, Report, November 30, 1867. Office of the Assistant Commissioner, Narrative Reports from Subordinate Officers, August 1865–December 1868, BRFAL, RG 105, NARA, M826-31.

171. Dempsey Turner, Complaint, November 30, 1867. Register of Complaints, Sardis, Mississippi, Letters Sent, September–November 1867, BRFAL, RG 105, NARA; James T. Currie, *Enclave: Vicksburg and Her Plantations, 1862–1870* (Jackson: University Press of Mississippi, 1980), 176.

172. Donald McIver to John McIver, May 15, 1867, John McIver Papers, Duke University, Durham, North Carolina.

173. Hattie Freeman to Mr. and Mrs. Wright, Columbus, November 11, 1869, American Missionary Association, Dillard University, Amistad Research Center, New Orleans, Louisiana.

174. Susan A. Mann, "Slavery, Sharecropping, and Sexual Inequality," 782–83; Wharton, *The Negro in Mississippi*, 70.

175. Jaynes argues that squads evolved into the sharecropping system in *Branches Without Roots*, 187–88.

176. DuBois, *Black Reconstruction in America, 1860–1880* (New York: Atheneum, 1962), 431.

177. Ransom and Sutch, *One Kind of Freedom*, 67, 70, 94–97; Davis, *Good and Faithful Labor*, 3; Jonathan M. Weiner, *Social Origins of the New South: Alabama, 1860–1885*, 69. Barbara Jeanne Fields, "The Advent of Capitalist Agriculture:

The New South in a Bourgeois World," in *Essays on the Postbellum Southern Economy*, ed. Thavolia Glymph and John J. Kushma (College Station: Texas A & M University Press, 1985), 83.

178. Currie, *Enclave: Vicksburg and Her Plantations*,170; Wharton, *The Negro in Mississippi*, 69; Ralph Shlomowitz, "The Origins of Southern Sharecropping," 592.

179. George P. Rawick, ed., *The American Slave: A Composite Autobiography*, Supplement, Series 1, Vol. 1: *Mississippi Narratives*, pt. 6 (Westport, Conn.: Greenwood Press, 1974), 278.

180. Litwack, *Been in the Storm So Long*, 220.

181. George P. Rawick, ed., *The American Slave*, Supplement, Series 1, Vol. 1, 161.

4. Male and Female Intimate Relationships

1. Pension File of George Washington, 304.839, 396.122, 5th Regiment, Record Group 15 (hereafter RG 15), National Archives and Records Administration (hereafter NARA), Washington, D.C.

2. Pension File of Thomas Brown, 147.977, 53rd Regiment, RG 15, NARA.

3. Historian Rebecca J. Scott wrote "However, one should not confuse the absence of legal marriage with an absence of perceived family responsibility, nor assume that hostile conditions made the formation of families impossible." *Slave Emancipation in Cuba: The Transition to Free Labor, 1860–1899* (Princeton: Princeton University Press), 17.

4. Herbert G. Gutman, *The Black Family in Slavery and Freedom, 1750–1925* (New York: Vintage Books, 1977), 32–33.

5. Barbara Bush, *Slave Women in Caribbean Society* (Bloomington: Indiana University Press, 1990), 100–102; Darlene Clark Hine, "Lifting the View, Shattering the Silence: Black Women's History in Slavery and Freedom," in *The State of Afro-American History: Past, Present, and Future*, ed. Darlene Clark Hine (Baton Rouge: Louisiana State University Press, 1986), 225.

6. Leslie A. Schwalm, *A Hard Fight For We: Women's Transition from Slavery to Freedom in South Carolina* (Urbana: University of Illinois Press, 1997), 248.

7. James Wilford Garner, *Reconstruction in Mississippi* (Gloucester, Mass.: Peter Smith, 1964), 287; Ira Berlin, Steven F. Miller, and Leslie S. Rowlands, ed., "Afro-American Families in the Transition from Slavery to Freedom," *Radical History Review* 42 (September 1988): 92, 98; Suzanne Lebsock, *The Free Women of Petersburg: Status and Culture in a Southern Town, 1784–1860*, 105–108.

8. Michael Tadman, *Speculators and Slaves: Masters, Traders, and Slaves in the Old South* (Madison: University of Wisconsin Press, 1989), 176.

9. The number and percentage of marriage licenses issued in Mississippi between 1865 and 1870 failed to show great differences in the percentages of marriages of whites and African Americans after the war and the majority of the marriages for both races were probably new marriages rather than freedpeople remarrying the slave spouses. In 1860 the African American population numbered 239,950, 56 percent of the total population. In 1866 approximately 500 more African Americans than whites received licenses and accounted for 54 percent of marriages. The 700 marriage licenses granted to African Americans in

1867 meant that African Americans comprised 55 percent of new marriages. In 1868 they accounted for 52 percent of new marriages; in 1869, 900 African Americans received marriage licenses (57 percent of all licenses granted that year in Mississippi). These numbers possibly indicate that these were primarily first marriages for both white and African Americans, given the fairly young population of Mississippi African Americans. If great numbers of slave couples were remarrying, it is likely that there would have been greater disparity in the percentages between the population of African Americans and whites getting married. In 1870 the number of freedpeople who married in Mississippi jumped to 1200, giving African Americans 61 percent of the new marriage licenses. This increase may have been caused in part by the confusion over the meaning of the 1868 Mississippi constitution. Garner, *Reconstruction in Mississippi*, 287; W. E. B. DuBois, *Black Reconstruction in America, 1868–1890* (Kingsport, Tenn.: Atheneum Publishers, 1962), 447; Gutman, *The Black Family in Slavery and Freedom*, 20, 187–88, 429.

10. Gutman, *The Black Family in Slavery and Freedom*, 429.

11. Francis A. Walker, *The Statistics of the Population of the United States, Ninth Census of the United States* (Washington, D.C.: Government Printing Office, 1872), 630–31.

12. D. S. Harriman to Merritt Barber, Panola, Mississippi, March 12, 1867. Office of the Assistant Commissioner, Narrative Reports from Subordinate Officers, August 1865–December 1868, BRFAL, RG 105, NARA, M826-31.

13. George P. Rawick, ed., *The American Slave: A Composite Autobiography*, Supplement, Series 1, Vol. 7: *Mississippi Narratives*, pt. 2 (Westport, Conn.: Greenwood Press, 1974), 526.

14. A. W. Preston, Endorsement, January 18, 1867. Office of the Assistant Commissioner, Endorsements Sent and Received, June 1865–December 1868, BRFAL, RG 105, NARA, M826-4.

15. Alvan Gillem to O. O. Howard, December 12, 1868. Office of the Assistant Commissioner, Press Copies of Letters of Sent, June 1865–April 1869, BRFAL, RG 105, NARA, M826-3; Gutman, *The Black Family in Slavery and Freedom*, 428. Freedpeople weren't the only ones confused. Herbert Gutman states that, "in November1865, the Mississippi legislature stamped approval on all slave marriages and declared their offspring 'legitimate for all purposes.'" In fact the Mississippi legislation disallowed all slave marriages and only legalized couples who cohabited in 1865. Gutman goes on to relate how one judge simply ignored the law in a custody case.

16. J. R. Webster, Report, February 7, 1868. Office of the Assistant Commissioner, Narrative Reports from Subordinate Officers, August 1865–December 1868, BRFAL, RG 105, NARA, M826-32.

17. Pension File of Joseph Duncan, 767.326, 567.264, 5th Regiment, RG 15, NARA.

18. Garner, *Reconstruction in Mississippi*, 287.

19. Pension File of Caesar Wilson, 294.985, 344.458, 5th Regiment, RG 15, NARA; Warren Brooks, 205.192, 186.147, 5th Regiment, RG 15, NARA; Floyd V. Calvert, *Reports of Cases in the Supreme Court for the State of Mississippi*, LIII (Boston: Little, Brown, and Co., 1877), 37–39, 45–46; Adams V. Adams, *Reports of Cases in the Supreme Court for the State of Mississippi*, LVII (Boston: Little, Brown,

and Co., 1880), 269–70. Although the statute in the 1865 constitution only applied to former slave couples, the 1869 law applied to all couples regardless of race. The passage of Civil Rights legislation at the federal level was interpreted as a prohibition of specific mention of race in legislation. The 1869 constitution deleted or changed passages from the 1865 Mississippi constitution that had referred specifically to African American freedmen. *Journal of the Proceedings in the Constitutional Convention of the State of Mississippi* (Jackson, Miss.: E. Stafford, 1871), 333.

20. Pension File of Frank Fletcher, 782.007, 599.542, 5th Regiment, RG 15, NARA.

21. Pension File of Joseph Duncan, 767.326, 567.264, 5th Regiment, RG 15, NARA.

22. Pension File of Lenn Bowling, 380.843 J, 3rd Regiment, RG 15, NARA.

23. George P. Rawick, ed., *The American Slave: A Composite Autobiography*, Supplement, Series 1, Vol. 9: *Mississippi Narratives*, pt. 4 (Westport, Conn.: Greenwood Press, 1974), 1431. Medora Peagram, *Reporter of Cases in the Supreme Court for the State of Mississippi*, XLIX, October term 1873, and April term, 1874 (Jackson, Mississippi: Pilot Publishing Co., Printers and Binders, 1874) 753, 755, 757 and George P. Rawick, ed., *The American Slave: A Composite Autobiography*, Supplement, Series 1, Vol. 10: *Mississippi Narratives*, pt. 5 (Westport, Conn.: Greenwood Press, 1974), 2234.

24. For more about laws that interpreted the validity of slave marriages, see Berlin et al., "Afro-American Families in the Transition from Slavery to Freedom," 98. The Maryland Assembly of 1867 "repealed many parts of the Black Code but among other things, did not allow a colored woman to be a competent witness against the white father of her child." DuBois, *Black Reconstruction in America*, 564.

25. Reed v. Moseley, *Mississippi and Southern Reporter Digest*, Vol. 23, February 16–September 21, 1898 (St. Paul: West Publishing Co., 1898), 76, 451; Andrews v. Simmons, *Mississippi and Southern Reporter Digest*, Vol. 10, October 28, 1891–May 25, 1892 (St. Paul: West Publishing Co., 1892), 65; Haines v. Haines, *Mississippi and Southern Reporter Digest*, Vol. 43, March 23–June 29, 1907 (St. Paul: West Publishing Co., 1907), 465.

26. Thomas H. Norton to John Whitney, August 19, 1867. Meridian, Mississippi, Letters Sent, July 1867–July 1868, BRFAL, RG 105, NARA.

27. P. P. Benjamin to S. C. Green, 30 May 1868. Office of the Assistant Commissioner, Registered Letters Received, June 1865–May 1869, BRFAL, RG 105, NARA, M826-23.

28. Alvan Gillem to O. O. Howard, December 12, 1868. Office of the Assistant Commissioner, Press Copies of Letters Sent, June 1865–April 1869, BRFAL, RG 105, NARA, M826-3.

29. George Corliss, Report, November 30, 1867. Office of the Assistant Commissioner, Narrative Reports from Subordinate Officers, August 1865–December 1868, BRFAL, RG 105, NARA, M826-31.

30. Theodore Wilson, Endorsement, September 3, 1867. Office of the Assistant Commissioner, Endorsements Sent and Received, June 1865–December 1868, BRFAL, RG 105, NARA, M826-4.

31. Reed v. Moseley; Andrews v. Simmons; Haines v. Haines.

32. Gutman, *The Black Family in Slavery and Freedom*, 70–74.

33. J. H. Chapman, Report, Vicksburg, April 10, 1868. Office of the Assistant Commissioner, Narrative Reports from Subordinate Officers, August 1865–December 1868, BRFAL, RG 105, NARA, M826-32.

34. T. S. Free to Samuel Thomas, September 9, 1865. Office of the Assistant Commissioner, Registers of Letters Received, June 1865–May 1869, BRFAL, RG 105, NARA, M826-9.

35. Pension Files of Robert Williams, 825.643 J. 597.764, 5th Regiment, RG 15, NARA; William Pleasant, 73.966, 541.171, 5th Regiment, RG 15, NARA; Solomon Griffin, 791.551, 564.716, 709.789, 5th Regiment, RG 15, NARA.

36. Pension Files of James Coleman, 373.043, 5th Regiment, RG 15, NARA; Alfred Johnson, 649.922 J. 566.335, 5th Regiment, RG 15, NARA; Watt Lee, 412.464 J. 577.520, 5th Regiment, RG 15, NARA.

37. Pension File of Henry Turner, 789.179 cert. 574.604, 5th Regiment, RG 15, NARA.

38. Pension File of James Dewar, 795.550, 573.380, 5th Regiment, RG 15, NARA.

39. Pension Files of Sam McCaskill, 145.087, 126.509, 3rd Regiment, RG 15, NARA; William Duncan, 126.417, 112.130, 5th Regiment, RG 15, NARA.

40. Pension Files of Joseph Wells, 128.576, cert. 115.572, 632.823, 5th Regiment, RG 15, NARA; Jeff Boose, 400.738, 3rd Regiment, RG 15, NARA.

41. Gutman, *The Black Family in Slavery and Freedom*, 392–96.

42. Linda Gordon, "Black and White Visions of Welfare: Women's Welfare Activism, 1890–1945," *Journal of American History* 78 (September 1991): 579.

43. Ira Berlin, Thavolia Glymph, Steven F. Miller, Joseph P. Reidy, Leslie S. Rowland, and Julie Saville, *The Wartime Genesis of Free Labor: The Lower South*, Series I, Volume III of *Freedom: A Documentary History of Emancipation, 1861–1867* (New York: Cambridge University Press, 1990), 698.

44. To the Freedpeople from E. E. Platt to Mr. Reskeys Hands, July 1, 1866. Natchez, Mississippi, Miscellaneous Records, August 1864–October 1865, BRFAL, RG 105, NARA. See Chapter 3 for the sacredness of the labor contract.

45. Leon F. Litwack, *Been in the Storm So Long: The Aftermath of Slavery* (New York: Alfred A. Knopf, 1979), 240.

46. Marriage Certificates, August 1865 and October 1865. Brookhaven, Mississippi, Miscellaneous Records, August 1865–November 1868, BRFAL, RG 105, NARA.

47. Clifton Lloyd Ganus, Jr., "The Freedmen's Bureau in Mississippi" (Ph.D. diss., Tulane University, 1953), 259.

48. Theodore Wiseman, Report, Sardis, Mississippi, August 31, 1867. Office of the Assistant Commissioner, Narrative Reports from Subordinate Officers, August 1865–December 1868, BRFAL, RG 105, NARA, M826-30.

49. George Corliss to A. W. Preston, Vicksburg, January 30, 1867. Pass Christian, Mississippi, Registered Letters Received, BRFAL, RG 105, NARA, M826-18.

50. James H. Shepley to Major A. W. Preston, June 30, 1867. Grenada, Mississippi, Registered Letters Received, BRFAL, RG 105, NARA, M826-20.

51. Susan Pedersen, "Gender, Welfare, and Citizenship in Britain during the Great War," *American Historical Review* 95 (October 1990): 996.

52. James H. Pierce to W. P. Drew, November 24, 1868. Sardis, Mississippi, Letters Sent, July and September–October 1868, BRFAL, RG 105, NARA, M826-13.

53. Roy P. Basler, "And for His Widow and His Orphan," *Quarterly Journal of the Library of Congress* 27 (October 1970): 293; *War of the Rebellion: A Compilation of the Official Records of the Union and Confederate Armies*, Series III (Washington, D.C.: Government Printing Office, 1910), 507; Megan J. McClintock, "Shoring Up the Family: Civil War Pensions and the Crisis of American Domesticity" (paper presented at the American Historical Association, Chicago, Illinois, December 28, 1991), 18; Theda Skocpol, *Protecting Soldiers and Mothers: The Political Origins of Social Policy in the United States* (Cambridge, Mass.: The Belknap Press of Harvard University Press, 1992), 138; Many women applied for a one-time bounty rather than apply for a monthly pension.

54. McClintock, "Shoring up the Family," 18–19.

55. Megan McClintock, "Civil War Pensions and the Reconstruction of Union Families," *Journal of American History* 83 (September1996): 473.

56. Clarissa Smith to Captain Weber, Vicksburg, June 10, 1865. Register of Letters, ProMarshall of the Freedmen, BRFAL, RG 105, NARA.

57. Pension File of Robert Drake, 145.055, 5th Regiment, RG 15, NARA.

58. O. C. French, Esq., Natchez, Mississippi, to William P. Drew, Washington, D.C., September 10, 1870. Natchez, Mississippi, Agent for the Payment of Bounties, Registered Letters Received, January 1869–April 1871, BRFAL, RG 105, NARA.

59. Pension File of George Hubbard, 304.430, 51st Regiment, RG 15, NARA.

60. Skocpol, *Protecting Soldiers and Mothers*, 596. Pedersen, "Gender, Welfare, and Citizenship in Britain," 998.

61. Amy E. Holmes, "'Such Is the Price We Pay': American Widows and the Civil War Pension System," in *Toward a Social History of the American Civil War: Exploratory Essays*, ed. Maris Vinovskis (Cambridge: Cambridge University Press, 1990), 172.

62. Pension File of John Brown, 387.412 J., 5th Regiment, RG 15, NARA.

63. Pension File of Aleck Coleman, 167.036, 3rd Regiment, RG 15, NARA.

64. Pension File of John Smith, 348.310, 5th Regiment, RG 15, NARA; Joseph Wells, 128.576, 5th Regiment, RG 15, NARA.

65. For a comparison with the North, see Elizabeth Hafkin Pleck, *Black Migration and Poverty: Boston, 1865–1900* (New York: Academic Press, 1979), 186–87.

66. Pension File of John Brown, 387.412, 5th Regiment, RG 15, NARA.

67. Pension File of Jacob Hart, 252.619, 203.817, 5th Regiment, RG 15, NARA.

68. Pension File of Thomas Toller, 801.281, 582.412, 5th Regiment, RG 15, NARA.

69. Pension File of John Smith, 348.310 J. 469.269, 5th Regiment, RG 15, NARA.

70. Pension File of Jeremiah Manney, 210.304, 5th Regiment, RG 15, NARA.

71. Gutman, *The Black Family in Slavery and Freedom*, 64, 114, 117; Paul A. David, Herbert G. Gutman, Richard Sutch, Peter Temin, and Gavin Wright,

Reckoning with Slavery: A Critical Study in the Quantitative History of American Negro Slavery (New York: Oxford University Press, 1976), 142.

72. Alonzo Sharkey, 3ʳᵈ Regiment, 120.208 J 438.423, RG 15, NARA; Gutman, *The Black Family in Slavery and Freedom*, 60.

73. Pension File of Wade Hamilton, 264.687, 273.744, 3ʳᵈ Regiment, RG 15, NARA.

74. Pension File of Wesley Thomas, 172.139, 224.634, 5ᵗʰ Regiment, RG 15, NARA.

75. George Corliss to Stuart Eldridge, April 9, 1866. Office of the Assistant Commissioner, Registered Letters Received, June 1865–May 1869, BRFAL, RG 105, NARA, M826-13.

76. George S. Smith, Columbus, to A. W. Preston, Vicksburg, July 11, 1867. Office of the Assistant Commissioner, Registered Letters Received, June 1865–May 1869, BRFAL, RG 105, NARA, M826-20; O. O. Howard, Washington, D.C., April 10, 1867, Sub District of Jackson. Office of the Assistant Commissioner, BRFAL, RG 105, NARA, M826-2.

77. Samuel Goozie, Monthly Report, Greenville, September 30, 1868. Office of the Assistant Commissioner, Narrative Reports from Subordinate Officers, August 1865–December 1868, BRFAL, RG 105, NARA, M826-33.

78. William Ross to A. W. Preston, Columbus, July 6, 1867, Office of the Assistant Commissioner, Registered Letters Received, June 1865–May 1869, BRFAL, RG 105, NARA, M826-20.

79. R. H. Cluse, Vicksburg, August 20, 1867, Respectfully returned by Alvan Gillem. Office of the Assistant Commissioner, Endorsements Sent and Received, June 1865–December 1868, BRFAL, RG 105, NARA, M826-4.

80. Gender roles had different meanings in different societies. See Elizabeth Fox-Genovese, *Within the Plantation Household: Black and White Women of the Old South* (Chapel Hill: University of North Carolina Press, 1988), 296.

81. Jacqueline Jones, *Labor of Love, Labor of Sorrow: Black Women, Work, and the Family, from Slavery to the Present* (New York: Vintage Books, 1985), 63.

82. Pickney Vaughn, Labor Contract, Lauderdale County, February 1866. Office of the Assistant Commissioner, Labor Contracts, June 1865–June 1868, BRFAL, RG 105, NARA, M826-50, Pension File of Benjamin Long, 127.192, 3ʳᵈ Regiment, RG 15, NARA; Pension File of Caesar Wilson, 294.985, 344.458, 5ᵗʰ Regiment, RG 15, NARA.

83. Pension File of Alfred Johnson, 649.922 J. 566.335, 5ᵗʰ Regiment, RG 15, NARA.

84. Pension File of Isaac Mackie, 322.326, J., 366.345, 5ᵗʰ Regiment, RG 15, NARA.

85. R. D. Montague, Report, October 31, 1867. Office of the Assistant Commissioner, Narrative Reports from Subordinate Officers, August 1865–December 1868, BRFAL, RG 105, NARA, M826-30.

86. Will of Daniel, Vernon, Miss., April 11, 1868. Filed under Office of the Assistant Commissioner, Labor Contracts, June 1865–June 1868, BRFAL, RG 105, NARA, M826-50; Joseph J. Hunter to Col. W. W. Rose, September 14, 1867. Macon, Mississippi, Letters Received, July 1867–December 1868, BRFAL, RG 105, NARA.

87. Pension File of Benjamin Long, 127.192, 3rd Regiment, RG 15, NARA; Jones, *Labor of Love, Labor of Sorrow*, 62–63.

88. Pension File of Leonard Barnes, 315.847, 250.920, 53rd Regiment, RG 15, NARA.

89. Pension File of John Brown, 387.412, 5th Regiment, RG 15, NARA.

90. W. Parker, Contract, De France, Hinds Co., February 4, 1868. Office of the Assistant Commissioner, Labor Contracts, June 1865–June 1868, BRFAL, RG 105, NARA, M826-50.

91. Pension File of Caesar Wilson, 294.985, 344.458, 5th Regiment, RG 15, NARA.

92. Ann Patton Malone, *Sweet Chariot: Slave Family and Household Structure in Nineteenth-Century Louisiana* (Chapel Hill: University of North Carolina Press, 1992), 230; Jones, *Labor of Love, Labor of Sorrow*, 62, 333; James Oliver Horton and Lois E. Horton, *Black Bostonians: Family Life and Community Struggle in the Antebellum North* (New York: Oxford University Press, 1986), 21; David et. al., *Reckoning with Slavery*, 147.

93. Pension File of Robert Caswell, 162.222, 146.201, 3rd Regiment, RG 15, NARA.

94. Thomas Smead, Vicksburg, Mississippi, January 3, 1868, List of Freedmen on "Oakwood" Plantation. Records Relating to the Division of Crops on Cotton Plantations, 1867–68, BRFAL, RG 105, NARA.

95. Robin D. G. Kelley, "'We Are Not What We Seem': Rethinking Black Working-Class Opposition in the Jim Crow South," *Journal of American History* 80 (June 1993): 84.

96. Mary Jones, Account, no date, 1867. Tupelo, Mississippi, Miscellaneous Records, November–December 1867, BRFAL, RG 105, NARA.

97. Ross H. Moore, "Social and Economic Conditions in Mississippi during Reconstruction" (Ph.D. diss., Duke University, 1937), 91.

98. George P. Rawick, ed., *The American Slave: A Composite Autobiography*, Supplement, Series 1, Vol. 8: *Mississippi Narratives*, pt. 3 (Westport, Conn.: Greenwood Press, 1974), 1134.

99. Charles Joyner, *Down by the Riverside: A South Carolina Slave Community* (Urbana: University of Illinois Press, 1984), 113.

100. Kelley, "'We Are Not What We Seem,'" 84.

101. Belle Kearney, *A Slaveholder's Daughter* (New York: Negro Universities Press, 1969), 55; Wharton, *The Negro in Mississippi*, 72; Robert L. Ransom and Richard Sutch, *One Kind of Freedom: The Economic Consequences of Emancipation* (Cambridge: Cambridge University Press, 1977), 4, 5.

102. George P. Rawick, ed., *The American Slave: A Composite Autobiography*, Supplement, Series 1, Vol. 10: *Mississippi Narratives*, pt. 5 (Westport, Conn.: Greenwood Press, 1974), 2077.

103. Mrs. Joseph Lowell to Capt. Joseph Lowell, February 26, 1867, Quitman Family, Southern Historical Collection, Chapel Hill, North Carolina; Litwack, *Been in the Storm So Long*, 116; Fox-Genovese, *Within the Plantation Household*, 222; Foner, *Reconstruction*, 79; Marietta Morrissey, *Slave Women in the New World: Gender Stratification in the Caribbean* (Kansas: University of Kansas Press, 1989), 54; Jones, *Labor of Love, Labor of Sorrow*, 69.

104. Winthrop D. Jordan, *White over Black: American Attitudes toward the Negro 1550–1812* (Baltimore, 1969), 136–67; Bertram Wyatt-Brown, *Southern Honor: Ethics and Behavior in the Old South* (New York: Oxford University Press, 1982), 307–24.

105. Fogel and Engerman suggest that slaves were prudish as opposed to promiscuous. Fogel and Engerman, *Time on the Cross*, 138. Elizabeth Fox-Genovese and Eugene D. Genovese, *Fruits of Merchant Capital: Slavery and Bourgeois Property in the Rise and Expansion of Capitalism* (New York: Oxford University Press, 1983), 140–41, argue against Fogel and Engerman.

106. Pension File of Lenn Bowling, 380.843 J., 3rd Regiment, RG 15, NARA.

107. Pension File of Robert Roberts, 317.426 J 519.390, 5th Regiment, RG 15, NARA.

108. Andrea E. Goldsmith, "Notes on the Tyranny of Language Usage," *Women's Studies International Quarterly* 3 (1980): 179–80.

109. Pension File of Wesley Thomas, 172.139, 224.634, 5th Regiment, RG 15, NARA.

110. Pension File of Hannibal Wallace, 375.899, 5th Regiment, RG 15, NARA.

111. Pension File of James Jones, 346.290, 53rd Regiment, RG 15, NARA.

112. Pension File of George Washington, 387.374, 371.908, 5th Regiment, RG 15, NARA.

113. Pension File of Moses West, 164.065, 5th Regiment, RG 15, NARA.

114. Pension File of Nathaniel Foreman, 121.340, 177.645, 5th Regiment, RG 15, NARA.

115. Pension File of Hubbard Reynolds, 163.950, 741.430, 5th Regiment, RG 15, NARA.

116. Pension File of Levi McLauren, 213.748, 58th Regiment, RG 15, NARA.

117. Pension File of Thomas Brown, 147.977, 445.087, 5th Regiment, RG 15, NARA.

118. Pension File of Caesar Wilson, 294.985, 344.458, 5th Regiment, RG 15, NARA.

119. Pension File of George Washington, 387.374, 371.908, 5th Regiment, RG 15, NARA; Pension File of Robert Caswell, 162.222, 146.201, 3rd Regiment, RG 15, NARA.

120. Pension File of Tobias Vassar, 165.958, 282.200, 198.334, 3rd Regiment, RG 15, NARA.

121. Pension File of James Toliver, 684.046, 615.530, 53rd Regiment, RG 15, NARA; Pension File of Jacob Horton, 627.635, 493.946, 3rd Regiment, RG 15, NARA.

122. Pension File of Richard Sled, 394.755, 389.853, 5th Regiment, RG 15, NARA.

123. Pension File of Thomas Brown, 147.977, 445.087, 53rd Regiment, RG 15, NARA; Pension File of Samuel Taylor, 210.144, 5th Regiment, RG 15, NARA.

124. Pension File of James Jones, 346.290, 53rd Regiment, RG 15, NARA.

125. Pension File of Samuel Taylor, 210.144, 5th Regiment, RG 15, NARA.

126. Pension File of James Mathey, 227.825, 268.203, 58th Regiment, RG 15, NARA; Pension File of William Taylor, 383.428, 5th Regiment, RG 15, NARA. Gutman, *The Black Family in Slavery and Freedom*, 74.

127. Pension File of Caesar Wilson, 294.985, 344.458, 5th Regiment, RG 15, NARA.

128. Linda Gordon, *Woman's Body, Woman's Right: A Social History of Birth Control in America* (New York: Penguin Books), 20; Frederick Engels, *The Origin of the Family, Private Property and the State* (Moscow: Progress Publishers, 1977 [1884]), 62; Louise A. Tilly and Joan W. Scott, *Women, Work, and Family* (New York: Holt, Rinehart and Winston, 1978), 25.

129. This was true in the Caribbean as well. Barbara Bush, *Slave Women in Caribbean Society*, 96.

130. Pension File of Joseph Duncan, 767.326, 567.264, 5th Regiment, RG 15, NARA.

131. Pension File of Benjamin Lee, 380.960, 5th Regiment, RG 15, NARA.

132. Pension File of Reuben Caston, 197.603, 282.131, 5th Regiment, RG 15, NARA; Pension File of Charles Hutchins, 178.142, 346.916, 457.840 cert. 457.840, 5th Regiment, RG 15, NARA; Pension File of Benjamin Lee, 380.960, 5th Regiment, RG 15, NARA; Pension File of Levi McLauren, 213.748, 58th Regiment, RG 15, NARA; Pension File of Wiley Taylor, 177.919, 5th Regiment, RG 15, NARA; Pension File of Wade Hamilton, 3rd Regiment, RG 15, NARA.

133. Pension File of Allen Burrell, 421.515, 331.801, 5th Regiment, RG 15, NARA.

134. Pension File of Levi McLauren, 213.748, J. 58th, Regiment, RG 15, NARA.

135. Pension File of Archie Hunt, 262.721, 268.081, 5th Regiment, RG 15, NARA.

136. Pension File of Benjamin Lee, 380.960, 5th Regiment, RG 15, NARA.

137. Pension File of Hannibal Wallace, 375.899, 5th Regiment, RG 15, NARA.

138. Pension File of Reuben Caston, 197.603 J, 282.131, 5th Regiment, RG 15, NARA.

139. Pension File of Allen Burrell, 421.515, 331.801, 5th Regiment, RG 15, NARA.

140. George P. Rawick, ed., *The American Slave: A Composite Autobiography*, Supplement, Series 1, vol. 10: *Mississippi Narratives*, pt. 5 (Westport, Conn.: Greenwood Press, 1974), 2211.

141. Pension File of Wade Hamilton, 264.687, 273.744, 3rd Regiment, RG 15, NARA.

142. Pension File of James Jones, 346.290, 53rd Regiment, RG 15, NARA.

143. Pension File of Levi McLauren, 213.748, 58th Regiment, RG 15, NARA.

144. Pension File of Allen Burrell, 421.515, 331.801, 5th Regiment, RG 15, NARA.

145. Pension File of Archie Hunt, 262.721, 268.081, 5th Regiment, RG 15, NARA.

146. P. P. Bergeoni, Woodville, Report, April 30, 1868. Office of the Assistant Commissioner, Narrative Reports from Subordinate Officers, August 1865–December 1868, BRFAL, RG 105, NARA, M826-32.

147. P. P. Bergeoni, Woodville, Report, June 30, 1868. Office of the Assistant Commissioner, Narrative Reports from Subordinate Officers, August 1865–December 1868, BRFAL, RG 105, NARA, M826-32.

148. Pension File of Benjamin Lee, 380.960, 5th Regiment, RG 15, NARA.

149. R. A. Hart, Testimony, June 27, 1867. Brookhaven, Mississippi, Miscellaneous Records, August 1865–November 1868, BRFAL, RG 105, NARA.

150. Pension File of George Hubbard, 145.205, 97.533, 51st Regiment, RG 15, NARA.

151. See Chapter 5 for further discussion of this issue.

152. Dimitri B. Shimkin notes that this practice has continued into the twentieth century. *The Extended Family in Black Societies* (The Hague: Mouton Publishers, 1978), 59.

153. Pension File of Richard Charleston, 155.642, 211.989, 58th Regiment, RG 15, NARA.

154. Gutman, *The Black Family in Slavery and Freedom*, 188–89; Wyatt-Brown, *Southern Honor*, 120. Wyatt-Brown notes the "mystique of names" for whites and the importance of lineage and naming for white southerners (p. 124); Niara Sudarkasa, "African and Afro-American Structure," in *Anthropology for the Nineties: Introductory Readings*, ed. Johnetta B. Cole (New York: The Free Press, 1988), 205.

155. Pension File of Leonard Barnes, 315.847, 250.920, 58th Regiment, RG 15, NARA; Deborah Gray White, *Ar'n't I A Woman? Female Slaves in the Plantation South* (New York: W.W. Norton, 1985), 109.

156. Pension File of Archie Branch, 168.398, 187.861, 58th Regiment, RG 15, NARA.

157. Pension File of Levi MacLaurin, 213.748, 58th Regiment, RG 15, NARA.

158. Pension File of Henry Carter, 178.418, 256.137, 58th Regiment, RG 15, NARA.

159. Pension File of Outlaw Hinton, 222.542, 175.86, 5th Regiment, RG 15, NARA.

160. Pension File of Leonard Barnes, 315.847, 250.920, 58th Regiment, RG 15, NARA.

161. Pension File of Isaac Harris, 237.517, 195.267, 58th Regiment, RG 15, NARA.

162. Pension File of Horace Stewart, 187.331, 518.689, 5th Regiment, RG 15, NARA. In *Southern Honor*, Wyatt-Brown discussed the same themes for southern whites. He wrote that southerners used "shame and humiliation" as childrearing techniques "in sharp contrast to the conscience building techniques of pious Yankees" (p. 118) and that "'blood' was not an abstract concept but a determination that could so type a child that a sense of unworthiness could well develop" (p. 119).

163. Nathan Williams, April 12, 1865. Natchez, Mississippi, Register of Complaints, December 1864–December 1868, BRFAL, RG 105, NARA.

164. Thomas Lee to John D. Moore, July 24, 1867. Corinth, Mississippi, Letters Sent, March 1867–December 1868, BRFAL, RG 105, NARA.

165. Hattie Freeman to Mr. and Mrs. Wright, November 11, 1869, Columbus, Mississippi. American Missionary Association, Amistad Research Center, Dillard University, New Orleans, Louisiana.

166. George P. Corliss, Complaints, September 30, 1867, East Pascogonis, Mississippi, Office of the Assistant Commissioner, Narrative Reports from Subordinate Officers, August 1865–December 1868, BRFAL, RG 105, NARA,

M826-30; other examples include J. H. Chapman to Col. James Biddle, Jackson, Mississippi, August 31, 1868. Vicksburg, Mississippi, Office of the Subcommissioner, Letters Sent, August–September 1868, BRFAL, RG 105, NARA; Aaron McDonald, Complaint, November 1868. Magnolia, Mississippi, Register of Complaints, August 1867–December 1868, BRFAL, RG 105, NARA.

167. Elizabeth Henderson, Complaint, September 12, 1867. Louisville, Mississippi, Register of Complaints, September 1867–November 1868, 190 BRFAL, RG 105, NARA.

168. M. Greaves to Alvan Gillem, February 6, 1868. Office of the Assistant Commissioner, Registered Letters Received, June 1865–May 1869, BRFAL, RG 105, NARA, M826-24.

169. Pension File of Jordan Fowler, 491.440, 53rd Regiment, RG 15, NARA; Pension File of Frank Fletcher, 782.007, 599.542, 5th Regiment, RG 15, NARA.

170. John Williams to M. Barber, Report, March 3, 1868. Office of the Assistant Commissioner, Narrative Reports from Subordinate Officers, August 1865–December 1868, BRFAL, RG 105, NARA, M826-32.

171. W. H. Eldridge to H. W. Smith, Report, September 30, 1867. Office of the Assistant Commissioner, Narrative Reports from Subordinate Officers, August 1865–December 1868, BRFAL, RG 105, NARA, M826-30.

172. Victoria E. Bynum, *Unruly Women: The Politics of Social and Sexual Control in the Old South* (Chapel Hill: University of North Carolina Press, 1992), 77, 82.

173. Pension File of Solomon Griffin, 795.551, 564.716, 709.789, 5th Regiment, RG 15, NARA.

174. Peter Gregory, Complaint, November 16, 1867. Louisville, Mississippi, Register of Complaints, September 1867–November 1868, BRFAL, RG 105, NARA.

175. J. Floyd Kind to Mallery, January 31, 1867, Natchez, Thomas Butler King Papers, Southern Historical Collection, University of North Carolina, Chapel Hill.

176. Pension File of Solomon Griffin, 795.551, 564.716, 709.789, 5th Regiment, RG 15, NARA.

177. W. H. Eldridge, Brookhaven, to Major A. W Preston, June 30, 1867. Office of the Assistant Commissioner, Registered Letters Received, June 1865–May 1869, BRFAL, RG 105, NARA, M826-18.

178. Lieutenant E. C. Gilbreath, Brookhaven, to A. W. Preston, July 31, 1867. Office of the Assistant Commissioner, Registered Letters Received, June 1865–May 1869, BRFAL, RG 105, NARA, M826-18.

179. *The Daily Clarion* (Jackson, Mississippi), April 1, 1866; Genovese, *Roll, Jordan, Roll*, 483–85; Malone, *Sweet Chariot*, 228–29; Schwalm, *A Hard Fight for We*, 261.

180. Sheri Parks, "Feminism in the Lives of Ordinary Black Women," *The Barnard Occasional Papers on Women's Issues* V (Summer 1990), 9.

181. Susan A. Mann, "Slavery, Sharecropping, and Sexual Inequality," *Signs* 14 (Summer 1989): 786, 789.

182. John Williams to M. Barber, Report, March 4, 1868. Office of the Assistant Commissioner, Narrative Reports from Subordinate Officers, August 1865–December 1868, BRFAL, RG 105, NARA, M826-32.

183. Pension File of Richmond Fay, 158.577, 120.432, 5th Regiment, RG 15, NARA; Amelia Symie to Joseph Addison, July 15, 1867, Joseph Addison Montgomery and Family Papers, Louisiana State University, Baton Rouge, Louisiana; Mr. McChristian, Complaint, June 9, 1868. Grenada, Mississippi, Registers of Complaints, July 1866–December 1868, BRFAL, RG 105, NARA; Allen P. Huggins, Yazoo County, to Colonel H. W. Smith, Report, August 31, 1867. Office of the Assistant Commissioner, Narrative Reports from Subordinate Officers, August 1865–December 1868, BRFAL, RG 105, NARA, M826-30.

184. Genovese, Roll, Jordan, Roll, 484.

185. Whitelaw Reid, After the War: A Southern Tour, May 1, 1865 to May 1, 1866 (Cincinnati: Moore, Wilstach and Baldwin, 1866), 540.

186. Samuel A. Agnew, Diary, July 14, 1869, Southern Historical Collection, Chapel Hill, North Carolina.

187. Camilia McKee, Complaint, November 8, 1867. Greenville, Mississippi, Register of Complaints, September–December 1867, BRFAL, RG 105, NARA; Eliza Glonn, Complaint, no date. Yazoo City, Mississippi, Registers of Complaints, November 1867–March 1868 and October–December 1868, BRFAL, RG 105, NARA; Allen P. Huggins to Col. H. W. Smith, Report, August 17, 1867. Office of the Assistant Commissioner, Narrative Reports from Subordinate Officers, August 1865–December 1868, BRFAL, RG 105, NARA, M826-30.

188. John Williams to Lieut. Merrit Barber, Report, January 3, 1868. Office of the Assistant Commissioner, Narrative Reports from Subordinate Officers, August 1865–December 1868, BRFAL, RG 105, NARA, M826-31; P. P. Bergeoni, Report, July 31, 1868. Office of the Assistant Commissioner, Narrative Reports from Subordinate Officers, August 1865–December 1868, BRFAL, RG 105, NARA, M826-33; Angeline Kahn, Complaint, August 1868. Magnolia, Mississippi, Register of Complaints, August 1867–December 1868, BRFAL, RG 105, NARA; Rachel, Complaint, December 7, 1867. Louisville, Mississippi, Register of Complaints, September 1867–November 1868, BRFAL, RG 105, NARA.

189. J. L. Tucker to Major Smith, November 24, 1866. Columbus, Mississippi, Registered Letters Received, March 1866–December 1868, BRFAL, RG 105, NARA.

190. W. H. Eldridge, Report, August 20, 1867. Office of the Assistant Commissioner, Narrative Reports from Subordinate Officers, August 1865–December 1868, BRFAL, RG 105, NARA; Harriet Buchanan, Complaint, no date. Corinth, Mississippi, Register of Complaints, BRFAL, RG 105, NARA; W. H. Eldridge to G. W. Filgo, August 20, 1867. Tupelo, Mississippi, Letters Sent, July 1867–May 1868, BRFAL, RG 105, NARA.

191. Anonymous to Captain E. E. Platt, August 24, 1867. Office of the Assistant Commissioner, Press Copies of Letters Sent, June 1865–April 1869, BRFAL, RG 105, NARA, M826-3; To Sandy Case (referred to in letter in Mr. Lamb), May 29, 1868. Brookhaven, Mississippi, Letters Sent, March 1866–December 1868, BRFAL, RG 105, NARA.

192. John Williams to M. Barber, Report, December 3, 1867. Office of the Assistant Commissioner, Narrative Reports from Subordinate Officers, August 1865–December 1868, BRFAL, RG 105, NARA, M826-32.

193. William K. White to Major City of Columbus, September 2, 1867. Columbus, Mississippi, Letters Sent Relating to Complaints, July–October 1867,

BRFAL, RG 105, NARA; George W. Corliss to D. S. Holmes, August 8, 1868. Lake Station, Mississippi, Letters Sent, November 1867–October 1868, BRFAL, RG 105, NARA.

194. Alvan Gillem to O. O. Howard, Washington, March 31, 1868. Office of the Assistant Commissioner, Assistant Commissioner, Press Copies of Letters Sent, BRFAL, RG 105, NARA, M826-3.

195. Clarissy Thompson, Complaint, November 11, 1868. Starkville, Mississippi, Letters Sent, April–July 1868, BRFAL, RG 105, NARA.

196. George D. Reynolds, May 1, 1865. Natchez, Mississippi, Miscellaneous Reports, 1865–1866, BRFAL, RG 105, NARA.

197. Thomas H. Norton to A. W. Preston, July 31, 1867. Office of the Assistant Commissioner, Registered Letters Received, June 1865–May 1869, BRFAL, RG 105, NARA, M826-19; George S. Smith to A. W. Preston, July 11, 1867. Office of the Assistant Commissioner, Registered Letters Received, BRFAL, RG 105, NARA, M816-20; W. G. Wedemeyer to Major Greene, July 15, 1868, Office of the Assistant Commissioner, Unregistered Letters Received, June 1865–May 1869, BRFAL, RG 105, NARA, M826-27.

198. George S. Smith to William H. Perkins, July 24, 1867. Columbus, Mississippi, Letters Sent Relating to Complaints, July–October 1867, BRFAL, Mississippi, RG 105, NARA.

199. George S. Smith to A. W. Preston, July 11, 1867. Office of the Assistant Commissioner, Registered Letters Received, June 1865–May 1869, BRFAL, RG 105, NARA, M826-20.

200. George Corliss, Friar Point, to Stuart Eldridge, April 9, 1866. Office of Assistant Commissioner, Registered Letters Received, June 1865–May 1869, BRFAL, RG 105, NARA, M826-13.

201. O. D. Greene, Letter, November 2, 1867. Office of Assistant Commissioner, Registers of Letters Received, June 1865–May 1869, BRFAL, RG 105, NARA, M826-7.

202. E. E. Platt to Henry Deeks, Esq., September 18, 1868. Brookhaven, Mississippi, Letters Sent, March 1866–December 1868, BRFAL, RG 105, NARA; J. H. Carr, Letter, June 13, 1867. Grenada, Mississippi, Registers of Letters Received, March 1866–December 1868, BRFAL, RG 105, NARA; Charity, Complaint, March 1868. Louisville, Mississippi, Register of Complaints, September 1867–November 1868, BRFAL, RG 105, NARA; Elizabeth Henderson, Complaint, September 12, 1867. Louisville, Mississippi, Register of Complaints, September 1867–November 1868, BRFAL, RG 105, NARA.

203. Robert P. Gardner to Peril Pradoe, October 24, 1866. Pass Christian, Mississippi, Letters Sent, April 1866–September 1867, BRFAL, RG 105, NARA.

204. Crawford Noblin, Complaint, July 4, 1868. Lake Station, Mississippi, Letters Sent, November 1867–October 1868, BRFAL, RG 105, NARA.

205. Elvina Edwards, Complaint, June 1868. Magnolia, Mississippi, Register of Complaints, August 1867–December 1868, BRFAL, RG 105, NARA.

206. P. P. Bergeoni, April 30, 1868, Office of the Assistant Commissioner, Narrative Reports from Subordinate Officers, August 1865–December 1868, M826-32, BRFAL, RG 105, NARA.

207. C. S. Swan to J. Tarbell, Hillsboro, Newton Station, April 27, 1869.

U.S. Army Continental Commands, 1821–1920, Part 7, Department of Arkansas, 7th Army Corps, 4th Military Districts, Office of Civil Affairs, #385, Letters Received March 1869–March 1870, Record Group 393 (hereafter RG 393), Box 21, NARA.

208. For example, see William White, Columbus, to Alvan C. Gillem, September 18, 1867, Registers of Letters Received. Office of the Assistant Commissioner, Bureau Period Records, BRFAL, RG 105, NARA, M826-7.

209. Henrietta Sykes, Affidavit, September 10, 1867. Columbus, Mississippi, Registers of Letters Received, March 1866–December 1868, BRFAL, RG 105, NARA.

210. A. Y. Harper, Endorsement, June 30, 1868, Office of the Assistant Commissioner, Endorsements Sent and Received, June 1865–December 1868, BRFAL, RG 105, NARA, M826-8.

211. United States Congress, 42nd Congress, Senate Report, No. 41, *Testimony taken by the U.S. Congress Joint Select Conditions of Affairs in the Late Insurrectionary States* (Washington, D.C.: Government Printing Office, 1872), 361.

212. Paul D. Escott, *Slavery Remembered: A Record of Twentieth-Century Slave Narrative* (Chapel Hill: University of North Carolina Press, 1979), 46, 43.

213. Genovese, *Roll, Jordan, Roll*, 33.

214. G. W. Sargeant, Natchez, to Mr. Gorton, 18 December 1861, vol 11, p. 233. Southern Historical Collection, Chapel Hill, North Carolina; Genovese, *Roll, Jordan, Roll*, 421.

215. Pension File of Warren Brooks, 205.192, 186.147, 5th Regiment, RG 15, NARA.

216. Albert Talmon Morgan, *Yazoo: or, On the Picket Line of Freedom in the South* (Washington, D.C.: Albert Talmon Morgan, 1884), 315.

217. Angeline Johns against John Humphreys, December 22, 1867. Canton, Mississippi, Register of Complaints, October 1867–April 1868, BRFAL, RG 105, NARA.

218. Thomas J. Wood to O. O. Howard, June 15, 1866. Letters Received by the Commissioner, May–August 1866, BRFAL, RG 105, NARA, M752-34; Samuel Gozee to John Tyler, October 3, 1868. Office of the Assistant Commissioner, Narrative Reports from Subordinate Officers, August 1865–December 1868, BRFAL, RG 105, NARA, M826-33.

219. Estelle B. Freedman and John D'Emilio, John, *Intimate Matters: A History of Sexuality in America* (New York: Harper and Row, 1988), 94.

220. John D. Moore to John Tyler, Report, October 30, 1868. Office of the Assistant Commissioner, Narrative Reports from Subordinate Officers, August 1865–December 1868, BRFAL, RG 105, NARA, M826-33; Gerda Lerner, ed., *Black Women in White America: A Documentary History* (New York: Vintage Books, 1973), 172–73.

221. Jacqueline Dowd Hall, "'The Mind That Burns in Each Body': Women, Rape, and Racial Violence," in *Powers of Desire, the Politics of Sexuality*, ed. Ann Snitow, Christine Stansell, and Sharon Thompson (New York: Monthly Review Press, 1983). Hall argued that "when the black woman seized the opportunity to turn her maternal and sexual resources to the benefit of her own family, sexual violence met her assertion of will" (p. 233).

222. John Perkins, Affidavit. Jackson, Mississippi, Subassistant Commission-er, Miscellaneous Records, 1865–1868, BRFAL, RG 105, NARA.

223. Lloyd Wheaton, Report, January 31, 1868. Corinth, Mississippi, Office of the Assistant Commissioner, Narrative Reports from Subordinate Officers, August 1865–December 1868, BRFAL, RG 105, NARA, M826-32.

224. United States Congress, 42nd Congress, Senate Report, No. 1, *Testimony taken by the U.S. Congress Joint Select Conditions of Affairs in the Late Insurrectionary States* (Washington, D.C.: Government Printing Office, 1872), 38.

225. Hall, "'The Mind that Burns in Each Body'," 332.

226. Pension File of Henry Carter, 145.205, 97.533, 58th Regiment, RG 15, NARA.

227. Pension File of Edward Ellicott, 225.720, 270.308, 5th Regiment, RG 15, NARA,

228. Pension File of Warren Brooks, 205.192, 186.147, 5th Regiment, RG 15, NARA.

229. Pension File of Horace Stewart, 187.331, 518.689, 5th Regiment, RG 15, NARA.

230. Wharton, *The Negro in Mississippi*, 87; Laws of Mississippi, Oct., Nov. and Dec., 1865 (Jackson: J. J. Shannon and Co., 1866), 87. In *Reconstruction in Mississippi*, historian James Wilford Garner recorded that "the first instance of intermarriage between the races in Mississippi occurred in Jackson in June 1866. It was the case of a negro and a white woman. They were tried in the circuit court, found guilty, and sentenced to imprisonment in the county jail for six months, and to pay a fine of $500 each. The military officers looked on with interest while the judge commented upon the depravity of the woman, but they did not interfere" (p. 114).

231. United States Congress, 42nd Congress, Senate Report, No. 11, *Testimony taken by the U.S. Congress Joint Select Conditions of Affairs in the Late Insurrectionary States* (Washington, D.C.: Government Printing Office, 1872), 559–60.

232. DuBois, *Black Reconstruction in America*, 372. Seventeen of the Mississippi delegates were African American, eighty-three were white.

233. Gutman, *The Black Family in Slavery and Freedom*, 400; *Journal of the Proceedings in the Constitutional Convention of the State of Mississippi* (Jackson, Miss.: E. Stafford, 1871), 542, 739.

234. Wharton, *The Negro in Mississippi*, 150.

235. W. J. Cash, *The Mind of the South* (New York: Vintage Books, 1941), 118; in *White over Black*, Winthrop Jordan wrote, "Any Negro insurrection, furthermore, threatened the white man's dominance, including his valuable sexual dominance, and hence the awful prospect of being overthrown was bound to assume a sexual cast" (p. 153). Martha Hodes, "The Sexualization of Reconstruction Politics: White Women and Black Men in the South after the Civil War," in *American Sexual Politics: Sex, Gender, and Race*, ed. John C. Fout and Maura Shaw Tantillo (Chicago: University of Chicago Press, 1993), 60; Robyn Wiegman, "The Anatomy of Lynching," in *American Sexual Politics*, 236.

236. Bynum, *Unruly Women*, 4, 9, 96.

237. Laura F. Edwards, *Gendered Strife and Confusion: The Political Culture of Reconstruction* (Urbana: University of Illinois Press, 1997), 15–16.

238. Gutman, *The Black Family in Slavery and Freedom*, 292–93. Morgan, *Yazoo*, 361.

239. Bynum, *Unruly Women*, 97.

240. A. J. Maize to O. D. Green, December 9, 1867. Jackson, Mississippi, Subassistant Commissioner, Unregistered Letters Received, January 1866–December 1868, BRFAL, RG 105, NARA.

241. William Page, Letter, April 6, 1867. Office of the Assistant Commissioner, Registered Letters Received, June 1865–May 1869, BRFAL, RG 105, NARA, M826-21.

242. Arthur Palmer Hudson, "An Attala Boyhood," *Journal of Mississippi History* IV (January1942): 62.

243. George P. Rawick, ed., *The American Slave: A Composite Autobiography*, Supplement, Series 1, Vol. 10: *Mississippi Narratives*, pt. 5 (Westport, Conn.: Greenwood Press, 1974), 1913.

244. United States Congress, 42nd Congress, Senate Report, No. 11, *Testimony taken by the U.S. Congress Joint Select Conditions of Affairs in the Late Insurrectionary States*, 849.

245. Ibid., 548.

246. Ibid., 470.

247. Ibid., 226.

248. Alvan Gillem to O. O. Howard, Washington, D.C., May 15, 1867, Office of the Assistant Commissioner, Press Copies of Letters Sent, BRFAL, RG 105, NARA, M826-2; Wharton, *The Negro in Mississippi*, 150.

249. E. H. Anderson, "A Memoir on Reconstruction in Yazoo City," *Journal of Mississippi History* 4 (October 1942): 188; Wharton, *The Negro in Mississippi*, 229.

250. Luke Ward Conerly, *Pike County, Mississippi, 1798–1979* (Nashville: Brandon Printing, 1909), 245.

251. T. S. Free, Letter, October 18, 1865. Natchez, Mississippi, Register of Letters Received, October 1865–March 1866, BRFAL, RG 105, NARA; Matilda Smith, Affidavit, October 16, 1865. Brookhaven, Mississippi, Miscellaneous Records, August 1865–November 1868, BRFAL, RG 105, NARA.

252. Conerly, *Pike County, Mississippi*, 245.

253. Melvin Grigsby, *The Smoked Yank*, 2d edition (Chicago: Regan Printing Co., 1891), 60.

254. Fox-Genovese, *Within the Plantation Household*, 292; Cash, *The Mind of the South*, 87; Jordan, *White Over Black*, 151–52; Forrest G. Wood, *The Arrogance of Faith: Christianity and Race in America from the Colonial Era to the Twentieth Century* (New York: Alfred A. Knopf, 1990), 203; Elsa Barkley Brown, "Intersections and Collision Courses: Women, Blacks, and Workers Confront Gender, Race, and Class," *Feminist Studies* 18 (Summer 1992): 305; Forrest G. Wood, *Black Scare: The Racist Response to Emancipation and Reconstruction* (Berkeley: University of California Press, 1970), 69; Charles Herbert Stember, *Sexual Racism: The Emotional Barrier to an Integrated Society* (New York: Elsevier Scientific Publishing Co., 1976), 41; Bynum, *Unruly Women*, 39; Evelyn Brooks Higginbotham, "African-American Women's History and the Metalanguage of Race," *Signs* 17 (Winter 1992): 262–64; bell hooks, *Ain't I a Woman: Black Women and Feminism* (Boston: South End Press, 1981), 33.

255. United States Congress, 42nd Congress, Senate Report, No. 11, *Testimony taken by the U.S. Congress Joint Select Conditions of Affairs in the Late Insurrectionary States*, 558.

256. Litwack, *Been in the Storm So Long*, 364; DuBois, *Black Reconstruction in America*, 136.

257. Skocpol, *Protecting Soldiers and Mothers*, 138. Although Skocpol contends that the "Pension Bureau was not formally racist," evidence exists of racist pension examiners. Examples can be found in the pension files of Gordon Fulgert, 320.012, 53rd Regiment, RG 15, NARA, and Leonard Barnes, 315.847, 250.920, 53rd Regiment, RG 15, NARA.

258. Pension File of Moses West, 164.065, 5th Regiment, RG 15, NARA.

259. Higginbotham, "African-American Women's History and the Metalanguage of Race," 265–66. Wendy Brown, "Finding the Man in the State," *Feminist Studies* 18 (Spring 1992): 9, 16. Brown argues that "State power is inevitably racialized as well as gendered and bourgeois." Linda Gordon, "Social Insurance and Public Assistance: The Influence of Gender in Welfare Thought in the United States, 1890–1935," *American Historical Review* 97 (February 1992): 44, 46.

260. Pension File of Solomon Griffin, 5th Regiment, RG 15, NARA.

261. Pension File of William Foster, 121.129, 114.998, 3rd Regiment, RG 15, NARA; Pension File of Gordan E. Fulgert, 320.012, 266.793, 53rd Regiment, RG 15, NARA. On another occasion the same pension examiner wrote about another freedwoman, "She is the 'lady's lady' of antebellum days. I venture no black skin except for [sic] husband ever came within her fond embraces. She would scorn a 'take up' with a nigger as much as any white lady. I was raised among her class and know her measurement." Foster pension file.

262. Isabel Quattlebaum, "Twelve Women in the First Days of the Confederacy," *Civil War History* VII (December 1961): 73; Leslie H. Owens, "The African in the Garden: Reflections about New World Slavery and Its Lifelines," in *The State of Afro-American History: Past, Present, and Future*, 33; George C. Rable, *Civil Wars: Women and the Crisis of Southern Nationalism* (Urbana: University of Illinois Press, 1991), 36; Wood, *Black Scare*, 69, 152.

263. Stember, *Sexual Racism*, 42; Hall, "'The Mind that Burns in Each Body'," 333.

264. Wyatt-Brown, *Southern Honor*, 297; Jordan, *White Over Black*, 474–75; "It is important to recognize that middle class women live the lives they do precisely because working-class women live the lives they do. White women and women of color not only live different lives but white women live the lives they do in large part because women of color live the ones they do." Barkley Brown, "Intersections and Collision Courses," 298

265. Fox-Genovese, *Within the Plantation Household*, 292; Cash, *The Mind of the South*, 235–36.

266. Carroll Smith-Rosenberg, "Dis-Covering the Subject of the 'Great Constitutional Discussion,' 1786–1789," *Journal of American History* 79 (December 1992): 861.

267. Wyatt-Brown, *Southern Honor*, 294, 295.

268. E. Franklin Frazier, *The Negro Family in the United States* (Chicago: University of Chicago Press, 1939), 74.

269. J. R. Chambers, Endorsement, November 7, 1867. Endorsements Sent and Received, Office of the Assistant Commissioner, June 1865–December 1868, BRFAL, RG 105, NARA, M826-4.

270. E. E. Platt, Report, September 1867. Office of the Assistant Commissioner, Narrative Reports from Subordinate Officers, August 1865–December 1868, BRFAL, RG 105, NARA, M826-30.

271. Barkley Brown, "Intersections and Collision Courses," 306.

272. Pension File of Thomas Toller, 801.281, 582.412, 5th Regiment, RG 15, NARA; Joseph Wells, 128.576, cert. 115.572, 632.823 5th Regiment, RG 15, NARA.

273. Pension File of Wade Hamilton, 264.687, 273.744, 3rd Regiment, RG 15, NARA.

274. Pension File of Charles Wabbs, 240.644, 5th Regiment, RG 15, NARA.

275. See George P. Rawick, ed., *The American Slave: A Composite Autobiography*, Supplement, Series 1, Vol. 10: *Mississippi Narratives*, pt. 5 (Westport, Conn.: Greenwood Press, 1974), 2151; James Oliver Horton, "Freedom's Yoke: Gender Conventions among Antebellum Free Blacks," *Feminist Studies* 12 (Spring 1986): 53. For the view that sexual indulgence negated emasculation, see Earl E. Thorpe, *Eros and Freedom in Southern Life and Thought* (Durham, North Carolina: Seeman Printery, 1967), 163.

276. Horton, "Freedom's Yoke," 55.

277. Edwards, *Gendered Strife and Confusion*, 187.

278. George M. Fredrickson, *The Black Image in the White Mind: The Debate on Afro-American Character and Destiny, 1817–1914* (New York: Harper Torchbooks, 1971), 188; DuBois, *Black Reconstruction in America*, 180.

279. DuBois, *Black Reconstruction in America*, 433.

280. Conerly, *Pike County, Mississippi*, 245.

281. DuBois, *Black Reconstruction in America*, 433.

282. Wharton, *The Negro in Mississippi*, 224–25.

283. George T. Swann to Capt. Gardner, June 13, 1866, Jackson, Mississippi, Subassistant Commissioner, Unregistered Letters Received, January 1866–December 1868, BRFAL, RG 105, NARA.

5. Families

1. Pension File of Thomas Toller, 801.281, 582.412, 5th Regiment, RG 15 (hereafter RG 15), National Archives and Records Administration (hereafter NARA), Washington, D.C.

2. Pension file of Thomas Brown, 147.977, 5th Regiment, RG 15, NARA.

3. Ira Berlin, Steven F. Miller, Leslie S. Rowland, "Afro-American Families in the Transition from Slavery to Freedom," *Radical History Review* 42(September 1988): 114; Herbert S. Gutman, *The Black Family in Slavery and Freedom, 1750–1925* (New York: Vintage Books, 1977).

4. Leslie A. Schwalm, *A Hard Fight for We: Women's Transition from Slavery to Freedom in South Carolina* (Urbana: University of Illinois Press, 1997), 67–68.

5. Suzanne Lebsock, *The Free Women of Petersburg: Status and Culture in a Southern Town, 1784–1868* (New York: W.W. Norton, 1984), 88–89; Dimitri B.

Shimkin, *The Extended Family in Black Societies* (The Hague: Mouton Publishers, 1978), 60–61; E. Franklin Frazier, *The Negro Family in the United States* (Chicago: University of Chicago Press, 1939), 106, 163–64, 180; Jacqueline Jones, *Labor of Love, Labor of Sorrow: Black Women, Work, and the Family from Slavery to the Present* (New York: Vintage Books, 1985), 104.

6. Eugene D. Genovese, *Roll, Jordan, Roll: The World the Slaves Made* (New York: Vintage Books, 1974), 450, 491; Herbert G. Gutman, "Persistent Myths about the Afro-American Family," *Journal of Interdisciplinary History* VI (Autumn 1975): 181–210; Leon F. Litwack, *Been in the Storm So Long: The Aftermath of Slavery* (New York: Alfred A. Knopf, 1979), 238; Susan A. Mann, "Slavery, Share-cropping, and Sexual Inequality," *Signs* 14 (Summer 1989): 796, 798; Orville Vernon Burton, *In My Father's House Are Many Mansions: Family and Community in Edgefield, South Carolina* (Chapel Hill: University of North Carolina Press, 1985), 13.

7. Robert William Fogel and Stanley L. Engerman, *Time on the Cross: The Economics of American Negro Slavery* (Boston: Little, Brown, and Co., 1974), 141–42.

8. Contract of Stephen Daggett, Pontotoc County, September 8, 1865, Labor Contracts, June 1865–June 1868, Office of the Assistant Commissioner. Records of the Bureau of Refuges, Freedmen, and Abandoned Lands (hereafter BRFAL), Mississippi, RG 105, NARA, M826-47.

9. C. N. Brown, Yazoo City, Contract, January 5, 1866. Office of the Assistant Commissioner, Labor Contracts, June 1865–June 1868, BRFAL, RG 105, M826-49.

10. For historians who use the term patriarchy, see Orville Vernon Burton, "Computers, History, and Historians: Converging Cultures?" *History Microcomputer Review* 7 (Fall 1991): 13–14; Eric Foner, *Reconstruction: America's Unfinished Revolution, 1863–1877* (New York: Harper and Row, 1988), 87–88; Roberta Sue Alexander, "Presidential Reconstruction: Ideology and Change," in *The Facts of Reconstruction: Essays in Honor of John Hope Franklin*, ed. Eric Anderson and Alfred A. Moss, Jr. (Baton Rouge: Louisiana State University Press), 48.

11. Gutman, *The Black Family in Slavery and Freedom*, 396.

12. Lebsock, *The Free Women of Petersburg*, 103, 111.

13. Elizabeth Fox-Genovese, *Within the Plantation Household: Black and White Women of the Old South* (Chapel Hill: University of North Carolina Press, 1988), 322; Molly Crocker Dougherty, *Becoming a Woman in Rural Black Culture* (New York: Holt, Rinehart and Winston, 1978), 107; Fogel and Engerman note that enslaved women in the southern United States maintained the highest fertility of all the slave populations in the Americas. *Time on the Cross*, 25, 29.

14. Pension File of Robert Graves, 637.803 J.D. 454.995, 58th Regiment, RG 15, NARA.

15. Susan Dabney Smedes, *Memorials of a Southern Planter* (Baltimore: Cushings and Barkley, 1887), 73.

16. Pension File of Charles Hutchins, 178.142, 346.916, cert. 457.840, 5th Regiment, RG 15, NARA. See also Pension File of Archie Branch, 168.398, 187.861, 58th Regiment, RG 15, NARA. Branch did not acknowledge a child although the mother believed he was the father.

17. Pension File of Benjamin Lee, 380.960, 5th Regiment, RG 15, NARA.

18. John W. Blassingame, *The Slave Community: Plantation Life in the Antebellum South* (New York: Oxford University Press, 1979), 172–73.

19. Fox-Genovese, *Within the Plantation Household*, 24.

20. Fogel and Engerman, *Time on the Cross*, 142. For more about slave men and masculinity, see James Oliver Horton, "Freedom's Yoke: Gender Conventions among Antebellum Free Blacks," *Feminist Studies* 12 (Spring 1986): 53.

21. Genovese, *Roll, Jordan, Roll*, 502.

22. Samuel Thomas to the Sheriff of Warren County, February 15, 1866. Press Copies of Letters Sent, Office of the Assistant Commissioner, BRFAL, RG 105, NARA, M826-1.

23. Gutman, *The Black Family in Slavery and Freedom*, 248.

24. Pension File of Ira Granberry, 388.731, 280.049, 51st Regiment, RG 15, NARA.

25. Frazier, *The Negro Family in the United States*, 180; Jones, *Labor of Love, Labor of Sorrow*, 62; Horton, "Freedom's Yoke," 55.

26. Joseph Craig, Complaint, November 9, 1867. Lake Station, Mississippi, Register of Complaints, BRFAL, RG 105, NARA.

27. W. Manning to A. C. Gillem, March 2, 1868. Narrative Reports from Subordinate Officers, M826-32; Edmond Cavin, Endorsement, August 2, 1868. Office of the Assistant Commissioner, Endorsements Sent and Received, June 1865–December 1868, M826-5; George Corliss to A. W. Preston, January 23, 1867. Vicksburg, Mississippi, Press Copies of Letters Sent. All in BRFAL, RG 105, NARA.

28. Transcript from the Journal of Complaints, Lake Station, Mississippi, January 13, 1868. Office of the Assistant Commissioner, Narrative Reports from Subordinate Officers, August 1865–December 1868, BRFAL, RG 105, NARA, M826-32.

29. W. E. Eldridge to A. Bogue Bilboe, June 26, 1867. Brookhaven, Mississippi, Letters Book, BRFAL, RG 105, NARA.

30. For an example, see Robert P. Gardner to A. W. Preston, July 22, 1867. Jackson, Mississippi, Letters Sent, BRFAL, RG 105, NARA.

31. J. Monroe Palmer to Capt. J. B. Holt, Rankin County, April 4, 1868. Jackson, Mississippi, Miscellaneous Records, BRFAL, RG 105, NARA.

32. Mark, Complaint, August 26, 1865. Monticello, Mississippi, Affidavits and Complaints, August–September 1865. BRFAL, RG 105, NARA; Henry Anthony, Complaint, August 20, 1867. Louisville, Mississippi, Register of Complaints, September 1867–November 1868, BRFAL, Mississippi, NARA; John Armstrong, Complaint, November 16, 1867. Sardis, Mississippi, Letters Sent, BRFAL, RG 105, NARA; John Thomas, Complaint, October 15, 1867. Sardis, Mississippi, Letters Sent, April–July 1868, BRFAL, RG 105, NARA; Thad Preuss, Oxford, Mississippi, to J. S. Sunderland, October 30, 1867. Office of the Assistant Commissioner, Narrative Reports from Subordinate Officers, August 1865–December 1868, BRFAL, RG 105, NARA, M826-30; George Corliss, East Pascognia, Mississippi, Report of Complaints, September 20, 1867. Office of the Assistant Commissioner, Narrative Reports from Subordinate Officers, August 1865–December 1868, BRFAL, RG 105, NARA, M826-30; J. H. Chapman, Report, July 1868. Office of the Assistant Commissioner, Narrative Reports from

Subordinate Officers, August 1865–December 1868, BRFAL, RG 105, NARA, M826-33; Jesse Lee, Complaint, September 13, 1867. Vicksburg, Mississippi, Letters Sent Relating to Complaints, July–September 1867, BRFAL, RG 105, NARA.

33. O. B. Foster to T. S. Free, August 9, 1865. Yazoo City, Mississippi, Registered Letters Received, June 1865–January 1866, BRFAL, RG 105, NARA; George Haller, Report, August 31, 1867. Office of the Assistant Commissioner, Narrative Reports from Subordinate Officers, August 1865–December 1868, BRFAL, RG 105, NARA, M826-30.

34. 42nd Congress, Senate Report, No. 41, Vol. 11, *Testimony Taken by the U.S. Congress Joint Select Committee on Conditions of Affairs in the Late Insurrectionary States* (Washington, D.C.: Government Printing Office, 1872), 505.

35. For examples of wives complaining on behalf of their husbands, see Andrew Thomas to Merritt Barber, January 31, 1868. Office of the Assistant Commissioner, Narrative Reports from Subordinate Officers, August 1865–December 1868, BRFAL, RG 105, NARA, M826-32; H. R. Williams, Endorsement returned, June 8, 1866. Jackson, Mississippi, Subassistant Commissioner, Endorsements Sent and Received, March 1866–August 1867, BRFAL, RG 105, NARA.

36. 42nd Congress, *Conditions of Affairs in the Late Insurrectionary States*, 488.

37. H. A. Cooper, Holly Springs, Mississippi, to John Tyler, Vicksburg, Mississippi, December 17, 1868; J. E. Towtelotte, Vicksburg, Mississippi, to John Tyler, Vicksburg, July 25, 1868, Letters Received, Office of Civil Affairs, RG 393, NARA.

38. Lebsock, *The Free Women of Petersburg*, 33.

39. John J. Knox to Alonzo Span, April 16, 1866. Meridian, Mississippi, Letters Sent, July 1867–July 1868, BRFAL, Mississippi, RG 105, NARA.

40. S. L. Bishop, Contract, January 1, 1866. Office of the Assistant Commissioner, Labor Contracts, June 1865–June 1868, BRFAL, RG 105, NARA Washington, M826-49.

41. Cornelius Ross, Contract, Hinds County, January 23, 1866. BRFAL, RG 105, NARA, M826-49.

42. Ismael Davis, Contract, no date, Office of the Assistant Commissioner, Labor Contracts, June 1865–June 1868, BRFAL, RG 105, NARA, M826-50.

43. E. J. Bowen, Contract, April 1, 1866. Office of the Assistant Commissioner, Labor Contracts, June 1865–June 1868, BRFAL, RG 105, NARA, M826-49.

44. William Wedemeyer to Cornelius Moore, April 22, 1868. Grenada, Mississippi, Letters Sent, March 1866–April 1868, BRFAL, RG 105, NARA.

45. U.S. v. Leer Austin, Jackson, Mississippi, Subassistant Commissioner, Miscellaneous Records, 1865–1868, BRFAL, RG 105, NARA.

46. Frazier, *The Negro Family in the United States*, 165.

47. B. P. Berry, Contract, January 22, 1867. Office of the Assistant Commissioner, Labor Contracts, June 1865–June 1868, BRFAL, RG 105, NARA, M826-50.

48. C. H. Jones, Contract, December 30, 1866. Office of the Assistant Commissioner, Labor Contracts, June 1865–June 1868, BRFAL, RG 105, NARA, M826-50.

49. James Hays, Contract, Holmes County, January 9, 1867. Office of the Assistant Commissioner, Labor Contracts, June 1865–June 1868, BRFAL, RG 105, NARA, M826-50; for another example, see Joel N. Moore, Contract, April 1866. Office of the Assistant Commissioner, Labor Contracts, June 1865–June 1868, BRFAL, RG 105, NARA, M826-50.

50. Proceeds of Cotton, August 28, 1868. Greenville, Mississippi, Miscellaneous Records, 1866–1868, BRFAL, RG 105, NARA.

51. L. J. F. Conyingham to William Tibald, Vicksburg, September 23, 1867. Greenville, Mississippi, Unregistered Letters Received, August 1867–October 1868, BRFAL, RG 105, NARA.

52. Pension File of James Jones E., 346.290, 53rd Regiment, RG 15, NARA.

53. George P. Rawick, ed., *The American Slave: A Composite Autobiography*, Supplement, Series 1, Vol. 7: *Mississippi Narratives*, pt. 2 (Westport, Conn.: Greenwood Press, 1974), 679.

54. Accounts with H. F. McWilliams, Carroll County, Mississippi. Office of the Assistant Commissioner, Labor Contracts, June 1865–June 1868, BRFAL, RG 105, NARA, M826-50.

55. Lawrence N. Powell, *New Masters: The Civil War and Reconstruction* (New Haven: Yale University Press, 1980), 90.

56. Thomas C. Holt, "The Essence of the Contract: The Articulation of Race, Gender, and Political Economy in British Emancipation Policy, 1838–1866," unpublished paper, University of Chicago, 1994. S. S. Sumner to Lieut. Merritt, November 3, 1867. Jackson, Mississippi, Subassistant Commissioner, Letters Sent, March 1866–December 1868, BRFAL, RG 105, NARA.

57. David R. Roediger, *The Wages of Whiteness: Race and the Making of the American Working Class* (London: Verso, 1991), 56; W. E. B. DuBois, *Black Reconstruction in America, 1860–1880* (New York: Atheneum, 1969), 172–73.

58. Donald G. Nieman, *To Set the Law in Motion: The Freedmen's Bureau and the Legal Rights of Blacks, 1865–1868* (Millwood, N.Y.: KTO Press, 1979), 39.

59. S. S. Sumner, Jackson, to Lieutenant Merritt Barber, Vicksburg, November 3, 1867. Monthly Report, Jackson, Mississippi, Subassistant Commissioner, Letters Sent, March 1866–December 1868, BRFAL, RG 105, NARA, M826-31.

60. A. Murdock, Ingleside, Mississippi, to Colonel Thomas, Vicksburg, Mississippi, July 17, 1865. Office of the Assistant Commissioner, Registers of Letters Received, June 1865–May 1869, BRFAL, RG 105, NARA, M826-6.

61. R. F. Petit to Major Preston, no date. Registered Letters Received, Office of the Assistant Commissioner, BRFAL, RG 105, NARA, M826-19.

62. W. W. Cheserblum to George Reynolds, De Kalb, April 18, 1866. Meridian, Mississippi, Registers of Letters Received, March 1866–February 1867, BRFAL, RG 105, NARA; Testimony of Emily Gully, March 19, 1866. Office of the Assistant Commissioner, Registered Letters Received, June 1865–May 1869, BRFAL, RG 105, NARA, M826-14; John J. Knox to Lieut. Stuart Eldridge, 15 June 1866. Meridian, Mississippi, Letters Sent, January 1866–February 1867, BRFAL, RG 105, NARA; Deposition in case of Orange v. Sundry Parties, July 1, 1865, sworn before A. Clarke. Statements of the various witnesses. Meridian, Mississippi, Affidavits and Complaints, BRFAL, RG 105, NARA; Stuart Eldridge to Major J. J. Knox, June 28, 1866. Meridian, Mississippi, Registered Letters Received, April–December 1866, BRFAL, RG 105, NARA; P. M. Preston to J. J.

Knox, March 23, 1866. Meridian, Mississippi, Unregistered Letters Received, July 1865–June 1868, BRFAL, RG 105, NARA; M. Preston to J. J. Knox, Meridian, Mississippi, March 23, 1868. Office of the Assistant Commissioner, Press Copies of Letters Sent, BRFAL, RG 105, NARA, M826-1; Capt. J. W. Sunderland to Alvan Gillem, August 18, 1867. Lauderdale, Mississippi, Endorsements Sent and Received, March 1867–October 1868, BRFAL, RG 105, NARA

63. John Power to Wesley Ward, September 21, 1867. Holly Springs, Mississippi, Letters Sent, September 1867–December 1868, BRFAL, RG 105, NARA.

64. John J. Knox to Alonzo Span, April 16, 1866. Meridian, Mississippi, Letters Sent, July 1867–July 1868, BRFAL, RG 105, NARA. See also Ira Berlin, Steven F. Miller, and Leslie S. Rowlands, "Afro-American Families in the Transition from Slavery to Freedom," 103.

65. Alvan Gillem, Endorsement returned, August 21, 1867. M826-4; J. W. Sunderland, Endorsement, September 16, 1867. Both documents in Office of the Assistant Commissioner, Endorsements Sent and Received, June 1865–December 1868, June 1865–December 1868, BRFAL, RG 105, NARA, M826-4.

66. Fanny Smart to Adam, February 13, 1866. Office of the Assistant Commissioner, Registered Letters Received, June 1865–May 1869, BRFAL, RG 105, NARA, M826-15; Litwack, *Been in the Storm So Long*, 234.

67. B. B. Wilkes to Provost Marshall E. Bamberger, West Station, February 21, 1866. Jackson, Mississippi, Acting Assistant Commissioner, Registered Letters Received, July 1865–March 1866, BRFAL, RG 105, NARA.

68. Pension File of Allen Burrell, 421.515, 331.801, 5th Regiment, RG 15, NARA.

69. DuBois, *Black Reconstruction in America*, 141–42.

70. S. S. Sumner, Report, October 1, 1867. Office of the Assistant Commissioner, Narrative Reports from Subordinate Officers, August 1865–December 1868, M826-30; G. S. Wilson, Complaint, September 2, 1867. Jackson, Mississippi, Register of Complaints, BRFAL, RG 105, NARA; Ira Berlin et al., "Afro-American Families in the Transition from Slavery to Freedom," 113–14; Gerald David Jaynes, *Branches without Roots: Genesis of the Black Working Class in the American South, 1862–1882* (New York: Oxford University Press, 1986), 121.

71. George Sheppey, June 5, 1868. Grenada, Mississippi, Registers of Complaints, July 1866–December 1868, BRFAL, RG 105, NARA.

72. Pension File of Solomon Griffin, 791.551, 564.716, 709.789, 5th Regiment, RG 15, NARA.

73. Lt. H. R. Williams, Jackson, June 1, 1866. Office of the Assistant Commissioner, Registers of Letters Received, June 1865–May 1869, BRFAL, RG 105, NARA, M826-6; Major General Wood, Jackson, Mississippi, Endorsements Sent and Received, March 1866–August 1867, BRFAL, RG 105, NARA.

74. H. F. McWilliams to Captain A. W. Allyn, no date, Office of the Assistant Commissioner, Labor Contracts, June 1865–June 1868, BRFAL, RG 105, NARA, M826-50.

75. H. F. McWilliams to Captain A. W. Allyn, no date. Office of the Assistant Commissioner, Labor Contracts, June 1865–June 1868, BRFAL, RG 105, NARA, M826-50.

76. Jones, *Labor of Love, Labor of Sorrow*, 332.

77. Molly Coalman, New Albany, to Gen. Ord, January 20, 1868. Office of the Assistant Commissioner, Unregistered Letters Received, August 1865–April 1869, BRFAL, RG 105, NARA, M826-27.

78. George Corliss to Edward M. Gresham, December 30, 1867. Lake Station, Mississippi, Letters Sent, November 1867–October 1868, BRFAL, RG 105, NARA.

79. Celia, Complaint, August 21, 1867. Office of the Assistant Commissioner, Narrative Reports from Subordinate Officers, Tupelo, Mississippi, BRFAL, RG 105, NARA, M826-30; John J. Cooke v. B. Hannum and Louisa, his wife, October Term, 1860, *Mississippi Reports* (Philadelphia: T. and J. W. Johnson, 1867), 423.

80. P. P. Bergeoni, Woodville, Mississippi, Report of Operations and Complaints for October 1868. Office of the Assistant Commissioner, Narrative Reports from Subordinate Officers, August 1865–December 1868, BRFAL, RG 105, NARA, M826-33.

81. Emily Bush, Affidavit, September 26, 1867. Macon, Mississippi, Letters Received, July 1867–December 1868, BRFAL, RG 105, NARA; P. P. Bergeoni, Report, July 31, 1868. Office of the Assistant Commissioner, Narrative Reports from Subordinate Officers, August 1865–December 1868, BRFAL, RG 105, NARA, M826-33.

82. Fred and Dinah Wilson to Col. Samuel Thomas, May 9, 1866. Office of the Assistant Commissioner, June 1865–May 1869, Registered Letters Received, BRFAL, RG 105, NARA, M826-17.

83. William S. Tidball to Major George S. Smith, October 25, 1867. Greenville, Mississippi, Unregistered Letters Received, August 1867–October 1868, BRFAL, RG 105, NARA.

84. See Wallace v. Godfrey, *The Federal Reporter*, Vol. 42, June–September (St. Paul: West Publishing Co., 1890), 814, 815.

85. B. Miles to Captain J. Holt, April 16, 1868. Jackson, Mississippi, Subassistant Commissioner, Unregistered Letters Received, January 1866–December 1868, BRFAL, RG 105, NARA.

86. W. H. Buford to William Wedemeyer, June 24, 1868. Grenada, Mississippi, Registers of Letters Received, March 1866–December 1868, BRFAL, RG 105, NARA.

87. P. P. Bergeoni, Report, September 30, 1868. Office of the Assistant Commissioner, Narrative Reports from Subordinate Officers, August 1865–December 1868, BRFAL, RG 105, NARA, M826-33.

88. John Williams, Report, November 15, 1868. Office of the Assistant Commissioner, Narrative Reports from Subordinate Officers, August 1865–December 1868, BRFAL, RG 105, NARA, M826-30.

89. Pension File of Alfred Johnson, 649.922, J 566.33, 5th Regiment, RG 15, NARA.

90. George P. Rawick, ed., *The American Slave: A Composite Autobiography*, Supplement, Series 1, Vol. 9: *Mississippi Narratives*, pt. 4 (Westport, Conn.: Greenwood Press, 1974), 1454.

91. DuBois, *Black Reconstruction in America*, 176.

92. James Ellis, letter to subcommissioner, May 19, 1866. Natchez, Missis-

sippi, Subassistant Commissioner, Registers of Letters Received, March 1866–
September 1867, BRFAL, RG 105, NARA.

93. Thomas A. Magee, July 14, 1866. Natchez, Mississippi, Registers of
Letters Received, March 1866–September 1867, BRFAL, RG 105, NARA; Tho-
mas Smith to E. Bamberger, February 1, 1866. Jackson, Mississippi, Registered
Letters Received, July 1865–March 1866, BRFAL, RG 105, NARA.

94. For examples of the Bureau apprenticing children of freedpeople, see
Vernon Lane Wharton, *The Negro in Mississippi, 1865–1890* (New York: Harper
and Row, 1965), 84; Samuel Thomas to O. O. Howard, February 3, 1866. Letters
Received by the Commissioner, M, October 1865–February 1866, BRFAL, RG
105, NARA, M752-22; Robert P. Gardner, Brookhaven, to General Wood, Vicks-
burg, May 14, 1866. Office of the Assistant Commissioner, Registered Letters
Received, June 1865–May 1869, BRFAL, RG 105, NARA, M826-14; Thomas J.
Wood, Endorsement returned, September 25, 1866. Office of the Assistant Commissioner, Endorsements Sent and Received, June 1865–December 1868, BRFAL,
RG 105, NARA, M826-4.

95. Samuel Thomas, Endorsement returned, February 2, 1866. Office of
the Assistant Commissioner, Endorsements Sent and Received, June 1865–December 1868, BRFAL, RG 105, NARA, M826-4; Victoria E. Bynum, *Unruly
Women: The Politics of Social and Sexual Control in the Old South* (Chapel Hill: University of North Carolina Press, 1992), 99.

96. Wharton, *The Negro in Mississippi*, 91.

97. Samuel Thomas to O. O. Howard, February 3, 1866. Letters Received
by the Commissioner, M, October 1865–February 1866, BRFAL, RG 105, NARA,
M752-22.

98. L. W. Dangerfield, letter to subassistant, January 8, 1866. Office of the
Assistant Commissioner, Registered Letters Received, June 1865–May 1869,
BRFAL, RG 105, NARA, M826-6.

99. A. C. Gillem, Endorsement Returned, June 22, 1868. Endorsements
Sent and Received, June 1865–December 1868, BRFAL, RG 105, NARA, M826-
5; Vina Flowers, Complaint, November 12, 1867. Friars Point, Mississippi, Register of Complaints, February–December 1868, BRFAL, RG 105, NARA; William Tims, letter, May 14, 1867. Jackson, Mississippi, Letters Sent, March
1866–December 1868, BRFAL, RG 105, NARA.

100. W. W. Chisalm to Major Knox, January 28, 1866. Jackson, Mississippi,
Subassistant Commissioner, Unregistered Letters Received, January 1866–December 1868, BRFAL, RG 105, NARA.

101. Thomas J. Wood, Endorsement, June 19, 1866. Office of the Assistant
Commissioner, Endorsements Sent and Received, June 1865–December 1868,
BRFAL, RG 105, NARA, M826-4.

102. April 10, 1866, *Daily Mississippi Clarion* (Jackson, Mississippi), 111.

103. Nelson Gill to E. Bamberger, January 19, 1866. Jackson, Mississippi,
Registered Letters Received, October 1867–December 1868, BRFAL, RG 105,
NARA.

104. Henry E. Rainals to Hiram, October 22, 1866. Meridian, Mississippi,
Letters Sent, July 1867–July 1868, BRFAL, RG 105, NARA.

105. Colonel Samuel Thomas to B. G. Humphreys, March 17, 1866. Merid-

ian, Mississippi, Unregistered Letters Received, July 1867–July 1868, BRFAL, RG 105, NARA.

106. C. C. Hubbard to Lieut. E. Bamberger, December 30, 1865. Jackson, Mississippi, Subassistant Commissioner, Registered Letters Received, July 1865–March 1866, BRFAL, RG 105, NARA.

107. Lloyd Wheaton, Endorsement, June 6, 1868. Corinth, Mississippi, Endorsements Sent and Received, March 1867–December 1868, BRFAL, RG 105, NARA; Albert P. Blaustein and Robert L. Zangrando, eds., *Civil Rights and the Black American: A Documentary History* (New York: Washington, D.C., 1970), 229–32.

108. For an example of the legal process parents needed to follow, see Charles A. Stovall to Major J. J. Knox, May 21, 1866. Meridian, Mississippi, Unregistered Letters Received, BRFAL, RG 105, NARA.

109. William M. Wiecek, "The Great Writ and Reconstruction: The Habeas Corpus Act of 1867," *The Journal of Southern History* XXXVI (November 1970): 531.

110. Thomas Smith to E. Bamberger, February 1, 1866. Jackson, Mississippi, Subassistant Commissioner, Registered Letters Received, July 1865–March 1866, BRFAL, RG 105, NARA; James Ellis, letter, May 19, 1866. Natchez, Mississippi, Subassistant Commissioner, Registers of Letters Received, March 1866–September 1867, BRFAL, RG 105, NARA.

111. E. H. Kessler to William Shields, October 23, 1867. Grenada, Mississippi, Registers of Letters Received, March 1866–December 1868, BRFAL, RG 105, NARA.

112. Pete Daniel, "Commentary: The Metamorphosis of Slavery, 1865–1900," *Journal of American History* 66 (June 1979): 92.

113. Apprentice Contracts with Louis Gest, November–December 1865. Macon, Mississippi, Miscellaneous Records, 1865–1867, BRFAL, RG 105, NARA.

114. Thomas Smith to Francis Goodwin, February 10, 1866. Jackson, Mississippi, Subassistant Commissioner, Letters Sent and Received, January–March 1866, BRFAL, RG 105, NARA.

115. Thomas Norton, Letter, July 30, 1867. Lauderdale, Mississippi, Registered Letters Received, March 1867–January 1868, BRFAL, RG 105, NARA.

116. O. D. Greene, Letter, September 14, 1867. Office of the Assistant Commissioner, Registers of Letters Received, June 1865–May 1869, BRFAL, RG 105, NARA, M826-7.

117. Mary Ann Elsey, Complaint, September 20, 1867. Magnolia, Mississippi, Register of Complaints, August 1867–December 1868, BRFAL, RG 105, NARA.

118. Mary Bragg, Endorsement, October 10, 1867. Office of the Assistant Commissioner, Endorsements Sent and Received, June 1865–December 1868, BRFAL, RG 105, NARA, M826-4; Winn Johnson to Major Knox, February 29, 1866. Meridian, Mississippi, Unregistered Letters Received, July 1865–June 1868, BRFAL, RG 105, NARA.

119. Calvin Aldridge to Lloyd Wheaton, February 26, 1868. Corinth, Mississippi, Unregistered Letters Received, May 1867–November 1868, BRFAL, RG 105, NARA.

120. Isaac Bennett to George Corliss, January 19, 1868. Lake Station, Mis-

sissippi, Registered Letters Received, BRFAL, RG 105, NARA; James Henderson
to George Corliss, March 19, 1868. Lake Station, Mississippi, Registered Letters
Received, BRFAL, RG 105, NARA.

121. H. H. Howard to General A. Ames, Carthage, April 14, 1869. Office of
Civil Affairs, Letters Received, RG 393, NARA.

122. John Knox to E. Bamberger, Meridian, Mississippi, March 10, 1866.
Meridian, Mississippi, Registered Letters Received, April–December 1866,
BRFAL, RG 105, NARA.

123. Ellen Lowe, Petition, October 19, 1867. Office of the Assistant Commissioner, Unregistered Letters Received, August 1865–April 1869, M826-27,
BRFAL, RG 105, NARA.

124. R. P. Gardner to William H. Eldridge, April 23, 1867. Jackson, Mississippi, Subassistant Commissioner, Letters Sent, March 1866–December 1868,
BRFAL, RG 105, NARA.

125. J. W. Sunderland to A. W. Preston, January 28, 1867. Office of the
Assistant Commissioner, Registers of Letters Received, June 1865–May 1869,
BRFAL, RG 105, NARA, M826-20.

126. George S. Smith to J. B. M. Callester, November 26, 1866. Columbus,
Mississippi, Letters Sent, March 1866–December 1868, BRFAL, RG 105, NARA.

127. Charles T. Howard, Letter, February 23, 1869. Office of the Assistant
Commissioner, Subassistant Commissioner, Registers of Letters Received, March
1866–September 1867, BRFAL, RG 105, NARA, M826-7.

128. Alfred H. Stone, Office of Acting Assistant Commissioner, Freedmen's
Bureau for Northern District of Mississippi, Jackson, Mississippi, September 28,
1865. Alfred H. Stone Collection, Department of Archives and History, Jackson,
Mississippi.

129. George Corliss, Report, September 30, 1867. Office of the Assistant
Commissioner, Narrative Reports from Subordinate Officers, August 1865–December 1868, BRFAL, RG 105, NARA, M826-30.

130. P. P. Bergeoni, Report, September 30, 1867. Office of the Assistant
Commissioner, Narrative Reports from Subordinate Officers, August 1865–December 1868, BRFAL, RG 105, NARA, M826-33.

131. P. L. Criglin, Contract, August 11, 1865. Office of the Assistant Commissioner, Labor Contracts, June 1865–June 1868, BRFAL, RG 105, NARA,
M826-45.

132. W. J. Benson with Lizzie Benson, Contract, July 16, 1866. Office of the
Assistant Commissioner, Labor Contracts, June 1865–June 1868, BRFAL, RG
105, NARA, M826-49.

133. Lyle Chandler, Contract, August 20, 1865. Office of the Assistant Commissioner, Labor Contracts, June 1865–June 1868, BRFAL, RG 105, NARA,
M826-45.

134. Mrs. Laura Waller, Contract, August 12, 1865. Office of the Assistant
Commissioner, Labor Contracts, June 1865–June 1868, BRFAL, RG 105, NARA,
M826-45.

135. William Shields to John M. Math, December 18, 1867. Grenada, Mississippi, Letters Sent, March 1866–April 1868, BRFAL, RG 105, NARA.

136. Phyllis Ann Johns, Affidavit, August 3, 1868. Jackson, Mississippi, Sub-

assistant Commissioner, Miscellaneous Records, 1865–1868, BRFAL, RG 105, NARA.

137. Edie Glover, Complaint, September 30, 1867. Jackson, Mississippi, Register of Complaints, January–December 1868, BRFAL, RG 105, NARA.

6. Kin Networks

1. Pension file of Archie Branch, 168.398, 187.861, 58th Regiment, Record Group 15 (hereafter RG 15), National Archives and Records Administration, Washington, D.C. (hereafter NARA).

2. Pension file of Thomas Brown, 147.977, 5th Regiment, RG 15, NARA.

3. Leon F. Litwack, *Been in the Storm So Long: The Aftermath of Slavery* (New York: Alfred A. Knopf, 1979), 230–38.

4. George P. Rawick, ed., *The American Slave: A Composite Autobiography*, Supplement, Series 1, Vol. 8: *Mississippi Narratives*, pt. 3 (Westport, Conn.: Greenwood Press, 1974), 804.

5. Richard Bartou, Esq., Oktibbeha Co., August 19, 1868. Columbus, Mississippi, Letters Sent, March 1866–December 1866, BRFAL, RG 105, NARA.

6. William K. White to A. C. Gillem, September 23, 1867. Office of the Assistant Commissioner, Endorsements Sent and Received, June 1865–December 1868, BRFAL, RG 105, NARA, M826-4.

7. Peggie Kelly, Starkville, Mississippi to William Peacock, Shelbyville, Tennessee, January 31, 1892. Mississippi Department of Archives and History, Jackson, Mississippi.

8. Crandall A. Shifflett, "The Household Composition of Rural Black Families: Louisa County, Virginia, 1888," *Journal of Interdisciplinary History* VI (Autumn 1975): 235–60. For an African context see Niara Sudarkasa, "African and Afro-American Family Structure," in *Anthropology for the Nineties: Introductory Readings*, ed. Johnetta B. Cole (New York: The Free Press, 1988), 202.

9. List of Negroes on B. Garland's Plantation in Hinds County, Mississippi, May 1865. Jackson, Mississippi, Subassistant Commissioner, Miscellaneous Records, 1865–1868, BRFAL, RG 105, NARA.

10. Leslie H. Owens, "The African in the Garden: Reflections About New World Slavery and its Lifelines," in *The State of Afro-American History: Past, Present, and Future*, ed. Darlene Clark Hine (Baton Rouge: Louisiana State University Press, 1986), 27.

11. H. F. Drummond, Contract, August 19, 1865. Office of the Assistant Commissioner, Labor Contracts, June 1865–June 1868, BRFAL, RG 105, NARA, M826-45.

12. J. A. Nixon, Contract, January 6, 1865. Office of the Assistant Commissioner, Labor Contracts, June 1865–June 1868, BRFAL, RG 105, NARA, M826-43; see also Reuben Davis, Contract, January 1, 1867. Office of the Assistant Commissioner, Labor Contracts, June 1865–June 1868, BRFAL, RG 105, NARA, M826-50.

13. George P. Rawick, ed., *The American Slave: A Composite Autobiography*, Supplement, Series 1, Vol. 9: *Mississippi Narratives*, pt. 4 (Westport, Conn.: Greenwood Press, 1974), 1611.

14. Pension File of James Tolliver, 684.046J, 615.530, 53rd Regiment, RG 15, NARA.

15. Pension File of Archie Branch, 168.398, 187.861, 58th Regiment, RG 15, NARA.

16. Pension File of Benjamin Lee, 380.960, 5th Regiment, RG 15, NARA.; Pension File of Nicholas Thomas, 197.568 J. 626.450, 5th Regiment, RG 15, NARA.

17. Pension File of Lee Vassar, 255.443, 201.542, 3rd Regiment, RG 15, NARA.

18. Pension File of George Hubbard, 304.430, 51st Regiment, RG 15, NARA.

19. Pension File of James Demar, 797.550, 573.380, 5th Regiment, RG 15, NARA.

20. Pension File of Archie Branch, 168.398, 187.861, 58th Regiment, RG 15, NARA.

21. Pension File of William Harris, 237.517, 195.267, 53rd Regiment, RG 15, NARA.

22. Pension File of Jacob Horton, 627.635, 493.946, 3rd Regiment, RG 15, NARA.

23. Alvan Gillem, Endorsement, September 18, 1867, Vicksburg, Mississippi. Office of the Assistant Commissioner, Endorsements Sent and Received, June 1865–December 1868, BRFAL, RG 105, NARA, M826-4.

24. Thad Preuss, Report, Oxford, September 30, 1867. Office of the Assistant Commissioner, Narrative Reports from Subordinate Officers, August 1865–December 1868, BRFAL, RG 105, NARA, M826-30.

25. T. S. Free to Samuel Thomas, September 9, 1865, Office of the Assistant Commissioner, Registers of Letters Received, June 1865–May 1869, BRFAL, RG 105, NARA, M826-9.

26. Dimitri B. Shimkin, *The Extended Family in Black Societies* (The Hague: Mouton Publishers, 1978), 72.

27. A sample of two counties from the 1870 Mississippi Census showed that less than 10 percent of the households contained women without an adult male. United States Bureau of Census, *Ninth Census of the United States* (Washington, D.C.: Government Printing Office), 1872.

28. Laura F. Edwards, *Gendered Strife and Confusion: The Political Culture of Reconstruction* (Urbana: University of Illinois Press, 1997), 147.

29. Frank Johnson to Robert P. Gardner, Jackson, July 31, 1867, Jackson, Mississippi, Subassistant Commissioner, Unregistered Letters Received, January 1866–December 1868, BRFAL, RG 105, NARA; R. P. Gardner to W. H. Eldridge, Brookhaven, May 13, 1867. Jackson, Mississippi, Subassistant Commissioner, Letters Sent, March 1866–December 1868, BRFAL, RG 105, NARA.

30. Caroline Holt to George Nelson, May 4, 1867. Yazoo City, Mississippi, Registered Letters Received, March–December 1867, BRFAL, RG 105, NARA.

31. Pension File of Wesley Thomas, 172.139, 224.634, 5th Regiment, RG 15, NARA.

32. Pension File of Caesar Wilson, 294.985, 344.458, 5th Regiment, RG 15, NARA.

33. Pension File of Henry Patterson, 156.614 cert. 500.651, 5th Regiment, RG 15, NARA.

34. Pension File of Leonard Barnes, 315.847, 250.920, 53rd Regiment, RG 15, NARA.

35. Pension File of Charles Wabbs, 240.644, 5th Regiment, RG 15, NARA.

36. Pension File of Joseph Duncan, 767.326, 567.264, 5th Regiment, RG 15, NARA.

37. Pension File of Wade Hamilton, 264.687, 273.744, 3rd Regiment, RG 15, NARA, and Jeff Boose, 400.738, 3rd Regiment, RG 15, NARA.

38. Pension File of Alfred Johnson, 649.922, J 566.335, 5th Regiment, RG 15, NARA.

39. Pension File of Frank Fletcher, 782.007, 599.542, 5th Regiment, RG 15, NARA.

40. Pension File of John Brown, 387.412, 5th Regiment, RG 15, NARA.

41. Pension File of Frank Fletcher, 782.007, 599.542, 5th Regiment, RG 15, NARA.

42. Henry H. Penniman to D. M. White, February 22, 1867. Office of the Assistant Commissioner, Registered Letters Received, June 1865–May 1869, BRFAL, RG 105, NARA, M826-19.

43. George S. Smith to Charles Moore, July 13, 1867. Columbus, Mississippi, Letters Sent Relating to Complaints, July–October 1867, BRFAL, RG 105, NARA.

44. James N. Shepley to A. W. Preston, May 9, 1867. Grenada, Mississippi, Letters Sent, March 1866–April 1868, BRFAL, RG 105, NARA.

45. John Williams to Lieut. M. Barber, November 15, 1867. Office of the Assistant Commissioner, Narrative Reports from Subordinate Officers, August 1865–December 1868, BRFAL, RG 105, NARA, M826-30.

46. W. L. Cadle to Major George D. Reynolds, September 11, 1865, Natchez, Mississippi, Southern District of Mississippi, Trimonthly and Monthly Reports of Freedmen, March 1864–January 1866, BRFAL, RG 105, NARA.

47. William Shields, Report, January 31, 1868. Office of the Assistant Commissioner, Narrative Reports from Subordinate Officers, BRFAL, RG 105, NARA, M826-32.

48. W.H. Offutt [to Major Tidball], September 6, 1867. Greenville, Mississippi, Registered Letters Received, August 1867–January 1868, BRFAL, RG 105, NARA.

49. H. Cox, Contract, July 1865, Office of the Assistant Commissioner, Labor Contracts, June 1865–June 1868, BRFAL, RG 105, NARA, M826-45.

50. G. B. Stallings, Contract, August 15, 1865, Office of the Assistant Commissioner, Labor Contracts, June 1865–June 1868, M826-46; Robert G. McDaniel, Contract, 8 January 1866. Office of the Assistant Commissioner, Labor Contracts, June 1865–June 1868, BRFAL, RG 105, NARA, M826-50.

51. Pension File of Thomas Ragland, 164.207, 5th Regiment, RG 15, NARA.

52. Pension File of Isaac Mackie, 322.326, 366.345, 5th Regiment, RG 15, NARA.

53. Pension File of Alonzo Sharkey, 120.208J, 438.423, 3rd Regiment, RG 15, NARA.

54. Mary Ann Ellesey to E. E. Platt, March 20, 1868. Brookhaven, Missis-

sippi, Registered Letters Received, November 1867–August 1868, BRFAL, RG 105, NARA.

55. George S. Smith to Hon. Judge of Probate, Monroe Co., May 28, 1866. Columbus, Mississippi, Letters Sent, March 1866–December 1868, BRFAL, RG 105, NARA; D. M. White to Ben S. Leonard, May 7, 1866. Brookhaven, Mississippi, Letters Sent, March 1866–December 1868, BRFAL, RG 105, NARA; Alvan Gillem, endorsement concerning Lucy Spencer, Office of the Assistant Commissioner, Endorsements Sent and Received, June 1865–December 1868, BRFAL, RG 105, NARA, M826-4; Preston to Captain R. P. Gardner, April 26, 1867. Office of the Assistant Commissioner, Press Copies of Letters Sent, June 1865–April 1869, BRFAL, RG 105, NARA, M826-2.

56. W.H. Eldridge to A. W. Smith, September 30, 1867. Office of the Assistant Commissioner, Narrative Reports from Subordinate Officers, August 1865–December 1868, BRFAL, RG 105, NARA, M826-30.

57. Hattie Freeman to Mr. and Mrs. Wright, November 11, 1869. American Missionary Association, Amistad Research Center, Dillard University, New Orleans, Louisiana.

58. Martha Jordan, Affidavit, December 25, 1867. Jackson, Mississippi, Subassistant Commissioner, Unregistered Letters Received, January 1866–December 1868, BRFAL, RG 105, NARA.

59. W. W. Whitchess [to William Wedemeyer], April 30, 1868. Grenada, Mississippi, Registers of Letters Received, March 1866–December 1868, BRFAL, RG 105, NARA.

60. Samuel Thomas to State of Mississippi, County of Warren, March 1, 1866. Office of the Assistant Commissioner, Press Copies of Letters Sent, June 1865–April 1869, BRFAL, RG 105, NARA, M826-1.

61. W.H. Eldridge to A. M. Scales, Esq., November 16, 1867. Tupelo, Mississippi, Letters Sent, July 1867–May 1868, BRFAL, RG 105, NARA; C. A. Beers, Yazoo City, to Major General Ord, June 16, 1867. Office of the Assistant Commissioner, Registered Letters Received, June 1865–May 1869, M826-19; W. H. Eldridge, Endorsement, August 6, 1867. Office of the Assistant Commissioner, Endorsements Sent and Received, June 1865–December 1868, BRFAL, RG 105, NARA, M826-4.

62. W.H. Eldridge to Richard Leadbetter, December 16, 1868. Yazoo City, Mississippi, Letters Sent, March 1867–December 1868, BRFAL, RG 105, NARA.

63. Pension File of Benjamin Lee, 380.960, 5th Regiment, RG 15, NARA.

64. H. Sweeney to Major General Wood, August 15, 1866. Vicksburg, Mississippi, Unregistered Letters Received, April 1866–October 1868, BRFAL, RG 105, NARA; Jeff C. Davis to assistant commissioner, January 2, 1867. Office of the Assistant Commissioner, Registers of Letters Received, June 1865–May 1869, BRFAL, RG 105, NARA, M826-6.

65. Pension File of Calvin Gaden, 266.613, 5th Regiment, RG 15, NARA.

66. Pension File of John Posey, 374.985, 5th Regiment, RG 15, NARA.

67. Enoch Williams, Corinth, Complaint, no date. Corinth, Mississippi, Register of Complaints, BRFAL, RG 105, NARA.

68. Thomas J. Wood to County of Warren, November 30, 1866. Office of the Assistant Commissioner, Press Copies of Letters of Sent, June 1865–April

1869, BRFAL, RG105, NARA, M826-2; Lewis and Laura Gardner to Thomas Wood, November 24, 1866. Office of the Assistant Commissioner, Registered Letters Received, June 1865–May 1869, BRFAL, RG 105, NARA, M826-14.

69. William P. Drew, Washington, D.C., to O. C. French Esq., Natchez, Mississippi, September 10, 1870. Natchez, Mississippi, Registered Letters Received, BRFAL, RG 105, NARA.

70. Allen P. Huggins to A. W. Preston, June 23, 1867. Yazoo City, Mississippi, Letters Sent, March 1867–December 1868, BRFAL, RG 105, NARA.

71. See Jacqueline Jones, *Labor of Love, Labor of Sorrow: Black Women, Work, and the Family, from Slavery to the Present* (New York: Vintage Books, 1985), 31, for fictitious kin in slavery.

72. Minnie Jenkins, Complaint, no date. Greenville, Mississippi, Register of Complaints, September–December 1867, BRFAL, RG 105, NARA.

73. Emily McCrane, Complaint, September 1868. Magnolia, Mississippi, Register of Complaints, August 1867–December 1868, BRFAL, RG 105, NARA.

74. Shimkin, *The Extended Family in Black Societies*, 169; Michael Wayne, *The Reshaping of Plantation Society: The Natchez District, 1860–1880* (Baton Rouge: Louisiana State University Press, 1983), 141; Susan A. Mann, "Slavery, Share-cropping, and Sexual Inequality," *Signs* 14 (Summer 1989): 791.

75. Ira Berlin, Steven F. Miller, and Leslie S. Rowlands, "Afro-American Families in the Transition from Slavery to Freedom," *Radical History Review* 42 (September 1988): 90.

76. Herbert G. Gutman, *The Black Family in Slavery and Freedom, 1750–1925* (New York: Vintage Books, 1977), 209–10.

77. Pension File of Charles Eagley, 165.787, 3rd Regiment, RG 15, NARA.

78. Joseph Einbry, Contract, August 15, 1865. Office of the Assistant Commissioner, Labor Contracts, June 1865–June 1868, BRFAL, RG 105, NARA, M826-46.

79. Litwack, *Been in the Storm So Long*, 196, 215; James L. Roark, *Masters without Slaves: Southern Planters in the Civil War and Reconstruction* (New York: W.W. Norton, 1977), 198; Wayne, *The Reshaping of Plantation Society*, 115.

80. William Shields to Merritt Barber, December 31, 1867. Office of the Assistant Commissioner, Narrative Reports from Subordinate Officers, August 1865–December 1868, BRFAL, RG 105, NARA, M826-31.

81. Thad Pruess, Letter, September 13, 1867. Office of the Assistant Commissioner, Registers of Letters Received, June 1865–May 1869, BRFAL, RG 105, NARA, M826-7; W. G. Wedemeyer, Letter, May 19, 1868. Office of the Assistant Commissioner, Registers of Letters Received, June 1865–May 1869, BRFAL, RG 105, NARA, M826-7; George Corliss, letter, May 4, 1868. Office of the Assistant Commissioner, Registers of Letters Received, June 1865–May 1869, BRFAL, RG 105, NARA, M826-7; J. L. S. Hill to A. W. Preston, October 15, 1866. Office of the Assistant Commissioner, Registered Letters Received, June 1865–May 1869, BRFAL, RG 105, NARA, M826-14; Robert Gardner to Major Preston, March 11, 1867. Office of the Assistant Commissioner, Registered Letters Received, June 1865–May 1869, BRFAL, RG 105, NARA, M826-18; Clifton Lloyd Ganus, Jr., "The Freedmen's Bureau in Mississippi" (Ph.D. diss., Tulane University, 1953), 389.

82. A. C. Gillem, Endorsement Returned, January 1, 1868. Office of the Assistant Commissioner, Endorsements Sent and Received, June 1865–December 1868, BRFAL, RG 105, NARA, M826-5.

83. S. C. Green to O. C. French, May 19, 1868. Lauderdale, Mississippi, Registered Letters Received, March 1867–January 1868, BRFAL, RG 105, NARA; A. C. Gillem, letter returned, November 5, 1868. Office of the Assistant Commissioner, Registers of Letters Received, June 1865–May 1869, BRFAL, RG 105, NARA, M826-7.

7. Communities

1. Pension File of James Mathey, 58th Regiment, 227.825, J, 268.203, RG 15 (hereafter RG 15), National Archives and Records Administration, Washington, D.C. (hereafter NARA).

2. Pension File of Thomas Brown, 147.977, 53rd Regiment, RG 15, NARA.

3. John W. Blassingame, *The Slave Community: Plantation Life in the Antebellum South* (New York: Oxford University Press, 1972); Eugene D. Genovese, *Roll, Jordan, Roll: The World the Slaves Made* (New York: Vintage Books, 1976); Charles Joyner, *Down by the Riverside: A South Carolina Slave Community* (Urbana: University of Illinois Press, 1984).

4. Pension File of James Brown, 406.868, 5th Regiment, RG 15, NARA.

5. Pension File of Henry Patterson, 156.614 cert. 500.651, 5th Regiment, RG 15, NARA.

6. Peter Kolchin, "Reevaluating the Antebellum Slave Community: A Comparative Perspective," *The Journal of American History* 70 (December 1983): 584–601.

7. Pension File of Nicholas Thomas, 197.568, J 626.450, 5th Regiment, RG 15, NARA.

8. Pension File of Frank Fletcher, 782.007, 599.542, 5th Regiment, RG 15, NARA.

9. Pension File of Samuel Williams, 168.903, 175.358, 5th Regiment, RG 15, NARA.

10. Pension File of Moses West, 164.065, 5th Regiment, RG 15, NARA.

11. Pension Files of Moses Wilson, 315.778, 273.769, 5th Regiment, RG 15, NARA.

12. Pension File of Nathaniel Forman, 121.340, 177.645, 5th Regiment, RG 15, NARA.

13. Pension File of James Gray, 390.751, 501.909, 5th Regiment, RG 15, NARA.

14. Pension File of Henry Patterson, 156.614, cert. 500.651, 5th Regiment, RG 15, NARA.

15. Pension File of Hapless Nash, 335.410, 235.274, 5th Regiment, RG 15, NARA.

16. Pension File of Alfred Johnson, 649.922 J. 566.335, 5th Regiment, RG 15, NARA.

17. Pension File of James Johnson, 294.416 OJ 578.302, 5th Regiment, RG 15, NARA.

18. Pension File of Henry Turner, 789.179, cert. 574.604, 5th Regiment, RG 15, NARA.

19. Pension File of Louis Caston, 388.190, 384.190, 5th Regiment, RG 15, NARA.

20. Pension File of Gadby Innis, 152.007, 5th Regiment, RG 15, NARA.

21. Pension File of Tod Welcome, 397.384, 440.081, 5th Regiment, RG 15, NARA.

22. Pension File of William Harris, 695.684 J., 538.313, 53rd Regiment, RG 15, NARA.

23. Pension Files of Lewis West, 174.998, 5th Regiment; Richard Roberts, 317.426 J 519.290, 5th Regiment; Hubbard Reynolds, 163.950, 741.430, 5th Regiment. All in RG 15, NARA.

24. Vernon Lane Wharton, *The Negro in Mississippi, 1865–1890* (New York: Harper and Row, 1965), 71; Gerald David Jaynes, *Branches without Roots: Genesis of the Black Working Class in the American South, 1862–1882* (New York: Oxford University Press, 1986), 189; Ronald L. F. Davis, *Good and Faithful Labor: From Slavery to Sharecropping in the Natchez District, 1860–1890* (Westport, Conn.: Greenwood Press, 1982), 178.

25. Mrs. Freshon, Complaint, October 1868. Magnolia, Mississippi, Register of Complaints, August 1867–December 1868, BRFAL, RG 105, NARA.

26. C. T. Lawson, October 23, 1867. Office of the Assistant Commissioner, Narrative Reports from Subordinate Officers, Subdistrict of McNutt, August 1865–December 1868, BRFAL, RG 105, NARA, M826-30. James T. Currie, *Enclave: Vicksburg and Her Plantations, 1863–1870* (Jackson: University Press of Mississippi, 1980), 77.

27. Pension File of Frank Fletcher, 782.007, 599.542, 5th Regiment; Pension File of Turner Roach, 337.590, cert. 260.142, 5th Regiment. Both in RG 15, NARA.

28. Pension File of Wade Hamilton, 264.687, 273.744, 3rd Regiment, RG 15, NARA.

29. Pension File of Henry Clark, 239.087, 305.330, 3rd Regiment, RG 15, NARA.

30. Pension File of Sam McCastle, 145.057, 126.509, 3rd Regiment, RG 15, NARA.

31. Ronald L. F. Davis, "The U.S. Army and the Origins of Sharecropping in the Natchez District—A Case Study," *The Journal of Negro History* LXII (January 1977): 79.

32. John Simmons, Contract, Yazoo Co., no date. Office of the Assistant Commissioner, Labor Contracts, June 1865–June 1868, BRFAL, RG 105, NARA, M826-49.

33. E. J. Castello to S. C. Greene, June 3, 1868. Office of the Assistant Commissioner, Mississippi, Registered Letters Received, June 1865–May 1869, BRFAL, RG 105, NARA, M826-23; Annie, Complaint, September 9, 1867. Louisville, Mississippi, Register of Complaints, September 1867–November 1868, BRFAL, RG 105, NARA; Eliza Roney, Complaint, June 1868. Magnolia, Mississippi, Register of Complaints, August 1867–December 1868, BRFAL, RG 105, NARA.

34. J. H. Chapman to S. G. Gaun, June 25, 1868. Vicksburg, Mississippi, Unregistered Letters Received, April 1866–October 1868, BRFAL, RG 105, NARA; George Chrittendon Bentham, *A Year of Wreck: A True Story* (New York: Harper and Brothers, 1880), 327–28.

35. J. Lowenstein, Contract, December 26, 1865. Mississippi, Office of the Assistant Commissioner, Labor Contracts, June 1865–June 1868, BRFAL, RG 105, NARA, M826-48.

36. Pension File of Sam McCaskill, 145.057, 126.509, 3rd Regiment, RG 15, NARA.

37. Pension File of Horace Stewart, 187.331, 518.689, 5th Regiment, RG 15, NARA.

38. Pension File of Levi McLauren, 213.748 J, 58th Regiment; Pension File of Watt Lee, 412.464 J, cert. 577.520, 5th Regiment; Pension File of Jacob Horton, 627.635, 493.946, 3rd Regiment. All in RG 15, NARA.

39. Pension File of James Johnson, 294.416 OJ 578.302, 5th Regiment, RG 15, NARA.

40. Deborah Jones, "Gossip: Notes on Women's Oral Culture," *Women's Studies International Quarterly* 3 (1980): 195; Elizabeth Fox-Genovese, *Within the Plantation Household: Black and White Women of the Old South* (Chapel Hill: University of North Carolina Press, 1988), 318.

41. Pension File of Nicholas Thomas, 197.586 J. 626.450, 5th Regiment, RG 15, NARA.

42. Pension File of Sam McCaskill, 145.057, 126.509, 3rd Regiment, RG 15, NARA.

43. Pension File of James Jones, 346.290, 53rd Regiment, RG 15, NARA.

44. Historian Deborah Gray White examined the strong female network that developed during slavery in segregated work areas such as trash gangs. The shift to sharecropping may have gradually lessened the intensity of relationships that White described. Under the family sharecropping system, freedwomen spent less time in the company of other women, particularly unrelated women. This suggests a possible weakening of closeness, although freedwomen continued to have close friendships with other women. The evidence suggests that the primary relationship of a married woman was with her spouse after the war. Deborah Gray White, *Ar'n't I a Woman?: Female Slaves in the Plantation South* (New York: Norton, 1985), 38.

45. George Haller, Report, June 1868. Officer of the Assistant Commissioner, Narrative Reports from Subordinate Officers, August 1865–December 1868, BRFAL, RG 105, NARA, M826-33.

46. G. Gordan Adams to Captain Gardner, March 20, 1867. Jackson, Mississippi, Subassistant Commissioner, Unregistered Letters Received, January 1866–December 1868, BRFAL, RG 105, NARA.

47. Sarah J. Foster, Application, November 26, 1871. Vicksburg, Mississippi, Agent for Payment of Bounties, Applications for Bounties, September 1868–March 1872, BRFAL, RG 105, NARA.

48. Pension File of Robert Drake, 143.055, 5th Regiment, RG 15, NARA.

49. Alexander Hamilton, Contract, August 17, 1865, Office of the Assistant Commissioner, Labor Contracts, June 1865–June 1868, BRFAL, RG 105, NARA, M826-45.

50. James O. Banks, Contract, August 12, 1865. Office of the Assistant Commissioner, Labor Contracts, June 1865–June 1868, BRFAL, RG 105, NARA, M826-45.

51. Dimitri B. Shimkin, *The Extended Family in Black Societies* (The Hague: Mouton Publishers, 1978), 58.

52. J. H. Chapman to William T. Drews, November 2, 1871, Vicksburg, Mississippi, Press Copies of Letters Sent, January 1869–March 1872, BRFAL, RG 105, NARA.

53. George P. Rawick, ed., *The American Slave: A Composite Autobiography*, Supplement, Series 1, Vol. 6: *Mississippi Narratives*, pt. 1 (Westport, Conn.: Greenwood Press, 1974), 267.

54. Pension File of Robert Drake, 143.055, 5th Regiment, RG 15, NARA.

55. George P. Rawick, ed., *The American Slave: A Composite Autobiography*, Supplement, Series 1, Vol. 7: *Mississippi Narratives*, pt. 2, 409–10.

56. Ibid., 409.

57. Pension File of Henry Ellison, 151.986, 194.705, 5th Regiment, RG 15, NARA.

58. Pension File of Henry Johnson, 166.519, 5th Regiment, RG 15, NARA.

59. Pension File of Aaron Jones, 166.523, 5th Regiment; same as William Smith, 169.277, 5th Regiment, RG 15, NARA.

60. Pension File of Jordan Meek, 336.679, 268.365, 5th Regiment, RG 15, NARA.

61. Pension File of Nathaniel Foreman, 121.340, 177.645, 5th Regiment, RG 15, NARA.

62. Pension File of Joseph Duncan, 767.326, 567.264, cert. 680.771, 5th Regiment, RG 15, NARA.

63. Pension File of Anderson Gradison, 158.739, 113.018, 5th Regiment, RG 15, NARA.

64. Pension File of Sam McCaskill, 145.057, 126.509, 3rd Regiment RG 15, NARA.

65. Pension File of Thomas Wesley, 172.139, 224.634, 5th Regiment, RG 15, NARA.

66. Pension File of Albert Johnson, 182.941, 222.782, 3rd Regiment, RG 15, NARA.

67. Pension File of Levi Hines, 417.339, 381.379, 5th Regiment, RG 15, NARA.

68. Lyle Chandler, Contract, August 20, 1865. Mississippi, Office of the Assistant Commissioner, Labor Contracts, June 1865–June 1868, BRFAL, RG 105, NARA, M826-45.

69. Rebecca Flournoy, Affidavit, August 17, 1867. Vicksburg, Mississippi, Letters Sent Relating to Complaints, July–September 1867, BRFAL, RG 105, NARA.

70. Thomas Andrew to Merritt Barber, Vicksburg, Report of Operations, January 1, 1868. Office of the Assistant Commissioner, Narrative Reports from Subordinate Officers, August 1865–December 1868, BRFAL, RG 105, NARA, M826-31; Martha, Complaints, March 1868. Louisville, Mississippi, Register of Complaints, September 1867–November 1868, BRFAL, RG 105, NARA; Caroline Burfet, Complaint, September 28, 1868. Natchez, Mississippi, Register of

Complaints, December 1864–December 1868, BRFAL, RG 105, NARA; Jim Williams to M. Barber, April 3, 1868. Office of the Assistant Commissioner, Narrative Reports from Subordinate Officers, August 1865–December 1868, BRFAL, RG 105, NARA, M826-32; P. P. Bergeoni, Report, December 1868. Office of the Assistant Commissioner, Narrative Reports from Subordinate Officers, August 1865–December 1868, BRFAL, RG 105, NARA, M826-33.

71. Celia Harrison, Complaint, August 10, 1867. Columbus, Mississippi, Registers of Complaints, August 1867–May 1868, BRFAL, RG 105, NARA.

72. A. S. Alden to A. W. Preston, Port Gibson, July 25, 1867. Port Gibson, Mississippi, Letters Received, June–September 1867, BRFAL, RG 105, NARA, M826-18.

73. Pension File of James Jones, 346.290, 53rd Regiment, RG 15, NARA.

74. William Tidwell to N. J. Nelson, December 21, 1867. Greenville, Mississippi, Letters Sent, March 1867–December 1868, Mississippi, BRFAL, RG 105, NARA.

75. P. P. Bergeoni, Narrative Report of Operations, Woodville, November 18, 1868. Office of the Assistant Commissioner, Narrative Reports from Subordinate Officers, August 1865–December 1868, BRFAL, RG 105, NARA, M826-33.

76. Mary Smith, Complaint, September 28, 1867. Louisville, Mississippi, Register of Complaints, September 1867–November 1868, BRFAL, RG 105, NARA; Laura F. Edwards, *Gendered Strife and Confusion: The Political Culture of Reconstruction* (Urbana: University of Illinois Press, 1997), 6.

77. James Wilford Garner, *Reconstruction in Mississippi* (Gloucester, Mass.: Peter Smith, 1964), 288; W. E. B. DuBois, *Black Reconstruction in America, 1860–1880* (New York: Atheneum, 1962), 447; William C. Harris, *The Day of the Carpetbagger: Republican Reconstruction in Mississippi* (Baton Rouge: Louisiana State University Press, 1979), 579.

78. Genovese, *Roll, Jordan, Roll*, 254; Randy J. Sparks, "Religion in Amite County, Mississippi, 1800–1861," in *Masters and Slaves in the House of the Lord: Race and Religion in the American South, 1740–1870*, ed. John B. Boles (Lexington: University Press of Kentucky, 1988), 60.

79. E. Franklin Frazier, *The Negro Family in the United States* (Chicago: University of Chicago Press, 1939), 172.

80. Amelia Symie to Joseph Addison, November 18, 1867. Joseph Addison Montgomery and Family Papers, Department of Archives and Manuscripts, Louisiana State University Library, Louisiana State University, Baton Rouge; Bentham, *A Year of Wreck*, 298.

81. Amelia Symie to Joseph Addison, November 18, 1867. Joseph Addison Montgomery and Family Papers, Department of Archives and Manuscripts, Louisiana State University Library, Louisiana State University, Baton Rouge, Louisiana.

82. Maria Waterbury, *Seven Years among the Freedmen* (New York: Books for Libraries Press, 1971), 154–55; Mechal Sobel, *The World They Made Together: Black and White Values in Eighteenth-Century Virginia* (Princeton: Princeton University Press, 1987), 202.

83. M. M Gillespie to Mt. Holt, May 24, 1868. Jackson, Mississippi, Subassistant Commissioner, Unregistered Letters Received, January 1866–December 1868, Mississippi, BRFAL, RG 105, NARA.

84. George P. Rawick, ed., *The American Slave: A Composite Autobiography*, Supplement, Series 1, Vol. 7: *Mississippi Narratives*, pt. 2 (Westport, Conn.: Greenwood Press, 1974), 757.

85. Wharton, *The Negro in Mississippi*, 165.

86. Waterbury, *Seven Years among the Freedmen*, 90.

87. James M. McPherson, *Battle Cry of Freedom: The Civil War Era* (New York: Oxford University Press, 1988), 564, 707, 843.

88. Benjamin Quarles, *The Negro in the Civil War* (Boston: Little, Brown, and Co., 1969), 184.

89. McPherson, *Battle Cry of Freedom*, 701, 702; Mary Frances Berry, "Military Policy Origins of the Thirteenth Amendment and the Civil Rights Act of 1866," in *Historical Judgments Reconsidered: Selected Howard University Lectures in Honor of Rayford W. Logan*, ed. Genna Rae McNeil and Michael R. Winston (Washington, D.C.: Howard University Press, 1988), 73, 75, 90; W. E. B. DuBois wrote, "It took in many respects a finer type of courage for the Negro to work quietly and faithfully as a slave while the world was fighting over his destiny, than it did to seize a bayonet and rush mad with fury or inflamed with drink, and plunge it into the bowels of a stranger. Yet this was the proof of manhood required of the Negro. He might plead his cause with the tongue of Frederick Douglass, and the nation listened almost unmoved. . . . But when he rose and fought and killed, the whole nation with one voice proclaimed him a man and brother. Nothing else made Negro citizenship conceivable, but the record of the Negro soldier as a fighter." *Black Reconstruction in America*, 104.

90. Forrest G. Wood, *Black Scare: The Racist Response to Emancipation* (Los Angeles: University of California Press, 1970), 148, 149.

91. DuBois, *Black Reconstruction in America*, 321, 341, 374; Wharton, *The Negro in Mississippi*, 139, 144; George M. Fredrickson, *The Black Image in the White Mind: The Debate on Afro-American Character and Destiny, 1817–1914* (New York: Harper Torchbooks, 1971), 183, 186; Ellen Carol DuBois, *Feminism and Suffrage: The Emergence of an Independent Women's Movement in America, 1848–1869* (Ithaca: Cornell University Press, 1978), 57.

92. Eleanor Flexner, *Century of Struggle: The Woman's Rights Movement in the United States* (New York: Atheneum, 1974), 143, 147, 149; Ellen Carol DuBois, *Feminism and Suffrage*, 60, 175. A gendered concept of citizenship began earlier than the nineteenth century in the United States; see Linda K. Kerber, "The Paradox of Women's Citizenship in the Early Republic: The Case of Martin vs. Massachusetts, 1805," *The American Historical Review* 97 (April 1992): 350; W. E. B. DuBois wrote, "In 1865, the right of all free Americans to be voters was unquestioned, and had not been questioned since the time of Andrew Jackson, except in the case of women, where it interfered with sex-ownership." *Black Reconstruction in America*, 191.

93. Wharton, *The Negro in Mississippi*, 146, 157.

94. Ira Berlin, *Slaves without Masters: The Free Negro in the Antebellum South* (New York: Vintage Books, 1976), 395.

95. James C. Cobb, *The Most Southern Place on Earth: The Mississippi Delta and the Roots of Regional Identity* (New York: Oxford University Press, 1992), 51.

96. Waterbury, *Seven Years among the Freedmen*, 90.

97. Thomas Holt, *Black over White: Negro Political Leadership In South Caro-*

lina during Reconstruction (Urbana: University of Illinois Press, 1977), 34–35. According to Holt, South Carolinian women, like Greek women of Lysistrata, "applied sanctions of the bedroom to whip male political defectors into conformity with self-interest." See also "Militancy and Black Women in Reconstruction Georgia," *Journal of American Culture* 1 (Winter1978), 841.

98. Albert Talmon Morgan, *Yazoo: Or, On the Picket Line of Freedom in the South* (Washington, D.C.: Albert Talmon Morgan, 1884), 236–37; historian E. Franklin Frazier, used the story of wearing Grant buttons and concluded that "only women accustomed to playing the dominant role in family and marriage relations (if we regard the slaves as having been married) would have asserted themselves as the Negro women in Mississippi did during the election of 1868." *The Negro Family in the United States*, 125. See also Julie Saville, *The Work of Reconstruction: From Slave to Wage Laborer in South Carolina, 1860–1870* (Cambridge: Cambridge University Press, 1994), 169–70.

99. Elsa Barkley Brown, "Many Ways of Being Political: Southern Women in the Nineteenth and Twentieth Centuries," *Newsletter of the Association of Black Women Historians* (October 1990): 6–7; Anna Julia Cooper, *A Voice from the South* (New York: Oxford University Press, 1988), 140; Thomas C. Holt, "'An Empire over the Mind': Emancipation, Race, and Ideology in the British West Indies and the American South," in *Region, Race, and Reconstruction: Essays in Honor of C. Vann Woodward*, ed. J. Morgan Kousser and James M. McPherson (New York: Oxford University Press, 1982), 299.

100. Jaynes, *Branches without Roots*, 284; Elizabeth R. Bethel, "Forming a Free Black Community," in *Promiseland: A Century of Life in a Negro Community* (Philadelphia: Temple University Press, 1981), 13. Bethel wrote that "Community and household autonomy were firmly grounded in the economic independence of land."

101. Jacqueline Dowd Hall, "'The Mind That Burns in Each Body': Women, Rape, and Racial Violence," in *Powers of Desire, and Politics of Sexuality*, ed. Ann Snitow, Christine Stansell, and Sharon Thompson (New York: Monthly Review Press, 1983), 332.

102. Susan A. Mann, "Slavery, Sharecropping, and Sexual Inequality," *Signs* 14 (Summer 1989), 782, 794; Catherine Clinton and Nina Silber, *Divided Houses: Gender and the Civil War* (New York: Oxford University Press, 1992), 318.

103. Gavin Wright, *Old South, New South: Revolutions in the Southern Economy since the Civil War* (New York: Basic Books, 1986), 65.

BIBLIOGRAPHY

Primary Sources

Unpublished

Samuel Andrew Agnew Diary. Southern Historical Collection, University of North Carolina, Chapel Hill, North Carolina.

James Allen, Allen Plantation Book. Mississippi Department of Archives and History, Jackson, Mississippi.

American Missionary Association Papers. Amistad Reseach Center, Dillard University, New Orleans, Louisiana.

Evernand Green Baker Diaries. Southern Historical Collection, University of North Carolina, Chapel Hill, North Carolina.

Records of the Bureau of Refugees, Freedmen, and Abandoned Lands, Record Group 105. National Archives and Records Service, Washington, D.C.

Pierce Butler Papers. Howard Tilton Memorial Library, Tulane University, New Orleans, Louisiana.

Eli Capell Papers. Department of Archives and Manuscripts, Louisiana State University Library, Louisiana State University, Baton Rouge, Louisiana.

Robert L. Caruthers Papers. Southern Historical Collection, University of North Carolina, Chapel Hill, North Carolina.

Anne Collins Papers. Southern Historical Collection, University of North Carolina, Chapel Hill, North Carolina.

Henry M. Crydenwise Papers. William R. Perkins Library, Duke University, Durham, North Carolina.

Harry St. John Dixon Papers. William R. Perkins Library, Duke University, Durham, North Carolina.

Alfred Wass Ellet Papers. William R. Perkins Library, Duke University, Durham, North Carolina.

Alexander K. Farrar Papers. Department of Archives and Manuscripts, Louisiana State University Library, Louisiana State University, Baton Rouge, Louisiana.

Fonsylvania Plantation Diary. Mississippi Department of Archives and History, Jackson, Mississippi.

James A. Gillespie and Family Papers. Department of Archives and Manuscripts, Louisiana State University Library, Louisiana State University, Baton Rouge, Louisiana.

Annie E. Jacobs Manuscript. "The Master of Doro Plantation: An Epic of the Old South." Unpublished Manuscript, Mississippi Department of Archives and History, Jackson, Mississippi.

Thomas Butler King Papers. Southern Historical Collection, University of North Carolina, Chapel Hill, North Carolina.

Francis Terry Leake Papers. Southern Historical Collection, University of North Carolina, Chapel Hill, North Carolina.

John McIver Papers. William R. Perkins Library, Duke University, Durham, North Carolina.

William Newton Mercer Papers. Department of Archives and Manuscripts, Louisiana State University Library, Louisiana State University, Baton Rouge, Louisiana.

Joseph Addison Montgomery and Family Papers. Department of Archives and Manuscripts, Louisiana State University Library, Louisiana State University, Baton Rouge, Louisiana.

Quitman Family Papers. Southern Historical Collection, University of North Carolina, Chapel Hill, North Carolina.

Isaac Shoemaker Diary. William R. Perkins Library, Duke University, Durham, North Carolina.

Alfred H. Stone Collection. Mississippi Department of Archives and History, Jackson, Mississippi.

Records of the Veterans Administration, Pension Case Files of the Bureau of Pensions and the Veterans Administration, 1981–1942, Record Group 15. National Archives and Records Service, Washington, D.C.

Published

Albert, Octavia V. *The House of Bondage.* Freeport, New York: Books for Libraries Press, 1972.

Anderson, E. H. "A Memoir on Reconstruction in Yazoo City." *Journal of Mississippi History* 4 (October 1942): 187–94.

Alverson, James Gibson, ed. *Memoirs of J. M. Gibson, Terrors of the Civil War and Reconstruction Days.* San Gabriel, California: James Gibson Alverson, 1966.

Bentham, George Chrittenden. *A Year of Wreck, A True Story.* New York: Harper and Brothers, 1880.

Berlin, Ira, Joseph P. Reidy, and Leslie S. Rowland. *The Black Military Experience*, Series II, Volume II of *Freedom: A Documentary History of Emancipation, 1861–1867.* New York: Cambridge University Press, 1982.

Berlin, Ira, Thavolia Glymph, Steven F. Miller, Joseph P. Reidy, Leslie S. Rowland, and Julie Saville. *The Wartime Genesis of Free Labor: The Lower South.* Series I, Volume III of *Freedom: A Documentary History of Emancipation, 1861–1867.* New York: Cambridge University Press, 1990.

Conerly, Luke Ward. *Pike County, Mississippi, 1789–1879.* Nashville: Brandon Printing, 1909.

Cooper, Anna Julia. *A Voice From the South.* New York: Oxford University Press, 1988.

Darst, Mary, ed. "The Vicksburg Diary of Mrs. Alfred Ingraham, (May 2–June 13, 1863)." *The Journal of Mississippi History* XLIV (May 1982): 148–179.

Eaton, John. *Grant, Lincoln and the Freedmen: Reminiscences of the Civil War.* New York: Longmans, Green, and Co., 1907.

The Federal Reporter. St. Paul: West Publishing Co, 1890.

Frederick, J. V. "An Illinois Soldier in North Mississippi: Diary of John Wilson, February 15–December 30, 1862." *Journal of Mississippi History* I (July 1939): 182–94.

Grigsby, Melvin. *The Smoked Yank.* 2d edition. Chicago: Regan Printing Co., 1891.

Hudson, Arthur Palmer. "An Attala Boyhood." *Journal of Mississippi History* IV (January 1942): 59–75.

Journal of the Proceedings in the Constitutional Convention of the State of Mississippi. Jackson, Mississippi: E. Stafford, 1871.

Kearney, Belle. *A Slaveholder's Daughter.* New York: Negro Universities Press, 1969.

Knox, Thomas W. *Camp-fire and Cotton Field: Southern Adventure in Time of War, Life with Union Army, and Residence on a Louisiana Plantation.* New York: Da Capo Press, 1969 [1865].

Morgan, Albert Talmon. *Yazoo; or, On the Picket Line of Freedom in the South.* Washington, D.C.: Albert Talmon Morgan, 1884.

Olmsted, Frederick Law. *Back Country.* New York: Burt Franklin, 1860.

Rawick, George P. *The American Slave: A Composite Autobiography.* Series 1. Westport, Connecticut: Greenwood Press, 1974.

Reid, Whitelaw. *After the War: A Southern Tour.* New York: Moore, Wilstach, and Baldwin, 1866.

Reports of Cases in the Supreme Court for the State of Mississippi. Boston: Little, Brown and Company, 1880.

Smedes, Susan Dabney. *Memorials of a Southern Planter.* Baltimore: Cushings and Barkley, 1887.

Smith, W. F., ed. "The Yankees in New Albany: Letter of Elizabeth Jane Beach, July 29, 1864", *The Journal of Mississippi History* II (January 1940): 46.

Southern Reporter. St. Paul: West Publishing Co., 1892.

United States Bureau of Census. *Ninth Census of the United States.* Washington, D.C.: Government Printing Office, 1872.

United States Congress, 42d, Senate Report, No. 41, Pt. 11.F *Testimony taken by the U.S. Congress Joint Select Committee on Conditions of Affairs in the Late Insurrectionary States.* Washington, D.C.: Government Printing Office, 1872.

Walker, Francis A. *The Statistics of the Population of the United States, Ninth Census of the United States.* Washington, D.C.: Government Printing Office, 1872.

War of the Rebellion: A Compilation of the Official Records of the Union and Confederate Armies. Series I–III. 70 vols. Washington, D.C.: Government Printing Office, 1880–1901.

Waterbury, Maria. *Seven Years Among the Freedmen.* 2d ed. Freeport, New York: Books for Libraries Press, 1971 [1891].

Yeatman, James E. *Report to the Western Sanitary Commission.* St. Louis: Western Sanitary Commission, 1864.

Newspaper

The Daily Mississippi Clarion, Jackson.

Secondary Sources

Published

Alexander, Roberta Sue. "Presidential Reconstruction: Ideology and Change."
    In *The Facts of Reconstruction: Essays in Honor of John Hope Franklin*, edited
    by Eric Anderson and Alfred A. Moss, Jr. Baton Rouge: Louisiana State
    University Press, 1991.
Arendt, Hannah. *On Violence*. New York: Harcourt, Brace and World, 1970.
Axinn, June and Herman Levin. *Social Welfare: A History of the American
    Response to Need*. New York: Longman Publishing Group, 1992.
Bardaglio, Peter. "The Children of Jubilee: African American Childhood in
    Wartime." In *Divided Houses: Gender and the Civil War*, edited by Catherine
    Clinton and Nina Silber. New York: Oxford University Press, 1992.
Basler, Roy P. "And For His Widow and His Orphan." *The Quarterly Journal of
    the Library of Congress* 27 (October 1970): 291–94.
Bederman, Gail. "'Civilization,' the Decline of Middle-Class Manliness, and
    Ida B. Wells's Antilynching Campaign (1892–94)." *Radical History Review*
    52 (Winter 1992): 5–32.
Belz, Herman. "The Freedmen's Bureau Act of 1865 and the Principle of No
    Discrimination According to Color." *Civil War History* XXI (September
    1975): 197–217.
Berlin, Ira. *Slaves Without Masters: The Free Negro in the Antebellum South*. New
    York: Vintage Books, 1976.
Berlin, Ira, Steven F. Miller, and Leslie S. Rowland. "Afro-American Families
    in the Transition from Slavery to Freedom." *Radical History Review* 42
    (September 1988): 89–121.
Berry, Mary F. "Military Policy Origins of the Thirteenth Amendment and the
    Civil Rights Act of 1866." In *Historical Judgments Reconsidered: Selected
    Howard University Lectures in Honor of Rayford W. Logan*, edited by Genna
    Rae McNeil and Michael Winston. Washington, D.C.: Howard University
    Press, 1988.
Bethel, Elizabeth R. *Promiseland: A Century of Life in a Negro Community*.
    Philadelphia: Temple University Press, 1981.
Bettersworth, John K. *Confederate Mississippi: The People and Policies of a Cotton
    State in War Time*. Baton Rouge: Louisiana University Press, 1943.
Bigelow, Martha Mitchell. "Freedmen of the Mississippi Valley, 1862–1865."
    Civil War History VIII (March 1962): 38–47.
Blassingame, John W. *The Slave Community: Plantation Life in the Antebellum
    South*. New York: Oxford University Press, 1979.
Blaustein, Albert P. and Robert L. Zangrando, eds. *Civil Rights and the Black*

American: A Documentary History. New York: Washington Square Press, 1970.

Boles, John B., ed. *Masters and Slaves in the House of the Lord: Race and Religion in the American South, 1740–1870*. Lexington: University Press of Kentucky, 1988.

Brown, Elsa Barkley. "African-American Women's Quilting: A Framework for Conceptualizing and Teaching African-American Women's History." *Signs* 14 (Summer 1989): 921–29.

———. "Many Ways of Being Political: Southern Women in the Nineteenth and Twentieth Centuries." *Newsletter of the Association of Black Women Historians* (October 1990): 1–8.

———. "'What Has Happened Here': The Politics of Difference in Women's History and Feminist Politics." *Feminist Studies* 18 (Summer 1992): 295–312.

Brown, Wendy. "Finding the Man in the State." *Feminist Studies* 18 (Spring 1992): 7–34.

Bruchey, Stuart, ed. *Cotton and the Growth of the American Economy, 1790–1860: Sources and Readings*. New York: Harcourt, Brace and World, 1967.

Burton, Orville Vernon. "Computers, History, and Historians: Converging Cultures?" *History Microcomputer Review* 7 (Fall 1991): 11–24.

———. *In My Father's House Are Many Mansions: Family and Community in Edgefield, South Carolina*. Chapel Hill: University of North Carolina Press, 1985.

Bush, Barbara. *Slave Women in Caribbean Society, 1650–1838*. Bloomington: Indiana University Press, 1990.

Bynum, Victoria E. *Unruly Women: The Politics of Social and Sexual Control in the Old South*. Chapel Hill: University of North Carolina Press, 1992.

Campbell, John. "Beyond Slavery: Market Activities of Female Slaves in the Cotton South." Paper presented at the conference "Women and the Transition to Capitalism in Rural America, 1760–1840," Northern Illinois University, DeKalb, Illinois, March 30—April 2, 1989.

Carter, Dan T. *When the War Was Over: The Failure of Self-Reconstruction in the South, 1865–1867*. Baton Rouge: Louisiana State University Press, 1985.

Cash, W. J. *The Mind of the South*. New York: Vintage Books, 1941.

Cimprich, John. *Slavery's End in Tennessee, 1861–1865*. University: University of Alabama Press, 1985.

Clinton, Catherine. *The Other Civil War: American Women in the Nineteenth Century*. New York: Hill and Wang, 1984.

———. "Reconstructing Freedwomen." In *Divided Houses: Gender and the Civil War*, edited by Catherine Clinton and Nina Silber. New York: Oxford University Press, 1992.

Cobb, James C. *The Most Southern Place on Earth: The Mississippi Delta and the Roots of Regional Identity*. New York: Oxford University Press, 1992.

Cohn, David L. *The Life and Times of King Cotton*. New York: Oxford University Press, 1956.

Cornish, Dudley Taylor. *The Sable Arm: Negro Troops in the Union Army, 1861–1865*. New York: W.W. Norton and Company, 1966.

Cruden, Robert. *The Negro in Reconstruction*. Englewood, New Jersey: Prentice Hall, 1969.

Currie, James T. *Enclave: Vicksburg and Her Plantations, 1863–1870*. Jackson: University Press of Mississippi, 1980.

Daniel, Pete. "Commentary: The Metamorphosis of Slavery, 1865–1900." *Journal of American History* 66 (June 1979): 88–99.

David, Paul A., Herbert G. Gutman, Richard Sutch, Peter Temin, and Gavin Wright. *Reckoning with Slavery: A Critical Study in the Quantitative History of American Negro Slavery*. New York: Oxford University Press, 1976.

Davis, Ronald L. F. "The U.S. Army and the Origins of Sharecropping in the Natchez District—A Case Study." *The Journal of Negro History* LXII (January 1977): 60–80.

————. *Good and Faithful Labor: From Slavery to Sharecropping in the Natchez District, 1860–1890*. Westport, Connecticut: Greenwood Press, 1982.

D'Emilio, John and Estelle B. Freedman. *Intimate Matters: A History of Sexuality in America*. New York: Harper and Row, 1988

Dougherty, Molly Crocker. *Becoming a Woman in Rural Black Culture*. New York: Holt, Rinehart and Winston, 1978.

Drago, Edmund L. "Militancy and Black Women in Reconstruction Georgia." *Journal of American Culture* 1 (Winter 1978): 838–63.

Du Bois, Ellen Carol. *Feminism and Suffrage: The Emergence of an Independent Women's Movement in America, 1848–1869*. Ithaca: Cornell University Press, 1978.

DuBois, W. E. B. *Black Reconstruction in America, 1860–1880*. New York: Atheneum, 1962.

Edwards, Laura F. *Gendered Strife and Confusion: The Political Culture of Reconstruction*. Urbana: University of Illinois Press, 1997.

————. "The Illusion of Freedom: Economic Development in Granville County, North Carolina, 1865–1900." Paper presented at the Newberry Seminar in Rural History, Chicago, Illinois, February 23, 1991.

Engerman, Stanley L. "Some Considerations Relating to Property Rights in Man." *Journal of Economic History* 33 (March 1973): 43–65.

Engerman, Stanley L., Manuel Moreno Fraginals, and Herbert S. Klein. "The Level and Structure of Slave Prices on Cuban Plantations in the Mid-Nineteenth Century: Some Comparative Perspectives." *The American Historical Review* 88 (December 1983): 1201–1218.

Engels, Frederick. *The Origin of the Family, Private Property and the State*. Moscow: Progress Publishers, 1977 [1884].

Escott, Paul D. *Slavery Remembered: A Record of Twentieth-Century Slave Narratives*. Chapel Hill: University of North Carolina Press, 1979.

Everly, Elaine C. "Marriage Registers of Freedmen." *Prologue: The Journal of the National Archives* 5 (Fall 1973): 150–54.

Fields, Barbara Jeanne. "The Advent of Capitalist Agriculture: The New South in a Bourgeois World." In *Essays on the Postbellum Southern Economy*, edited by Thavolia Glymph and John J. Kushma. College Station: Texas A & M University Press, 1985.

Fields, Barbara J. *Slavery and Freedom on the Middle Ground: Maryland during the Nineteenth Century*. New Haven: Yale University Press, 1985.

Flexner, Eleanor. *Century of Struggle: The Woman's Rights Movement in the United States*. New York: Atheneum, 1974.

Fogel, Robert W. and Stanley L. Engerman. "Explaining the Relative Efficiency of Slave Agriculture in the Antebellum South." *The American Economic Review* 67 (June 1977): 275–96.

———. *Time on the Cross: The Economics of American Negro Slavery*. Boston: Little, Brown and Company, 1974.

Foner, Eric. *Free Soil, Free Labor, Free Men: The Ideology of the Republican Party before the Civil War*. New York: Oxford University Press, 1970.

———. *Reconstruction: America's Unfinished Revolution, 1863–1877*. New York: Harper and Row, 1988.

Fout, John C. and Maura Shaw Tantillo. *American Sexual Politics: Sex, Gender, and Race since the Civil War*. Chicago: University of Chicago Press, 1993.

Fox-Genovese, Elizabeth. *Within the Plantation Household: Black and White Women of the Old South*. Chapel Hill: University of North Carolina Press, 1988.

Fox-Genovese, Elizabeth and Eugene D. Genovese. *Fruits of Merchant Capital: Slavery and Bourgeois Property in the Rise and Expansion of Capitalism*. New York: Oxford University Press, 1983.

Franklin, John Hope. *Reconstruction: After the Civil War*. Chicago: University of Chicago Press, 1961.

Frankel, Noralee. "From Slave Women to Free Women: The National Archives and Black Women's History in the Civil War Era." *Prologue: Quarterly of the National Archives and Records Administration* 29 (Summer 1997): 100–104.

———. "The Southern Side of 'Glory': Mississippi African-American Women during the Civil War." *Minerva: Quarterly Report on Women and the Military* VIII (Fall 1990): 28–37.

Frazier, E. Franklin. *The Negro Family in the United States*. Chicago: University of Chicago Press, 1939.

Fredrickson, George M. *The Black Image in the White Mind: The Debate on Afro-American Character and Destiny, 1817–1914*. New York: Harper Torchbooks, 1971.

Friedman, Lawrence J. *The White Savage: Racial Fantasies in the Postbellum South*. Englewood Cliffs, New Jersey: Prentice Hall, 1970.

Garner, James Wilford. *Reconstruction in Mississippi*. Gloucester, Massachusetts: Peter Smith, 1964.

Genovese, Eugene D. *The Political Economy of Slavery: Studies in the Economy and Society of Slave South*. New York: Vintage Books, 1967.

———. *Roll, Jordan, Roll: The World the Slaves Made*. New York: Vintage Books, 1976.

———. *The World the Slaveholders Made: Two Essays in Interpretation*. New York: Vintage Books, 1969.

Gerteis, Louis S. *From Contraband to Freedman: Federal Policy toward Southern Blacks, 1861–1865*. Westport, Connecticut: Greenwood Press, 1973.

Glatthaar, Joseph T. *Forged in Battle: The Civil War Alliance of Black Solders and White Officers*. New York: The Free Press, 1990.

Glymph, Thavolia, and John J. Kushma, eds. *Essays on the Postbellum Southern Economy*. College Station: Texas A & M University Press, 1985.

Glymph, Thavolia. "Freedpeople and Ex-Masters: Shaping a New Order in the
    Postbellum South, 1865–1868." In *Essays on the Postbellum Southern Econo-
    my*, edited by Thavolia Glymph and John J. Kushma. College Station:
    Texas A & M University Press, 1985.
Goldsmith, Andrea E. "Notes on the Tyranny of Language Usage." *Women's
    Studies International Quarterly* 3 (1980): 179–191.
Gordon, Linda. "Black and White Visions of Welfare: Women's Welfare
    Activism, 1890–1945." *The Journal of American History* 78 (September
    1991): 559–90.
———. "Social Insurance and Public Assistance: The Influence of Gender in
    Welfare Thought in the United States, 1890–1935." *The American His-
    torical Review* 97 (February 1992): 19–54.
———. *Woman's Body, Woman's Right: A Social History of Birth Control in
    America*. New York: Penguin Books, 1977.
Gray, Lewis Cecil. *History of Agriculture in the Southern United States to 1860*.
    Vol. 1. Washington: Carnegie Institution of Washington, 1933.
Greenberg, Kenneth S. "The Civil War and the Redistribution of Land: Adams
    County, Mississippi, 1860–1870." *Agricultural History* 52 (April 1978): 292–
    307.
Gutman, Herbert G. *The Black Family in Slavery and Freedom, 1750–1925*. New
    York: Vintage Books, 1977.
———. "Persistent Myths About the Afro-American Family." *Journal of
    Interdisciplinary History* VI (Autumn 1975): 181–210.
Hall, Jacquelyn Dowd. "'The Mind That Burns in Each Body': Women, Rape,
    and Racial Violence." In *Powers of Desire: The Politics of Sexuality*, edited by
    Ann Snitow, Christine Stansell, and Sharon Thompson. New York:
    Monthly Review Press, 1983.
———. "Partial Truths." *Signs* 14 (Summer 1989): 902–11.
Harris, William C. *The Day of the Carpetbagger: Republican Reconstruction in
    Mississippi*. Baton Rouge: Louisiana State University Press, 1979.
Hewitt, Nancy A. "Multiple Truths: The Personal, the Political, and the
    Postmodernist in Contemporary Feminist Scholarship." Memphis: Center
    for Research on Women, January 1992 (revised version of closing address
    presented at the Second Southern Conference on Women's History,
    University of North Carolina-Chapel Hill, June 8, 1991).
Higginbotham, Evelyn Brooks. "African-American Women's History and the
    Metalanguage of Race." *Signs* 17 (Winter 1992): 251–74.
Hine, Darlene Clark. "Lifting the Veil, Shattering the Silence: Black Women's
    History in Slavery and Freedom." In Darlene Clark Hine, *The State of
    Afro-American History: Past, Present, and Future*. Baton Rouge: Louisiana
    State University Press, 1986.
———. "Rape and the Inner Lives of Black Women in the Middle West:
    Preliminary Thoughts on the Culture of Dissemblance." *Signs* 14 (Summer
    1989): 912–20.
———. *The State of Afro-American History: Past, Present, and Future*. Baton
    Rouge: Louisiana State University Press, 1986.
Hine, Darlene Clark and Kate Wittenstein "Female Slave Resistance: The

Economics of Sex." In *The Black Woman Cross-Culturally*, edited by Filomina Chioma Steady. Cambridge, Massachusetts: Shenkman Publishing Company, 1981.

Hodes, Martha. "The Sexualization of Reconstruction Politics: White Women and Black Men in the South after the Civil War." In *American Sexual Politics: Sex, Gender, and Race since the Civil War*, edited by John C. Fout and Maura Shaw Tantillo. Chicago: University of Chicago Press, 1993.

Holmes, Amy E. "'Such Is the Price We Pay': American Widows and the Civil War Pension System." In *Toward a Social History of the American Civil War: Exploratory Essays*, edited by Maris A. Vinovskis. Cambridge: Cambridge University Press, 1990.

Holt, Thomas. *Black over White: Negro Political Leadership in South Carolina during Reconstruction*. Urbana: University of Illinois Press, 1977.

————. "'An Empire over the Mind': Emancipation, Race, and Ideology in the British West Indies and the American South." In *Region, Race, and Reconstruction: Essays in Honor of C. Vann Woodward*, edited by J. Morgan Kousser and James M. McPherson. New York: Oxford University Press, 1982.

————. "The Essence of the Contract: The Articulation of Race, Gender, and Politics in British Emancipation Policy, 1838–1866." Unpublished paper, Chicago, Illinois, 1994.

————. *The Problem of Freedom: Race, Labor, and Politics in Jamaica and Britain, 1832–1938*. Baltimore: Johns Hopkins University Press, 1992.

————. "Reflections on Race-Making and Racist Practice: Toward a Working Hypothesis." Paper presented at the Newberry Seminar in American Social History, Chicago, Illinois, May 30, 1991.

hooks, bell. *Ain't I a Woman: Black Women and Feminism*. Boston: South End Press, 1983.

Horton, James Oliver. "Freedom's Yoke: Gender Conventions among Antebellum Free Blacks." *Feminist Studies* 12 (Spring 1986): 51–76.

Horton, James Oliver and Lois E. Horton. *Black Bostonians: Family Life and Community Struggle in the Antebellum North*. New York: Holmes and Meier Publishers, 1979.

Hurtado, Ada. "Relating to Privilege: Seduction and Rejection in the Subordination of White Women and Women of Color." *Signs* 14 (Summer 1989): 833–55.

Jaynes, Gerald David. *Branches without Roots: Genesis of the Black Working Class in the American South, 1862–1882*. New York: Oxford University Press, 1986.

Jensen, Joan M. *With These Hands: Women Working on the Land*. Old Westbury, New York: The Feminist Press, 1981.

Jones, Deborah. "Gossip: Notes on Women's Oral Culture." *Women's Study International Quarterly* 3 (1980): 193–98.

Jones, Jacqueline. *Labor of Love, Labor of Sorrow: Black Women, Work, and the Family, from Slavery to the Present*. New York: Vintage Books, 1985.

Jordan, Winthrop D. *White and Black: American Attitudes toward the Negro, 1550–1812*. Baltimore: Penguin Books, 1969.

Joyner, Charles. *Down by the Riverside: A South Carolina Slave Community*. Urbana: University of Illinois Press, 1984.

Kellogg, Susan. "Hegemony out of Conquest: The First Two Centuries of
    Spanish Rule in Central Mexico." *Radical History Review* 53 (Spring 1992):
    27–48.
Kelley, Robin D. G. "'We Are Not What We Seem': Rethinking Black Work-
    ing-Class Opposition in the Jim Crow South." *Journal of American History*
    80 (June 1993): 75–112.
———. *Hammer and Hoe: Alabama Communists during the Great Depression.*
    Chapel Hill: University of North Carolina Press, 1990.
Kerber, Linda K. "The Paradox of Women's Citizenship in the Early Republic:
    The Case of *Martin vs. Massachusetts,* 1805." *American Historical Review* 97
    (April 1992): 349–78.
Kolchin, Peter. "Reevaluating the Antebellum Slave Community: A Compara-
    tive Perspective." *Journal of American History* 70 (December 1983): 579–601.
Kulikoff, Allan. "Uprooted Peoples: Black Migrants in the Age of the Revolu-
    tion, 1790–1820." In *Slavery and Freedom in the Age of the American
    Revolution,* ed. Ira Berlin and Ronald Hoffman. Charlottesville: University
    Press of Virginia, 1983.
Lebergott, Stanley. *Manpower in Economic Growth: The American Record since
    1800.* New York: McGraw-Hill Book Company, 1964.
Lebsock, Suzanne. *The Free Women of Petersburg: Status and Culture in a
    Southern Town, 1784–1860.* New York: W.W. Norton, 1984.
Lerner, Gerda, ed. *Black Women in White America: A Documentary History.* New
    York: Vintage Books, 1973.
Litwack, Leon F. *Been in the Storm So Long: The Aftermath of Slavery.* New York:
    Alfred A. Knopf, 1979.
Loewen, James W. and Charles Sallis, ed. *Mississippi: Conflict and Change.* New
    York: Pantheon Books, 1974.
Malone, Ann Patton, *Sweet Chariot: Slave Family and Household Structure in
    Nineteenth-Century Louisiana.* Chapel Hill: University of North Carolina
    Press, 1992.
Mandle, Jay B. *The Roots of Black Poverty: The Southern Plantation Economy After
    the Civil War.* Durham: Duke University Press, 1978.
Manfra, Jo Ann and Robert R. Dykstra. "Serial Marriage and the Origins of the
    Black Stepfamily: The Rowanty Evidence." *Journal of American History* 72
    (June 1985): 18–44.
Mann, Susan A. "Slavery, Sharecropping, and Sexual Inequality." *Signs* 14
    (Summer 1989): 774–98.
Manning, Patrick. "Contours of Slavery and Social Change in Africa." *American
    Historical Review* 88 (October 1983): 835–57.
McClintock, Megan J. "Civil War Pensions and the Reconstruction of Union
    Families." *Journal of American History* 83 (September 1996): 456–80.
———. "Shoring up the Family: Civil War Pensions and the Crisis of American
    Domesticity." Paper presented at the annual meeting of the American
    Historical Association, Chicago, Illinois, December 28, 1991.
McNeil, Genna Rae and Michael Winston, eds. *Historical Judgments Reconsid-
    ered: Selected Howard University Lectures in Honor of Rayford W. Logan.*
    Washington, D.C.: Howard University Press, 1988.

McPherson, James M. *Battle Cry of Freedom: The Civil War Era*. New York: Oxford University Press, 1988.

———. *The Negro's Civil War: How American Negroes Felt and Acted during the War for the Union*. New York: Vintage Books, 1965.

Mohr, Clarence L. *On the Threshold of Freedom: Masters and Slaves in Civil War Georgia*. Athens: University of Georgia Press, 1986.

Moore, John Hebron. *Agriculture in Ante-Bellum Mississippi*. New York: Bookman Associates, 1958.

Morrissey, Marietta. *Slave Women in the New World: Gender Stratification in the Caribbean*. Lawrence: University Press of Kansas, 1989.

Nieman, Donald G. *To Set the Law in Motion: The Freedmen's Bureau and the Legal Rights of Blacks, 1865–1868*. Millwood, New York: KTO Press, 1979.

Novak, Daniel A. *The Wheel of Servitude: Black Forced Labor after Slavery*. Lexington: University Press of Kentucky, 1978.

Owens, Leslie H. "The African in the Garden: Reflections about New World Slavery and Its Lifelines." In *The State of Afro-American History: Past, Present, and Future*, ed. Darlene Clark Hine. Baton Rouge: Louisiana State University Press, 1986.

Painter, Nell Irvin. *Exodusters: Black Migration to Kansas after Reconstruction*. New York: Alfred A. Knopf, 1977.

Parent, Anthony S., Jr. and Susan Brown Wallace. "Childhood and Sexual Identity under Slavery." In *American Sexual Politics: Sex, Gender, and Race since the Civil War*, ed. John C. Fout and Maura Shaw Tantillo. Chicago: University of Chicago Press, 1993.

Parks, Sheri. "Feminism in the Lives of Ordinary Black Women." *Barnard Occasional Papers on Women's Issues* V (Summer 1990): 1–14.

Pedersen, Susan. "Gender, Welfare, and Citizenship in Britain during the Great War." *American Historical Review* 95 (October 1990): 983–1006.

Phillips, Ulrich Bonnell. *American Negro Slavery*. New York: D. Appleton Century Company, 1933.

Pleck, Elizabeth Hafkin. *Black Migration and Poverty: Boston, 1865–1900*. New York: Academic Press, 1989.

Powdermaker, Hortense. *After Freedom: A Cultural Study in the Deep South*. New York: Atheneum, 1969.

Powell, Lawrence N. "The American Land Company and Agency." *Civil War History* XXI (December 1975): 293–308.

———. *New Masters: Northern Planters during the Civil War and Reconstruction*. New Haven: Yale University Press, 1980.

Quarles, Benjamin. *The Negro in the Civil War*. Boston: Little, Brown, and Company, 1969.

Quattlebaum, Isabel. "Twelve Women in the First Days of the Confederacy." *Civil War History* VII (December 1961): 69–79.

Rable, George C. *Civil Wars: Women and the Crisis of Southern Nationalism*. Urbana: University of Illinois Press, 1991.

Ransom, Robert L. and Richard Sutch. *One Kind of Freedom: The Economic Consequences of Emancipation*. Cambridge: Cambridge University Press, 1977.

Richardson, Joe Martin. *Christian Reconstruction: The American Missionary*

Association and Southern Blacks, 1861–1890. Athens: University of Georgia Press, 1986.

Ripley, C. Peter. "The Black Family in Transition: Louisiana, 1860–1865." *Journal of Southern History* XLI (August 1975): 369–80.

Roark, James L. *Masters without Slaves: Southern Planters in the Civil War and Reconstruction.* New York: W.W. Norton, 1977.

Robinson, Armstead L. "'Worser dan Jeff Davis': The Coming of Free Labor during the Civil War, 1861–1865." In *Essays on the Postbellum Southern Economy,* ed. Thavolia Glymph and John J. Kushma. College Station: Texas A & M University Press, 1985.

Roediger, David R. *The Wages of Whiteness: Race and the Making of the American Working Class.* London: Verso, 1991.

Rose, Nancy E. "Gender, Race, and the Welfare State: Government Work Programs from the 1930s to the Present." *Feminist Studies* 19 (Summer 1993): 319–42.

Rosen, Hannah. "Struggle over Freedom: Sexual Violence during the Memphis Riot of 1866." Paper presented at the Berkshire Conference on the History of Women, Poughkeepsie, New York, June 1993.

Ross, Steven Joseph. "Freed Soil, Freed Labor, Freed Men: John Eaton and the Davis Bend Experiment." *The Journal of Southern History* XLIV (May 1978): 213–32.

Royce, Edward. *The Origins of Southern Sharecropping.* Philadelphia: Temple University Press, 1993.

Sansing, David G., ed. *What Was Freedom's Price?* Jackson: University Press of Mississippi, 1978.

Saville, Julie. *The Work of Reconstruction: From Slave to Wage Laborer in South Carolina, 1860–1870.* Cambridge: Cambridge University Press, 1994.

Schwalm, Leslie A. *A Hard Fight for We: Women's Transition from Slavery to Freedom in South Carolina.* Urbana: University of Illinois Press, 1997.

Scott, Rebecca J. "Defining the Boundaries of Freedom in the World of Cane: Cuba, Brazil, and Louisiana after Emancipation." *American Historical Review* 99 (February 1994): 70–102.

———. *Slave Emancipation in Cuba: The Transition to Free Labor, 1860–1899.* Princeton: Princeton University Press, 1985.

Shifflett, Crandall A. "The Household Composition of Rural Black Families: Louisa County, Virginia, 1880." *Journal of Interdisciplinary History* VI (Autumn 1975): 235–60.

Shimkin, Dimitri B. *The Extended Family in Black Societies.* The Hague: Mouton Publishers, 1978.

Shlomowitz, Ralph. "The Origins of Southern Sharecropping." *Agricultural History* 53 (July 1979): 557–75.

———. "Plantations and Smallholding: Comparative Perspectives from the World Cotton and Sugar Cane Economies, 1865–1939." *Agricultural History* 58 (January 1984): 1–16.

Skocpol, Theda. *Protecting Soldiers and Mothers: The Political Origins of Social Policy in the United States.* Cambridge: Harvard University Press, 1992.

Sifakis, Stewart. *Who Was Who in the Civil War.* New York: Facts on File, 1988.

Smith-Rosenberg, Carroll. "Dis-Covering the Subject of the 'Great Constitutional Discussion,' 1786–1789." *Journal of American History* 79 (December 1992): 841–73.

Sobel, Mechal. *The World They Made Together: Black and White Values in Eighteenth-Century Virginia*. Princeton: Princeton University Press, 1987.

Sparks, Randy J. "Religion in Amite County, Mississippi, 1800–1861." In *Masters and Slaves in the House of the Lord: Race and Religion in the American South, 1740–1870*, ed. John Boles. Lexington: University Press of Kentucky, 1989.

———. "'The White People's Arms Are Longer Than Ours': Blacks, Education, and the American Missionary Association in Reconstruction History." *The Journal of Mississippi History* LIV (February 1992): 1–27.

Stampp, Kenneth M. *The Peculiar Institution: Slavery in the Ante-Bellum South*. New York: Vintage Books, 1956.

Stanley, Amy Dru. "Conjugal Bonds and Wage Labor: Rights of Contract in the Age of Emancipation." *The Journal of American History* 75 (September 1988): 471–500.

Steckel, Richard H. "Slave Marriage and the Family." *Journal of Family History* 5 (Winter 1980): 406–21.

Stember, Herbert. *Sexual Racism: The Emotional Barrier to an Integrated Society*. New York: Elsevier Scientific Publishing Company, 1976.

Sudarkasa, Niara. "The Status of Women in Indigenous African Societies." *Feminist Studies* 12 (Spring 1986): 91–104.

———. "African and Afro-American Family Structure." In *Anthropology for the Nineties: Introductory Readings*, ed. Johnetta B. Cole. New York: The Free Press, 1988.

Sutch, Richard. "The Breeding of Slaves for Sale and the Westward Expansion of Slavery, 1850–1860." In *Race and Slavery in the Western Hemisphere: Quantitative Studies*, ed. Stanley Engerman and Eugene D. Genovese. Princeton: Princeton University Press, 1975.

Sutch, Richard and Robert L. Ransom. "Sharecropping: Market Response or Mechanism of Race Control?" In *What Was Freedom's Price?*, ed. David S. Sansing. Jackson: University Press of Mississippi, 1978.

Sydnor, Charles Sackett. *Slavery in Mississippi*. New York: D. Appleton-Century, 1933.

Tadman, Michael. *Speculators and Slaves: Masters, Traders, and Slaves in the Old South*. Madison: University of Wisconsin Press, 1989.

Thorpe, Earl E. *Eros and Freedom in Southern Life and Thought*. Durham, North Carolina: Seeman Printery, 1967.

Tilly, Louise A. and Joan W. Scott. *Women, Work, and Family*. New York: Holt, Rinehart, and Winston, 1978.

Walker, Cam. "Corinth: The Story of a Contraband Camp." *Civil War History* XX (March 1974): 5–17.

Wayne, Michael. *The Reshaping of Plantation Society: The Natchez District, 1860–1880*. Baton Rouge: Louisiana State University, 1983.

Weiner, Jonathan. *Social Origins of the New South: Alabama, 1860–1885*. Baton Rouge: Louisiana State University Press, 1978.

Wharton, Vernon Lane. *The Negro in Mississippi, 1865–1890*. New York: Harper and Row, 1965.

White, Deborah Gray. *Ar'n't I a Woman?: Female Slaves in the Plantation South*. New York: Norton, 1985.

Wiecek, William M. "The Great Writ and Reconstruction: The Habeas Corpus Act of 1867." *Journal of Southern History* XXXVI (November 1970): 530–48.

Wiegman, Robyn. "The Anatomy of Lynching." In *American Sexual Politics: Sex, Gender, and Race since the Civil War*, ed. John C. Fout and Maura Shaw Tantillo. Chicago: University of Chicago Press, 1993.

Wiley, Bell Irvin. *Confederate Women*. Westport, Connecticut: Greenwood Press, 1975.

———. *Southern Negroes 1861-1865*. New Haven: Yale University Press, 1969.

———. "Vicissitudes of Early Reconstruction Farming in the Lower Mississippi Valley." *Journal of Southern History* III (November 1937): 440–56.

Wood, Forrest G. *The Arrogance of Faith: Christianity and Race in America from the Colonial Era to the Twentieth Century*. New York: Alfred A. Knopf, 1990.

———. *Black Scare: The Racist Response to Emancipation*. Los Angeles: University of California Press, 1970.

Woodman, Harold. "The Reconstruction of Cotton Plantations in the New South." In *Essays on the Postbellum Southern Economy*, ed. Thavolia Glymph and John J. Kushma. College Station: Texas A & M University Press, 1985.

Wright, Gavin. *Old South, New South: Revolutions in the Southern Economy since the Civil War*. New York: Basic Books, 1986.

Wyatt-Brown, Bertram. *Southern Honor: Ethics and Behavior in the Old South*. Oxford: Oxford University Press, 1983.

Unpublished: Dissertations

Bercaw, Nancy. "Politics of Household during the Transition from Slavery to Freedom in the Yazoo-Mississippi Delta, 1861–1876." Ph.D. diss., University of Pennsylvania, 1996.

Everly, Elaine Cutler. "The Freedmen's Bureau in the National Capital." Ph.D. diss., George Washington University, 1972.

Ganus, Clifton Lloyd, Jr. "The Freedmen's Bureau in Mississippi." Ph.D. diss., Tulane University, 1953.

Moore, Ross H. "Social and Economic Conditions in Mississippi during Reconstruction." Ph.D. diss., Duke University, 1937.

Schwalm, Leslie A. "The Meaning of Freedom: African-American Women and Their Transition from Slavery to Freedom in Lowcountry South Carolina." Ph.D. diss., University of Wisconsin, 1994.

INDEX

DR. NORALEE FRANKEL is Assistant Director on Women, Minorities, and Teaching at the American Historical Association. She is the author of *Break Those Chains at Last: African Americans 1860–1880* and the co-editor of *Gender, Class, Race, and Reform in the Progressive Era*.